"The American Statesmen Series was a pathbreaking venture in its time; and the best proof of its continuing vitality for our time lies in the testimony of the introductory essays written by eminent scholars for the volumes of the Chelsea House edition—essays that not only explain the abiding value of the texts but in many cases represent significant scholarly contributions on their own.

"Chelsea House is contributing vitally to the scholarly resources of the country—and, at the same time, helping us all to understand and repossess our national heritage."
                    —Professor Arthur M. Schlesinger, jr.

Andrew Jackson

American Statesmen Series

The Home of Andrew Jackson

ANDREW JACKSON
WILLIAM GRAHAM SUMNER

INTRODUCTION BY
ROBERT V. REMINI

American Statesmen Series
GENERAL EDITOR
ARTHUR M. SCHLESINGER, JR.
ALBERT SCHWEITZER PROFESSOR OF THE HUMANITIES
THE CITY UNIVERSITY OF NEW YORK

CHELSEA HOUSE
NEW YORK, LONDON
1980

Cover design by Zimmerman Foyster Design

Library of Congress Cataloging in Publication Data

Sumner, William Graham, 1840-1910.
    Andrew Jackson.

    Reprint of the ed. published by Houghton,
Mifflin, Boston, which was issued as v. 17 of
American statesmen.
    Includes index.
    1. Jackson, Andrew, Pres. U. S., 1767-1845.
2. United States--Politics and government--1829-
1837.   3. Presidents--United States--Biography.
I. Title.   II. Series: American statesmen ;
v. 17.
[E382.S9583 1980]   973.5'6'0924 [B]
ISBN 0-87754-176-0   80-18576

1- 83 GIFT

Chelsea House Publishers
Harold Steinberg, Chairman & Publisher
Andrew E. Norman, President
A Division of Chelsea House Educational Communications, Inc.
70 West 40 Street, New York 10018

CONTENTS

ILLUSTRATIONS
FOLLOWING PAGE 288

BLAZING THE WAY
Arthur M. Schlesinger, jr.

THE ORIGINAL AMERICAN STATESMEN SERIES
consisted of thirty-four titles published between
1882 and 1916. Handsomely printed and widely read, the Series made a notable contribution
to the popular appreciation of American history. Its creator was John Torrey Morse, Jr.,
born in Boston in 1840, graduated from Harvard
in 1860 and for nearly twenty restless years
thereafter a Boston lawyer. In his thirties he
had begun to dabble in writing and editing; and
about 1880, reading a volume in John Morley's
English Men of Letters Series, he was seized by
the idea of a comparable set of compact, lucid
and authoritative lives of American statesmen.

It was an unfashionable thought. The cele-
brated New York publisher Henry Holt turned
the project down, telling Morse, "Who ever
wants to read American history?" Houghton,
Mifflin in Boston proved more receptive, and
Morse plunged ahead. His intention was that
the American Statesmen Series, when com-

plete, "should present such a picture of the development of the country that the reader who had faithfully read all the volumes would have a full and fair view of the history of the United States told through the medium of the efforts of the men who had shaped our national career. The actors were to develop the drama."

In choosing his authors, Morse relied heavily on the counsel of his cousin Henry Cabot Lodge. Between them, they enlisted an impressive array of talent. Henry Adams, William Graham Sumner, Moses Coit Tyler, Hermann von Holst, Moorfield Storey and Albert Bushnell Hart were all in their early forties when their volumes were published; Lodge, E. M. Shepard and Andrew C. McLaughlin in their thirties; Theodore Roosevelt in his twenties. Lodge took on Washington, Hamilton and Webster, and Morse himself wrote five volumes. He offered the authors a choice of $500 flat or a royalty of 12.5¢ on each volume sold. Most, luckily for themselves, chose the royalties.

Like many editors, Morse found the experience exasperating. "How I waded among the fragments of broken engagements, shattered pledges! I never really knew when I could count upon getting anything from anybody." Carl Schurz infuriated him by sending in a two-volume life of Henry Clay on a take-it-or-leave-it basis. Morse, who had confined Jefferson,

John Adams, Webster and Calhoun to single volumes, was tempted to leave it. But Schurz threatened to publish his work simultaneously if Morse commissioned another life of Clay for the Series; so Morse reluctantly surrendered.

When a former Confederate colonel, Allan B. Magruder, offered to do John Marshall, Morse, hoping for "a good Virginia atmosphere," gave him a chance. The volume turned out to have been borrowed in embarrassing measure from Henry Flanders's *Lives and Times of the Chief Justices*. For this reason, Magruder's *Marshall* is not included in the Chelsea House reissue of the Series; Albert J. Beveridge's famous biography appears in its stead. Other classic biographies will replace occasional Series volumes: John Marshall's *Life of George Washington* in place of Morse's biography; essays on John Adams by John Quincy Adams and Charles Francis Adams, also substituting for a Morse volume; and Henry Adams's *Life of Albert Gallatin* instead of the Series volume by John Austin Stevens.

"I think that only one real blunder was made," Morse recalled in 1931, "and that was in allotting [John] Randolph to Henry Adams." Half a century earlier, however, Morse had professed himself pleased with Adams's *Randolph*. Adams, responding with characteristic self-deprecation, thought the "acidity" of his account "much too decided" but blamed the "excess of acid" on the acidulous subject. The book was indeed hostile but nonetheless stylish. Adams also wrote a life of Aaron Burr, presumably for the Series. But Morse thought Burr no statesman, and on his advice, to Adams's extreme irritation, Henry Houghton of Houghton, Mifflin rejected the manuscript. "Not bad that for a damned bookseller!" said Adams. "He should live for a while at Washington and know our *real* statesmen." Adams eventually destroyed the work, and a fascinating book was lost to history.

The definition of who was or was not a "statesman" caused recurrent problems. Lodge told Morse one day that their young friend Theodore Roosevelt wanted to do Gouverneur Morris. "But, Cabot," Morse said, "you surely don't expect Morris to be in the Series! He doesn't belong there." Lodge replied, "Theodore . . . *needs the money*," and Morse relented. No one objected to Thomas Hart Benton, Roosevelt's other contribution to the Series. Roosevelt turned out the biography in an astonishing four months while punching cows and chasing horse thieves in the Badlands. Begging Lodge to send more material from Boston, he wrote that he had been "mainly evolving [Benton] from my inner consciousness; but when he leaves the Senate in 1850 I have nothing whatever to go by. .... I hesitate to give him a wholly fictitious date of death and to invent all the work of his later years." In fact, T.R. had done more research than he pretended; and for all its defects, his *Benton* has valuable qualities of vitality and sympathy.

Morse, who would chat to Lodge about "the aristocratic upper crust in which you & I are imbedded," had a fastidious sense of language. Many years later, in the age of Warren G. Harding, he recommended to Lodge that the new President find someone "who can clothe for him his 'ideas' in the language customarily used by educated men." At dinner in a Boston club, a guest commented on the dilemma of the French ambassador who could not speak English. "Neither can Mr. Harding," Morse said. But if patrician prejudice improved Morse's literary taste, it also impaired his political understanding. He was not altogether kidding when he wrote Lodge as the Series was getting under way, "Let the Jeffersonians & the Jacksonians beware! I will poison the popular mind!!"

Still, for all its fidelity to establishment values, the American Statesmen Series had distinct virtues. The authors were mostly from outside the academy, and they wrote with the confidence of men of affairs. Their books are

generally crisp, intelligent, spirited and read-
able. The Series has long been in demand in
secondhand bookstores. Most of its volumes
are eminently worth republication today, on
their merits as well as for the vigorous expression they give to an influential view of the
American past.

Born during the Presidency of Martin Van
Buren, John Torrey Morse, Jr., died shortly
after the second inauguration of Franklin D.
Roosevelt in 1937. A few years before his
death he could claim with considerable justice
that his Series had done "a little something in
blazing the way" for the revival of American
historical writing in the years to come.

New York
May, 1980

INTRODUCTION
TO THE
CHELSEA HOUSE EDITION
Robert V. Remini

WILLIAM GRAHAM SUMNER'S biography of
Andrew Jackson occupies a unique position in
the historiography of the middle period of
American history. Of all the early biographies
of Old Hickory, it alone offers a distinct point
of view about both the man and the era that
bears his name. Less than a viable interpretation of either man or era but much more than a
mere recitation of historical and biographical
events, Sumner's study advances and defends
many of the author's most cherished opinions
about society, economics and politics. This
book tells the reader almost as much about the
author as it does about its subject.

William Graham Sumner was born on October 30, 1840, in Paterson, New Jersey, and was
educated at Yale and Oxford. Ordained a priest
in the Episcopal church, he served as curate
and pastor before recognizing that the church
provided only a limited outlet for his wide-

ranging interests and talents. Thus, in 1872, he accepted the newly created chair of political and social science at Yale University and became deeply involved in the study of the origins of social institutions. Prodigious in research and untiring in his work habits, he all but educated himself as a sociologist and economist. He mastered a dozen languages in the process and studied, among other things, anatomy, biology and higher mathematics.

Sumner espoused the Darwinian theory of evolution as applied to human society by the English writer Herbert Spencer. Like other Spencerians in this country, Sumner argued that species evolved through adaptation to a changing environment and that human progress resulted through the struggle for life in which the weak perished and the strong survived. Men were incapable of advancing this process, and their interference only delayed evolutionary progress by enabling the weak to survive. Any effort at social reform, therefore, constituted a useless waste of time and energy.

As a sociologist, and one of the first of that breed in the United States, Sumner contributed original research in the unexplored field of human customs. His *Folkways*, published in 1907, explained the natural forces working within society and emphasized the necessity of allowing them full play. The question Sumner had posed in his book *What Social Classes Owe to Each Other* (1883) he now virtually answered in a single word: nothing. Perhaps his most important scholarly work was the monumental four-volume *Science of Society,* completed and published in 1927 by A. G. Keller, his successor at Yale.

Equally opinionated about economics, Sumner was an active and vociferous advocate of laissez faire. Government involvement in the affairs of business he deplored as unwarranted and dangerous. He attacked any regulation of industry. The operations of finance, he said, had a regular and natural pulse that the government must respect and leave alone. He warned against the tendency in his own day to criticize big business, and he pronounced the evolution of trusts a normal and desirable phenomenon. He was just as adamantly opposed to tariffs, subsidies, and any other form of state aid to business as he was to legislation regulating the conduct of the marketplace. He particularly worried over the rage for free silver that dominated the political and economic scene during the final decades of the nineteenth century. Any inflationary device to stimulate the economy violated the basic tenets of Sumnerian dogma. The United States had prospered and grown over the last half-century, he contended, because it had been remarkably free of controls of any kind. The frontier experience had not only shaped the nation's success but had proved the importance of adaptation for survival.

Most of these notions found expression in Sumner's biography of Jackson; Old Hickory proved an excellent vehicle for the propagation of his ideas. Jackson's early poverty and struggle; his life on the frontier; his rise to financial, military and political success; and, most particulary, his war against the Bank of the United States as President—all these conveniently served the cause of Social Darwinism and laissez faire. The degree to which Sumner tailored his subject to his own intellectual needs can be judged by the amount of space and effort he allotted to the first forty-five years of Jackson's life compared to his treatment of the Relief War in Kentucky following the Panic of 1819. They are virtually the same. The remainder of the book, once Sumner seats Old Hickory in the White House, is almost totally concerned with the Bank, the tariff and internal improvements. Clearly, then, this study is less a biography than a history of Jackson's administration.

Sumner lacked interest in anything other than the economic issues of the middle period.

Indian removal failed to excite him, and although his strong moral convictions surface
regularly in the biography, he makes no moral
judgment about Jackson's Indian policy. Nor
does he appreciate Old Hickory's foreign policy; he hardly troubles himself to understand
the objectives motivating the President (but
then, subsequent biographers have also failed
to treat Jackson's conduct of foreign affairs
adequately). In addition, Sumner faults the
President's handling of the nullification controversy, the one area where contemporaries and
future historians praised Jackson for defusing
an explosive situation and thereby preserving
the Union. Sumner argues that the controversy
developed in large measure because of Jackson's
own failures in handling the dispute between
Georgia and the Supreme Court. His insistence
that the President should have enforced a pre-
sumed Court order against Georgia indicates
how little he understood the case or the decision of the Court. Today many historians credit
Jackson with statesmanlike prudence and wisdom in responding to the dispute.

As for Jackson personally, Sumner is almost
relentlessly critical. He respects his subject's
rise from poverty and obscurity to power and
influence but deplores Jackson's flawed moral
character, his emotional excesses and his pen-
chant for personal rencounter. He characterizes

the President's actions as Napoleonic. He accuses him of acting on his own initiative to undertake dangerous and unwarranted experiments involving public institutions. He tends to reduce Jackson's motivation to "spite, pique, instinct, prejudice, or emotion"—a judgment some later historians accepted uncritically. He trivializes the President's goals and says that his influence sank to the "nature of an incident or an accident." After establishing what should have been Jackson's "true" objectives and personal creed—individual liberty, free institutions, the "non-interference theory," opposition to all state action on internal improvements and tariffs, and intelligent discussion and disciplined reason in the conduct of public affairs—Sumner concludes that Old Hickory "stumbled along through a magnificent career," occasionally championing a worthy cause without really appreciating it (obviously the Bank question) and leaving behind "distorted and discordant elements" fit only to "produce turmoil and disaster in the future." The tyranny of Jackson's popularity, Sumner further argues, extinguished reason and common sense in the resolution of public questions. "Representative institutions are degraded on the Jacksonian theory," he declares, "just as they are on the divine-right theory, or on the theory of the democratic empire."

All of which demonstrates how a popular President and authentic folk hero can get himself and his career mangled by an unsympathetic biographer with an ideological ax to grind. Still, Sumner's judgments and criticism constitute most of the book's continuing value. His strong statements about a highly controversial individual command attention and response, and some of his views still elicit respect from modern historians.

And the book has other merits. It provides a detailed, acute and perceptive analysis (for its time and size) of the Bank War, one of the most significant and heroic battles in the history of the republic. If Sumner is highly critical of Jackson's actions during the War, he is equally rough on Nicholas Biddle. He condemns the banker's theory of paper money as "vicious and false"; he describes another Biddle effort as "meretricious and dazzling" and a "cover up"; he calls the Bank's operations distressingly inadequate.

In addition to his excellent account of the Bank War, Sumner includes unusual and valuable information, quite unique for its time, about land distribution, tariff schedules, court cases and certain social phenomena. For example, he mentions the urban violence that periodically erupted during the Jacksonian era over racial and economic problems. Not until the

1970s did historians "rediscover" these significant social events.

Sumner took considerable care in preparing this volume. A glance at his bibliography confirms the remarkable range of his research among nearly all the primary sources available to him at the time. In addition, he enjoyed the special advantage of reading and using a major collection of Jackson's letters to his close friend and confidant, William B. Lewis (most of which are now housed in the New York Public Library). Sumner did not take full advantage of the collection—choosing only "the material in these letters which was useful for my purpose"—but he handled what he did choose with professional skill and attention to accuracy.

At the time Sumner wrote his study only one biography of Jackson merited (and still merits) a commanding place in the historiography of its subject. James Parton's three-volume *Life of Andrew Jackson*, published in 1859 and 1860, not only provided an immense amount of information not available elsewhere but also sketched the important outlines of Jackson's personality and character. Subsequent biographies have drawn heavily upon this work for all aspects of Old Hickory's career. Moreover, Parton wrote with a sweep and sense of excitement that complement his subject. Sumner, on the other hand, adds nothing to our knowledge of Jackson personally. And his writing falls far short of Parton's. Sumner's style brightens occasionally—his analyses of Van Buren and Calhoun possess a distinctive flair—but such instances are rare. However, where Parton ends his massive study of Jackson's life and achievements on an ambiguous note—he repeatedly applauds several of Jackson's triumphs but comes down hard on the principle of rotation—Sumner is quite definite in his judgments and clear in his evaluation. The virtue of Sumner's biography is the clarity of its statement.

Early in the twentieth century the first so-called scholarly biography of Jackson was published by John Spencer Bassett. Its author had the advantage of access to a large collection of Jackson material deposited in the Library of Congress. For the first time much of Jackson's career could be documented, but Bassett still offered nothing new by way of interpretation of his subject or the era in which he lived. The same might be said about Marquis James's two-volume *Life of Andrew Jackson,* published in 1933 and 1937. Though written with dash and style and impressively researched, James's biography offered only a one-dimensional

Jackson: hero, patriot, nationalist. For something more substantial a reader needed to return to Sumner.

Except for the breathtaking interpretations
of Frederick Jackson Turner and Charles Beard,
whose exciting and important views of the
whole sweep of American history could be applied to the Jacksonian era in part, nothing
specifically aimed at understanding the unique-
ness of Jackson and his times was attempted
until Arthur M. Schlesinger, jr., published *The
Age of Jackson* in 1945. This monograph constituted a major breakthrough in Jacksonian
scholarship. It challenged the historical profession to reexamine and rethink the entire age,
and it provoked a flood of articles, books and
dissertations that grappled with virtually every
aspect of Jacksonianism. Schlesinger established
a fixed point from which all modern scholarship takes its start or determines its position.

Although Schlesinger's approach to Jackson
and his cronies was distinctly favorable, much
of modern scholarship is quite critical. Some of
this is due to the anti-hero movement of the
1960s and 1970s, some to the modern consciousness of the plight of the Indians and the
role Jackson played in their agonizing removal,
and some to concern about the "imperial presidency" and Jackson's part in the expansion of

presidential powers. The range of discontent is quite extensive. Part of the problem is that there has not been a real interpretative and scholarly biography of Jackson himself since Sumner's study. As he was in life, Jackson continues to be controversial. That is part of his enduring fascination. And until some historian succeeds in providing a critical analysis of Old Hickory's life and achievements, Sumner's forceful statement remains a valuable, provocative, and instructive point of view.

Chicago, Illinois
April, 1980

SELECT BIBLIOGRAPHY

Bassett, John Spencer. *The Life of Andrew Jackson*. 2 vols. New York, 1911.

James, Marquis. *The Life of Andrew Jackson*. 2 vols. Indianapolis and New York, 1933, 1937.

Meyers, Marvin. *The Jacksonian Persuasion: Politics and Belief*. Stanford, 1957.

Parton, James. *Life of Andrew Jackson*. 3 vols. New York, 1859, 1860.

Pessen, Edward. *Jacksonian America: Society, Personality, and Politics*. Homewood, Illinois, 1978.

Remini, Robert V. *Andrew Jackson and the Course of American Empire, 1767-1821*. New York, 1977.

Rogin, Michael Paul. *Fathers and Children: Andrew Jackson and the Subjugation of the American Indian*. New York, 1975.

Schlesinger, Arthur M., jr. *The Age of Jackson*. New York, 1945.

VanDeusen, Glyndon G. *The Jacksonian Era, 1828-1845*. New York, 1959.

Ward, John William. *Andrew Jackson: Symbol of an Age*. New York, 1955.

White, Leonard D. *The Jacksonians: A Study in Administrative History, 1829-1860*. New York, 1954.

PREFACE TO THE 1899 EDITION

THE fourth group of biographies in this series covers the period of Domestic Politics, the Tariff and Slavery being the matters of chief interest. It comprises the lives of Andrew Jackson, Martin Van Buren, Henry Clay, Daniel Webster, John C. Calhoun, Thomas H. Benton, and Lewis Cass.

With the election of Andrew Jackson the United States turned a political corner and set out upon a new course. It is noteworthy that, beginning with Washington, each successive president is included in this series until we close the line with Jackson's successor, Van Buren. But after Van Buren went out of office in March, 1841, not another president finds a place until we come to the inauguration of Lincoln in March, 1861. Of the propriety of all the inclusions of the first list no question can be raised, unless possibly a mild doubt as to Monroe; concerning the exclusion of all the incumbents of the second period, covering twenty years, the editor certainly feels no doubt that his judgment has been correct, nor has he

ever known disapproval to be expressed among all
the numerous criticisms and suggestions which he
has heard concerning the series. Now this so
strongly marked difference between the two lists
cannot be attributed to two continuous series of
accidents; to assert this would be to tax even
blind credulity too far. There must be, and in
fact there is, an underlying reason.

At the time of Jackson's triumph over Adams,
Democracy, though not at first under that name,
had been in power ever since Jefferson won his
campaign in 1800–1801. Jackson also was a Democrat, but with what a change in the signification
of the word! Between Jeffersonian Democracy
and Jacksonian Democracy there was indeed a
great gulf. Jefferson had believed in the people
upon the basis, tacitly understood, that they should
always select for the places of power men like himself, who to natural ability should also add that
aptitude for administering the government which
might be supposed to spring from a broad education in historical and political directions, and a
career of steadily widening experience in public
affairs. If he had found them using their creative
power in order to elevate men of not more than
ordinary intellectual calibre and of little artifi-
cially acquired fitness, he would have indignantly
rebuked them for betraying just expectations.

Upon this ground the selection of Jackson would have offended him deeply, and not without reason; for certainly that selection, though natural, did not show the element of soundness in the popular judgment, and was unfortunate in its results. Two or three inducements led to it. Jackson was the "hero of New Orleans," and the mass of the people, in whom the peace-loving Jefferson so implicitly believed, adored military heroes. They made Harrison president because of Tippecanoe; they made Taylor president because of the Mexican war; and for the same reason they long dangled the same office before the eyes of Scott, who never had quite the political skill to grasp it. Yet Jackson was no very great hero, after all. His famous victory was chiefly due to the blunders of his opponent; and, though an opponent's blunders are an entirely justifiable means for triumphing over him, yet a victory thus won ought not to stand as a sole and all-sufficient reason for great military distinction. But Jackson's violent temperament corroborated the general impression that he was a great fighter. This domineering quality also pleased the multitude; for all who have observed such phenomena will agree that the democratic crowd, while boisterously abusing a dominant class, will always obsequiously set over themselves a masterful individual. Furthermore,

it was much in Jackson's favor that he was an ignorant man, fully as devoid as the average citizen
could be of all the training, through books or
practice, which had theretofore been commonly
regarded as constituting the odious superior qualifications of a detestable upper class.

Selected for such reasons, Jackson responded
generously to the tastes of his following. He dis-
graced his office by the "Kitchen Cabinet," and
by all the mal-odorous and undignified scandal of
Peggy O'Neil. A low personal element permeated
the administration and banished real statesmanship. Devotion to himself was the only quality
which he found essential for the office-seeker. He
has generally been accused of having foisted upon
the country that noxious practice expressed by
the aphorism: To the victors belong the spoils.
But he really did much worse than this; for perhaps some spoils must be allowed to the *victors ;*
perhaps, even, they ought to be so allowed; but
his reading was, or would have been, had the saying been then in vogue : To the *victor* belong the
spoils; — and he himself was the victor.

Sometimes he may have deserved credit for his
actions. Thus it has been held by many excellent
authorities that, though the methods of the campaign against the Bank of the United States were
open to severe criticism, yet the destruction of

that institution was fortunate for the country. Not improbably this is a correct opinion, though it is difficult to speak with entire assurance when, of the two alternatives, only one has been brought to the test of experience. He won, also, great fame by his repression of the secession movement in South Carolina. But he did not wholly merit this fame. The outburst of his furious temper came at a critical moment, and brought a most happy result. But careful study of the facts shows that this outburst far outran what he was really ready to do. He was giving alarming indications of weakening when the recession instead of the secession of the Palmetto State left him in possession of another lucky victory — a victory which, as many writers have shown, must not be too curiously examined.

Like Jefferson, Jackson enjoyed the privilege of naming his successor, and he gave the honor to Van Buren. It is my opinion that Van Buren has never had justice done to him. He is too commonly regarded as a man of moderate capacity, little strength of character, and a somewhat too suave deportment. He certainly presented a strong contrast to his predecessor, and the nation which had learned to worship Jacksonian outbursts could hardly be expected to be enthusiastic over Van Buren's urbanity. He was unfortunate, moreover, in having his incumbency marked by the terrible financial disasters of that ever-memorable year, 1837. He was no more responsible for them, and no more able to cure them, than if the outbreak had been of cholera or small-pox; indeed, he was much less so. But of course the multitude looked to him for a remedy, and, getting none, they contemned him as incompetent. In point of fact, while no one would think of saying that Van Buren was very great intellectually or very strong as a controller of men or events, yet he really had much of the statesman in him; he had distinct policies, and reasons for them, and he pursued them intelligently. Later on in his career he showed that, though of a temperament to which quarreling was distasteful, yet he had genuine moral and political principles to which he would adhere in the face of opponents and against his own selfish interests. His life in this series seems to me a very interesting and able presentation of a period which has not generally been well appreciated. If we measure him with those who had gone before him, he seems of moderate dimensions, but in comparison with those who came after him he appears almost distinguished. With him, as has been said, we bid a long farewell to presidential biographies; but his exclusion would have been a great error; he was really a man of mark.

Between the time when John Quincy Adams left the presidency and Abraham Lincoln came to it, some brilliant reputations reached their zenith, and many great changes took place. Webster, Clay, Calhoun, will rise to the memory of every reader; their great battles, their superb oratory, seem almost to call for Homeric description. But it will not do for me to magnify my office, and to forget that I am writing merely a brief — or what should be a brief — prefatory introduction to a group or period. One general remark, however, I must find room for, in order to call attention to the new development of political life in the country. By the time that Monroe left office the United States had escaped from European entanglements; the French Revolution was burned out; we had only to forget our brush with Great Britain. Then for a while a political calm succeeded; there were almost no politics at all, only personal scrambling of politicians. But before Jackson was comfortably established in the White House, a new order of business was already well to the front. For a long while thereafter the country was to be occupied with domestic affairs. Questions of internal policy absorbed the people. There was first the tariff and then slavery; while in a practical direction the Southwest and the Northwest were growing rapidly in importance,

politically as well as in every other respect. The
lives of Benton and Cass tell these especial stories
of the growth of the new regions; while all the
lives combine to tell the stories of tariff and slavery conflicts. The tariff rose and fell, — I do not
mean financially, but as a topic of political discussion. But slavery kept very steadily rising, with
few and brief intervals of rest, until finally it
crowded out all else and absorbed all popular
interest for itself alone. To my mind, I must
say that this new condition presents itself as more
satisfactory than either the calm, or the foreign
excitements, which had preceded it. To see American statesmen busied with American affairs is
vastly more gratifying than to see them, with at
least one eye askance, scanning the doings of other
peoples. Nor in the histories of many nations and
eras does the reader find an episode more intensely
exciting, more fascinating in all the swayings of
the struggle, than was the anti-slavery movement.
What moral qualities, what intellectual wrestlings,
what defeats and victories, and renewals of the
unwearying contest, does not one witness! It is
a narrative which cannot stale ; which can never,
by repetition, lose its freshness ; and the stories of
the lives of those engaged in that quarter-century
of strife will never, I hope, cease to enthrall American readers.

Further it may be said that it is in the history
of this period that the distinctive national character is most strongly marked. As a natural consequence of the fact that the people were wholly
engrossed in their own affairs, they began to
develop traits sufficiently peculiar to themselves
to differentiate them from other peoples. In the
earlier years Americans had grown *out of* English
colonists, but now they had grown *away* from
them. With our own special domestic interests
and our own internal policies, we began also to
have our own characteristics infused through the
people at large, and finding expression in those
who were engaged in the conduct of our public
affairs. The reader who wants to study genuine
Americanism must seek its establishment in the
administration of the second Adams, and watch
its rapid and strong development from that time
until the death of Mr. Lincoln. It is not only
the questions of that era, but the statesmen also,
that were American. Their lives are full of instruction and suggestion in this respect, and the
interest which this quality confers upon them is
very great. In a great measure this condition
comes to an end, perhaps only temporarily, at or
soon after the close of the civil war, collaterally
with the rapid growth of material prosperity which
then occurred, and with the accompanying inunda-

tion of many foreign and alien elements. For the time being, we have ceased to be homogeneous, and it is hard to say what is the American character to-day, or indeed whether any such character is now established. We have the power and consideration which come with wealth and numbers; perhaps we are developing a new and it may be a grander national character; certainly we are becoming what is vaguely called cosmopolitan; but in getting much we are also parting with something, — we are losing, or have actually lost, the group of distinguishing traits which marked the period to which this group of our series belongs. That period had very definite boundaries; it was of exceptional importance, and its great men command an unusual measure of interest and attention. It may be differentiated as the era of Americanism, nationalism, nativism, by whichever phrase one may prefer to describe the new and original conditions, political, moral, and social, of the country.

JOHN T. MORSE, JR.

September, 1898.

AUTHOR'S PREFACE
TO THE
1899 EDITION

THIS new edition of this book has been revised
line by line, and the corrections, amendments, and
additions, which have been collected during the
sixteen years since it was first written, are now
incorporated in it. I have had the very great
advantage of using a collection of unpublished letters of Jackson to William B. Lewis, 250 in number, the property of the Messrs. Ford. I have
been allowed to avail myself of all the material in
these letters which was useful for my purpose ;
and I have now to make my acknowledgments to
the owners of them for their courtesy and generosity. In the quotations from Jackson's letters I
have reproduced the original exactly, as respects
spelling, punctuation, and capitals, not even cor-
recting obvious slips of the pen, or inaccuracies
of an old man. It is left to the reader to make
such allowances where necessary. As I have been
under strict injunctions not to increase the size of
the book, I have cancelled much which was intended, in the first edition, to elucidate events or
proceedings of Jackson's time, but which did not

strictly belong to it.   The cancelled passages were especially important in Chapters VIII., IX., and X. of the first edition.   The great number of excellent works which have been added to the literature of American history within sixteen years make these passages less necessary.   On the whole, therefore, I have curtailed the history and extended the biography.

W. G. SUMNER.

Yale University, October, 1898.

ANDREW JACKSON

CHAPTER I

THE FIRST FORTY-FIVE YEARS OF JACKSON'S LIFE

In the middle of the last century a number of Scotchmen and Scotch-Irishmen migrated to the uplands of North and South Carolina. Among these was Andrew Jackson, who came over in 1765, with his wife and two sons, being accompanied also by several neighbors and connections from Carrickfergus, County Antrim, Ireland. They appear to have been led to the spot at which they settled, on the upper waters of the Catawba river, by the fact that persons of their acquaintance in Ireland had previously found their way thither, under special inducements which were offered to immigrants.[1] The settlement was called the Waxhaw Settlement, and was in Mecklenburg County, North Carolina, but close to the South Carolina

---

[1] 2 Hewitt, 13, 268, 272. A bounty was offered equal to the cost of passage. Ship captains became immigration agents.

For the full titles of books referred to, see the list at the end of the volume.

boundary. Andrew Jackson had no capital, and
never became an owner of land. In 1767 he died.
His son Andrew was born within a few days of
the father's death, March 15, 1767. Parton fixes
his birthplace in Union County, North Carolina;
Kendall in South Carolina. In Jackson's Proclamation of 1832, in a letter of December 24,
1830,[1] and in his will, he speaks of himself as a
native of South Carolina.

It appears that Andrew Jackson's mother abandoned the settlement which her husband had commenced, and it is probable that she owed much to
the assistance of her relatives and connections while
Andrew was a child. Circumstances of birth more
humble than those of this child can scarcely be
imagined. It was not, probably, hard to sustain
life in such a frontier community. Coarse food
was abundant; but to get more out of life than
beasts get when they have enough to eat was no
doubt very difficult. The traditions of Jackson's
education are vague and uncertain. Of book-learning and school-training he appears to have got
very little indeed.

The population of the district was heterogeneous,
and, when the Revolutionary War broke out, the
differences of nationality and creed divided the
people by opposing sympathies as to the war. The
English penetrated the district several times in the
hope of winning recruits and strengthening the
tories. On one of these raids Andrew Jackson

[1] 39 Niles, 385.

was wounded by an officer, who struck him because he refused to brush the officer's boots. He and his brother were taken prisoners to Camden. The war cost the lives of both Andrew's brothers, and also that of his mother, who died while on a journey to Charleston to help care for the prisoners there. Andrew Jackson accordingly came to entertain a vigorous hatred of the English from a very early age. In 1781 he was alone in the world. What means of support he had we do not know, but, after trying the saddler's trade, he became, in 1784, a student of law at Salisbury, North Carolina. The traditions collected by Parton of Jackson's conduct at this time give us anything but the picture, so familiar in political biography, of the orphan boy hewing his way up to the presidency by industry and self-denial. If the information is trustworthy, Jackson was gay, careless, rollicking, fond of horses, racing, cock-fighting, and mischief. Four years were spent in this way.

It is necessary to note the significance of the fact that a young man situated as Jackson was should undertake to " study law."

In the generation before the Revolution the intellectual activity of the young men, which had previously been expended in theology, began to be directed to the law. As capital increased and property rights became more complicated there was more need for legal training. In an agricultural community there was a great deal of leisure at certain seasons of the year, and the actual outlay

required for an education was small. The standard
of attainments was low, and it was easy for a
farmer's boy of any diligence to acquire, in his
winter's leisure, as much book-learning as the best
colleges gave. In truth the range of ideas, among
the best classes, about law, history, political science,
and political economy, was narrow in the extreme.
What the aspiring class of young men who were
self-educated lacked, as compared with the technically "educated," was the bits of classical and
theological dogmatism which the colleges taught
by tradition, and the culture which is obtained by
frequenting academical society, however meagre
may be the positive instruction given by the institution. What the same aspiring youths had in
excess of the regularly educated was self-confidence, bred by ignorance of their own short-com-
ings. They were therefore considered pushing
and offensive by the colonial aristocracy of place-
holders and established families, who considered
that "the ministry" was the proper place for
aspiring cleverness, and that it was intrusive when
it pushed into civil life. The restiveness of the
aspiring class under this repression was one of the
great causes of the Revolution. The lawyers became the leaders in the revolt everywhere. The
established classes were, as classes, tories. After
the war the way was clear for every one who wanted
office, or influence, or notoriety, to attain these
ends. The first step was to study law. If a young
man heard a public speaker, and was fired by the

love of public activity and applause, or if he became engaged in political controversy, and was
regarded by his fellows as a good disputant, or if
he chanced to read something which set him thinking, the result was very sure to be that he read
some law. The men, whose biographies we read
because they rose to eminence, present us over and
over again the same picture of a youth, with only
a common school education, who spends his leisure
in reading law, while he earns his living by teach-
ing or by farm work. Those, however, whose biographies we read are only the select few who
succeeded, out of the thousands who started on the
same road, and who were arrested by one circum-
stance or another, which threw them back into the
ranks of farmers and store-keepers. We shall see
that Andrew Jackson so fell back into the position
of a farmer and store-keeper. Chance plays a
great *rôle* in a new community, just as it does in a
primitive civilization. Chance had very much to
do with Jackson's career. We have no evidence
that he was dissatisfied with his circumstances, and
set himself to work to get out of them, or that he
had any strong ambition towards which the law
was a step. There is no proof that he ever was an
ambitious man; but rather the contrary. He never
learned any law, and never to the end of his
life had a legal tone of mind; even his admirer,
Kendall, admits this.[1] His study of law had no
influence on his career, and no significance for his

[1] *Jackson*, 109.

character, except that it shows him following the
set or fashion of the better class of young men of
his generation. If conjecture may be allowed, it
is most probable that he did not get on well with
his relatives, and that he disliked the drudgery of
farming or saddle-making. A journey which he
made to Charleston offers a very possible chance
for him to have had his mind opened to plans and
ideas.

In 1789, Jackson's friend, John McNairy, was
appointed judge of the Superior Court of Law
and Equity of the District of Mero, *i. e.*, Davidson, Sumner, and Tennessee Counties, Tennessee.
McNairy and Jackson were admitted to the bar at
Greenville, in May, 1788, the Court sitting there,
under the authority of the State of North Carolina,
without interruption, for the first time after the
Franklin troubles.[1] Jackson arrived in Tennessee in the fall of 1789 or the spring of 1790. He
settled in Jonesboro. Tennessee was then a wild
frontier country, in which the whites and Indians
were engaged in constant hostilities. It was shut
off from connection with the Atlantic States by the
mountains, and its best connection with civilization
was down the Ohio and Mississippi rivers. Such
frontier communities have always had a peculiar
character. In them the white man has conformed,

---

[1] Haywood, 194. Haywood writes Frankland. Allison (29) says
that Sevier's Correspondence shows that the State was named
after Franklin. Inasmuch as Allison claims to have searched
court records, etc., his dates, etc., are here followed.

in no small degree, to the habits and occupations
of the Indians. Cut off from tools, furniture,
clothing, and other manufactured articles such as
civilized men use, he has been driven to such substitutes as he could produce by bringing his intelligence to bear on the processes and materials used
by the Indians. Living where game is abundant,
and where the forests make agriculture difficult,
he has often sunk back to the verge of the hunt-
ing stage of civilization.[1] The pioneers, so much
lauded in song and story, were men who first broke
the path into the wilderness, but who derogated
from the status of their race to do it. They became
incapacitated for the steady labor of civilized industry, and when the country became so filled up
that game was scarce, agriculture a necessity, and
"law" began to be recognized and employed, the
pioneers moved on into the wilderness. In their
habits they were idle and thriftless, and almost
always too fond of strong drink. The class of
settlers who succeeded them were but little better
in their habits, although they began to clear the
forests and till the soil. They were always very

[1] See Collins's *Kentucky*, Putnam's *Middle Tennessee*, Ford's *Illinois*, and Kendall's *Jackson*, 74. To "indianize" was a current
term for this social phenomenon. The worst manifestation of it
was the adoption of the custom of scalping, and the acts of
legislation by which bounties were offered for scalps, even for
those of women and children. During the war of the Revolution
there were, in the mountains of East Tennessee, white people
"more savage than the Indians. They possess every one of their
vices but not one of their virtues." 2 Hanger, 404.

litigious. Court day was an occasion which drew the men to the county town, forming an event in a monotonous existence, and offering society to people oppressed by isolated life. This concourse of people furnished occasion for gossip and news-mongering, and the discussion of the affairs of everybody for miles around. "Public opinion" took control of everything. Local quarrels involved the whole county sooner or later. Friend-ships, alliances, feuds, and animosities grew up and were intensified in such a state of society. If there was an election pending, the same concourse of people furnished an opportunity for speech-mak-ing and argument. The institution of "stump-speaking" was born and developed in these cir-cumstances. In the court itself the parties to the suits and the jury enjoyed a place before the public eye. The judge and the counsel made reputation day by day. The lawyers, as actual or prospective candidates for office, were directly and constantly winning strength with the electors. They passed from the bar to the stump or the tavern parlor, and employed the influence which their eloquence had won in the court room to advance the in-terests which they favored in the election. There are features of American democracy which are inexplicable unless one understands this frontier society. Some of our greatest political abuses have come from transferring to our now large and crowded cities maxims and usages which were con-venient and harmless in backwoods county towns.

Another feature of the frontier society which it is important to notice is, that in it the lack of capital and the intimacy of personal relations led to great abuses of credit. Idleness, drink, debt, and quarrels produced by gossip have been the curses of such society. The courts and the lawyers were always busy with the personal collisions which arose where no one was allowed to practise any personal reserve, where each one's business was everybody's business, where gossip never rested, and where each one was in debt to some others.

In such a state of society the public prosecutor is the general of the advancing army of civilization. He has to try to introduce law and order, the fulfilment of contracts, and the recognition of rights into the infant society. This was the task which Jackson undertook in Tennessee. It required nerve and vigor. The western counties of North Carolina were in a state of anarchy, resulting from the attempt to set up the State of Franklin, and the population were so turbulent and lawless that the representative of legal order was at open war with them. There had been civil war in the district for four years.

The proceedings by which the State of Franklin was brought into existence were suggested and carried out upon principles and notions which can only be characterized as *squatterism*. The colonists at the outset, especially those of New England, took their stand on squatterism, without reflection or question. The primary standpoint or

view on which it rests is the notion that a group
of people who find themselves in what the New
Englanders called a *"vacuum domicilium"* (putting it in Latin to give it emphasis since it lacked
contents) may hold a mass meeting, and create a
state, without regard to the jurisdiction of some
political body already existing, which has historical
and legal authority over the territory in which they
are. Many conflicts arose in the colonial history
from the collision between squatterism and constituted authority, and three or four very important
cases have occurred in the federal history.[1] Franklin was the first. The conflict is always attended
by big declarations about "liberty" on the part of
the squatters, and when they are forced to submit
to law and constitutional order, great irritation is
sure to be produced.

The Indians and whites were also engaged in
the final struggle of the former before yielding
their hunting-grounds to the cultivation of the
white man. Jackson had to travel up and down
the country in the discharge of his duties, when he
was in danger of his life upon the road. He
brought all the required force and virtue to the
discharge of the duties of this office. He pursued
his way without fear and without relenting. He
made strong enemies, and he won strong friends.
Kendall says that Jackson settled at Nashville,
because the debtors there tried to drive him away,
he having taken some collection cases.[2] His merits

[1] See p. 446.   [2] Kendall's *Jackson*, 90.

as prosecutor[1] are vouched for by the fact that
Governor Blount said of him, in reference to certain intruders on Indian lands who were giving
trouble, " Let the District Attorney, Mr. Jackson,
be informed. He will be certain to do his duty,
and the offenders will be punished." [2] As to the
administration of justice in such a society, the colonial records show how slight were the guarantees
of civil liberty against popular power. Allison[3]
proves it again in his description of the primitive
court of Tennessee and its proceedings.

Among the earliest settlers of Middle Tennessee
(1780) was John Donelson, who had been killed
by the Indians before Jackson migrated to Tennessee.[4] Jackson boarded with the widow Donelson.
In the family there were also Mrs. Donelson's
daughter, Rachel, and the latter's husband, Lewis
Robards. Robards, who seems to have been of a
violent and jealous disposition, had made injurious
charges against his wife with reference to other
persons, and he now made such charges with reference to Jackson. Robards had been married in
Kentucky under Virginia law. There was no law

---

[1] He was appointed district attorney by Washington in 1791,
after the western counties of North Carolina were ceded. The
cession was made that the State might no longer be obliged to
pay expenses incurred in Indian wars, which the western people
were charged with provoking in order to create claims which the
eastern counties must pay. Hayward, 214 ; Allison, 26.

[2] Putnam, 351.

[3] Chap. iii.

[4] Putnam, 613 *et seq.*; Kirke, 7.

of divorce in Virginia. Robards, in 1790, petitioned the Legislature of Virginia to pass an act
of divorce in his favor, making an affidavit that
his wife had deserted him, and was living in adultery with Jackson. The Legislature of Virginia
passed an act authorizing the Supreme Court of
Kentucky to try the case with a jury, and, if the
facts proved to be as alleged, to grant a divorce.[1]
Robards took no action for two years. September
27, 1793, he obtained a divorce from the Court of
Quarter Sessions of Mercer County, Kentucky.[2]
In the mean time, Jackson and Mrs. Robards, upon
information of the legislative act of 1790, which
they assumed, or were informed, to be an act of
divorce, were married at Natchez, in July or August, 1791. In January, 1794, upon hearing of
the action of the Mercer County Court, they were
married again.[3] The circumstances of this marriage were such as to provoke scandal at the time,
and the scandal, which in the case of a more obscure man would have died out during thirty years
of honorable wedlock, came up over and over again
during Jackson's career. It is plain that Jackson
himself was to blame for contracting a marriage
under ambiguous circumstances, and for not protecting his own wife's honor by proper precautions,

[1] 13 Va. Stat. at Large, 227; Dec. 20, 1790.
[2] The decree was for desertion and adultery. It is given in
full in *Truth's Advocate*, 17. (1828.)
[3] *Telegraph Extra*, p. 33. Report of a Jackson committee in
1828.

such as finding out the exact terms of the act of the Legislature of Virginia. He clung to this lady until her death, with rare single-mindedness and devotion, although she was not at all fitted to share the destiny which befell him. He cherished her memory until his own death in a fashion of high romance. An imputation upon her, or a reflection upon the regularity of his marriage, always incensed him more than any other personal attack. Having put her in a false position, against which, as man and lawyer, he should have protected her, he was afterward led, by his education and the current ways of thinking in the society about him, to try to heal the defects in his marriage certificate by shooting any man who dared to state the truth; that said certificate was irregular.

Jackson was a member of the convention which met at Knoxville, January 11, 1796, and framed a Constitution for the State of Tennessee. There is a tradition that he proposed the name of the river as the name of the State.[1] This Constitution established a freehold qualification for voting and holding the chief offices, and declared that the people of Tennessee had an inalienable right to navigate the Mississippi river to its mouth. The federalists in Congress opposed the admission of Tennessee, because it was a raw frontier community; but it was admitted June 1, 1796. In the autumn Jackson was elected the first federal representative. A year later, Blount, one of the senators from Ten-

[1] Ramsey, 655.

nessee, having been expelled, Jackson was appointed senator in his place.   He held this position
only until April, 1798, when he resigned.

In December, 1796, therefore, at the age of
thirty, Jackson first came in contact with a society
as cultivated as that of Philadelphia then was.
Except for the brief visit to Charleston in 1783,
above referred to, he had seen no society but that
of western North Carolina and Tennessee.   He
came to Philadelphia just as the presidential election of 1796 was being decided.   Tennessee voted
for Jefferson, and we may believe that whatever
political notions Jackson had were Jeffersonian.
He identified himself with the opposition to Washington's administration in the most factious and
malicious act which it perpetrated, namely, the
vote against the address to Washington at the
close of his administration.   He and Edward Livingston were two out of twelve in the House who
refused to vote for the address.   It is not known
what Jackson's reasons were.   Some refused to
vote that Washington's administration had been
wise.   Others objected to the hope that Washington's example would guide his successors.[1]   The
grounds of objection to the administration were
Jay's treaty and Hamilton's financial measures.   In
the light of history the " irreconcilable " minority
which opposed these measures to the bitter end
must stand condemned.

[1] In 1830 Livingston attempted an elaborate defence of his
vote.   He tried to distinguish between Washington and his administration.   Hunt's *Livingston*, 340.

In the Senate, Jackson voted, with only two others, against a bill to authorize the President to buy or lease cannon foundries, in view of possible war with France. He voted against a bill to authorize the arming of merchant ships ; in favor of an embargo ; against a proviso that the United States should not be bound to cancel the Indian title to land on behalf of any State.[1]

We know nothing of any activity or interest shown by Jackson in any measure save a claim of Hugh L. White, and an act to reimburse Tennessee for expenses incurred in an Indian war. Tennessee thought that the federal government was slow and negligent about defending her against the Indians. The federal government thought that Tennessee was hasty and aggressive towards the Indians. It had inherited the burden against which North Carolina had revolted.[2] Jackson secured payment of this claim of Tennessee while he was in the House, to the great advantage of his popularity at home.

We must infer from his conduct that he did not enjoy political life and did not care for it. He certainly did not become engaged in it at all, and he formed no ties which he found it hard to break at a moment's warning. He does not appear to have made much impression upon anybody at Philadelphia. In the "History of the United States in 1796 " (p. 244) he is quoted for an account of the Nickajack expedition, against the Indian strong-

---

[1] Annals of Congress ; 5th Congress, I. 485–532.
[2] See p. 11, n. 1.

hold, in 1794. Gallatin recalled him years afterwards as " a tall, lank, uncouth-looking personage,
with long locks of hair hanging over his face, and
a cue down his back tied in an eel-skin; his dress
singular, his manners and deportment that of a
rough backwoodsman." [1] Jefferson said of him, in
1824: " When I was President of the Senate he
was a senator, and he could never speak on account
of the rashness of his feelings. I have seen him attempt it repeatedly, and as often choke with rage." [2]
There is, however, ample testimony that Jackson,
later in life, was distinguished and elegant in his
bearing, when he did not affect roughness and in-
elegance, and that he was able to command enco-
miums upon his manners from the best bred ladies
in the country.

Jackson was a " Judge of the Superior Courts "
of Tennessee from 1798 to June 1804. Overton's
Reports (1 Tennessee) cover this period, but the
reports are meagre and undated (beginning in
1791), and those which appear to belong to Jackson's time deal with only petty and unimportant
cases. It is stated here that he resigned, " having
been previously appointed a general of the militia."

While Jackson was on the bench, he and ex-Governor Sevier were in feud with each other. The
origin of the quarrel is obscure, and not worth
picking out from the contradictory backwoods gossip in which it probably originated. It is enough
to notice that the two men were too much alike in

[1] 4 Hildreth, 692.   [2] Webster's *Corr.* 371.

temper to be pleased with each other. Sevier was fifty-seven years old in 1801, and had been a leading man in the country for twenty years. Jackson was only thirty-four in that year, and a rising man, whose success interfered with Sevier's plans for himself. In 1802 the field officers of the militia tried to elect a major-general. Sevier and Jackson were the candidates. The election resulted in a tie. The governor, Archibald Roane, who had the casting vote, threw it for Jackson. Jackson had not taken part in the Nickajack expedition, or otherwise done military service, so far as is known, except as a private in an Indian fight in 1789. On that occasion one of his comrades described him as " bold, dashing, fearless, and mad upon his enemies." [1] In 1803 Sevier was elected governor, and he and the judge-major-general drew their weapons on each other when they met. Each had his faction of adherents, and it was only by the strenuous efforts of these persons that they were prevented from doing violence to each other. Kendall says that Jackson's popularity was increased by his quarrel with Sevier. [2] Parton gives letters of Jackson from this period which are astonishingly illiterate for a man in his position, even when all the circumstances are taken into consideration. Jackson was made a trustee of the Nashville Academy in 1793.[3]

He wanted to be made governor of the Territory of Orleans after the purchase, and the Tennessee

[1] Putnam, 318.   [2] Kendall's *Jackson*, 108.   [3] Putnam, 410.

delegation urged Jefferson to appoint him. A letter from William Henderson of Sumner County, Tennessee, has been published, which was written to dissuade the President from this appointment. I " view him as a man of violent passions, arbitrary in his disposition, and frequently engaged in broils and disputes. . . . He is a man of talents, and, were it not for those despotic principles, he might be a useful man." [1]

In 1804 Jackson was once more a private citizen, a planter, and a store-keeper. Neither politics nor law had apparently touched any chord of interest in him. The turning point in his career was the vote which made him major-general of militia, but the time had not yet arrived for him to show that all there was in him could be aroused when there were public enemies to be crushed. He had been engaged in trade for six years or more before 1804, and was now embarrassed. He devoted himself to business for several years.

Mention has already been made of the general abuse of credit in the frontier communities. Money is scarce because capital is scarce, and is so much needed that the community is unwilling to employ any of it in securing a value currency. It is true that the people always have to pay for a value currency, whether they get it or not, but they always cheat themselves with the notion that cheap money is cheap. Food and fuel are abundant, but everything else is scarce and hard to get. Hopes

[1] N. Y. *Times*, Dec. 26, 1897.

are strong and expectations are great. Each man gives his note, which is a draft on the glorious future; that is, every man makes his own currency as he wants it, and the freedom with which he draws his drafts is as unlimited as his own sanguine hopes. The hopes are not unfounded, but their fruition is often delayed. Continued renewals become necessary, and liquidation is put off until no man knows where he stands. A general liquidation, with a period of reaction and stagnation, therefore, ensues upon any shock to credit. In Tennessee, between 1790 and 1798, land was used as a kind of currency; prices were set in it, and it was transferred in payment for goods and services. During the same period there was a great speculation in new land throughout the country. Prices of land were inflated, and extravagant notions of the value of raw land prevailed. After the crisis of 1798, land fell in value all over the country, to the ruin of thousands of speculators. Values measured in land all collapsed at the same time. Jackson was entangled in the system of credit and land investments, but he seems to have worked out of his embarrassments during the next three or four years, after which he abandoned trade and became a planter only.

Another feature of this early southwestern frontier society which excites the surprise and contempt of the modern reader is, that store-keepers and farmers and lawyers, who lived by their labor, and had wives and children dependent on them, are found constantly quarrelling, and in all their quarrels are found mouthing the "code of honor." The earlier backwoodsmen quarrelled and fought as above described, but they fought with fists and knives, on the spur of the moment, as the quarrel arose. It was a genteel step in advance, and marked a new phase of society, when the code of the pistol came into use, and the new higher social caste prided itself not a little on being "gentlemen," because they kept up in the backwoods a caricature drawn by tradition and hearsay from the manners of the swaggerers about the courts of France and England a century before. Andrew Jackson was a child of this society, an adherent of its doctrines, and in his turn a propagandist and expounder of them. He proved himself a quarrelsome man. Instead of making peace he exhausted all the chances of conflict which offered themselves. He was remarkably genial and gentle when things went on to suit him, and when he was satisfied with his companions. He was very chivalrous about taking up the cause of any one who was unjustly treated and was dependent. Yet he was combative, and pugnacious, and over-ready to adjust himself for a hostile collision whenever there was any real or fancied occasion. The society in which he lived developed, by its fashions, some of his natural faults.

In 1795 he fought a duel with a fellow lawyer named Avery, over some sparring which had taken place between them in a court room, when they were opposing counsel. His quarrel with Sevier has been mentioned. While on the bench he also quarrelled with his old friend Judge McNairy, on account of an appointment made by the judge which injured an old friend of both.[1] In 1806 he fought a duel with Charles Dickinson, who had spoken disparagingly of Mrs. Jackson in the course of a long quarrel which involved, besides Jackson, three or four others, and which was a capital specimen of the quarrels stirred up by the gossip and backbiting of men who had too much leisure. This was the real cause of Jackson's anger, although on the surface the quarrel was about a strained and artificial question of veracity concerning a bet on a horse-race, and it was inflamed by some sarcastic letter-writing in the local newspaper, and by some insulting epithets. Jackson's friends declared that there was a plot to drive Jackson out of the country. Each man meant to kill the other. They met May 30, 1806. Jackson was wounded by a bullet which grazed his breast and weakened him for life. Dickinson was mortally wounded, and died the same evening. Jackson told General Harding that he was afraid of Dickinson, who was a good shot. He also affirmed that he had not an ungovernable temper, but often pretended that he had, for effect.[2] Many persons who were intimate with him later believed that this was true.

Jackson had made the acquaintance of Burr

[1] Kendall's *Jackson*, 105.
[2] 2 *Southern Bivouac*, 667.

when in Congress. In 1805 Burr visited Jackson,
and made a contract with him for boats for the
expedition down the Mississippi. The people of
Kentucky and Tennessee had always regarded it
as a vital interest of theirs to have the free navigation of the Mississippi. They believed that all
Indian hostilities were incited by the Spaniards at
New Orleans.[1] So long as a foreign power held
the mouth of the river, plots were formed for separating the trans-Alleghany country from the Atlantic States, the strength of which plots lay in
the fact that the tie of interest which made the
basis of a union with the holder of New Orleans
was stronger than the tie of interest which united
the two sides of the Alleghanies.[2] In 1795 the
United States by treaty with Spain secured a right
of deposit at New Orleans for three years, and
these separation plots lost all their strength. The
" Annual Register " for 1796 (anti-federalist) very
pertinently pointed out to the western people the
advantages they enjoyed from the Union. " If
they had been formed into an independent republic,
the court of Madrid would have scorned to grant
such a free navigation " [3] (*i. e.*, as it granted in
the treaty of 1795). Spain ceded Louisiana to
France by the secret treaty of St. Ildefonso, October 1, 1800. This treaty became known in 1802
after the peace of Amiens. In the same year

---

[1] Haywood's *Tennessee, passim ;* Allison, 91.

[2] Butler's *Kentucky*, chap. xi ; Allison, 89, 92.

[3] *Ann. Reg.* (1796) p. 83.

Spain, which still held possession of Louisiana, withdrew the right of deposit, and the western country was thrown into great excitement. In 1803 the whole matter of the navigation of the Mississippi was settled by the purchase of Louisiana by the United States, but then a new set of questions was opened. In the treaty of 1795 Spain had acknowledged the parallel of 31° as the boundary of Florida from the Mississippi to the Chattahoochee, although she had been slow about surrendering posts held by her north of this line and east of the Mississippi. Hence there had been complaints and bad feeling. Now a new question arose as to how far Louisiana extended east of the Mississippi river, and this question was of great importance to the Gulf territories, because if, by the Louisiana purchase, the United States had become owner of the territory east as far as the Perdido, then the Gulf coast, with the valuable harbor of Mobile, was available for the whole Southwest. Spain denied that Louisiana included anything east of the Mississippi except the city of New Orleans, and the bit of territory south and west of the Iberville and the two lakes.[1] The territory remained in dispute, and the relations between the two countries continued to be bad, until Florida was purchased in 1819. In 1802 a treaty was made with Spain for the payment by her of claims held by American citizens, but Spain

[1] See the decision of the Supreme Court of the United States in Foster *v.* Neilson, 2 Peters, 253.

did not ratify the treaty until 1818. She had her grievances also, at first about Miranda's expedition, and afterwards about aid to her revolted colonies. In 1810 the President ordered the Governor of Orleans to occupy the territory as far as the Perdido, and to hold it in peace and order, subject to the final decision of the pending controversy with Spain. In 1812, Congress, by two acts, divided the country east as far as the Perdido into two parts, and added one part to Louisiana, which was admitted as a State, and the other part to the Mississippi territory.

It has seemed convenient to pursue these proceedings up to this point, because future reference to them will be necessary. To return now to Burr and his expedition: — It will be understood what were the relations of the United States to Spain in 1805 and 1806, and especially what part of those relations peculiarly affected the people of the Southwest at that time. Their collisions with Spain no longer concerned New Orleans, but West Florida and Mobile. It is still a mystery what Burr really intended.[1] Napoleon's career had fired the imagination of men of a military and romantic turn all over the world. It is quite as reasonable an explanation of Burr's scheme as any other that he was reserving all his chances, and meant to do much or little, according to the turn of events, and that he did not himself define to himself what he was aiming at. His project had an unmistak-

---

[1] Safford's *Blennerhasset;* 2 *Amer. Whig Rev.* No. 2.

able kinship with the old plans for setting up a republic of the Mississippi, with its capital at New Orleans.[1] For that, however, he was ten years too late. If he had intended to go on a filibustering expedition against the Spaniards in Mexico, he would have obtained secret aid and sympathy in Kentucky and Tennessee, and the aid which he did get was given under that belief.[2] If his scheme was aimed in any manner against the United States he could not find any aid for it. Since the purchase of Louisiana, and the accession to power in the Union of the party to which the great majority of the western people belonged, there was no feeling for Burr to work on.[3]

In 1805 Burr found a cordial welcome and aid. He was evidently trying to use Jackson without startling him. His letter of March 24, 1806, which Parton gives,[4] is a very crafty letter, for the purpose of engaging Jackson's name and influence to raise troops for his enterprise without defining it. In 1806 Burr was again in Nashville. His proceedings then aroused suspicion. It appears that Jackson was mystified. He did not know whether he ought to aid Burr or oppose him, or aid him secretly and oppose him openly. It seems to be very clear, however, that he took sides against Burr, if Burr was against the United States. Jan-

[1] 2 Wilkinson, 196; Gayarré, *Louisiana under Spanish Dominion;* 2 Pickett, ch. xxix.

[2] 2 *Amer. Reg.* (1807) 103, note.

[3] Cf. Jefferson's Message of January 22, 1807.

[4] 1 Parton, 313.

uary 15th he wrote to Campbell, member of the House of Representatives, and gave November as the time when he first heard of a plan to seize New Orleans, conquer Mexico, carry away the Western States, and set up a great empire.[1] He says that he was indignant at being the dupe of such an enterprise, and that he called Burr to account. Burr denounced and ridiculed the notion that he intended anything hostile to the United States.[2] He claimed to have the secret countenance of the Secretary of War. It seems that Jackson must have been convinced afterwards that Burr had been calumniated and unjustly treated. He was at Richmond as a witness in Burr's trial. He there made a public speech against Jefferson. Jackson had previously been ill-disposed towards Jefferson because Jefferson did not give him the office of Governor of Orleans. Jackson's strong personal contempt and dislike for General Wilkinson, the commander at New Orleans, who appeared as Burr's accuser, also influenced his judgment.[3] Throughout his life he was unable to form an unbiassed opinion on a question of fact or law, if he had any personal relations of friendship or enmity with the parties.

From 1806 to 1811 Jackson appears to have led

[1] *Telegraph Extra*, 481 *et seq.*

[2] When Burr was arrested in Kentucky he gave his word of honor to his counsel that he intended nothing against the United States. Kendall's *Jackson*, 120.

[3] His hatred of Wilkinson was greatly strengthened afterwards, but he shows it, and the influence of it, in his letter to Campbell.

the life of a planter without any noticeable incident.
The next we hear of him, however, he is committing
another act of violence. Silas Dinsmore, the Indian agent, refused to allow persons to pass through
the Indian country with negroes, unless they had
passports for the negroes. It was his duty by law
to enforce this rule. There were complaints that
negroes ran away or were stolen. His regulation,
however, interfered with the trade in negroes. This
trade was then regarded as dishonorable. It has
been charged that Jackson was engaged in it, and
the facts very easily bear that color. He passed
through the Indian country with some negroes
without hindrance, because Dinsmore was away,
but he took up the quarrel with the agent, and
wrote to Campbell to tell the Secretary of War
that, if Dinsmore was not removed, the people of
West Tennessee would burn him in his own agency.
There is a great deal of fire in the letter, and not
a little about liberty and free government.[1] Dinsmore was suspended, and things took such a turn
that he lost his position and was reduced to poverty. Parton gives a story of an attempt by Dinsmore, eight years later, to conciliate Jackson. This
attempt was dignified, yet courteous and becoming.
Jackson repelled it in a very brutal and low-bred
manner. Dinsmore did not know until 1828, when
he was a petitioner at Washington, and the papers
were called for, that Jackson had been the cause
of his ruin.[2]

[1] 34 Niles, 110.   [2] 8 Adams, 61.

The time was now at hand, however, when Andrew Jackson would have a chance to show how he could serve his country. At the age of forty-five he had commenced no career. He was a prominent man in his State, but he had held no political offices in it, and had not, so far as we know, been active in any kind of public affairs, although we infer that he had discharged all his duties as general of militia. He had shown himself a faithful friend and an implacable enemy. Every man who has this character is self-centred. He need not be vain or conceited. Jackson was not vain or conceited. He never showed any marked selfishness. He had a great deal of *amour propre*. All things which interested him at all took on some relation to his person, and he engaged his personality in everything which interested him. An opinion or a prejudice became at once for him a personal right and interest. To approve it and further it was to win his gratitude and friendship. To refute or oppose it was to excite his animosity. There was an intensity and vigor about him which showed lack of training. His character had never been cultivated by the precepts and discipline of home, or by the discipline of a strict and close society, in which extravagances of behavior and excess of *amour propre* are promptly and severely restrained by harsh social penalties. There is, to be sure, a popular philosophy that home breeding and culture are of no importance. The fact, however, is not to be gainsaid that true honor, truthfulness, suppression of undue personal feeling, self-control, and courtesy are inculcated best, if not exclusively, by the constant precept and example, in earliest childhood, of high-bred parents and relatives. There is nothing on earth which it costs more labor to produce than a high-bred man. It is also indisputable that home discipline and training ingrain into the character of men the most solid and valuable elements, and that, without such training, more civilization means better food and clothes rather than better men. It is characteristic of barbarians to put their personality always at stake, and not to distinguish the man who disputes their notions from the man who violates their rights. It is possible, however, that the military virtues may flourish where moral and social training are lacking. Jackson was unfortunate in that the force of his will and the energy of his executive powers had never been disciplined, but the outbreak of the second war with England afforded him an arena on which his faults became virtues.

CHAPTER II

IN no place in the world was Napoleon more ardently admired than in the new States of this country. The popular enthusiasm about him in those States lasted long after he was rated much more nearly at his true value everywhere else in the world. The second war with England was brought on by the policy, the opinions, and the feelings of the South and West, represented by a young and radical element in the Jeffersonian party. The opinion in the South and West, in 1811 and 1812, was that Napoleon was about to unite the Continent for an attack on England, in which he was sure to succeed, and that he would thus become master of Europe and the world. It was thought that it would be well to be in at the death on his side. It is not necessary to point out in any detail the grounds for this opinion which might have been put forward at that time, or to show the partial and distorted information on which it was founded. It is certain that the persons who held this notion were very ill-informed on European politics, and their opinions were strongly biassed by party conflicts at home. For twenty years the domestic politics of the United States had been organized on sympathy with one or the other of the belligerent parties in Europe. This country was weak in a military point of view, but commercially it would have been a great advantage to either belligerent to have free intercourse with the United States, and to keep his enemy from it. The English policy towards the United States was arrogant and insolent. That of France was marked by duplicity and chicanery. Party spirit here took possession of the people to such an extent that the federalists made apology for any injury from England, no matter how insolent, and the democrats could not see any wrong in the acts of Napoleon, in spite of the evident fact that he was using this country for his own selfish purposes while cajoling it with shameless lies. The course of the weak neutral between two such belligerents was very difficult.

Washington succeeded in maintaining neutrality by Jay's treaty, but at the cost of bitter hostility at home. Adams was driven to the verge of war with France by his party, but succeeded in averting war, although his party was destroyed by the reaction. Jefferson cannot be said to have had any plan. The statesmen of his party tried to act on the belligerents by destructive measures against domestic commerce and industry, chastising ourselves, as Plumer said, with scorpions, in order to beat the enemy with whips. They tried one measure after another. No measure had a rational origin or effect calculated and adjusted to the circumstances of the case.   Each was a new blunder. The republican rulers in France, in 1792, could do nothing better for a man who claimed protection from the Jacobin mobs than to put him in prison, so that the mob could not get at him.   Jefferson's embargo offered the same kind of protection to American shipping.   Before the embargo, merchants and ship-owners went to sea at great risk of capture and destruction; after it, they stayed at home and were sure of ruin.   Jefferson has remained a popular idol, and has never been held to the responsibility which belonged to him for his measures.   The alien and sedition laws were not nearly so unjust and tyrannical [1] as the laws for enforcing the embargo, and they did not touch one man where the embargo laws touched hundreds. The commercial war was a device which, if it had been sensible and practical, would have attained national ends by sacrificing one group of interests and laying a much inferior burden on others.   New England was denounced for want of patriotism because it resisted the use of its interests for national purposes, but as soon as the secondary effects of the embargo on agriculture began to be felt, the agricultural States raised a cry which overthrew the device.   Yet criticisms which are justified by the most conclusive testimony of history fall harmlessly from Jefferson's armor of popular platitudes

[1] See Carey's *Olive Branch*, page 50, for the opinion of a democrat on these laws after party spirit had cooled down.

and democratic sentiments. He showed the traits which we call womanish. He took counsel of his feelings and imagination; he planned measures like the embargo, whose scope and effect he did not understand. He was fiery when deciding initiatory steps, like the rejection of the English treaty; vacillating and timid when he had to adopt measures for going forward in the path which he had chosen. His diplomacy, besides being open to the charge that it was irregular and unusual, was transparent and easily turned to ridicule. It was a diplomacy without lines of reserve or alternatives, so that, in a certain very possible contingency, it had no course open to it. Jefferson finally dropped the reins of government in despair, and, on a theory which would make each presidential term last for three years and eight months, with an interregnum of four months, he left the task to his successor. He had succeeded in keeping out of war with either belligerent, but he had shaken the Union to its foundations. The extremists in the democratic party now came forward, and began to push Madison into a war with England, as the extreme federalists had pushed Adams into war with France. Madison, therefore, had to inherit the consequences of Jefferson's policy. An adherent of Jefferson describes the bequest as follows: "Jefferson's honest experiment, bequeathed to Madison, to govern without army or navy, and resist foreign enemies without war, proved total failures, more costly than war and much more odious to the people, and dangerous to the Union.''[1]

The young and radical democrats, amongst whom Clay was prominent, were restive under the predominance of the older generation of democrats of revolutionary fame, and their favorites. The young democrats wanted to come forward without the patronage of the Virginia leaders. The presidential election of 1812 was the immediate occasion of their action. The Jeffersonian policy had produced irritation at home and humiliation abroad. The natural consequence was a strong war spirit. It was believed that the country would not really be engaged in military operations, because England would be fully occupied in Europe; that Canada could be conquered; that we should come in on the winning side at the catastrophe of the great conflict in Europe; and that all this would be very popular in the South and West. Madison was compelled greatly against his will to yield to the war party, as a condition of his reëlection.[2] England pointed out that Napoleon had not complied with the terms of the American demands on both belligerents, but had falsified a date and told a lie. She withdrew her orders in council, and there remained only impressment as the ostensible cause of war. September 12, 1812, Admiral Warren offered an armistice. Madison refused it unless the practice of impressment was suspended. War-

---

[1] Ingersoll, 70.
[2] *Statesman's Manual*, 348. 1 Colton's *Clay*, 161.

ren had not power to agree to this. For purposes of redress the war was, therefore, unnecessary, and the United States was duped into it by Napoleon, so far as its avowed causes were concerned.[1]

General Jackson offered his services, with those of 2500 volunteers, as soon as he heard of the declaration of war. January 7, 1813, he set out under orders for New Orleans, an attack on that place being regarded as a probable movement of the enemy. Jackson threw himself into the business with all his might, and at once displayed activity, vigilance, and skill. His letter to the Secretary of War when he started shows with what enthusiasm he set to work. He assured the Secretary that his men had no " constitutional scruples," but would, if so directed, plant the American eagle on the walls of Mobile, Pensacola, and St. Augustine. In March he was at Natchez engaged in organizing his force, and waiting for orders. While there he had a quarrel with General Wilkinson on a question of rank. Thomas H. Benton, who was serving under Jackson, thought Jackson wrong on the point in question. This produced discord between him and Jackson.

Suddenly Jackson received orders to dismiss his troops, as it did not appear that the enemy were intending to attack New Orleans. He was, of course, greatly chagrined at this order. He was also enraged at the idea of disbanding his men, without pay or rations, five hundred miles from

[1] See 1 Gallatin's Writings, 517; 2 ditto, 196, 211, 499.

home, to find their way back as best they could.
A subsequent order repaired part of this error by
ordering pay and rations, but Jackson hired transportation on his own responsibility, and marched
his men home in a body.   Thomas H. Benton, in
June following, succeeded in obtaining from the
federal authorities reimbursement of the expenses
which Jackson had incurred.

This act of Benton would perhaps have extinguished the memory of the trouble about rank at
Natchez, but, in the mean time, Jackson had stood
second to another man in a duel with Jesse Benton,
brother of Thomas.   A feud was speedily created
out of this by the gossip and tale-bearing already
described.   Up to this time Jackson had had as
many enemies as friends, but his course in leading
home the troops from Natchez had made him very
popular.   His conduct in acting as second in the
duel, although chivalrous in one point of view, was
overbearing in another.   He threatened to horsewhip Thomas Benton, and a rencontre between him
and the two brothers took place in a tavern at
Nashville.   Blows and shots were exchanged, and
Jackson came away with a ball in his shoulder,
which he carried for twenty years.   This affair
occurred September 4, 1813.[1]

The great Indian chief Tecumseh had been trying for years to unite all the red men against the
whites.[2]   There would have been an Indian war if
there had been no war with England, but the latter

[1] *Cf.* 1 Sargent, 225.   [2] Drake's *Tecumseh.*

war seemed to be Tecumseh's opportunity. Among
the southwestern Indians he found acceptance only
with the Creeks, who were already on the verge of
civil war, because some wanted to adopt civilized
life, and others refused.[1] The latter became the
war party, under Weatherford, a very able half-
breed chief. The first outbreak in the Southwest,
although there had been some earlier hostilities,
was the massacre of the garrison and refugees at
Fort Mims, at the junction of the Alabama and
Tombigbee rivers, August 30, 1813. There were
553 persons in the fort, of whom only five or six
escaped.[2] If Tecumseh had lived, and if the English had been able to give their attention to an
alliance with him, he would have united the Indians from the Lakes to the Gulf, and the "young
democrats" would have found out what sort of a
business it may be to start a war for party effect.
The result of the massacre at Fort Mims was that
Alabama was almost abandoned by whites. Terror
and desire for revenge took possession of Georgia
and Tennessee. September 25th, the Tennessee
Legislature voted to raise men and money to aid
the people of the Mississippi territory against the
Creeks. Jackson was still confined to his bed by
the wound which Benton had given him. He and
Cocke were the two major-generals of the militia
of Tennessee. They concerted measures. As soon
as he possibly could, Jackson took the field. Geor-

[1] Folio State Papers, 1 *Indian Affairs*, 845 fg.
[2] 2 Pickett, 206.

gia had a force in the field under General Floyd. General Claiborne was acting at the head of troops from Louisiana and Mississippi. This Indian war had a local character and was outside the federal operations, although in the end it had a great effect upon them. Up to this time little had been known at Washington of Jackson, save that he had been a friend of Burr, an enemy of Jefferson, and that he had just acted in a somewhat insubordinate manner at Natchez, reflecting on the administration and winning popularity for himself.

The Creek war [1] was remarkable for three things: (1) the quarrels between the generals, and the want of concert of action; (2) lack of provisions; (3) insubordination in the ranks. Partly on account of the lack of provisions, for which he blamed General Cocke (as it appears, unjustly), Jackson fell into a bitter quarrel with his colleague and junior officer. The lack of provisions, and consequent suffering of the men, was one cause of insubordination in the ranks, but the chief cause was differences as to the term of enlistment. The enlistment was generally for three months, and constant recruiting was necessary to keep up the army in the field. A great deal of nonsense has been written and spoken about pioneer troops. Such troops were always insubordinate [2] and home-

[1] See Eaton's *Jackson* and Pickett's *Alabama*. On Tecumseh and the Prophet see *Smithsonian Rep.* 1885, Pt. ii. p. 200. The Prophet is described there as a vain sneak.

[2] See descriptions of Kentucky militia in Kendall's *Autobio-*

sick, and very dependent for success on enthusiasm
for their leader and a prosperous course of affairs.
For these reasons the character of the commander
was all-important to such an army. On three occasions Jackson had to use one part of his army to
prevent another part from marching home, he and
they differing on the construction of the terms of
enlistment. He showed very strong qualities under
these trying circumstances. He endured delay with
impatience, but with fortitude, and without a suggestion of abandoning the enterprise,[1] although he
was in wretched health all the time. He managed
his soldiers with energy and tact. He understood
their dispositions. He knew how to be severe with
them without bringing them to open revolt, and
he knew how to make the most efficacious appeals
to them.

In the conduct of the movements against the
enemy his energy was very remarkable. So long
as there was an enemy unsubdued Jackson could
not rest, and could not give heed to anything else.
Obstacles which lay in the way between him and
such unsubdued enemy were not allowed to deter
him. This restless and absorbing determination
to reach and crush anything which was hostile was
one of the most marked traits in Jackson's charac-

graphy, 124, 131, and description of a muster and training in 2
Lambert's *Travels*, 192. The western soldiers of this period re-
semble very closely the colonial troops of 60 or 70 years before.

[1] To Governor Blount, who proposed that he should retire from
the expedition, Jackson wrote a strenuous remonstrance, even an
admonition. Eaton's *Jackson*, 101.

ter. It appeared in all his military operations, and he carried it afterwards into his civil activity. He succeeded in his military movements. This gave him the confidence and adherence of his men. The young men of the State then hastened to enlist with him, and his ranks were kept well filled, because one who had fought a campaign with him, and had a story to tell, became a hero in the settlement. Jackson's military career and his popularity thus rapidly acquired momentum from all the circumstances of the case and all the forces at work. He was then able to enforce discipline and obedience, by measures which, as it seems, no other frontier commander would have dared to use.

On the 14th of March, 1814, he ordered John Wood to be shot for insubordination and assault on an officer. This was the first of the acts of severity committed by Jackson as a commanding officer, which were brought up against him in the presidential campaigns when he was a candidate. Wood was technically guilty. He acted just as any man in the frontier army, taught to reverence nobody and submit to no authority, would have acted under the circumstances. If it had not been for the great need of enforcing discipline, extenuating circumstances which existed would have demanded a mitigation of the sentence. Party newspapers during a presidential campaign are not a fair court of appeal to review the acts which a military commander in the field may think necessary in order to maintain discipline. Jackson showed in this case that he was not afraid to do his duty, and that he would not sacrifice the public service to curry popularity.

At the end of March, Jackson destroyed a body of the Creeks at Tohopeka, or Horse-Shoe Bend, in the northeast corner of the present Tallapoosa County, Alabama. With the least possible delay he pushed on to the last refuge of the Creeks, the Hickory Ground, at the confluence of the Coosa and Tallapoosa, and the Holy Ground a few miles distant. The medicine men, appealing to the superstition of the Indians, had taught them to believe that no white man could tread the latter ground and live. In April the remnant of the Creeks surrendered or fled to Florida, overcome as much by the impetuous and relentless character of the campaign against them as by actual blows. Fort Jackson was built on the Hickory Ground. The march down through Alabama was a great achievement, considering the circumstances of the country at the time. Major-General Thomas Pinckney, of the regular army, came to Fort Jackson, April 20th, and took command. He gave to Jackson's achievements the most generous recognition both on the spot and in his reports. April 21, 1814, the West Tennessee militia were dismissed, and they marched home.

The Creek campaign lasted only seven months. In itself considered, it was by no means an important Indian war, but in its connection with other military movements it was very important.

Tecumseh had been killed at the battle of the Thames in Canada, October 5, 1813. His scheme of a race war died with him. The Creek campaign put an end to any danger of hostilities from the southwestern Indians, in alliance either with other Indians or with the English. It was henceforth possible to plan military operations and pass through the Indian territory without regard to the disposition of the Indians. This state of things had been brought about very summarily, while military events elsewhere had been discouraging.

This campaign, therefore, was the beginning of Jackson's fame and popularity, and from it dates his career. He was forty-seven years old. On the 31st of May he was appointed a major-general in the army of the United States, and was given command of the department of the South. He established his headquarters at Mobile in August, 1814. That town had been occupied by Wilkinson, April 13, 1813. There were fears of an attack either on Mobile or New Orleans. English forces appeared, and took post at Pensacola. Jackson naturally desired to attack the enemy where he found him. The relations of the parties must be borne in mind.[1] Spain was a neutral and owned Florida, but the boundaries of Florida were in dispute between Spain and the United States. Jackson would not have been a southwestern man if he had not felt strongly about that dispute. We have seen[2] that one of Jackson's first thoughts,

[1] See page 23.   [2] See page 35.

when war with England broke out, was that Florida
might be conquered. Now Spain appeared to be
allowing England to use Florida as a base of operations. Jackson wrote to Washington for leave to
attack Pensacola. It did not suit his temper to
sit still under a great anxiety as to which spot on
a long coast might be chosen by the enemy as the
point of attack. The Secretary of War (Arm-
strong) replied to Jackson's application that it was
necessary, before invading Spanish territory, to
know certainly whether Spain voluntarily yielded
the use of her territory to England. This letter
did not reach Jackson until the war was over. All
Jackson's letters of this period to the State and
federal authorities have a tone of lecturing which
gives deep insight into the character of the man.
He meant no disrespect, but the case seemed so
clear to him that he set it forth with an unconscious
directness of language which violated official forms.

Jackson had but a very small force at Mobile,
very inadequately provided with any of the neces-
saries of war. The government at Washington
was falling to pieces. On the 24th of August
the English captured Washington and burned the
public buildings. Jackson could not obtain either
assistance or orders. September 14th, the English
attacked Fort Bowyer, on Mobile Point, and were
repulsed with energy and good fortune. They
retired to Pensacola. Jackson advanced against
Pensacola without orders from Washington, and
reached that place November 6th, with 3000 men.

He easily stormed the town. The Spaniards surrendered the forts near the town. The English
blew up the fort at Barrancas and departed.[1] Jackson immediately returned to Mobile, fearing a
new attack there. This energetic action against
Pensacola, which a timid commander would have
hesitated to take, although the propriety of it could
not be seriously questioned, was the second great
step in the war in the South. If the Creeks had
not been subdued, Mobile could not have been
defended. If Pensacola had not been captured,
New Orleans could not have been defended three
months later. Jackson had extraordinary luck, but
he deserved it by his energy and enterprise. All
the accidents fell out in his favor, and all contributed to his final success.

On the 2d of December, 1814, Jackson reached
New Orleans, where he expected the next blow to
fall. Nothing had been done there to prepare for
defence, and no supplies were there, — not even
arms. Edward Livingston and a Frenchman named
Louaillier were alone active even in preparing
the minds of the people for defence. Jackson
declared martial law as a means of impressing soldiers and sailors, and began preparations for defending the city, in spite of discouragements and
the lack of all proper means. He seemed to be
possessed by a kind of frenzy or fanaticism at the
idea of any one "invading" American territory.
As soon as he heard of the landing effected by the

[1] 7 Niles, 271. Latour, 44 *et seq.*

English after they had destroyed the flotilla on the lakes, he set out to meet them with such forces as he had. He arrested their advance as far from the city as possible, pushed on his preparations with redoubled energy and activity, and was indefatigable in devising and combining means of defence. " The energy manifested by General Jackson spread, as it were, by contagion, and communicated itself to the whole army. I shall add, that there was nothing which those who composed it did not feel themselves capable of performing, if he ordered it to be done. It was enough that he expressed a wish, or threw out the slightest intimation, and immediately a crowd of volunteers offered themselves to carry his views into execution." [1] He made the utmost of all the means he possessed and devised substitutes for what he lacked. He enlisted free colored men in spite of the great dissatisfaction which this caused.[2] Thus, with every day that passed, his position became stronger. The enemy were veteran troops, amply provided with all the best appliances of war, but, as it appears, not well commanded. An energetic advance on their part, at the first moment, would have won the city. It was, however, Jackson who made the energetic advance at the first moment, and he never let them get any farther.

Both parties courted the alliance of the pirates of Barataria. When the English made the first overtures, Jackson denounced them for seeking

[1] Latour, Preface, p. 17.   [2] Gayarré, 359, 409, 505.

alliance with "pirates and hellish banditti." The
pirates thought that their interest lay with the
Americans and joined them. Then Jackson called
them "privateers and gentlemen." In the American histories they have generally been lauded as
"patriots." [1] Jackson's proclamations were bombastic imitations of those of Napoleon. It is not
known who wrote the earlier ones. Some of his
later ones, at New Orleans, are attributed to Livingston.

The story of the battle which took place is a
strange one. Everything fell out favorably for
Jackson as if by magic. The English lost their
way, fired into each other, adopted foolish rumors,
disobeyed orders, neglected precautions. The two
parties built redoubts out of the same mud, and
cannonaded each other all day through a dense
smoke. At night the American works were hardly
damaged, while the English works were battered
to pieces and the cannon dismounted. On the 8th
of January, 1815, the English made their grand
assault on Jackson's works. Latour says that they
were over-confident, and that they disregarded the
obstacles. They were repulsed with great slaughter.
Their loss in general and field officers was especially remarkable. Only on the west bank of the
river did the English gain some advantage. General Jackson said then — and he always afterwards
refused to withdraw the assertion, in spite of the
remonstrances of General Adair, and in spite of a

[1] 19 *National Magazine,* 358; Gayarré, 353.

long controversy — that the Kentucky troops on
the west side "ingloriously fled."[1] This is worth
noticing only because it shows that Jackson would
not recede from what he thought true, either to
soothe wounded pride or to win popularity. If the
English had had a little larger force on the west side,
they would have won that position, and would have
more than counterbalanced all Jackson's success on
the east bank, for the batteries on the west bank
could easily have been made to command Jackson's
camp and works. The English withdrew after
their repulse. Their loss, January 8th, was over
2000 killed, wounded, and missing; Jackson's was
seven killed and six wounded.[2] The treaty of
peace had been signed at Ghent December 24,
1814, two weeks before the battle took place.
Before the English attempted any further operations in Louisiana, the news of the peace was received. They captured Fort Bowyer in a second
attack, February 12, 1815.

A brilliant victory was the last thing any one in
the United States had expected to hear of from
New Orleans. The expectations under which the
war had been undertaken had all been disappointed. Canada had not been conquered. The
United States had ranged itself with the defeated,

---

[1] 7 Niles, 373. Latour, App. 52. Latour makes an apology
for the Kentuckians, p. 174.

[2] Latour, App. 55, 153. See accounts of the battle in Cable's
History of New Orleans, in 10th Census, *Social Statist.* II, 255
fg.; Walker's *Jackson;* Gleig's *Campaigns*.

and not with the successful party in Europe. The
war had been more than nominal, but on land it
had been anything but glorious. Only on the sea
did the few frigates which the federalists had built,
while they controlled the federal government, vin-
dicate the national honor by brilliant successes.
Jefferson's *a priori* navy of gunboats had disappeared and been forgotten. The war party had
looked upon Gallatin as their financier. He had
told them in 1809 that war could be carried on
without taxes, but they had squandered, against
his remonstrances, resources on which he relied
when he so declared, and they had refused to recharter the Bank as he desired. When the war
broke out he went to Russia as one of the peace
commissioners. There was no one competent to
succeed him, and the democrats never forgave him
for the embarrassments which they suffered in trying to manage the finances.[1] He did not resign
his secretaryship, but was superseded February 9,
1814. Good democrats thought that sending him
abroad was a repetition of the course they had
blamed in Jay's case.[2] It certainly was a very
strange policy to leave the treasury without a regular head in war-time. The banks suspended, the
currency fell into confusion, heavy taxation became
necessary, and the public finances were brought to
the verge of bankruptcy. The party which had
made such an outcry about direct taxes, national

[1] See Ingersoll, 74.
[2] Carey's *Olive Branch*, 63.

bank, and eight per cent loans, imitated Hamilton's system of direct taxes and excise throughout. They were discussing a big paper-money bank on the day (February 13th) when news of the Treaty of Ghent reached Washington, and they would have adopted it if the war had continued. They sold six per cent bonds for eighty and eighty-five in a currency of bank rags depreciated twenty or twenty-five per cent. A grand conscription bill was also in preparation, and the Hartford convention had just adjourned, having done much or little according as peace or war might make it expedient to put one sense or another on ambiguous phrases. When Napoleon fell, and England was left free to devote her attention to this country as her only remaining foe, the war took on a new aspect. June 13, 1814, Gallatin wrote home that a large force was fitting out in England against America. Admiral Cochrane wrote to Monroe that he had orders to devastate the coasts of the United States. The first conditions of peace talked of by England involved cession of territory in Michigan and the Ohio territory, as well as concessions of trading privileges and navigation of the Mississippi, — terms which could not be accepted until after a great deal more hard fighting. The feeling here in the autumn of 1814 was one of deep despondency and gloom.[1] The victory of New Orleans was

[1] See *Niles's Register*, vol. 7; Pres. Message, 1814; 1 Goodrich, Letter xxx.; Carey's *Olive Branch*, preface 4th and 6th ed. Ingersoll finds room for the opinion that the prospects for 1815 were bright.

the cause of boundless delight, especially because
the news of it reached the North at just about the
same time as the news of peace, and there was no
anxiety about the future to mar the exultation.
The victory was a great consolation to the national
pride, which had been sorely wounded by military
failures, and by the capture of Washington. The
power of Great Britain had been met and repulsed
when put forth at its best, and when the American
resources were scanty and poor. To the administration and the war party the victory was political
salvation. The public plainly saw, however, that
the federal administration had done nothing for
the victory. Jackson had been the soul of the defence from the beginning, and to his energy and
perseverance success was due. He therefore got
all the credit of it, and the administration was only
too glad to join in the plaudits, since attention was
thereby diverted from its blunders and failure.
These facts explain Jackson's popularity. In the
space of time between September, 1813, and January, 1815, he had passed from the status of an obscure Tennessee planter to that of the most distinguished and popular man in the country.

In the treaty of peace nothing was said about
impressment, the "principle" of which was what
the United States had been striving about ever
since 1806, and which was the only cause of the
war. The war was therefore entirely fruitless as to
the causes which were alleged for it at the outset.
What the course of things might have been, if

a wiser statesmanship had adopted Monroe and
Pinkney's treaty, and pursued a steady course of
peace and industrial growth, so far as the state of
the world would allow, is a matter of speculation ;
but, in the course which things did take, there are
especial and valuable features of our history which
are to be traced to the second war with England
as their origin.   The discontent of New England
faded away at once, and there was a stronger feeling of nationality and confidence throughout the
country than there ever had been before.[1] From
that time on the Union had less of the character
of a temporary experiment.   The country had also
won respect abroad, and was recognized in the
family of nations as it had not been before.   From
1789 to 1815 the European nations were absorbed
by European politics and war.   At the end of this
period they turned to find that a new nation had
begun to grow up on the western continent.   The
Americans had shown that they could build ships
of war, and sail them, and fight them on an equal
footing.   To the military states of Europe this was
a fact which inspired respect.

To return to our more immediate subject : There
had been another dispute about terms of enlistment at Fort Jackson in September, 1814. About
200 men, some of whom broke open a store-house
to get supplies, and indulged in expressions and
acts of contempt for authority, marched home without the consent of their commanding officer. Most

[1] Gallatin expressed this opinion.   1 Gallatin's Writings, 700.

of them came back; some being compelled, others
thinking better of it, and others after assuaging
their homesickness. A large number were put
under arrest and tried by court-martial. Six were
condemned to death, and, by Jackson's orders,
were executed at Mobile, February 21, [?] 1815.[1]
The question of law involved was a difficult one.
The men took the risk of acting on their own view
of that question, while they were under military
law. The tribunal was competent, the law undis-
puted, and the proceedings regular, but attempts
were made to make political capital out of the incident, when Jackson became a candidate. There
had never been such discipline in an American
army,[2] least of all in the West. Jackson, and Lewis
on his behalf, did not avow and defend, although
some of his adherents did do so, on the ground of
need of discipline. Lewis denied that Jackson ordered the execution. He wrote, at different times,
versions of the story which are not strictly accord-
ant. In 1827 Jackson wrote to Lewis that the
men were sentenced to be shaved and drummed out
of camp, but that even this sentence was not to
be executed. " There was no punishment on any
one of them inflicted, or my orders were violated." [3]
The formal finding of the court with his approval

[1] From the documents as given in 34 Niles, 55 (1828). Report
of a Committee of the House friendly to Jackson.
[2] Jackson's apologists made much of an alleged parallel case
under Washington.
[3] Ford MSS.

and order for execution is in 34 Niles, 73. The
noticeable thing is that, in this case, quite excep-
tionally, he tried to deny and evade responsibility
for something which he had done.

After the English departed from New Orleans
Jackson relaxed none of his vigilance, but continued to strengthen his force by all the means at
his command. In this he acted like a good and
wise commander, who did not mean to be caught.
He could not assume that the enemy would not
make another attack, and he knew nothing yet of
the peace. He maintained the attitude of alert
preparation until he was sure that the war was at
an end. He maintained martial law in the city,
and he administered it with rigor. Evidently he
thought that a proclamation of martial law set
aside the *habeas corpus* and all civil law.[1] The
possession of absolute and arbitrary power did not
have a good effect on him. The exhilaration and
self-confidence of success and flattery affected his
acts. It appears that he did not respect all the
inhabitants of the city; for which he had ample
reason.[2] They were a motley crowd, and he thought
that some of them were not ready to do what he
thought they ought to do to defend the city.[3] Any
one who would not go to the last extreme for that
object could count on Jackson's contempt. He
meant to hold the city in such shape that he could

---

[1] Gayarré, 608; Martin, 402.
[2] See Cable's *History of New Orleans.*
[3] See his defence in reply to Hall's writ, 8 Niles, 246.

make every man in it contribute to its defence, if the occasion should arise. Frenchmen had certain privileges for twelve years, under the treaty of 1803. They had generally coöperated in the defence, but, after the English departed, they sought certificates of nationality in order to secure the privileges and exemptions to which they were entitled. To Jackson this seemed like shirking a share of the common burdens. Livingston, who had been on an embassy to the English fleet, brought back news, on the 18th of February,[1] of the peace. Jackson would not alter his attitude or proceedings on account of this intelligence, because it came through the enemy, although it was transmitted in a formal and polite note from the English naval commander, and the English officers acted on it. Jackson, in an address to his army, said that it was only a newspaper report. It was a "bulletin" from Jamaica, dated February 13.[2] February 24, Governor Claiborne wanted martial law abolished. On February 28th, Jackson ordered all who had certificates of French nationality to go to Baton Rouge before March 3d, on the ground

[1] Latour says on the 10th. This date has been regarded as important for the question whether Jackson knew, before he allowed the six militiamen to be executed, that peace had been made. The order for execution was signed at New Orleans, January 22, and it was to be executed four days after its promulgation at Mobile. In Dallas's letter to Jackson of April 12, mention is made of a letter of Jackson of February 6, which showed that he had received that intelligence then.

[2] Gayarré, 579, 623.

that he would have no man in the city who was not
bound to help defend it. March 8th he suspended
this order, except as to the French consul, a man
who had lost an arm in the American revolution.
There had been almost civil war between the
French and American residents. March 3d the
same Louaillier, who had been conspicuous as an
advocate of energetic defence, wrote an article for
a local paper, criticising the order of February
28th, and urging that martial law should be abolished. The English troops had all departed about
six weeks before.[1] The editor, when called to account for this article, gave up his contributor.
Louaillier was arrested March 4th, under a law
against "lurking" near camps and forts. Judge
Hall, of the United States District Court, issued a
writ of *habeas corpus* for him. Jackson received
news of the peace from Washington on March 6th,
but by some blunder the courier did not bring the
document containing the official notification. On
that day Jackson convened a court-martial to try
Louaillier. He sent an officer to arrest Judge
Hall, and to obtain from the clerk of the court the
original writ of *habeas corpus*. The writ was written on the back of the petition for it,[2] on the 5th,
which was Sunday; therefore it was dated on the
6th. Jackson seized the original writ in order to

[1] Gayarré, 616.
[2] Martin, 397. It appears that the writ was submitted to the
judge with the date, the 5th, and that he changed the date in
signing it.

prove the "forgery" of the date. In 1842 he laid
great stress on this alteration of the date. He
seemed to think that it bore materially on the
question whether Hall was guilty, by the writ, of
inciting to mutiny in his camp,[1] but although he
had, what was called in the documents of the time,
"persuasive evidence" of peace on the 6th, he
maintained his military organization two days
longer. On the 8th he disbanded the militia. On
the same day Dick, the District Attorney of the
United States, obtained from a State judge a *habeas corpus* for Hall. Jackson arrested and imprisoned Dick with Louaillier. He arrested the
State judge too, but soon released him and Dick.
The court-martial struck out all the charges against
Louaillier except one (illegal and improper conduct), for want of jurisdiction, and acquitted him
on that. Jackson disapproved of this finding, and
defended his own proceedings. On the 11th of
March he sent Hall four miles out of the city and
released him. Louaillier was kept in prison until
the official document announcing the peace was received, March 13th. On the 22d of March the
United States District Court ordered Jackson to
show cause why an attachment should not issue
against him for contempt of court, in wresting an
original document from the court, disobeying the
writ of *habeas corpus*, and imprisoning the judge.
Jackson refused to answer save by a general vindication of his proceedings. This the judge refused

[1] Several letters in the Ford MSS. and 62 Niles, 326.

to hear, and fined him $1000.[1] Jackson tried to
escape by saying that his actions were against Hall,
the *man*, not against Hall, the *judge*. In 1842
Tyler recommended Congress to refund the fine
without reflecting on the court. J. Q. Adams said
in a speech, January 6, 1843, that this was auction-
eering for the presidency, all the factions desiring
Jackson's support.[2] In 1844 Congress refunded
the fine with interest, — total $2700. In a letter
to L. F. Linn, March 14, 1842,[3] Jackson refers to
the fine as having been laid because he declared
martial law. He wrote to Lewis, in 1843 : —

"It surely was one of the greatest usurpations in Hall
recorded in the history of the world — he usurped the
power of the holy inquisition to charge, try, and condemn
me, unheard in open violation of the constitution & all
law — he had no legal power for his proceedings & In-
gersol has clearly shewn it, and I trust it will be fully
investi-[gated] now whilst I am living, that the people
may see, who were the tyrants & who the usurper of
power."[4]

In this incident Jackson displayed some of the
faults of which he afterwards showed many in-

[1] Report of a committee of the House of Representatives; 64
Niles, 61 (1843). Cf. the account in 8 Niles, 246, and Judge
Hall's response, *Ibid.*, 272 (1815).

[2] 63 Niles, 312.

[3] 62 Niles, 212. For Jackson's own story of the fine, see 62
Niles, 326.

[4] Ford MSS. The best account of the trial, etc., is by Judge
Martin, who was in New Orleans at the time, and was a competent
observer and historian. His account has been followed above.

stances. He spoiled his military success by this
unnecessary collision with the civil authority. He
proved himself wrong-headed and persistent in a
course in which every step would have warned him
of his error, if he had been willing to learn. Being
committed by his first passionate and hasty step,
he was determined to push through on the course
he had adopted. He knew with reasonable certainty from February 18, and to a moral certainty
from the 6th of March, that the war was at an end.
All these mischievous proceedings took place on
and after the latter date. A very little concession
and good-will at any time would have avoided the
whole trouble, but Jackson acted as if he was determined to grind out of the opposing elements in
the situation all the friction of which they were
capable.

April 12th, Dallas, acting Secretary of War,
wrote a dispatch to Jackson, asking for explanations
of the proceedings, which were rehearsed in detail,
and very accurately, according to reports which had
reached Washington. " The President views the
subject in its present aspect, with surprise and so-
licitude ; but in the absence of all information
from yourself, relative to your conduct and the
motives for your conduct, he abstains from any decision, or even the expression of an opinion, upon
the case, in hopes that such explanations may be
afforded as will reconcile his sense of public duty
with a continuance of the confidence which he re-
poses in your judgment, discretion, and patriotism."

As the matter was all past and dead, and no one desired to mar the exultation of the public or the personal satisfaction of Jackson, it was allowed to drop.

In the autumn of 1815 Jackson was in Washington, conferring with the War Department about the peace footing of the army. In the spring of 1816 he was at New Orleans on business of his military department.

CHAPTER III

ANDREW JACKSON took no important part in
the election of 1816. He had favored Monroe in
1808, and he preferred him to the other candidates
in 1816. Crawford was, at this time, Jackson's
pet dislike. The reason for this was that Crawford, as Secretary of War, had modified Jackson's
treaty with the Creeks, about which the Cherokees,
deeming the terms unjust to them, had appealed
to the President. Jackson made a personal quarrel with a public man for not acting as he, Jackson,
wanted him to act in the discharge of his duty.
Jackson resumed the negotiation, and bought again
the lands ceded before. As the people of Tennessee, Georgia, and Alabama were interested in the
cession, Jackson, by re-obtaining it after it had
been surrendered, greatly increased his popularity.[1]

November 12, 1816, a letter, signed by Jackson,
was addressed to Monroe, immediately after his
election to the presidency, urging the appointment
of Wm. Drayton, of South Carolina, as Secretary
of War. Wm. B. Lewis, Jackson's neighbor and
confidential friend, husband of one of Mrs. Jack-

[1] 11 Niles, 143.

son's nieces, wrote this letter. As Parton says,
one has no trouble in distinguishing those letters
signed Jackson, but which have been copied and
revised by Lewis, Lee, Livingston and others, from
those which have not been through that process. A
part of this letter was connected with a land speculation, but the political part of it seems gratuitous
and impertinent. It is, in fact, introduced by an
apology. It is difficult to see its significance and
that of others which Jackson wrote during this
winter (1816–17), unless he was being used to
advance an intrigue on behalf of Drayton about
which we have no other information. The ideas
and suggestions are not at all such as would arise
in Jackson's mind. Drayton had been a federalist.
He belonged to the South Carolina aristocracy.
No ties of any kind are known to have existed
between him and Jackson, either before or after
this time. Jackson said in 1824 that he did not
know Drayton in 1816.[1] Drayton was not appointed.

These well-composed letters failed entirely of their
immediate object; and they reposed in obscurity
for seven years. Lewis was an astonishingly farsighted man. We shall see abundant proofs, hereafter, of his power to put down a stake where he
foresaw that he would need to exert a strain a little
later, but it does not seem credible that he can
have foreseen and prepared for the ultimate purpose which these letters served. His own account,

[1] 26 Niles, 162.

endorsed on a MS. copy of this especial letter, and
dated 1835, is : —

"Gen. Jackson furnished the rough draft, from which
the letter was prepared by the undersigned. The original letter will be found, if examined, to be in my
hand-writing. The ideas are the General's and the
language mine. It contained sentiments so patriotic and
liberal I thought them worthy the Hero of New Orleans,
and deserved to be handed down to posterity. So
strongly was this opinion impressed upon my mind, at
the time, that I took a copy, unknown to him, to be
placed in the hands of his future biographer, should the
original fail to find its way to the public. This precau-
tion, however, turned out to be unnecessary, as it was
unexpectedly brought to light, about eleven years ago,
and has been frequently published since. It was called
out by Gen. Jackson's political enemies, when he was
first a candidate for the presidency. They, understanding such a letter had been written to Mr. Monroe,
resolved on having it published, under the belief it would
ruin him in the estimation of the republican party in
Pennsylvania, with whom he was a great favorite, but
in this they reckoned without their host. Instead of
weakening, it evidently strengthened him, and was one
of the principal causes of his receiving the highest electoral vote in 1824, and was probably the means of
securing his election in 1828." [1]

He engineered the "calling out" and the production of the letter, in 1824, himself.

In the course of his argument on behalf of Drayton, Jackson was led (in the letters) to discuss

[1] Ford MSS.

the general theory of appointments, and to urge
Monroe to abandon the proscription of the federalists, to appoint them to office, and to promote
reconciliation and good-will.   He declared that he
would have hung the leaders of the Hartford convention, if he had been in command in the eastern
department in 1815.   In 1823 and 1824 the letters
were used with great effect to draw federalists to
the support of Jackson.   They were delighted with
the tone and sentiment of them,[1] although a few
winced at the reference to the Hartford convention.
In 1828 the other aspect of the letters rather pre-
dominated.   The democrats were not quite pleased
that Jackson should have urged Monroe to appoint
federalists and disregard party.[2]

Monroe was being acted upon, when Jackson
wrote to him, from the other side, by those who
wanted him to favor the Monroe faction in the republican party.   He had enough to do to maintain
himself between the two demands.   He answered
Jackson, admitting the high principle of the course
Jackson advocated, but setting forth a theory of
appointments more conformable to the exigencies
of party politics.

April 22, 1817, Jackson published an order to his
department forbidding his subordinates to obey any
order from the War Department not issued through

[1] Binns, 249.
[2] The whole correspondence, 26 Niles, 163 *et seq.* See comments quoted, *ibid.*, p. 219. For the disapproval of the democrats, see Binns, 246.

him. He had been much and justly annoyed at incidents in the service under him, of which he had not been informed beforehand, and also by direct orders issued from Washington, which interfered with his arrangements and frustrated them without his knowledge. On the merits of the question he was in the right, but his public "order" produced an unnecessary scandal and public collision in a case where a proper private representation to the department would have answered every purpose. Crawford was transferred to the treasury in October, 1816. There was difficulty in filling the position of Secretary of War. Calhoun was appointed October 8, 1817. He conceded the point claimed by Jackson, reserving only the cases of emergency.

Some persons informed Jackson that General Scott had animadverted upon his action in the matter just mentioned, and had characterized it as mutiny. September 8, 1817, Jackson wrote a fiery letter to Scott, calling him to account. Scott replied that, in private conversation, he had said that the order of April 22d was mutinous as to the future, and a reflection on the President, the Commander-in-Chief, as to the past. He disclaimed any personal feeling. Jackson replied in a very insulting letter, in which the well-battered question, Who of us two is the gentleman? did good service again, and he wound up with a challenge to a duel. Scott declined the challenge on the ground of religious scruples and patriotic duty. The correspondence was almost immediately published. It created another scandal, for the public was not edified to see two of the first officers of the army engaged in such a quarrel.[1] Niles, who at this time greatly admired Jackson, and who is always a good representative of the average citizens of his time, refrained from publishing the correspondence until April, 1819.[2] In this case, again, Jackson showed evidence of an ungovernable temper and a willingness to profit by every opportunity for a quarrel.

There was, however, more public fighting at hand.

There were in Florida many refugee Indians of the Creek nation, who were hostile to the United States, and many runaway negroes. During the war the English had sought such aid as they could get from these persons in their operations against the United States. They had built a fort on the Appalachicola River, about fifteen miles from its mouth, and had collected there an immense amount of arms and ammunition. The English officers who were operating in Florida acted with a great deal of arbitrary self-will. They were not under strict responsibility to their own government. They were operating on Spanish territory. They were stirring up Indians and negroes, and were not commanding a regular or civilized force. It is difficult to understand some of their proceedings in any point of view, and other of their doings certainly would not have been sanctioned by the English

[1] 14 Niles, 295 ; 4 Adams, 323.   [2] 16 Niles, 121.

government, if known to it. The officers were able to gratify their own malice without responsibility.

When the war ended, the English left the arms and ammunition in the fort. The negroes seized the fort, and it became known as the " Negro Fort." The authorities of the United States sent General Gaines to the Florida frontier with troops, to establish peace on the border. The Negro Fort was a source of anxiety both to the military authorities and to the slave-owners of Georgia, and, according to some accounts, the first step was its investment. It is otherwise stated that the American authorities undertook to bring supplies up the Appalachicola for a fort which they were building in Georgia, and that the boats were fired on, after which the troops marched down from Georgia and invested the fort, having received permission to do so from the Spanish authorities at Pensacola, who also very unwillingly saw a great fortress established in their territory, and held by negroes and Indians.[1] The fort was bombarded. A hot shot penetrated one of the magazines, and the whole fort was blown to pieces, July 27, 1816. There were three hundred negro men, women, and children and twenty Choctaws in the fort; two hundred and seventy were killed. Only three came out unhurt, and these were killed by the allied Indians.[2]

[1] Document A, 55.
[2] See Wait's *State Papers*, vii. 478, 482 ; viii. 126-135 ; ix. 41-49 ; 154-198.

Spain was engaged in hostilities with her revolted colonies in America. Filibusters and privateers took advantage of this state of things to carry on a certain grade of piracy and the slave-trade. Amelia Island, on the northeast coast of Florida, had been infested by smugglers, slavers, and freebooters ever since the war with England. In 1817 the island was occupied by a filibuster named McGregor, and later by another named Aury. They pretended to desire to render Florida independent, and there was a measure of honest intention in their plans, but the island was a nest of outlaws and a nuisance. The troops of the United States took possession of the island and drove the freebooters out, because Spain was not able to do so. Old causes of complaint against Spain with respect to Florida have been described above.[1] The hostile Indians and the freebooters were new causes of annoyance. The Georgians were also annoyed that their slaves found an easy refuge in Florida. It had been amply proved that Spain could not fulfil the duties which devolved upon her as owner of Florida. Yet she strenuously insisted that her sovereignty should be respected.[2] For all these reasons the United States was very anxious to buy Florida.

During 1817 there were frequent collisions on the frontiers between white men and Indians. Ex-Governor Mitchell of Georgia, the Indian agent, the fairest and best informed witness who appeared

[1] See page 23.   [2] Document A, 55.

before the committee of Congress in 1818–19, deposed that the blame for these collisions was equal, that one party was as often the aggressor as the other, and that the lawless persons in Florida were especially to blame for acts of injury which provoked retaliation.[1] When Gaines wrote to the chief Kenhigee that his Indians had killed white men, the chief replied that four Indians had been killed for every white man.[2] The reports which were sent North were, as usual in such cases, only such as tended to show an aggressive disposition on the part of the Indians.[3]

On the 20th of November, General Gaines sent a force of two hundred and fifty men to Fowltown, the headquarters of the chief of the "Redsticks," or hostile Creeks. They approached the town in the early morning, and were fired on. An engagement followed. The town was taken and burned. Gaines's dispatch to the Governor of Georgia puts the number of Indians killed at four.[4] Ex-Governor Mitchell of Georgia, quoted above, said, "This fact was, I conceive, the cause of the Seminole war." It is, however, fair to say that Mitchell was unfriendly to Gaines and to Jackson.[5] The Indians of that section, after this, began general hostilities, attacked the boats which were ascending the Appalachicola, and massacred the persons in them. Gaines states no reason at

[1] 16 Niles, 85.   [2] Document A, 140.
[3] See the items of news from Florida in 13 Niles.
[4] 13 Niles, 296.   [5] 43 Niles, 80.

all for sending a force against Fowltown, except that he had invited the chief to visit him, in order to find out "whether his hostile temper had abated." The chief refused to come. The friendly Indians said that the Fowltown Indians had been hostile ever since the last war. Therefore Gaines sent a force equal to the number of Indians in the town "to bring the chief and warriors, and, in the event of resistance, to treat them as enemies." When the Indians saw this force approaching they fired on it, stood fire once, and then ran away. Their property was then all destroyed, and the United States had an Indian war on its hands.

In December, on receipt of intelligence of the battle at Fowltown and the attack on the boats, Jackson was ordered to take command in Georgia. He wrote to President Monroe: "Let it be signified to me through any channel (say Mr. J. Rhea [1]) that the possession of the Floridas would be desirable to the United States, and in sixty days it will be accomplished." Much was afterwards made to depend on this letter. Monroe was ill when it reached Washington, and he did not see or read it until a year afterwards, when some reference was made to it.[2] Jackson construed the

[1] This name is found at the head of a movement, in 1810, to set up a filibuster state in Florida. Rhea signed "as President" an application, dated at Baton Rouge, for the admission of such state to the Union. It is couched in such terms as to call for the covert approval of the United States before becoming explicit. 7 Wait's *State Papers*, 482.

[2] 8 Adams, 249.

orders which he received from Calhoun from the standpoint of this letter. He also afterwards affirmed that Rhea wrote to him that the President approved of his suggestions;[1] but he could not produce that letter. He had burned it.[2] He certainly supposed, however, that he had the secret concurrence of the administration in conquering Florida. In 1811 orders were given to General Matthews to sound the inhabitants of East Florida as to coming into the Union ; also not to let any foreign nation occupy Florida.[3] Any one who knew this might well infer that the authorities at Washington would not be scrupulous about invading Florida.

When the orders to take command reached Jackson, the Governor of Tennessee was absent from Nashville. Jackson proceeded to raise troops in Tennessee on his own responsibility; he being authorized to call on the governors of the States which were neighbors to the scene of war. He pushed on his preparations with great energy and

[1] 8 Adams, 404.

[2] Memorandum by Jackson, 1837. He told Henry Lee, who was astonished that he had burned the letter, that " it was at the earnest personal request of Mr. Rhea, and Mr. Rhea stated at the earnest request of Mr. Munroe, as my health was delicate and I might die without destroying that confidential letter, which was strictly confidential and I had promised him that as soon as I reached home I would burn it — and having so promised I did burn and made that memorandum on the margin to show I had complied with my promise." He wanted Lee to testify that he had seen the entry on the margin of the letter-book opposite Jackson's letter to Monroe. Ford MSS.

[3] 9 Wait's *State Papers*, 41.

celerity. His acts were approved both by the State and federal authorities. He advanced through Georgia with great haste, and was on the Florida frontier in March, 1818. He ordered part of his provisions sent to Fort Scott by the Appalachicola, on which the Spaniards had no. fort, and he sent word to the Spanish commander at Pensacola that, if the fort at Barrancas hindered his supply boats from ascending the Escambia, he should consider it an act of hostility to the United States. These were, to say the least, very aggressive proceedings against a nation with which we were at peace, for a man who had been thrown into paroxysms of rage and energy at the idea of a redcoat resting on the soil of Louisiana during a public war. Jackson immediately advanced to St. Mark's, which place he captured. On his way down the Appalachicola he found the Indians and negroes at work in the fields, and unconscious of any impending attack. Some of them fled to St. Mark's. His theory, in which he supposed that he was supported by the administration, was that he was to pursue the Indians until he caught them, wherever they might go; that he was to respect Spanish rights as far as he could consistently with that purpose; and that the excuse for his proceedings was that Spain could not police her own territory, or restrain the Indians. Jackson's proceedings were based on two positive but arbitrary assumptions: (1) That the Indians got aid and encouragement from St. Mark's and Pensacola. (This the Spaniards

always denied, but perhaps another assumption of
Jackson might be mentioned : that the word of a
Spanish official was of no value.)   (2) That Great
Britain kept paid emissaries employed in Florida
to stir up trouble for the United States.   This
latter assumption was a matter of profound belief
generally in the United States.   Niles's reports
and criticisms of events in Florida all proceed
from that assumption.[1]   The English government
disavowed every transaction of Colonel Nichols
with the Indians which took definite shape and
could be dealt with at all.   The Indians whom he
took to England were kindly treated, but were not
encouraged to look to England for any assistance
or countenance.   It was not easy to break off the
connections which had been established, and destroy
the hopes which had been raised, during the war,
but there is not the slightest evidence that the
English government did not act in good faith, or
that it was busy in such contemptible business as
employing emissaries to stir up some two thousand savages to wage a frontier war on the United
States, after peace had been concluded.   Jackson's
assumption, however, had serious import for two
unfortunate individuals.

A Scotchman, Alexander Arbuthnot, was found
by Jackson in St. Mark's.   When the fort was
taken, Arbuthnot mounted his horse to ride away,
but he was seized, and put in confinement.   He
was an Indian trader, who had been in Florida for

[1] 14 Niles; all the articles on Florida.

many years. He had established as intimate and
friendly relations as possible with the Indians for
his own security and advantage in trade. He had
also sympathized with the Indians, and had exerted
himself in their behalf in many quarters.

Several American vessels of war lay in the bay
of St. Mark's to coöperate with the land forces.
By displaying English colors on these ships, two
Indian chiefs, Hillis Hajo (or Francis) and Himol-
lemico, were enticed on board and made prisoners.
They were hung by Jackson's order. They had
tortured and massacred prisoners after the Indian
fashion, but no one has ever explained by what law
or usage known in the service of the United States
they were put to death, when thus captured, not
even on the field of battle, but by a very questionable trick.

Jackson pushed on with the least possible delay
to the Suwanee River, where were the headquarters
of Boleck (Billy Bowlegs), the Seminole chief.
Arbuthnot had a trading-post there. When he
had heard of Jackson's advance, he had written
to his son, who was his agent at Boleck's village,
to carry the goods across the river. Through
this letter the Indians got warning in time to cross
the river and take to the swamps. Their escape
enraged Jackson. He had already regarded Arbuthnot as one of the British emissaries. He now
considered Arbuthnot's letter an overt act of interference in the war. The town was burned by
Jackson. In its neighborhood he captured an

Englishman named Robert Ambrister, an ex-lieutenant in the British marines, and nephew of the Governor of New Providence. This man was carried as a prisoner to St. Mark's, the troops being on their way home, and the war being over. A court-martial was convened at St. Mark's. Arbuthnot was tried for (1) inciting the Creek Indians to war against the United States; (2) being a spy and aiding the enemy; (3) inciting the Indians to murder two white men named. The court found him guilty of the first charge and of the second except of being a spy, and condemned him to be hung. There was no evidence at all against him on any charge.[1] His business in Florida was open and obvious. He had always advised the Indians to peace and submission. His letter to his son was not open to censure. Can traders be executed if their information, not transmitted through the lines, frustrates military purposes? As Arbuthnot construed the Treaty of Ghent the Indians were to have their lands restored, and he told them so. There was so much room for this construction that diplomatic measures were necessary to set it aside. Peace had been made with the Creeks before the Treaty of Ghent was made.

Ambrister was tried for inciting the Indians and levying war. His case was different. He had no ostensible business in Florida. He was an adven-

---

[1] Report of the trial in full, 15 Niles, 270. All the documents about the Negro Fort and the invasion of Florida are in Document A.

turer, and it is not clear what he hoped or intended. He threw himself on the mercy of the court. He was condemned to be shot. This sentence was reconsidered, and he was then condemned to fifty lashes and a year of hard labor. Jackson disapproved of the reconsideration, revived the first sentence, and ordered both men to be executed. April 29, 1818, he left St. Mark's, having detached a force to hold that place and to execute the sentence. The same day both men were executed. Arbuthnot was seventy years old; Ambrister was thirty-three.

It was as a mere incident of his homeward march that Jackson turned aside and captured Pensacola, May 24, 1818, because he was told that some Indians had taken refuge there. He deposed the Spanish government, set up a new one, and established a garrison. He then continued his march homewards. On his way he heard of an attack by Georgia militia on the villages of friendly and allied Indians, and he became engaged in a fiery correspondence with Governor Rabun of Georgia about that affair.[1] He was in the right, but it was another case in which by violence he provoked anger and discord, when he might have accomplished much more by a temperate remonstrance.

In the whole Florida matter we see Jackson proceeding to summary measures on inadequate facts and information. He "knew" how the matter

[1] Documents in the Supplement to 15 Niles, 56.

stood by the current prejudices and assumptions, not by evidence and information. This was the tone of his mind. Notions and prepossessions which once effected a lodgment in his mind, because circumstances gave them a certain plausibility, or because they fell in with some general prejudice or personal bias of his, immediately gained for him the character of obvious facts or self-evident truths. He then pursued such notions and prepossessions to their last consequences, and woe to any one who stood in the way.[1]

General Jackson had, in five months, broken the Indian power, established peace on the border, and substantially conquered Florida. This five months and the eighteen months service in 1813–15 were all the actual service he ever saw. The Seminole war was, in its relations and effects, one of the most important events in our history, but in itself it was one of the most insignificant of our Indian campaigns. Jackson had an overwhelming force. The report of the Senate committee of 1819 puts his force at 1,800 whites and 1,500 friendly Indians. The hostile Indians were never put by anybody at a higher number than 2,000. This committee put them at 1,000, not over half of whom, at any one time, were in front of Jackson. The allied Indians did all the fighting. They lost

[1] "It was easy to see that he was not a man to accept a difference of opinion with equanimity, but that was clearly because, he being honest and earnest, Heaven would not suffer his opinions to be other than right." Quincy; *Figures*, 355.

twenty men in the campaign. Not one white man was killed. The number of hostile Indians killed is put at sixty.[1]

The trouble with Jackson's achievements was that he had done too much. The statesmen and diplomatists could not keep up with him, and the tasks he threw on them were harder than those he performed in the field. The administration was not aware that it had authorized him to violate neutral territory. Federal administrations in those days were always timid. They did not know the limits of their power, or what they dared do. Monroe was especially timid. His administration wanted to buy Florida, not conquer it. They did not thank Jackson for plunging them into such a difficulty with Congress and with England and Spain all at once. The two Indian captives who had been hung had no friends, but their execution was an awkward thing to justify before the civilized world. The execution of the two Englishmen was likely to provoke a great deal of diplomatic trouble. Jackson had been perfectly sure about the law. He laid it down in the order for the execution. "It is an established principle of the law of nations that any individual of a nation making war against the citizens of any other nation, they being at peace, forfeits his allegiance, and becomes an outlaw and a pirate." If the facts are admitted, such a person undoubtedly forfeits his allegiance, and cannot demand the protection of his sovereign,

[1] Perkins, 113.

whatever may happen to him. On this ground
the English government took no steps in relation
to the execution of Arbuthnot and Ambrister, beyond an inquiry into the facts of their alleged
complicity in the war,[1] and that inquiry was not
pushed as we may hope that the government of
the United States will push the inquiry, if an
American citizen is ever executed as Arbuthnot was.
The doctrine of Jackson's order, that a person who
engages in a war to which his country is not a
party becomes an outlaw and pirate, will not stand.
As has been well said, there were a large number
of foreigners in the American army during the
Revolution, who, on this doctrine, would, if captured by the English, have forfeited their lives.
The United States would have protected any such
persons by retaliation or otherwise. The Creeks
were not a nation in international law, they were
not the possessors of the soil on which they lived
and fought; there had never been a declaration of
war; yet they were not rebels against the United
States, and it could not be denied that they had
some belligerent rights. Whatever rights they
had, the Englishmen, even if they had been complete and unquestioned allies, must also have been
entitled to from the American authorities. If,
then, the Indians were not to be hunted down
like wild beasts, or executed by court-martial, if
captured, for levying war on the United States,

[1] 1 Rush, 473. "War might have been produced on this occasion 'if the ministry had but held up a finger.'" (488.)

the Englishmen were executed without right or
law. There never was any proof that anybody
incited the Indians. The attack on Fowltown pre-
cipitated hostilities in a situation where lawless
men and savages, by mutual annoyance, outrage,
and retaliation, had prepared the warlike temper.
When the matter was investigated this appeared,
and it was seen that Jackson had acted unjus-
tifiably, because without evidence or law. The
popular feeling, however, would not allow him
to be censured. Niles, who well represents the popular temper, believed in the emissary theory, and
when that theory broke down he became angry.[1]
He also expressed the popular feeling with great
exactness in this paragraph: " The fact is that
ninety-nine in a hundred of the people believe
that General Jackson acted on every occasion for
the good of his country, and success universally
crowned his efforts. He has suffered more hard-
ships, and encountered higher responsibilities, than
any man living in the United States to serve us,
and has his reward in the sanction of his government and the approbation of the people." With
this dictum the case was dismissed, and the matter
stood so that General Jackson, having done important public military service, could not be called
to account, although he had hung four persons
without warrant of law. His popularity had already begun to exercise a dispensing power in his
favor. A committee of the House of Representa-

[1] See his editorial, 16 Niles, 25.

tives,[1] at the next session, reported a vote of censure
on him for the execution of the Englishmen, but
the House, after a long debate, refused to pass it.

Jackson's proceedings came up in Monroe's cabinet on the question what to do with him and his
conquests. Calhoun was vexed at Jackson's insubordination to the War Department. He wanted
Jackson censured. The President and the whole
cabinet, with the exception of Adams, disapproved
of Jackson's conduct in invading Florida, and
were ready to disavow his proceedings and make
reparation.[2] On Adams would fall the labor of
vindicating Jackson's proceedings diplomatically,
if the administration should assume the responsibility for them. He avowed himself ready to
undertake the task, and to perform it substantially
on the grounds on which Jackson justified himself. It was agreed that Pensacola and St. Mark's
should be restored to Spain, but that Jackson's
course should be approved and defended on the
grounds that he pursued his enemy to his refuge, and that Spain could not do the duty which
devolved on her. The President, however, coun-
termanded an order which Jackson had given to
Gaines to seize St. Augustine because some Indians
had taken refuge there. All the members of the
cabinet agreed to the policy decided on, and all
loyally adhered to it, the secret of their first opinion
being preserved for ten years. Calhoun wrote to
Jackson in accordance with the agreement, con-

[1] 15 Niles, 394.   [2] 2 Gallatin's *Writings*, 117.

gratulating and approving.   Jackson inferred that
Calhoun had been his friend in the cabinet all the
time, and that his old enemy, Crawford, had been
the head of the hostile party.   " There is one fact
I wish Mr. Munroe to know — that Mr. Wm. H.
Crawford, whatever his pretensions are, is not his
friend — and facts can be produced on this head —
I know he is my enemy — and I also know he
is a base man — " [1]   The political history of this
country was permanently affected by the personal
relations of Jackson to Calhoun and Crawford on
that matter.   Monroe had a long correspondence
with Jackson to try to reconcile him to the surrender of the forts to Spain.   In that correspondence
Jackson did not mention the Rhea letter.

At the next session of Congress (1818–19) the
proceedings in Florida were made the subject of
inquiry, and were at once involved in the politics
of the day.   Clay was in opposition to the administration because he had not been made Secretary of
State.   He refused the War Department and the
mission to England.   His opposition was factious.
After the administration assumed the responsibility
for Jackson's doings, Clay opened the attack on
them.   Here began the feud between Clay and
Jackson.   The latter was in a doubly irritable
state of mind between the flatterers on one side
and the critics on the other.   The personal element
came to the front.   Any one who approved of his
acts was his friend ; any one who criticised was his

[1] Ford MSS.   Jackson to Lewis, Dec. 8, 1817.

enemy; whether any personal feeling was brought
to the discussion of a question of law and fact or
not. There are some facts which look as if Clay
and Crawford had begun to regard Jackson as a
possible competitor for the presidency. Crawford
was in communication with the committees on the
Seminole war, apparently instigating action, while
Calhoun tried to quell the excitement and avert
action, out of loyalty to the decision adopted by
the administration of which he was a member.[1]
The Georgian friends of Crawford in Congress
led the attack on Jackson.[2] Crawford and Calhoun were enemies. Adams was writing dispatches
and preparing instructions, by which, both with
England and Spain, he succeeded in vindicating
Jackson's proceedings. He said that he could not
regard a man of Jackson's distinguished services
like any other man.[3] He therefore yielded to the
prevailing current of the time, and incurred a large
responsibility for saving Jackson from censure,
and making possible his later career. He and
Jackson were, at this time, friends, and one scheme
was to make Jackson Vice-President on a ticket
with Adams.[4] Adams's defence of Jackson was

---

[1] See Lacock's letter of June 25, 1832, in answer to Jackson's
interrogatories.   43 Niles, 79.

[2] 8 Adams, 240.   [3] 5 Adams, 473.

[4] Adams said (in 1824) that the vice-presidency would be a
nice place for Jackson's old age. Jackson was four months older
than Adams. This is not so ridiculous as it would be if Jackson
had not pleaded old age and illness as a reason why he should not
go to the Senate in 1823. See 6 Adams, 633.

very plausible, and it was fortified line by line with references to the documentary proofs, yet if it had been worth any one's while, either in England or this country, to examine the alleged proofs, as any one may do now, verifying his references, all the case against Arbuthnot would have been found baseless. Adams quotes a certain letter as proof that Arbuthnot was not truly a trader, but had concealed purposes. The letter bears no testimony at all to the fact alleged.[1] Rush cited to the English minister another proof of this, which is equally frail, and only proves that Arbuthnot had taken trouble to try to serve the Indians out of pity for them.[2] His letter to his son, besides warning him to save as much as possible of their property, contained a message to Boleck not to resist the Americans.[3] The Senate committee reported February 24, 1819 (Lacock's Report), strongly against Jackson on all the points from the independent recruiting down to the taking of Pensacola.[4] No action was taken. Jackson had been in Washington during the winter watching the proceedings. He attended one of the President's drawing-rooms. "From the earnestness with which the company pressed round him, the eagerness with which multitudes pushed to obtain personal introductions to him, and the eye of respect and gratitude which from every quarter

[1] Document A, 20, cf. 147.
[2] 2 Rush, 52, cf. Document A, 215.
[3] Document A, 137.   [4] 16 Niles, 33.

beamed upon him, it had as much the appearance
of being his drawing-room as the President's."[1]
In February he made an excursion as far north
as New York. He was received everywhere with
enthusiasm. There was a story that he was so
angry at some of the proceedings in censure of
him that he went to the Senate chamber to waylay
some persons who had displeased him. He denied
this.

In 1819 the purchase of Florida was effected,
although the treaty was not ratified until February
22, 1821. In this treaty the western boundary of
the Louisiana purchase was for the first time defined. Adams, while the negotiations were pending, consulted Jackson about the boundary to be
contended for. Jackson " said there were many
persons who would take exception to our receding
so far from the boundary of the Rio del Norte,
which we claim, as the Sabine, and the enemies of
the administration would certainly make a handle
of it to assail them; but the possession of the
Floridas was of so great importance to the southern frontier of the United States, and so essential
even to their safety, that the vast majority of the
nation would be satisfied with the western boundary as we propose, if we obtain the Floridas."[2]
Monroe and his cabinet seem to have cared just as
little for Texas. Adams's diary shows that he was
not heartily supported in the efforts he was willing
to make to push the line westward. Jackson's

[1] 4 Adams, 243.   [2] Adams, 238-9.

opinion about claiming Texas was of no value, but the fact that he was consulted showed the amount of respect and consideration which the administration was willing to pay to him. In 1836, and again in 1843, Adams, citing his diary, declared that Jackson had been consulted, and had approved the Florida treaty. Jackson contradicted and denied it in a violent and insulting manner.

In the spring of 1821 Jackson was appointed Governor of Florida, under the belief that the public would be glad to see him so honored. On July 21st of the same year he published general orders,[1] taking leave of his army, a reduction having been made by which he had been thrown out. In these orders, or in a postscript to them, he managed to come into collision with his colleague and senior, Major-General Brown, then chief in command of the army of the United States, by taking up and criticising an order " signed Jacob Brown," especially in regard to the punishment for desertion. Brown was a New York militia general, some eight years younger than Jackson, who had distinguished himself, in the general ill-success of the war, by some small successes on the northern frontier. He seemed to be the coming military hero of the war until he was eclipsed by Jackson. He took precedence of Jackson by seniority of appointment, and so became chief in command. It had become evident now that Jackson needed much room in the world for all his jealousies and ani-

[1] 21 Niles, 53.

mosities, and that his fellow-men must put up with a great deal of arrogance and misbehavior on his part. His popularity shielded him. He had become a privileged person, like a great French nobleman of the last century. To offend him was to incur extraordinary penalties. To get in his way was to expose one's self to assaults which could not be resented as they would be if they came from another man. All this he had won by military success. At least it seemed fair to expect that he would observe military discipline and decorum. But he did not do so, and no one dared to call him to account.

Congress did not have time to legislate for the territory of Florida, after the treaty was ratified, before the end of the session. An act was passed extending to the new territory only the revenue laws and the law against the slave-trade. Jackson was appointed Governor in April, with all the powers of the Captain-General of Cuba and the Spanish Governors of Florida, except that he could not lay taxes or grant land.[1] His position was therefore a very anomalous one, — an American Governor under Spanish law, of an American territory not yet under the Constitution and laws of the United States. Long delays, due to dilatoriness and inefficiency, postponed the actual cession until July 17th. Meanwhile Jackson was chafing and fuming, and strengthening his detestation of all Spaniards.

[1] His commission in full, 22 Niles, Supp. 148.

In September certain persons represented to Jackson that papers which were necessary for the protection of their interests were being packed up, and would be carried away by the Spanish ex-Governor, contrary to the treaty. There were five or six sets of papers about property and land grants[1] which were missing. There had been complaints against the Spaniards for granting lands belonging to the Crown between the making and the ratification of the treaty. Jackson no doubt believed the worst against them. The persons who claimed his aid were weak and poor. With characteristic chivalry and impetuosity, he sent an officer to seize the papers. The ex-Governor, Callava, refused to give up any papers unless they were described, and a demand for them was addressed to him as Spanish commissioner. He and Jackson seem to have worked at cross-purposes unnecessarily. It is hard to make out what the misunderstanding was (although the use of two languages might partly account for it), unless Jackson was acting under his anti-Spanish bias. Jackson ended by sending Callava to the calaboose. Parton, who gives some special and interesting details derived from Brackenridge, the alcalde and interpreter, says that Callava saw the ridiculous side of the affair, and that he and his friends "made a night of it" in the calaboose. Jackson sent an officer to Callava's house to take the papers, and then ordered Callava to be discharged.

[1] 21 Niles, 150.

Eligius Fromentin, of Louisiana, had been appointed judge of the western district of Florida. He, upon application, issued a writ of *habeas corpus* for Callava. Jackson summoned Fromentin before him to show cause why he had interfered with Jackson's authority as Governor of the Floridas with the powers of the Captain-General of Cuba, as "Supreme Judge," and as "Chancellor." Fromentin sent an excuse on the ground of illness. The next day he went to see Jackson, and after a fierce interview each prepared a "statement" to send to Washington. Callava went to Washington to seek satisfaction. Some of his friends published, at Pensacola, a statement in his defence. Thereupon Jackson ordered them out of Florida at four days' notice, on pain of arrest for contempt and disobedience, if they were found there later. After all, the heirs of Vidal, who stirred up the whole trouble, were, according to Parton, indebted to the Forbes firm, against which they wanted to protect themselves.[1] This would not affect their right and interest in securing papers properly theirs. Whether the papers were being carried away, and did properly belong to the claimants, is not known.[2]

"I have no time," wrote Jackson to Lewis, Sept. 21, 1821, "to write to a friend, my civil, military,

[1] 2 Parton, 638. See Vidal's Heirs *vs.* J. Innerarity, 22 Niles, Supp. 147.

[2] All the documents are in Folio State Papers, 2 *Miscellan.*, 199. The important papers are in 21 Niles.

and Judicial Functions keep me constantly engaged as you will see from the news papers, that I am on some occasions for Justice sake, to use energetic measures, but one thing you and my friends may rely on, that I have acted with great caution and prudence, and that my conduct when investigated will be as much approved as any act of my life."

About the time of the trouble with Callava, Worthington, the Secretary and acting Governor of East Florida, was having a contest with Coppinger, the Spanish Governor of East Florida, about papers which the former seized under Jackson's orders.

Here, then, was another trouble which Jackson had prepared, in about six months' service, for his unhappy superiors. He was ill and disgusted with his office. He resigned and went home in October. It is plain that he had acted from a good motive against Callava, and, being sure of his motive, he had disregarded diplomatic obligations, evidence, law, propriety, and forms of procedure. Those things only enraged him because they balked him of the quick purpose, born of his sense of justice, and of his sympathy with an *ex parte* appeal to his power. Such a man is a dangerous person to be endowed with civil power. As to his quarrel with Fromentin, it was a farce. If Jackson had been a man of any introspection, he must have had, ever after, more charity for the whole class of Spanish governors, when he saw what an arrogant fool he had made of himself while endowed with indefinite and irresponsible power.[1]

Monroe's cabinet unanimously agreed that, as the only laws which had been extended to Florida were the revenue laws and those against the slave-trade, Fromentin's jurisdiction was limited to those laws,[2] and he could not issue a writ of *habeas corpus.* The President, Calhoun, and Wirt thought that he was not amenable for his error to Jackson. Adams took Jackson's part in this matter also. He said that Fromentin had violated Jackson's authority.[3] The cabinet discussed the subject for three days without reaching a decision. They were greatly perplexed as to the law and justice of the matter, and also as to its political effect. Congress took it up, and the newspapers were filled with it. At first the tide of opinion was against Jackson, but his popularity reacted against it, and the affair did not hurt him.

In 1823 Jackson was offered the mission to Mexico. He declined it. Soon afterwards he published in the Mobile "Register" a letter stating his reasons for declining. These reasons were a reflection on the administration, because they showed cause why no mission ought to be sent. The letter was calculated to win capital out of the

[1] "Although inebriety may be necessary to awaken the brute in man, absolute power suffices to bring out the fool." Taine, 3 *Revolution*, 267.

[2] For Fromentin's own theory of his action, which was plainly erroneous, see 21 Niles, 252.

[3] 5 Adams, 359, 368 to 380.

appointment at the expense of the administration
which had made it.[1]   Monroe must have been often
reminded of what Jefferson said to him, in 1818,
when he asked whether it would not be wise to
give Jackson the mission to Russia : " Why, good
G—d, he would breed you a quarrel before he
had been there a month ! " [2]

[1] 24 Niles, 280.   [2] 4 Adams, 76.

CHAPTER IV

ELECTION OF 1824

THE Congressional caucus met April 8, 1820.
The question was whether to nominate any candidates for President and Vice-President. Adams
says that the caucus was called as part of a plan
to nominate Clay for Vice-President. About forty
members of Congress attended. R. M. Johnson
offered a resolution that it was inexpedient to
nominate candidates. This resolution was adopted,
and the caucus adjourned.[1] Monroe received, at
the election, every electoral vote save one, which
was cast by Plumer, in New Hampshire, for Adams.
Tomkins was reëlected Vice-President, but he received fourteen less votes than Monroe. His reputation was declining. In raising money for the
public service during the war he had engaged his
own credit. His book-keeping was bad, and his
accounts and the public accounts became so entangled that he could not separate them.[2] The trouble was that, in order to show himself a creditor,
he had to include in his accounts interest, commissions, damages, allowances, etc., with interest on
them all ; that is, all the ordinary and extraordi-

[1] 5 Adams, 58, 60.   [2] 1 Hammond, 508 *et seq.*

nary charges which a broker would make for finding funds for an embarrassed client. If these
charges were all allowed, Tomkins could claim no
credit for patriotism. If he was to keep the credit
of extraordinary patriotism, he was a debtor. In
1816 he was very popular and had high hopes of
the presidency. In 1824 he retired neglected and
forgotten. He died in June, 1825.

During Monroe's second term each of the personal factions was intriguing on behalf of its chief,
and striving to kill off all the others. There were
no real issues. On the return of peace in 1815, the
industries which had grown up here during the
war, to supply needs which could not, under the
then existing laws, be supplied by importation, found
themselves threatened with ruin. The tariff of
1816, although its rates were of course far below
the "double duties" which had been levied during
the war, was supposed at the time to be amply protective. It had been planned to that end. The
embargo, non-intercourse, and war had created entirely artificial circumstances, which were a heavy
burden on the nation as a whole, but which had
given security and favor to certain manufacturing
industries. There was no way to "protect" the
industries after peace returned except to reproduce
by taxes the same hardship for everybody else,
and the same special circumstances for the favored
industries, as had been produced by embargo and
war. In 1819 a great commercial crisis occurred,
which prostrated all the industry of the country

for four or five years. So long as vicious and depreciated currencies existed in Europe, there was less penalty for a vicious currency here ; but as fast as European currencies improved after the return of peace, gold and silver began to go to the countries of improving currency, and away from the countries where the currency still remained bad. The "hard times" were made an argument to show that more protection was needed; that is, that the country had been prosperous during war, and that the return of peace had ruined it, unless taxes could be devised which should press as hard as the war had done. The taxes had not indeed been made so heavy as that, and so more were needed. Currency theorists also arose to anticipate all the wisdom of later days. They proved that the people of the United States, with a great continent at their disposal, could not get out of the continent an abundance of food, clothing, shelter and fuel because they had not enough bits of paper stamped "one dollar" at their disposal. The currency whims, however, hardly got into politics at that period.

In 1820 a strong attempt was made to increase the tariff, to do away with credit for duties, and to put a check on sales at auction. As the presidential election was uncontested, power to carry these bills could not be concentrated. In 1824 the case was different. No faction dared vote against the higher tariff for fear of losing support.[1] The

[1] 24 Niles, 324.

tariff was not, therefore, a party question. The act was passed May 22, 1824, by a combination of Middle and Western States against New England, and on a combination of the iron, wool, hemp, whiskey, and sugar interests. New England, as the commercial district, was then for free trade.

Jackson had been elected to the Senate in the winter of 1823-24. Parton brings the invaluable testimony of William B. Lewis as to the reason why and the way in which Jackson was elected.[1] John Williams had been senator. His term expired. He was an opponent of Jackson. He was a candidate for reëlection, and was so strong that no Jackson man but Jackson himself could defeat him. Hence the men who were planning to make Jackson President, of whom Lewis was the chief, secured Jackson's election to the Senate. While the tariff question was pending, a convenient person — Dr. Coleman, of Warrenton, Va. — was found to interrogate Jackson about it. His letter in reply was the first of the adroit letters or manifestoes by means of which the Jackson managers carried on the campaign in Jackson's favor. They developed this art of electioneering in a way then not conceived of by other factions. The letter to Coleman was a model letter of its kind. It said nothing clear or to the point on the matter in question. It used some ambiguous phrases which the reader could interpret to suit his own taste. It muddled the question by contradictory suggestions,

[1] 3 Parton, 21.

bearing upon it from a greater or less distance, and from all points of view, and it failed not to introduce enough glittering platitudes to make the whole pass current. Jackson voted for the tariff. He wrote to Lewis, May 7, 1824: —

"The articles of National Defence & National Independence, I will with my vote, foster & protect, without counting on cents & dollars; so that our own manufacturers shall stand on a footing of fair competition with the labourers of Europe. In doing this, the articles all being of the product of our own country, tends to promote the agriculturists, whilst it gives security to our nation & promotes Domestic Labour. The balance of the bill I look to with an eye to Revenue alone, to meet the national debt. These articles of National defence, are Hemp, iron, lead, & coarse woollen, and from the experience of last war every patriot will justify me in this course — & if they do not, my own conscience approves, & I will follow it regardless of any consequences." [1]

He also voted for a number of internal improvement schemes. These votes were afterwards quoted against him.[2]

Jackson was therefore fairly started as a candidate for the presidency. Among all the remarkable accidents which opened his way to the first position in the country, it was not the least that he had William B. Lewis for a neighbor and friend. Lewis was the great father of the wire-pullers. He first practised in a masterly and scientific way

[1] Ford MSS.   [2] 38 Niles, 285.

the art of starting movements, apparently spontaneous, at a distance, and in a quarter from which
they win prestige or popularity, in order that these
movements may produce, at the proper time and
place, the effects intended by the true agent, who,
in the mean time, prepares to be acted on by the
movement in the direction in which, from the beginning, he desired to go. On this system political
activity is rendered theatrical. The personal initiative is concealed. There is an adjustment of
rôles, a *mise en scène*, and a constant consideration
of effect. Each person acts on the other in pre-
arranged ways. Cues are given and taken, and the
effect depends on the fidelity of each to his part.
The perfection of the representation is reached
when the audience or spectators are disregarded
until the finale, when the chief actor, having reached
the *dénoûment* towards which he and his comrades
have so long been laboring, comes to the footlights
and bows to the "will of the people." Lewis
showed great astuteness in his manœuvres. There
was nothing vulgar about him. There was a certain breadth of generalship about his proceedings.
He was very farsighted and prudent. He had the
great knowledge required by the wire-puller, —
knowledge of men, good judgment of the influences which would be potent, if brought to bear on
each man or group. He knew the class amongst
whom Jackson's popularity was strongest. He
knew their notions, prejudices, tastes, and instincts.
He knew what motives to appeal to. He wrote

very well. When he wanted to go straight to a
point he could do so. When he wanted to produce effects or suggest adroitly, without coming to
the point, he could do that too. He also knew
Jackson well. He no doubt sincerely loved and
admired Jackson. He threw his whole soul into
the undertaking to elect Jackson, but he never
showed very markedly selfish or interested purposes in that connection. So long as Jackson was
uninformed or unprejudiced on any matter, he was
at the disposition of any one who had won his confidence, and who desired to influence him on that
matter. He could then be led to accept any view
of it which was put before him in a way to strike
his mind. Lewis knew how to put a thing before Jackson's mind. However, when Jackson had
adopted any view or notion, his mind became set
or biassed, and it was not easy, even for those who
first influenced him, to deflect his mind from rigid-
ity of inference, or his conduct from direct deduction. He often outstripped the wishes and
intentions of those who had moved him first. To
contradict him, at that stage, would have been to
break friendship. Lewis treated him with great
tact, and influenced him very often, but he did
not control him or manage him. It would have
been a good thing for the country if no worse
man than Lewis had ever gained influence over
Jackson.

No doubt many people saw, as early as 1815,
Jackson's availability as a presidential candidate.

Aaron Burr wrote to his son-in-law, Alston, Nov. 20, 1815,[1] urging that Jackson should be brought forward as a candidate by whose might the caucus could be overthrown. Jackson wrote to Lewis, in 1844, about "the book lately publeshed" "called the history of the last congress," "which undertakes to state the manner of my being brought out for the Presedency, and which says it *originated* with " "Col Burr & the militant Federalists." " I have to state that it is a base falsehood, that I ever received a letter from Col Burr on that subject, — or that I ever received a request from any Federalist to become a candidate for the Presidency —   That I received many from such republicans as Edward Livingston, as early as 1816 & 17 — to permit my name to be brought out for the Presedency is certainly true, but which I answered promptly I could not yield to their solicitation — "[2] Adams recognized Jackson's strength, as a candidate, in 1818: "There is a considerable party disposed to bring forward Jackson as a candidate, and the services of his late campaign would have given him great strength, if he had not counteracted his own interest by several of his actions in it,"[3] having alienated Georgia, Kentucky, Virginia, all State rights men and Governors of States.

Parton obtained from Lewis a description of the first steps towards Jackson's nomination. Lewis tells how he used Jackson's letters to Monroe to win influential federalists to Jackson's support. It

[1] Mayo, 171.   [2] Ford MSS.   [3] 4 Adams, 198.

was after Jackson's return from Florida, in 1821, that the project was definitely decided upon. At first Jackson rejected, with some temper, the suggestion that he could or would run for President. He did not consider himself the right sort of man, and he felt old and ill. In the spring of 1822 Lewis went to North Carolina, and worked up his connections there for Jackson. On the 20th of July, 1822, the Tennessee Legislature made the formal nomination. During the next two years Jackson's supporters were gaining connections and undermining the caucus, for he was an independent candidate and a "disorganizer," because he was raised up outside of the machine, and without any consultation with the established party authorities.

Certain features of Jackson's character have appeared already. We have seen some of his elements of strength and some of his faults. The nation wanted to reward him for military achievements and for a display of military virtues. They had discarded dukedoms, pensions, ribbons, and orders, and they had no sign of national gratitude to employ but election to civil office. So far Jackson had not made public display of any qualities but those of a military man, and violence, indiscretion, obstinacy, and quarrelsomeness. In the campaign, those who opposed him called him a "murderer." The only incidents of his life which the biographer can note, aside from his military service, are successive acts of impropriety and bad judgment. Senator Mills wrote of him that "he was considered extremely rash and inconsiderate; tyrannical and despotic in his principles. A personal acquaintance with him has convinced many who had these opinions that they were unfounded. He is very mild and amiable in his disposition, of great benevolence, and his manners, although formed in the wilds of the West, exceedingly polished and polite. Everybody that knows him, loves him, and he is exactly the man with whom *you* [his wife] would be delighted. . . . He has all the ardor and enthusiasm of youth and is as free from guile as an infant. . . . A personal acquaintance with him has dissipated all my prejudices. . . . But with all Gen. Jackson's good and great qualities, I should be sorry to see him President of the United States. His early education was very deficient, and his modes of thinking and habits of life partake too much of war and military glory." [1] Negatively, however, there was more to be said for Jackson. He was above every species of money vice; he was chaste and domestic in his habits; [2] he was temperate in every way; he was not ambitious in the bad sense. Judge McNairy "speaks of Gen. Jackson as being less addicted to the vices and immoralities of youth, than any young man with whom he was acquainted; that he

[1] Mills's *Letters*, 31.

[2] The only contrary suggestion known is in Binns, 245. "This rough soldier, exposed all his life to those temptations which have conquered public men whom we still call good, could kiss little children with lips as pure as their own." Quincy; *Figures*, 367.

never knew of his *fighting cocks*, or gambling, and, as for his being a *libertine*, as has been charged, the Judge says he was distinctly the reverse of it. The truth is, as everybody here well knows, Gen. Jackson never was fond of any kind of sport, nor did he indulge in any except occasionally for amusement, but Horse-racing. This his friends are willing to admit, but even this he has quit for many years. I believe ever since the year 1810 or 1811." [1]

There were already four other candidates in the field, who all belonged to the democratic-republican party. Niles gives an instance in which seven democrats met at Philadelphia, who all were for Schulze, the democratic candidate for Governor. Each candidate for President had a supporter among them, and no candidate had over two.[2] De Witt Clinton was not altogether out of consideration. A caucus of the South Carolina Legislature nominated Lowndes.[3]

John Quincy Adams stood first among the candidates by his public services and experience. He was fifty-seven years old. He went to Europe with his father when he was eleven years old, and studied there for several years. He.was, through his father, intimate from his earliest youth with public and diplomatic affairs. As far as education and early training could go, he had the best outfit for

[1] Lewis to Haywood (1827); copy in Ford MSS.
[2] 24 Niles, 369.
[3] 5 Adams, 468.

a statesman and diplomat. He enjoyed great respect. Those who thought that a man ought to
advance to the presidency through lower grades of
public employment looked upon him as the most
suitable candidate. He was not a man of genius,
but one of wide interests, methodical habits, and
indefatigable industry. It is hard to see what he
ever did, from his earliest youth, for amusement
and entertainment. He would have been a better
statesman if he had been more frivolous. He was
unsocial in his manners, had few friends, and repelled those who would have been his friends. So
far as we can learn, he engaged in no intrigues
for the presidency. He certainly had the smallest
and least zealous corps of workers. His weakness
was that the great body of the voters did not have
any feeling that a man with the qualifications which
he possessed was needed for the presidential office.
He had been a democrat since 1807, when he went
over to the administration party because he believed
that the New England federalists were plotting
secession. His soundness in "democratic principles" was doubted. He was earnestly disliked by
all the active politicians. In the campaign he was
called a "tory." He was charged with offering,
at Ghent, to yield to the English the right of
navigating the Mississippi, if they would renew
the rights to fish in Canadian waters; that is, with
offering to sacrifice a western interest to serve an
eastern one. He published a small volume to expose the untruth of this charge and the character

of the evidence by which it was supported.[1] In
his own opinion, this attack helped him.[2] He was
in favor of the tariff as it stood in 1824. He
thought that it gave enough protection. He was
also in favor of internal improvements, but thought
that they might be abused.[3] He was accused of
undemocratic care for etiquette, and also of sloven-
liness in dress. Mrs. Adams gave a ball in honor
of Jackson, January 8, 1824. "It is the universal
opinion that nothing has ever equalled this party
here, either in brilliancy of preparation or elegance
of the company." [4]

Calhoun enjoyed great popularity in New England, in New York city, and in Pennsylvania, as
well as at home. He was forty-two years old,
and was the "young men's candidate." He had
actively favored the tariff of 1816 and the Bank,
and also plans for internal improvements. In
October, 1822, Adams wrote: "Calhoun has no
petty scruples about constructive powers and State
rights." [5] "He is ardent, persevering, industrious,
and temperate, of great activity and quickness of
perception and rapidity of utterance; as a politician, too theorizing, speculative and metaphysical,
— magnificent in his views of the powers and
capacities of the government and of the virtue,
intelligence, and wisdom of the *people*. He is
in favor of elevating, cherishing, and increasing

---

[1] The Duplicate Letters, the Fisheries and the Mississippi.
[2] 6 Adams, 263.   [3] 6 Adams, 353, 451.
[4] Mills's *Letters*, 30.   [5] 6 Adams, 75.

all the institutions of the government, and of a
vigorous and energetic administration of it.   From
his rapidity of thought, he is often wrong in
his conclusions, and his theories are sometimes
wild, extravagant, and impractical.   He has always
claimed to be, and is, of the democratic party, but
of a very different class from that of Crawford;
more like Adams, and his schemes are sometimes
denounced by his party as ultra-fanatical.   His
private character is estimable and exemplary, and
his devotion to his official duties is regular and
severe, but he is formidably opposed on the ground
of his youth, his inexperience, his heterodoxy in
politics, and his ambition." [1]   Calhoun and Adams
had been strong friends, and there was some idea
of putting Calhoun on the ticket with Adams until
1822, when some members of Congress nominated
Calhoun for President.[2]   Webster preferred Calhoun to all the other candidates.[3]   His brother
wrote that Calhoun was the second choice of New
Hampshire.[4]   Calhoun took the War Department
in 1817, when it was in great disorder.   He had
to bear a great deal of abuse before he got it in
order, but later he was much praised for the system
he had introduced.[5]   He and Crawford were especial rivals, because Crawford was the " regular "

[1] Mills's *Letters*, 28.
[2] 6 Adams, 42.
[3] 1 Curtis's *Webster*, 218, 236.
[4] 1 Webster's *Correspondence*, 323.
[5] 26 Niles, 50.   Adams thought this praise undeserved.   7
Adams, 446.

Virginia and Southern candidate. In 1822 attempts were made to injure Calhoun by an investigation of a contract for building the Rip Raps at Old Point Comfort. The contract was private, not competitive. He was exonerated by a committee of the House.[1] As we shall see, Calhoun withdrew his name before the election.

Crawford was the regular candidate. He was fifty-two years old. In 1798 he had been an " Addresser," that is, an orthodox federalist.[2] He had also been a supporter of the old Bank, and had been the leader in the Senate for the renewal of its charter. He had also opposed the embargo.[3] He had been very eagerly working for eight years to reach the presidency. In the campaign he was called an "intriguer." As Secretary of the Treasury, during the crisis of 1819, he had a very difficult task to perform. He had undertaken even more than his duty required, for he had aimed to " do justice " between the banks, and to keep them from encroaching upon each other. To this end he distributed his deposits, and in some cases favored certain banks. When the crash came his funds were locked up in some of these banks. He was then open to the charge, which Ninian Edwards made over the signature "A. B.," that he had used the treasury funds to win political capital, and had corruptly put the funds in unsound banks. Crawford was exonerated by a committee of the

[1] 22 Niles, 251.   [2] 24 Niles, 132.
[3] Cobb, 143.

House, but he barely escaped ruin.[1] "He is a
hardy, bold, resolute man, with the *appearance* of
great frankness and openness of character, unpol-
ished and somewhat rude in his manners, and very
far inferior to Mr. Adams in learning and attainments. He has, however, a strong, vigorous mind,
and has made himself what he is by his own active
efforts. . . . He is now at the head of those who
are here termed radicals " [extreme State rights
men].[2]   He introduced the limited period of service, by the Act of May 15, 1820, into the Treasury
Department. This act limits the period of office
of all persons engaged in collecting the revenue to
four years, at the expiration of which time they go
out of office or come up for reappointment.[3]   It is
one of the most important steps in the history of
the abuse of the civil service. Crawford was believed by his colleagues to have sacrificed the administration to make capital for himself. Adams
says that Crawford and Monroe quarrelled to the
verge of violence during the last months of the
administration.[4]   In order to win strength for
Crawford, Van Buren was nominated for Vice-
President by the Legislature of Georgia. This
proposition was overwhelmed by ridicule.[5]   Craw-

1 Folio State Papers ; 5 *Finance.*   Edwards said that he made
the charge under promises of support from Monroe, Jackson, Calhoun, and Adams.   Ford's *Illinois*, 63.

2 Mills's *Letters*, 28.

8 7 Adams, 424.

4 7 Adams, 81.

5 Cobb, 209.

ford was physically disabled from September, 1823,
to September, 1824.   He could not sign his name,
and was apparently a wreck.   He used a fac-simile
stamp on public papers, or it was used by a member of his family under his direction.

" Adams, Jackson, and Calhoun, all think well of
each other, and are united at least in one thing, to
wit, a most thorough dread and abhorrence of Crawford.   Mr. Clay stands by himself, and, with many
excellent qualities, would be more dangerous at the
head of the government than either of the others.
Ardent, bold, and adventurous in all his theories, he
would be, as is feared, rash in enterprise, and inconsiderate and regardless of consequences.   His
early education was exceedingly defective, and his
morals have been not the most pure and correct." [1]
Clay had already assumed the championship of
the protective system.   He had been one of the
strongest opponents of the re-charter of the first
Bank.   He had also made " sympathy with nations
struggling for liberty " one of his points, and had
been zealous for the recognition of the South American republics.   He was a great party leader.   He
had just the power to win men to him and to inspire personal loyalty, which Adams had not.   On
the other hand, he lacked industry.   He was eloquent, but he never mastered any subject which
required study.   His strength lay in facility and
practical tact.   He was forty-seven years old.   He
was stigmatized as a " gambler " by his opponents

[1] Mills's *Letters*, 32.

in the campaign. From 1820 to 1823 he was not in public life, but was retrieving his private fortunes. His enemies said that his affairs had been embarrassed by gambling. He was Speaker from 1815 to 1820, and again from 1823 to 1825. He was one of the commissioners who made the treaty of Ghent.

The Crawford men wanted a congressional caucus in 1824, because they had control of the machine. The supporters of the other candidates opposed any caucus, but secretly, because the caucus was now an established institution. The opponents of the caucus found a strong ally in Niles, who opened fire on the caucus in his "Register" without any reserve. His sincerity and singleness of purpose are beyond question. He did not use his paper to support any candidate. He was an old Jeffersonian republican of 1798, and he believed sincerely in all the "principles." He assailed the caucus, because in his view it usurped the right of the people to govern themselves. He denounced it steadily for more than a year, and he succeeded in casting odium upon it. The Legislatures of New York and Virginia passed resolutions in favor of a caucus, because these two States, while united, could control the presidency through the caucus. New York being rent by democratic faction fights, and Virginia being led by a close oligarchy, New York became an appendage to Virginia in their coalition. Tennessee, South Carolina, Alabama and Maryland adopted resolutions against the caucus. The legislature of Pennsylvania declared against a "partial caucus." [1]

The caucus met in the chamber of the House of Representatives February 14, 1824.[2] Of 216 democrats in Congress, 66 were present. Two, who were ill at home, sent proxies. If proxies were allowable, the members of Congress, when assembled in presidential caucus, must have been regarded as independent powers, possessed of a prerogative, like peers or sovereigns. The vote was: Crawford, 64; Adams, 2; Jackson, 1; Macon, 1: i. e., all but the Crawford men stayed away. Gallatin was nominated for Vice-President by 57 votes. An address was published, defending the caucus, and arguing its indispensability to the party.[3] Some question was raised about Gallatin's eligibility on account of his foreign birth, but he possessed the alternative qualification allowed by the Constitution. He had been a commissioner at Ghent and a friend of Crawford. His nomination did not strengthen the ticket. There was still a great deal of rancor against him for forsaking the Treasury Department when the war of 1812 broke out.[4] He soon withdrew his name because the caucus was so unpopular.

Martin Van Buren was chief engineer of the last congressional caucus. He was senator from New

[1] 6 Adams, 232.
[2] 25 Niles, 388.
[3] 25 Niles, 391.
[4] See a strong expression of it as late as 1832 in 42 Niles, 435.

York.   He and his friends, under the new Constitution of 1821, had established a very efficient
party organization, which they had well in hand.
They were known as the Regency, and they had
renewed the alliance with Virginia to control the
machine and elect Crawford.   A project which
threatened to mar their scheme was the proposition, in 1823, to take the election of presidential
electors from the Legislature of New York and give
it to the people.   The Regency-Tammany party
opposed this, as it would render useless all their
machinery.   The advocates of the change, who were
the opponents of Crawford, Tammany, and the
Regency, formed the "people's party."   Clinton
was for Jackson, so he was allied with the people's
party against Crawford.   Although Clinton was
the soul of the canal enterprise, he was removed
from his office of canal commissioner to try to
break up this combination.   It would never do for
the Regency to oppose directly and openly a proposition to give the election to the people.   When
the law was proposed, the Regency managed to
twist it into such preposterous shape that a general
ticket was to be voted for, and if there should not
be a majority (which, with four in the field, was a
very probable result) the State would lose its vote.
The bill passed the House, but was defeated in the
Senate.[1]   The popular indignation was so great
that the next Legislature was carried by the people's party, and a joint ticket of electors was

[1] 2 Hammond, 132.

elected, on which were 25 Adams men, 7 Clay men, and 4 Crawford men.[1] Some of them must have changed their votes before the election.

A federalist convention at Harrisburg, Pennsylvania, February 22, 1824, nominated Jackson.[2] At a primary meeting at Philadelphia, Dallas withdrew Calhoun's name from the first place and nominated him for the second. Calhoun was strong in Pennsylvania, but Jackson had superseded him. This move was a coalition of Jackson and Calhoun. Jackson wrote to Lewis, from Washington, March 31, 1824: —

"On the subject of M[r] Calhoune, I have no doubt myself, but his friends acted agreeable to his understanding & instructions; & that he is sincere in his wishes — some have doubted this, but I have not — and I can give you when we meet reasons that will convince you I cannot be mistaken — as far as his friends to the south have acted, it is conformable to this; & I have no doubt but both the Carolinas will unite in my support — You have seen the result of Pennsylvania — New York is coming out — and it is said some of the Newengland States; a few weeks will give us the result of the movement of New York — if Crawford is not supported in that State I have but little doubt but he will be droped, and from what you will see in the National intelligences of this morning M[r] Clay taken up. I have no doubt if I was to travel to Boston where I have been invited that it would ensure my election — But this I cannot do —

[1] 27 Niles, 186. Hammond's statement is obscure. See 1 Hammond, 177.

[2] 1 Sargent, 41.

I would feel degraded the ballance of my life— If I
ever fill that office it must be the free choice of the
people— I can then say I am the President of the
nation—and my acts shall comport with that character." [1]

The understanding was that Jackson would take
only one term, and that his friends would then
secure the succession to Calhoun.

The democratic convention at Harrisburg, March
4th, was stampeded for Jackson. Only one vote was
given against him.[2] Another democratic convention, called "regular," was convened August 9th.
It repudiated Jackson and adhered to Crawford.[3]
Jackson and his followers were denounced as "disorganizers." The Albany "Argus" said of Jackson, "It is idle in this State, however it may be in
others, to strive even for a moderate support of
Mr. Jackson. He is wholly out of the question as
far as the votes of New York are in it. Independently of the disclosures of his political opinions, he
could not be the republican candidate. He is respected as a gallant soldier, but he stands, in the
minds of the people of this State, at an immeasurable distance from the executive chair." [4] The
"Argus" swallowed its words a little later, without
a sign of indigestion. It knew that, when the democratic Leviathan takes a self-willed freak, he is
the wisest leader who follows most humbly. After
it had reversed itself, any one who held the very

[1] Ford MSS.   [2] 26 Niles, 20.
[3] 1 Sargent, 42.   [4] Quoted 49 Niles, 188.

ANDREW JACKSON

judicious opinion embodied in this paragraph was denounced by it as a "federalist," which was as much as to say, an enemy of the American people. Niles says that Calhoun opposed Jackson in a public speech, in 1822, because he was the candidate of the Bank of the United States, and his election would unite "the purse and the sword."[1] Jefferson said: "I feel very much alarmed at the prospect of seeing General Jackson President. He is one of the most unfit men I know of for the place. He has had very little respect for laws or constitutions, and is, in fact, an able military chief. His passions are terrible. . . . He has been much tried since I knew him, but he is a dangerous man."[2] On the contrary, Jackson's courtly bearing won for him all the ladies. Webster wrote: "General Jackson's manners are more presidential than those of any of the candidates. He is grave, mild, and reserved. My wife is for him decidedly."[3] Jackson's friends induced him to have a kind of reconciliation with Scott, Clay, and Benton. The last was a supporter of Clay, but when Clay was out of the contest he turned to Jackson.[4] Adams says that Benton joined Jackson after Jackson's friends obtained for him the nomination as minister to Mexico. When Adams came in he would not

[1] 22 Niles, 73.
[2] 1 Webster's *Correspondence*, 371.
[3] 1 Webster's *Correspondence*, 346. See, also, Quincy, *Figures*, 363.
[4] He went first to Crawford, then to Jackson. Cobb, 215.

ratify the appointment.[1] During the winter some sort of a peace was made between Jackson and Crawford.[2]

The result of the electoral vote was: Jackson, 99; Adams, 84; Crawford, 41; Clay, 37. For Vice-President the vote was: Calhoun, 182; Sanford, 30; Macon, 24; Jackson, 13; Van Buren, 9; Clay, 2; blank, 1. New York voted: Jackson, 1; Adams, 26; Crawford, 5; Clay, 4. The electors were chosen by the Legislature in Delaware, Georgia, Louisiana, New York, South Carolina, and Vermont. In the other States the popular vote stood (in round numbers): Jackson, 155,800; Adams, 105,300; Crawford, 44,200; Clay, 46,500. The second choice of Clay's States (Ohio, Kentucky, and Missouri) was Jackson. In Pennsylvania, Jackson had 36,000 votes, and all the others together had less than 12,000. Only about one third of the vote of the State was polled, because it was known that Jackson would carry it overwhelmingly.[3] Ten years later Adams wrote about the people of Pennsylvania, " whose fanatical passion for Andrew Jackson can be compared to nothing but that of Titania, Queen of the Fairies, for Bottom after his assification." [4]

The intriguing for the election now entered on a new stage. Clay was out of the contest in the House, but he had great influence there, and it has often been asserted that the House would have

[1] 6 Adams, 522.   [2] 6 Adams, 478, 485.
[3] 27 Niles, 186.   [4] 9 Adams, 160.

elected him if his name had come before it as one
of the three highest. He was courted by all parties.
It would be tedious to collect the traces of various
efforts to form combinations. The truth seems to
be this: Washington was filled during the winter
with persons, members of Congress and others, who
were under great excitement about the election.
All sorts of busybodies were running about, talking and planning, and proposing what seemed to
each to be good. Persons who were in Washington, and were cognizant of some one line of intrigue,
or of the activity of some one person, have left
records of what they saw or heard, and have vehemently maintained each that his evidence gives
the only correct clew to the result. Each candidate's name is connected with some intrigue, or
some proposition for a coalition. In no case is the
proposition or intrigue brought home to the principal party as a conscious or responsible partici-
pator, and yet it appears that the negotiations
were often of such a character that they could
have been taken up and adopted, if they had
proved satisfactory.

The election in the House took place February
9, 1825. On the first ballot, Adams obtained the
votes of thirteen States, Jackson of seven, and
Crawford of four. For the first few days Jackson seemed to bear his defeat good-naturedly,
although he had written to Lewis, as early as
January 29:—

"You will see from the public Journals the stand M^r
Clay has taken for Mr Adams — This was such an un-
expected course, that self-agrandizement, and corruption,
by many are attached to his motives — . . .

"Intrigue, corruption, and sale of public office is the
rumor of the day — How humiliating to the american
character that its high functionaries should so conduct
themselves, as to become liable to the imputation of
bargain & sale of the constitutional rights of the
people." [1]

He met Adams on the evening of the election
at the President's reception, and bore himself much
the better of the two.[2]

It was soon rumored that Clay was to be Secretary of State. After a few days he accepted
that post. The charge of a corrupt bargain between him and Adams was then started. It was
an inference from Clay's appointment, and nothing
more. Any man can judge to-day, as well as any
one could in 1824, whether that fact leads straight
and necessarily to that inference. Not a particle
of other evidence ever was alleged. We have
never had any definition of the proper limits of
combinations, bargains, and pledges in politics, but
an agreement to make Clay Secretary of State, if
made, could not be called a *corrupt* bargain. He
was such a man that he was a fit and proper
person for the place. No one would deny that.
Therefore no public interest would be sacrificed or
abused by his appointment. A corrupt bargain

[1] Ford MSS.   [2] Cobb, 226; 1 Curtis's *Buchanan*, 43.

must be one in which there is collusion for private
gain at the expense of the public welfare. Bargains which avoid this definition must yet be toler-
ated in all political systems, although they impair
the purity of any system.

The men around Jackson — Eaton, Lewis, Livingston, Lee, Swartwout — knew the value of the
charge of corrupt bargain for electioneering purposes, and the political value of the appeal to Jackson's supporters on the ground that he had been
cheated out of his election. Did not they first
put the idea into Jackson's head that he had been
cheated by a corrupt bargain? Is not that the explanation of his change of tone from the lofty
urbanity of the President's assembly to the rancorous animosity of a few days afterwards? Such a
conjecture fits all the circumstances and all the
characters. The men around Jackson might see
the value of the charge, and use it, without ever
troubling themselves to define just how far they believed in it; but Jackson would not do that. Such
a suggestion would come to him like a revelation,
and his mind would close on it with a solidity of
conviction which nothing ever could shake. February 20th, he wrote to Lewis : —

" But when we see the predictions verified on the result of the Presidential election — when we behold two
men — political enemies, and as different in political sentiments as any men can be, so suddenly unite ; there must
be some unseen cause to produce this political phenomena
— This cause is developed by applying the rumors be-

fore the election, to the result of that election, and to the tendering of and the acceptance of the office of Sec. of State by Mr Clay. These are facts that will confirm every unbiasased mind, that there must have been & were a secret understanding between Mr Adams & Mr Clay of and concerning these scems of corruptoon, that has occasioned Mr Clay to abandon the will, and wishes of the people of the west, and to form the coalition so extraordinary as the one he has done.

.   .   .   .

.   .   From Mr Clays late conduct, my opinion of him, long ago expressed, is best realized — from his conduct on the Seminole question, I then pronounced him a political Gambler —   .   .   .   I have, *now*, no doubt, but I have had opposed to me all the influence of the Cabinet, except Calhoune — would it not be well that the papers of Nashville & the whole State should speak out, with moderate but firm disapprobation of this corruption — to give a proper tone to the people & to draw their attention to the subject — When I see you I have much to say — There is more corruption than I anticipated; and as you know I thought there was enough of it." [1]

Benton always scouted the notion of the bargain. [2] He says that he knew before Adams did, that Clay intended to vote for Adams. [3] Benton would not follow Clay. Clay and Jackson had had no intercourse since the Seminole war affair. The Tennessee delegation patched up a reconcilia-

[1] Ford MSS.

[2] *Ibid.*

[3] 1 Benton, 48; see his letter of Dec. 27, 1827, in *Truth's Advocate*, 63.

tion in 1824.[1]   Clay's reason for voting for Adams
was that Crawford was incapacitated by broken
health,[2] and that a military hero was not a fit person
to be President.   January 8th Clay wrote to F. P.
Blair [3] that the friends of all the candidates were
courting him, but that he should vote for Adams.
January 24th Clay and the majority of the Ohio
and Kentucky delegations declared that they would
vote for Adams.   In a letter to F. Brooke, January
28, 1825, Clay stated that he would vote for Adams
for the reasons given.[4]   The Clay men generally
argued that if Jackson was elected he would keep
Adams in the State Department.   It would then
be difficult, in 1828, to elect Clay, another western
man ; but Adams would have more strength.   If
Adams should be elected in 1824, the election of
Clay, as a western man, in 1828, would be easier,
especially if Adams would give him the Secretaryship.[5]   On the 25th of January, the day after the
western delegations came out for Adams, an anonymous letter appeared in the " Columbian Observer," of Philadelphia, predicting a bargain between
Adams and Clay.   Kremer, member of the House

[1] Clay's Speech, 1838; 54 Niles, 68.

[2] Crawford was taken to the Capitol for a few hours, a day or
two before the election, but he was apparently a wreck.   Cobb,
218.

[3] Blair and Kendall, in 1824, were Clay men.   They were both
active, in 1825, in urging Clay men to vote for Adams.   40 Niles,
73 ; *Telegraph Extra*, 300 *et seq.*

[4] 27 Niles, 386.

[5] *Telegraph Extra*, 321.

from Pennsylvania, avowed his responsibility for
the letter, although it has generally been believed
that he could not have written it.   Clay demanded
an investigation in the House, and a committee was
raised, but Kremer declined to answer its interrogatories.   The letter was another case of the general device of laying down anchors for strains which
would probably need to be exerted later.   It would
not do for Kremer to admit that the assertion in
the letter was only a surmise of his.   It certainly
was a clever trick.   The charge would either prevent Clay from going into Adams's cabinet, lest he
should give proofs of the truth of the imputation,
or, if he did go into the cabinet, this letter would
serve as a kind of evidence of a bargain.   Immediately after the inauguration, Kremer made this
latter use of it in an address to his constitutents.[1]
On the 20th of February, Jackson wrote a letter
to Lewis, in which he affirmed and condemned the
bargain.   Lewis published this letter in Tennessee.
February 22d, Jackson wrote a letter to Swartwout,
in which he spoke very bitterly of Clay, and resented Clay's criticism of him as a " military
chieftain."   He sneered at Clay as *not* a military
chieftain.   But he did not allege any bargain.
Swartwout published this letter in New York.[2]
Both letters were plainly prepared by Jackson's
followers for publication.   Clay replied at the end
of March in a long statement.[3]

Jackson remained in Washington until the mid-

28 Niles, 21.   [2] 28 Niles, 20.   [3] 28 Niles, 71.

dle of March.   He was present at the inauguration,
and preserved all the forms in his public demeanor
towards Adams.[1]   His rage was all directed against
Clay.   In the Senate there were fifteen votes
against Clay's confirmation, but no charges were
made there.[2]   On his way home Jackson scattered
the charge as he went.   It is to his own lips that
it is always traceable, when it can be brought home
to anybody.   Up to this time it is questionable
whether Jackson was more annoyed or pleased at
being run for President.   Now that the element of
personal contest was imported into the enterprise,
his whole being became absorbed in the determination to achieve victory.   There was now a foe to
be crushed, a revenge to be obtained for an injury
endured.   He did not measure his words, and the
charge gained amplitude and definiteness as he
repeated it.   In March, 1827, Carter Beverly, of
North Carolina, wrote to a friend an account of a
visit to Jackson, and a report of Jackson's circumstantial assertion, at his own table, that Clay's
friends offered to support Jackson, if Jackson
would promise not to continue Adams as Secretary
of State.   Beverly's letter was published at Fay-
etteville, North Carolina.[3]   In June, Jackson
wrote to Beverly an explicit repetition over his
own signature.[4]   The charge had now a name and
a responsible person behind it, — Jackson himself.

[1] 28 Niles, 19.
[2] Branch made some allusions and vague comments.   33 Niles,
22.   [3] 32 Niles, 162.   [4] 32 Niles, 315.

Clay at once called on him for his authorities and proofs. Jackson named Buchanan as his authority.[1] Buchanan had been one of the active ones[2] that winter, but he had blundered. He now made a statement which was not straightforward either way, but it did not support Jackson's statement. He distinctly said that he had never been commissioned by the Clay men for anything he had said to Jackson about appointing Adams.[3] Clay then called on Jackson to retract, since his only authority had failed. Jackson made no answer. He never forgave Buchanan. In 1842, Carter Beverly wrote to Clay that the charge had never been substantiated, and that he regretted having helped to spread it.[4] At Maysville, in 1843, Adams made a solemn denial of the charge.[5] May 3, 1844, Jackson reiterated the charge in a letter to the "Nashville Union." He said: "Of the charges brought against Mr. Adams and Mr. Clay at that time, I formed my opinions, as the country at large did, from facts and circumstances which were indisputable and conclusive, and I may add that this opinion has undergone no change."[6] Of course this means that he inferred the charge from Clay's appointment, never had any other ground for it, and therefore had as much ground in 1844 as in 1825. Clay never escaped the odium of this charge while he lived. At Lexington, Ky., in 1842, he

[1] 32 Niles, 415.   [2] Markley's Letter, 33 Niles, 167.
[3] 32 Niles, 416; 1 Curtis's *Buchanan*, 42, 511.
[4] 61 Niles, 403.   [5] 11 Adams, 431.   [6] 66 Niles, 247.

said that he thought he should have been wiser if he had not taken office under Adams.[1]

On the publication of Adams's " Diary," probably all students of American political history turned to see what relations with Clay were noted in the winter of 1824–25. Clay and Adams had never been intimate. Their tastes were by no means congenial. There was an " adjourned question of veracity " outstanding between them, because Clay had given vague support to the charge against Adams about the fisheries and the Mississippi, and Adams had challenged him to produce the proof, which would impeach Adams's own story of the negotiations at Ghent. Clay had never answered. December 17, 1824, Letcher, as one of Clay's nearest friends, called on Adams. " The drift of all Letcher's discourse was . . . that Clay would willingly support me, if he could thereby serve himself, and the substance of his *meaning* was, that if Clay's friends could *know* that he would have a prominent share in the administration, that might induce them to vote for me, even in the face of instructions. But Letcher did not profess to have any authority from Clay for what he said, and he made no definite propositions." [2] January 1, 1825, Clay and Adams met by Letcher's intervention.[3] Adams recorded in 1828[4] that Letcher told him, January 2, 1825, that Kentucky would vote for him. January 9th Clay told Adams that he should

---

[1] 62 Niles, 291.　　　　　　[2] 6 Adams, 447.
[3] *Cf.* 8 Adams, 337 (1831).　　[4] 7 Adams, 462.

vote for him, and said that Crawford's friends and Adams's friends had approached him with personal considerations. January 21st Scott, of Missouri, who held the vote of that State, told Adams that he wanted Clay to be in the administration. Adams replied that he could give no assurances, but that, in looking for a western man, he could not overlook Clay. On the same day, in answer to fears that he would proscribe the federalists, he answered that he would try to break up the old parties. February 3d Webster called on Adams about the proscription of the federalists.[1] Adams said that he could give no assurances about his cabinet, but would try to harmonize parties.[2]

The Jackson men found another grievance in the election of Adams. They revived a doctrine which had been advocated in 1801, to the effect that the House of Representatives ought simply to carry out "the will of the people," as indicated by the plurality vote. Benton is the chief advocate of this doctrine.[3] He faces all the consequences of it without flinching. He says plainly that there was a struggle "between the theory of the Constitution and the democratic principle." The Constitution

[1] The federalists all hated Adams for "ratting." In 1828, Timothy Pickering was a Jackson man; not that he loved democracy more, but that he hated Jackson less. 34 Niles, 246.

[2] 1 Curtis's *Webster*, 237.

[3] 31 Niles, 98, gives a homely but very pungent criticism of Benton's doctrine. It consists in showing what the "will of the people" is, when the State divisions, Senate equality, and negro representation are taken into account.

gives to the House of Representatives the right and power to elect the President in a certain contingency. There is no provision at all in the Constitution for the election of President by a great national democratic majority. The elected President is the person who gets a majority of the votes constitutionally described and cast, and the power and right of the House of Representatives, in the contingency which the Constitution provides for, is just as complete as that of the electoral college in all other cases. But the electoral college by no means necessarily produces the selection which accords with the majority of the popular vote. The issue raised by Benton and his friends was therefore nothing less than constitutional government *versus* democracy. The Constitution does not put upon the House the function of raising a plurality vote to a majority, for the obvious reason that it would be simpler to let a plurality elect. The Constitution provides only specified ways for ascertaining "the will of the people," and that will does not rule unless it is constitutionally expressed. That is why we are, fortunately, under a constitutional system, and not under an unlimited and ever-changing democracy. Benton and those who agreed with him were, as he avows, making an assault on the Constitution, when they put forward their doctrine of the function of the House. On that doctrine the Constitution is every one's tool while it answers his purposes, and the sport of every faction which finds it an obstacle, if they can only manage to carry an election. Their might and their right become one and the same thing, — guarantees of each other. Such a doctrine is one of the most pernicious political heresies. A constitution is to a nation what self-control under established rules of conduct is to a man. The only time when it is of value is just the time when the temptation to violate it is strong, and that is the time when it contravenes temporary and party interests.

In its practical aspects, also, the election of 1824 showed how pernicious and false Benton's doctrine is. "The will of the people," to which he referred as paramount, was an inference only. The moment we depart from constitutional methods of ascertaining the will of the people, we shall always be driven to inferences which will, in the last analysis, be found to rest upon nothing but party prejudices and party hopes. In the vote of 1824 the facts were as follows: Clay's States indicated, as their second choice, Jackson. Jackson's friends inferred that, if Clay had not been running, Jackson would have carried those States and would have been elected. Going farther, however, we find that in New Jersey and Maryland the Crawford men supported Jackson to weaken Adams. In North Carolina, Adams men supported Jackson to weaken Crawford. In Louisiana, Adams men and Jackson men combined to weaken Clay.[1] Hence Jackson got the whole or a part of the vote of these four

[1] 1 *Annual Register*, 40.

States by bargain and combination. How many more undercurrents of combination and secondary intention there may have been is left to conjecture. What then becomes of the notion of "the will of the people," as some pure and sacred emanation only to be heard and obeyed? No election produces any such pure and sacred product, but only a practical, very limited, imperfect, and approximate expression of public opinion, by which we manage to carry on public affairs. The "*demos krateo* principle," to use Benton's jargon, belongs in the same category with Louis Fourteenth's saying: *L'état, c'est moi.* One is as far removed from constitutional liberty as the other.

Let it be noted, however, that this suggestion of Benton was far more than a preposterous notion which we can set aside by a little serious discussion. He touched the portentous antagonism which is latent in the American system of the State, — the antagonism between the democratic principle and the constitutional institutions. The grandest issue that can ever arise in American political life is whether, when that antagonism is developed into active conflict, the democratic principle or the constitutional institution will prevail.

Crawford went home to Georgia, disappointed, broken in health, his political career entirely ended. He recovered his health to some extent. He became a circuit judge, and gave to Calhoun, five years later, very positive evidence that he was still alive. He died in 1834.

CHAPTER V

ADAMS'S ADMINISTRATION

THE presidential office underwent a great change at the election of 1824. The congressional caucus had, up to that time, proceeded on the theory that the President was to be a great national statesman, who stood at the head of his party, or among the leaders of it. There were enthusiastic rejoicings that "King Caucus" was dethroned and dead. What killed the congressional caucus was the fact that, with four men running, the adherents of three of them were sure to combine against the caucus, on account of the advantage which it would give to the one who was expected to get its nomination. However, it was a great error to say that King Caucus was dead. Looking back on it now, we see that the caucus had only burst the bonds of the chrysalis state and entered on a new stage of life and growth.

Jackson was fully recognized as the coming man. There was no fighting against his popularity. The shrewdest politician was he who should seize upon that popularity as an available force, and prove capable of controlling it for his purposes. Van Buren proved himself to be the man for this func-

tion. He usurped the position of Jackson leader
in New York, which seemed by priority to belong
to Clinton. He and the other Crawford leaders
had had a hard task to run a man who seemed to
be physically incapacitated for the duties of the
presidency, but when Crawford's health broke
down it was too late for them to change the whole
plan of their campaign. After the election they
joined the Jackson party. The " era of good feeling " had brought into politics a large number of
men,[1] products of the continually advancing political activity amongst the less educated classes, who
were eager for notoriety and spoils, for genteel living without work, and for public position. These
men were ready to be the janizaries of any party
which would pay well. They all joined the opposition, because they had nothing to expect from the
administration. All the factions except the Adams
faction, that is to say, all the federalists and all the
non-Adams personal factions of the old republican
party, went into opposition. These elements were
very incoherent in their political creeds and their
political codes, but they made common cause.[2]
They organized at once an opposition of the most
violent and factious kind. Long before any political questions arose, they developed a determination
to oppose to the last whatever the administration
should favor. They fought for four years to make

[1] 3 *Ann. Reg.* 10.
[2] The new groupings caused intense astonishment to simple-
minded observers. See 32 Niles, 339.

capital for the next election, as the chief business of Congress. John Randolph, who by long practice had become a virtuoso in abuse, exhausted his powers in long tirades of sarcasm and sensational denunciations, chiefly against Clay. The style of smartness which he was practising reached its climax when he called the administration an alliance of Blifil and Black George, the Puritan and the Black-leg. He and Clay fought a duel, on which occasion, however, Randolph fired in the air. After Jackson's election, Randolph was given the mission to Russia, and was guilty of a number of the abuses which he had scourged most freely in others. He had to endure hostile criticism, as a matter of course, and he learned the misery of a public man forced to make "explanations" under malignant charges. He proved to be as thin-skinned as most men of his stamp are when their turn comes.[1]

Van Buren initiated the opposition into the methods and doctrines of New York politics. Ever since the republicans wrested that State from the federalists, in 1800, they had been working out the methods of organization by which an oligarchy of a half dozen leaders could, under the forms of democratic-republican self-government, control the State. As soon as the federalists were defeated, the republicans broke up into factions. Each faction, when it gained power, proscribed the others. Until 1821 the patronage, which was the cohesive

[1] 2 Garland's *Randolph*, 339.

material by which party organization was cemented,
was in the hands of a " council" at Albany. After
1821 the patronage, by way of reform, was converted into elective offices. It then became necessary to devise. a new system adapted to this new
arrangement, and all the arts by which the results
of primaries, conventions, committees, and cau-
cuses, while following all the forms of spontaneous
action, can be made to conform to the programme
of the oligarchy or the Boss, were speedily developed. If now the presidency was no longer to be
the crown of public service, and the prize of a very
limited number of statesmen of national reputation, — if it was conceivable that an Indian fighter
like Jackson could come within the range of choice,
— then the presidency must be ever after the position reserved for popular heroes, or, in the absence
of such, for "available" men, as the figure-heads
with and around whom a faction of party leaders
could come to power. ·King Caucus was not dead,
then. He had lost a town and gained an empire.
It remained to develop and extend over the whole
country an organization of which the public service
should constitute the network. There would be
agents everywhere to receive and execute orders,
to keep watch, and to make reports. The central
authority would dispose of the whole as a general
disposes of his army. The general of the "outs"
would recruit his forces from those who hoped for
places when the opposition should come in. As
there were two or three "outs" who wanted each

place held by those who were "in," recruits were not lacking. It was during Adams's administration that the opposition introduced on the federal arena the method of organizing federal parties by the use of the spoils, which method had been previously perfected in the State politics of New York.

The opposition invented and set in action two or three new institutions. They organized local Jackson committees' up and down the country, somewhat on the plan of the old revolutionary committees of correspondence and safety. It was the duty of these committees to carry on a propaganda for Jackson, to contradict and refute charges against him, to make known his services, to assail the administration, and to communicate facts, arguments, reports, etc., to each other. Jackson had had a "literary bureau" at work in Washington in 1824. He wrote to tell Lewis who the writers were, viz. Eaton, Houston, and Isaacs. He mentioned a case in which Eaton was conducting both sides of a discussion, on the approved plan, under two pseudonyms.[1] Partisan newspaper writing was also employed to an unprecedented extent. The partisan editor, who uses his paper to reiterate and inculcate statements of fact and doctrine designed to affect the mind of the voter, was not a new figure in politics, but now there appeared all over the country small local newspapers, edited by men who assumed the attitude of party advocates, and pursued one side only of

[1] Ford MSS.

all public questions, disregarding truth, right, and justice, determined only to win. In 1826, at Calhoun's suggestion, an "organ" was started at Washington, the "Telegraph," edited by Duff Green, of Missouri. The organ gave the key to all the local party newspapers.

Adams showed, in his inaugural, some feeling of the unfortunate and unfair circumstances of his position. He said : " Less possessed of your confidence in advance than any of my predecessors, I am deeply conscious of the prospect that I shall stand more and oftener in need of your indulgence." In October, the Legislature of Tennessee nominated Jackson for 1828, and he appeared before the Legislature to receive an address and to make a reply. He resigned the senatorship in a very careful and well-written letter,[1] in which he urged (referring, as everybody understood, to Clay's appointment) that an amendment to the Constitution should be adopted forbidding the appointment to an office in the gift of the President of any member of Congress during, or for two years after, his term of office in Congress.[2] In this letter he said that the senatorship had been

[1] 29 Niles, 156.

[2] Robert G. Harper once testified in a court of law his personal belief, founded on general knowledge and inference, that Burr could have been elected in 1801, if he would have used " certain means," and his belief that Jefferson did use those means. 23 Niles, 282. He referred to the appointment by Jefferson to lucrative offices of Linn, of New Jersey, and Claiborne, of Tennessee (each of whom controlled the vote of a State), and also

given to him in 1823 without effort or solicitation;
also that he made it a rule neither to seek nor decline office. In his speech before the Legislature
he spoke more freely of the corruption at Washington, from which he sought to escape by resign-
ing.[1] He now had Livingston, Eaton, Lee, Van
Buren, Benton, Swartwout, Duff Green, and Lewis
managing his canvas, some of them at Washington
and some in Tennessee. They kept close watch
over him, and maintained constant communication
with each other.

The first overt acts of the opposition were the
objection to Clay's confirmation, and the rejection
of the treaty with Colombia. Clay had been a
champion of the South American republics, and
everything in the way of intimacy with them was
capital for him. These votes occurred in March,
1825. The "Annual Register," commenting, over
a year later, on these votes, said: "The divisions
which had been taken on the foregoing questions
[those mentioned] left little doubt that the new
administration was destined to meet with a sys-
tematic and organized opposition, and, previous to
the next meeting of Congress, the ostensible
grounds of opposition were set forth at public

of Livingston, who could have divided the vote of New York. 36
Niles, 197. According to a return made to a call by Congress
in 1826, the number of members of Congress appointed to office
by the Presidents down to that time was: by Washington, 10; by
Adams, 13; by Jefferson, 25; by Madison, 29; by Monroe, 35;
by J. Q. Adams, in his first year, 5. 36 Niles, 267.

[1] 1 *Ann. Reg.* 21.

dinners and meetings, so as to prepare the community for a warm political contest until the next election."[1] The public was greatly astonished at the uproar among the politicians. The nation acquiesced in the result of the election as perfectly constitutional and regular, and it cost great effort to stir up an artificial heat and indignation about it. The "bargain" formed the first stock or capital of the opposition. The claim that Jackson had been cheated out of his election was the second. This became an article of the political creed, and it was the most efficacious means of stirring up party rage, although no one could tell how he was cheated. It was a splendid example of the power of persistent clamor without facts or reason. Some attempt was made to get up a cry about "family influence," but this did not take. The charge of bargain and fraud was so assiduously reiterated that, in 1827, there were six senators and forty representatives who would not call on the President.[2] It was during the session of 1825–26 that the discordant elements of the opposition coalesced into a party,[3] the democratic party of the next twenty years. Near the end of the session a prominent Virginia politician declared that the combinations for electing Jackson in 1828 were already formed.[4]

[1] 1 *Ann. Reg.* 38.
[2] 7 Adams, 374. The federal members of Congress would not visit Madison in 1815. 1 Curtis's *Webster*, 135.
[3] 1 *Ann. Reg.* 22.   [4] *Ibid.*

It was proposed to adopt a constitutional amendment taking away the contingent power of the
House to elect a President, but no agreement could
be reached. A committee on executive patronage
was raised, in reality to provide electioneering material. This committee reported six bills, the most
important of which provided that the President
might not appoint to office any person who had
been a member of Congress during his own term
in the presidential office, and that the President, if
he should remove any officer, should state his
reasons to the Senate on the appointment of a successor. No action was taken.

The topic, however, on which the opposition
most distinctly showed their spirit was the Panama
mission. Benton misrepresents that affair more
grossly than any other on which he touches. The
fact is that the opposition were forced by their
political programme to oppose a measure which it
was very awkward for them to oppose, and they
were compelled to ridicule and misrepresent the
matter in order to cover their position. Sargent [1]
tells a story of an opposition senator, who, when
rallied on the defeat of the opposition, in the vote
on confirming the commissioners, replied: "Yes,
they have beaten us by a few votes after a hard
battle; but if they had only taken the other side
and refused the mission, we should have had
them!" The opposition vehemently denounced
the Monroe doctrine. They would not print the

[1] 1 Sargent, 117.

instructions to the commissioners because these would have refuted the exaggerated denunciations. It was not until 1829 that public opinion forced the printing.[1]

Adams had strong convictions about points of public policy. He held that it was the duty of the President to advise and recommend to Congress such measures as he thought desirable in the public interest, and then to leave to Congress the responsibility if nothing was done. He therefore set out in his messages series of acts and measures which he thought should be adopted. He thereby played directly into the hands of the opposition, for they then had a complete programme before them of what they had to attack. Adams held the active theory of statesmanship. He was not content to let the people alone. He thought that a statesman could foresee, plan, prepare, open the way, set in action, encourage, and otherwise care for the people. To him the doctrine of implied powers meant only that the Constitution had created a government complete and adequate for all the functions which devolved upon it in caring for all the interests which were confided to it. He regarded the new land as a joint possession of all the States, the sale of which would provide funds which ought to be used to build roads, bridges, and canals, and to carry out other works of internal improvement, which, as he thought, would open up the continent to civilization.[2] He cared more for internal

[1] They are to be found, 4 *Ann. Reg.* 29.   [2] 9 Adams, 162.

improvements than for a protective tariff.[1] He
wanted a national university and a naval school.
He favored expenditures on fortifications and a
navy and an adequate army. He wanted the
federal judiciary enlarged and a bankruptcy law
passed. Some of the opposition found the party
exigency severe, which forced them to oppose all
the points in this programme. In 1824 Crawford
had been the only stickler for State rights and
strict construction. Calhoun and his friends had
been on the other side. The old-fashioned pet-
tifogging of the strict constructionists, and the
cast-iron dogmatism of the State rights men, were
developed in the heat of the factious opposition of
1825–29. All that, however, before that time had
been considered extreme or " radical." Van Buren,
on his reëlection to the Senate in 1827, wrote a
letter in which he promised to recover for the
States the "rights of which they had been deprived by construction," and to save what rights
remained.[2] Hammond expresses the quiet astonishment which this created in the minds of the people,
even democrats like himself, who were not aware
that the States had suffered any wrong, especially
at the hands of the existing administration. The
country was in profound peace and stupid prosperity, and the rancor of the politicians seemed
inexplicable. The public debt was being refunded
advantageously. Immigration was large and growing. The completion of the Erie Canal in 1825

[1] 8 Adams, 444.   [2] 2 Hammond, 246.

opened up the great lakes to navigation, and the
adjacent country to settlement.   Public affairs were
in fact dull.   The following passage from the
" Annual Register " shows the impression made by
the agitation at Washington : [1] —

"Nearly all the propositions which were called for
by the popular voice were defeated, either from want
of time for their consideration, or by an influence
which seemed to exert itself for the sole purpose of
rendering those who administered the government unpopular.   The community was generally disappointed
as to the results of the session. . . . Many of the
members were new to political life. . . . Others were
predetermined to opposition, and from the first as-
sembling of Congress devoted themselves to thwarting
the measures which its [the administration's] friends
urged upon the consideration of Congress.   The Vice-
President and his friends were most prominent in this
class of politicians. . . . The manner, too, in which the
opposition attacked the administration displayed an ex-
asperated feeling, in which the community did not
sympathize, and a general suspicion was felt that its
leaders were actuated by private griefs, and that the
public interests were neglected in their earnest struggle
for power.   The pride of the country, too, had received
a deep wound in the prostration of the dignity of the
Senate."

Calhoun appointed committees hostile to the
administration, which could not bring their own
party to the support of their reports.   He also
ruled that it was not the duty of the Vice-Presi-

[1] 1 *Ann. Reg.* 149.

dent to preserve order, save upon the initiative of
some senator on the floor. Great disorder occurred, and John Randolph especially took advantage of this license. The Senate was led, at the
end of the session of 1825–26, to take from the
Vice-President the duty of appointing the committees of the Senate. Letters which appeared in
one of the Washington newspapers, signed " Pat-
rick Henry," criticising Calhoun's course, were
ascribed to the President. Answering letters,
signed " Onslow," were ascribed to the Vice-President.[1]

Adams took no steps to create an administration
party. He offered the Treasury to Crawford, who
refused it. He then gave it to Rush, who had
voted against him. The Secretaries of War and
of the Navy had likewise supported other candidates.[2] Adams refused to try to secure the election of Jeremiah Mason, an administration man, to
the Senate.[3] He had declared, before the election,
that he should reward no one, and proscribe no
one. He adhered to this faithfully. Clay urged
him to avoid pusillanimity on the one hand, and
persecution on the other.[4] The election being
over, Clay said that no officer ought to be allowed
" to hold a conduct in open and continual dispar-
agement of the administration and its head."
Adams replied that, in the particular case under
discussion (collector at New Orleans), there had

[1] Harper's *Calhoun*, 31.   [2] Perkins, 289.
[3] 7 Adams, 14.   [4] 6 Adams, 546.

been no overt act; that four fifths of all the custom-house officers had been unfavorable to his (Adams's) election, and were now in his power; that he had been urged to sweep them all away; that he could not do this as to one without opening the question as to all, and that he would enter on no such policy. In 1826 Clay urged Adams to remove the custom-house officers at Charleston and Philadelphia. Adams refused, although he thought that these officers were using the subordinate offices in their control against the administration.[1] He appointed federalists when he thought that they were better qualified than other candidates. This did not conciliate the federalists, and it aroused all " the wormwood and the gall " of the old party hatred.[2] In 1827 Clay and others urged him to confine appointments to friends. He refused to adopt that rule.[3] He expressed the belief that the opposition were spending money to poison public opinion through the press, but he would not do anything for Binns, an administration editor.[4] In June, 1827, he refused to go to Philadelphia, to make a speech in German to the farmers, at the opening of the canal, because he objected to that style of electioneering.[5] In October, 1827, Clay made a warm protest against Adams's action in retaining McLean, the Postmaster-General. Clay alleged that McLean was using the post-office patronage actively against the administration.

[1] 7 Adams, 163.   [2] 7 Adams, 207.   [3] 7 Adams, 257.
[4] 7 Adams, 262.   [5] 7 Adams, 297.

McLean hated Clay and loved Calhoun,[1] but he claimed to be a loyal friend of the administration. Adams would not believe him a traitor.[2] A campaign story was started that Adams's accounts with the Treasury were not in order. Clay desired that Adams would correspond with an election committee in Kentucky, and refute the charge. Adams refused, because he disapproved of the western style of electioneering and stump-speaking.[3] Binns, an Irish refugee, editor of the "Democratic Press" of Philadelphia, ought by all affinities to have been a supporter of Jackson, but he took the wrong turning after Crawford's disappearance, and became a supporter of Adams. He plaintively describes the results. He tried to talk to Adams about appointments. "I was promptly told that Mr. President Adams did not intend to make any removals. I bowed respectfully, assuring the President that I had no doubt the consequence would be that he would himself be removed so soon as the term for which he had been elected had expired. This intimation gave the President no concern, and assuredly did in no wise affect his previous determination." [4] Binns, however, was wise in his generation.

Adams's administration had a majority in the Senate until the 20th Congress met in 1827, when both Houses had opposition majorities. Adams says that this was the first time in the history of

[1] 7 Adams, 364.   [2] 7 Adams, 343.
[3] 7 Adams, 347.   [4] Binns, 250.

the country that such had been the case.[1] The
session of 1827–28 was almost entirely occupied in
manufacturing political capital. A committee on
retrenchment and reform presented a majority and
a minority report. The majority expressed alarm
at the increasing expenditures of the federal government, and the extravagance of the administration. The minority said that no expenditures had
been made which Congress had not ordered, and
that the expenditures had not increased unduly,
when the size and population of the country were
considered. It was charged that large sums had
been spent in decorating the President's house,
especially the "East Room." Congress had appropriated $25,000 for the White House, of which
$6,000 had been spent. The rest was returned to
the Treasury. As soon as Jackson was elected,
the " Courier and Enquirer " said that the " East
Room " was very shabby, and would at once be
made decent.[2] There was no attempt to be fair or
truthful in these charges. They were made solely
with a view to effect. Clamor and reiteration
availed to spread an opinion that the administration had been extravagant.

The campaign of 1828 was conducted, on both
sides, on very ruthless methods. Niles said that
it was worse than the campaign of 1798.[3] Campaign extras of the " Telegraph " were issued
weekly, containing partisan material, refutations
of charges against Jackson, and slanders on Ad-

[1] 7 Adams, 367.   [2] Quoted 37 Niles, 229.   [3] 35 Niles, 33.

ams and Clay. The Adams party also published a monthly of a similar character : " Truth's Advocate and Monthly Anti-Jackson Expositor." The country was deluged with pamphlets on both sides. These pamphlets were very poor stuff, and contain nothing important on any of the issues, and no contribution to history. They all appeal to low tastes and motives, prejudices and jealousies. Binns issued a number of hand-bills, each with a coffin at the head, known as " coffin hand-bills," setting forth Jackson's bloody and lawless deeds.[1] One Jackson hand-bill had a broad-axe cut of John Quincy Adams driving off with a horsewhip a crippled old soldier who dared to speak to him and ask an alms. In short, campaign literature took on a new and special development in this campaign, and one is driven to wonder whether the American people of that day were such that all this drivel and vulgarity could affect their votes.

Against Jackson was brought up his marriage, and all the facts of his career which could be made the subject of unfavorable comment. Against Adams were brought charges that he gave to Webster and the federalists, in 1824, a corrupt promise; that he was a monarchist and aristocrat; that he refused to pay a subscription to turnpike stock on a legal quibble; that his wife was an Englishwoman; that he wrote a scurrilous poem

[1] Binns says that he issued these hand-bills and was mobbed in 1824. It seems that his memory failed him.

against Jefferson in 1802 ; that he surrendered a young American servant-woman to the Emperor of Russia; that he was rich; that he was in debt; that he had long enjoyed public office; that he had received immense amounts of public money, namely, the aggregate of all the salaries, outfits, and allowances which he had ever received; that his accounts with the Treasury were not in order; that he had charged for constructive journeys; that he had put a billiard-table in the White House at the public expense;[1] that he patronized duellists (Clay) ; that he had had a quarrel with his father, who had disinherited him; that he had sent out men in the pay of the government to electioneer for him; that he had corrupted the civil service; that he had used the federal patronage to influence elections. The federalists, in their turn, charged him with not having kept his promise to Webster.

McLean's conduct towards the end of Adams's term caused more and more complaint. He had been a Methodist minister, and some administration men did not want him dismissed lest the Methodists should be offended.[2] Bache, the postmaster at Philadelphia, was a defaulter. McLean had known it for eighteen months. Finally he removed Bache, and appointed Thomas Sergeant, who had been allied with Ingham, Dallas, and other Jackson men. Adams would not remove McLean.[3]

[1] Levi Woodbury was especially shocked at this. Plumer's *Plumer*, 513.

[2] 7 Adams, 540.   [3] 8 Adams, 8, 25, 51.

In October, just before the election, but too
short a time before it to have any effect on it,
Adams became involved in a controversy with
William B. Giles about the circumstances and
motives of his (Adams's) going over to the administration in 1807. On account of revelations
which were made in this controversy, Adams was
involved in another with the descendants of the
old high federalists, who called him to account for
allegations that the federalists of 1803–1809 were
secessionists. The controversy developed all the
acrimony of the old quarrel between the Adamses
and the high federalists. John Quincy Adams
prepared a full statement of the facts on which he
based his opinions and statements, but it was not
published until 1877.[1]

Lewis wrote to Hayward of Cincinnati, March
28, 1827, urging that the Clinton men should take
sides, as the Calhoun men had done, which " will
give them equally as strong claims on the friends
of Gen. Jackson, but unless they do this they have
no right to expect the support of his friends, unless
it be from motives of Patriotism alone." " Their
silence heretofore has subjected them to the imputation of a want of candor. They ought to know
that if the schemes of Adams, Clay and Webster
are carried into effect; that he [Clinton] never
can be President. If Old Hickory shall be elected
he will set a better example — it is not my opinion

[1] *New England Federalism*, by Henry Adams. See also Plumer's *Plumer*, and Lodge's *Cabot*.

he could be induced to serve more than one term." [1] In September, the Tammany General Committee and the Albany "Argus" came out for Jackson,[2] as it had been determined, in the programme, that they should do. A law was passed for casting the vote of New York in 1828 by districts. The days of voting throughout the country ranged from October 31st to November 19th.[3] The votes were cast by the Legislature in Delaware and South Carolina; by districts in Maine, New York, Maryland, Tennessee; elsewhere, by general ticket. Jackson got 178 votes to 83 for Adams. The popular vote was 648,273 for Jackson; 508,064 for Adams.[4] Jackson got only one vote in New England, namely, in a district of Maine, where the vote was, Jackson, 4,223; Adams, 4,028.[5] New York gave Jackson 20; Adams, 16. New Jersey and Delaware voted for Adams. Maryland gave him 6, and Jackson 5. Adams got not a single vote south of the Potomac or west of the Alleghanies. In Georgia no Adams ticket was nominated.[6] Tennessee gave Jackson 44,293 votes, and Adams 2,240. Parton has a story of an attempt, in a Tennessee village, to tar and feather two men who dared to vote for Adams.[7] Pennsylvania gave Jackson 101,652 votes; Adams, 50,848. For Vice-

[1] Copy in Ford MSS.   [2] 2 Hammond, 258.

[3] *Telegraph Extra*, 565.

[4] 3 *Ann. Reg.* 31. The figures for the popular vote vary in different authorities.

[5] 35 Niles, 177.   [6] See page 228.   [7] 3 Parton, 151.

President, Richard Rush got all the Adams votes;
Calhoun got all the Jackson votes except 7 of
Georgia, which were given to William Smith, of
South Carolina.

General Jackson was therefore triumphantly
elected President of the United States, in the name
of reform, and as the standard-bearer of the people,
rising in their might to overthrow an extravagant, corrupt, aristocratic, federalist administration,
which had encroached on the liberties of the people,
and had aimed to corrupt elections by an abuse
of federal patronage. Many people believed this
picture of Adams's administration to be true. Andrew Jackson no doubt believed it. Many people
believe it yet. Perhaps no administration, except
that of the elder Adams, is under such odium.
There is not, however, in our history any administration which, upon a severe and impartial scrutiny,
appears more worthy of respectful and honorable
memory.[1] Its chief fault was that it was too good
for the wicked world in which it found itself. In
1836 Adams said, in the House, that he had never
removed one person from office for political causes,
and that he thought that was one of the principal
reasons why he was not reëlected.[2] The "Annual
Register"[3] aptly quoted, in regard to Adams, a
remark of Burke on Lord Chatham: "For a wise
man he seemed to me, at that time, to be governed
too much by general maxims. In consequence of

[1] See Morse's *J. Q. Adams.*   [2] 50 Niles, 194.
[3] 3 *Ann. Reg.* 34.

having put so much the larger part of his opposers into power, his own principles could not have any effect or influence in the conduct of affairs. When he had executed his plan he had not an inch of ground to stand upon. When he had accomplished his scheme of administration, he was no longer a minister."

CHAPTER VI

THE "RELIEF" SYSTEM OF KENTUCKY

BEFORE entering upon the history of Jackson's administration it is necessary to notice a piece of local history, to which frequent subsequent reference must be made, on account of influences exerted on national politics. A great abuse of paper money and banking took place in the Mississippi Valley between 1818 and 1828. It was an outcome of the application of political forces to the relations of debtor and creditor. It necessarily followed that political measures were brought into collision with constitutional provisions, and with judicial institutions as the interpreters and administrators of the same, in such points as the public credit, the security of contracts, the sanctity of vested rights, the independence of the judiciary, and its power to pass on the constitutionality of laws. A struggle also arose between squatterism and law in respect to land titles, which involved the same fundamental interests and issues of civil liberty and civilization. Currency, banks, land titles, stay laws, judge-breaking, disunion, and the authority of the federal judiciary, were the matters at stake, and all were combined and reacting on

each other. Kentucky was the scene of the strongest and longest conflict between the constitutional
guarantees of vested rights and the legislative measures for relieving persons from contract obligations, when the hopes under which those obligations
were undertaken had been disappointed by actual
experience. It was from Kentucky, also, that the
influences arose which were brought to bear on
national politics.

It is worth while to see what historical antecedents had educated the people of Kentucky up to
the extravagant opinions and conduct of 1820–30.

The sources of the trouble lie far back in the
colonial history of Virginia and North Carolina,
where false and evil traditions were started which,
when carried to Kentucky and Tennessee, produced
more gross and extravagant consequences. There
had been excessive speculation in all the colonies,
and all had imitated more or less the action of
Massachusetts, in 1640, when a crisis produced ruin
to indebted speculators, and when it was ordered
that goods taken on execution should be transferred
to the creditor at a valuation put on them by three
neighbors as appraisers.[1] There was some justification for such a law when there was no market, so
that goods offered at auction were harshly sacrificed. Appraisement laws, however, in a community where all were indebted, and where each in
turn became appraiser for his neighbors, were a
gross abuse of the forms of law.

[1] Felt, 23.

A case of judge-breaking, in connection with a disputed land-title (due to the slovenly land system of Virginia), occurred, in Kentucky, in 1795.[1] An attempt had been made, by the State, to quiet titles, and to give security to landholders, by appointing commissioners, who gave certificates to possessors. Very many of the latter were squatters, and paper titles were extant which underlay their claims. The Court of Appeals of the State would not allow the certificates to preclude an examination of a claim and an award of justice, as the law and the facts might require. In this it aroused the rage of the squatter element. Two judges, Muter and Sebastian, made the decision; Wallace dissenting. At the next session of the Legislature an attempt was made to remove the two judges by an address to the Governor, but there were only three majority for it in the House, while two thirds were required. The House then summoned the two judges before it, but they refused to appear on grounds of the independence of the judiciary. The House passed resolutions denouncing the judgment and impugning the integrity or mental capacity of the judges. The Senate, by a majority of one, passed similar resolutions. At the next term, Muter joined Wallace in reversing the decision and ordering a new trial. There was a new appeal and affirmation of the second decision.[2]

A system of selling State lands on credit began

[1] McConnell *vs.* Kenton, Hughes's Ky. Rep. 257.
[2] Butler, 252.

in 1797, which had a very unfortunate effect in creating a body of debtors to the State. For fifteen years law upon law was passed, fluctuating between the motive of collecting what was due to the State, and that of showing leniency to the debtor. Innumerable acts of grace to individuals were passed.

It was another peculiarity of Kentucky legislation that the judiciary system of the State was changed again and again, and also that numerous acts were passed in relief of negligent and delinquent officers.

Judge Muter experienced in his own person the hardship of life in a community which does not respect vested rights. He was retired, in 1806, on an old age pension of $300, but pensions were unpopular, and his was repealed in 1809, in spite of the Governor's veto.

Another incident which contributes to the same manifestation of the popular temper was a law of 1808, that "all reports" of decisions in England since July 4, 1776, "shall not be read nor considered as authority in any of the courts of this commonwealth." The lawyers held that no one could violate this except by reading *all the reports*, etc.; but the decisions, although cited, were not read in court.[1] This State also tried the popular whim of lay judges.

During the period of inflation east of the Alleghanies (1812–15),[2] the States west of the Alleghanies had plenty of silver, and were free from

---

[1] Littell's Rep. Pref.   [2] See page 268.

financial disturbance. At the session of 1817–18, the Legislature of Kentucky plunged that State into the inflation system by chartering forty banks, which were to issue notes redeemable in Bank of Kentucky notes.[1] The popular party was now under the dominion of a mania for banks, as the institutions for making the poor rich. Clamorous demands were, at the same time, made for a share in the blessings which the Bank of the United States was to shower over the country, and two branches were established, one at Lexington and one at Louisville. Prices immediately began to rise; specie was exported; contracts were entered into, in the expectation of a constant advance of the "wave of prosperity." All hastened to get into debt, because to do so was not only the way to get rich, but the only way to save one's self from ruin. In June, 1819, it is reported: "The whole State is in considerable commotion. The gross amount of debts due the banks is estimated at ten millions of dollars. . . . Several county meetings have been held. Their purpose is: (1) a suspension of specie payments; (2) more paper money; (3) an extra session of the Legislature to pass some laws on this emergency. What did we tell the people of Kentucky when they littered their banks?"[2]

In 1819 the banks of Tennessee and Kentucky

[1] The Bank of Kentucky was founded in 1806, with capital $1,000,000, half contributed by the State; to begin business when $20,000 were subscribed. Sumner; *Hist. of Banking in the U. S.*, 59.

[2] 16 Niles, 201.

and nearly all in Ohio suspended specie payments.[1]
The bubble had now exploded. Liquidation was
inevitable, and the indebted speculators were
ruined. Then came the outcry for relief, that is,
for some legislative measures which would, as they
thought, make the bubble mount again long enough
for them to escape, or suspend the remedies of
creditors so that liquidation might be avoided.
The local banks generally ascribed their ruin to
the Bank of the United States. They over-issued
their notes, which accumulated in the branch of
the Bank, that being the strongest holder. These
notes were presented for redemption. The local
banks construed that as "oppression," and eagerly
warded off all responsibility from themselves by
representing themselves as the victims of an alien
monster, which crushed them while they were trying to confer blessings on the people about them.
The big Bank was bad enough, but the plea of the
local banks was ingeniously false. It availed, however, to turn the popular indignation altogether
against the Bank of the United States.

July 26, 1820, the Bank of Tennessee was established, to last until 1843, with a branch at Knoxville. Its amount of issue was $1,000,000. Its notes
were to be loaned on mortgage security under an
apportionment between the counties, according to
the taxable property in 1819.[2] There was already

---

[1] On the history of the banks of the whole Mississippi Valley
at this time see Sumner; *Hist. Banking in U. S.*
[2] 18 Niles, 452; Gouge, 39.

a Bank of Tennessee, which would have nothing
to do with the new "bank." The Legislature of
Tennessee also passed a law that both real and
personal property, sold under execution, should be
redeemable within two years by paying the purchaser ten per cent advance. Jackson was a prominent and energetic opponent of the relief system.[1]
While the bill for the above bank was pending he
wrote to Lewis as follows: —

"Have you seen the Bill now before the Legislature
of our state to establish a loan office — If you have,
permit me to ask, have you ever seen as wicked &
pernicious a thing attempted by a set of honest Legislatures acting under the santity of an oath — and such a
palbable infringement of both the federal & state constitutions — If you have I would thank you to tell me
when and where. I did not believe that corruption &
wickedness had obtained such an ascendancy in the mind
of any man, to originate such a bill and still much less,
that a majority of the Legislature would be imposed
upon by false colouring & false reasoning to pass such a
Bill — but I have been mistaken, it has passed to a third
reading & will pass into a law unless stopped in its
Carreer by the voice of the people — I learn to day
that a meeting will be in the lower end of Sumner &
one in the lower end of Wilson & one at Mʳ Sanders
store in Davidson this day to remonstrate against it
the people are unanimous I am told on this subject —
They find it a desperate & wicked project in its details
& one which strikes at the vital principles of the charter
of their liberties, and their dearest rights & are all alive

[1] Sumner; *Hist. Banking*, 148.

upon the subject, and I expect will be unanimous in their remonstrance against it, as no good can grow out of it & much evil — I do hope that the good people of Nashvill will unite in their hearty remonstrance against it, & that they will be aided by the grand Jury early next week: if early in the week; it will stop the evil of the passage of the law, or be a sure pledge that it will be repealed next session.

"I hope you and Mr Derby will not sit silent & let such a wicked — profligate & unconstitutional law pass without your exertions to prevent it — a law that will disgrace the state, destroy all credit abroad, and all confidence at home — I will endeavour to send you on Sunday a copy of the resolutions [illegible] tomorrow — I trust they will be such that you & all honest men will approve — answer this by the bearer." [1]

This letter was indorsed on the back by Lewis: "Mr. Grundy was the originator of the *wicked* and *corrupt* measure referred to by the General in this letter." This accounts to some extent for Jackson's active opposition to the measure.

Lewis reminded Jackson, in 1839, that they had always differed on "financial matters," and referred to the following letter, written in answer to the one just quoted, in proof : —

"I have both seen, and read with attention, the law, or Bill, now before the Legislature, authorising the establishment of a Loan Office; and altho I think it a dangerous experiment, and that by passing it we will be hazarding much, yet I hope and am inclined to think, it will not be fraught with such consequences as your lively

[1] Ford MSS.

interest for the prosperity of the State, have induced
you to believe. . . . The members of the Legislature, I
am told, and particularly some of your warmest friends,
think your remarks about them, when in Murfresborough,
were very harsh. Members of Assembly, acting under
the sanctity of an oath do not like to be told that by
voting for certain measures they have been guilty of
perjury. Such harshness, my dear General, is calculated
to do yourself an injury without producing the desired
good. Mildness universally has a much more salutary
effect; it often convinces the understanding without
wounding the feelings. Your enemies will, and are already giving a high colouring to the observations you
made in Murfresboro'. the other day."

Fifteen months later Jackson wrote from Florida:

"I regret the scenes that you relate, you may rest
assured it has greatly injured the reputation of the
State, and I have no doubt will have a tendency to open
the eyes of the sober virtuous part of the community, to
the proflegate conduct of a party in Tennessee whose
conduct has destroyed its character and its best interests,
your paper here is not worth $\frac{50}{100}$ to the dollar and this
depreciation falls upon the labourers — There is no
county that can stand this long — and I expect if the
assembly can be swayed by Mr Grandy the governor, &
party, that we will have a few more million of raggs —
as I do not mean to have much to do with this ragg
business, I console myself with the prayer "May the
lords will be done.""

In June, 1821, the Court of Appeals of Tennessee pronounced the relief system of that State
unconstitutional, and it came to an end.

The forty banks and the two branches of the Bank of the United States, in Kentucky, went into operation in 1817. The Bank of Kentucky could not therefore sustain its former circulation. It imported $240,000 in silver, and reduced its circulation, November, 1818, to $195,000. Nevertheless, it fell heavily in debt during 1818 and 1819 to the branches of the Bank of the United States.[1] In November, 1819, the latter bank ordered the debt to be collected. The Bank of Kentucky suspended and compromised. Its notes were at fifteen per cent discount. A great reduction of the paper was forced, because the Bank of the United States came in to demand payment. May 4, 1820, the stockholders of the Bank of Kentucky voted to suspend specie payments. This suspension became permanent. Intense rage was excited against the Bank of the United States. Kentucky had laid a tax of $60,000 on each of the branches of the national Bank, in January, 1819. At the same time the Supreme Court of the United States declared the Bank constitutional.[2] In December the Kentucky Court of Appeals unanimously sustained the State tax, on the ground that the Bank was unconstitutional. Two judges thought that they must yield to the Supreme Court of the United States. The third, Rowan, thought that they ought to stand out and force further trial in the interest of State rights.[3]

---

[1] Kendall's *Autobiography*, 203. [2] See page 166.
[3] Kendall's *Autobiography*, 205.

December 15, 1819, the Legislature of Kentucky passed, over a veto, a law [1] to suspend for sixty days sales under executions, if the defendant gave bonds that the goods levied on should be forthcoming at the end of that time. The Bank of the Commonwealth of Kentucky was established November 29, 1820, as a further " relief " measure for the benefit of the debtors, victims of the forty banks of 1817. As a further measure of relief a replevin law was passed, December 25, 1820, according to which the debtor was to have two years in which to redeem, under an execution, unless the creditor should endorse on the note that he would take notes of the Bank of the Commonwealth, if the debtor could pay them. Another act was passed, December 21, 1821, which forbade the sale of land on execution, unless it should bring three fourths of its value as appraised by a jury of neighbors. The Bank of the Commonwealth was authorized to issue notes for three millions of dollars. It had no stockholders. The president and directors were elected annually by the Legislature. Their salaries were paid by the State. They were incorporated. The notes were issued in loans on mortgage security, and were apportioned between the counties in proportion to the taxable property in each in 1820. Loans were to be made, in 1820, only to those who needed them, " for the purpose of paying his, her, or their just debts," or to purchase the products of the country for exportation.

[1] Kendall's *Autobiography*, 227.

The bank had twelve branches. Its funds were to be: (1) all money *thereafter* paid in for land warrants, or for land west of the Tennessee river; (2) the produce of the stock owned by the State in the Bank of Kentucky, after that bank should be wound up; (3) the unexpended balances in the treasury at the end of the year. The profits of the bank were to go to the State. Stripped of all pretence, therefore, the bank was the State treasury, put into the hands of a commission elected by the Legislature, and incorporated. Its funds were the current receipts of the treasury from land, and its current balance, if it had one; also the capital already invested in the old bank, whenever that should be released, which never was done. The notes of the bank were legal tender to and from the State. The Legislature appropriated $7,000 to buy books, paper, and plates for printing the notes. This is all the real capital the bank ever had. It was, therefore, just one of the grand swindling concerns common at that period, so many of which are described in the pages of Niles and Gouge.[1]

In 1822 Judge Clark, of the Circuit Court of Kentucky, declared the replevin law of that State unconstitutional.[2] He was cited before the House of Representatives of the State, and an effort was

[1] 46 Niles, 211.

[2] 23 Niles, Supp. 153 (supplement to the 22d vol.). The judge's decision, the legislative proceedings, and the judge's defence are there given.

made to have him removed by the Governor on
the resolution of the Legislature. The vote was
59 to 35 ; not two thirds, as required by the Constitution for this method of removal. In this year
the Legislature used its power in the election of
directors of the old Bank of Kentucky to put in
" relief " men who would make that bank accept
Commonwealth notes. The effect was that the
stock of the old bank at once fell to fifty, and it
suspended.[1] In October, 1822, a specie dollar was
worth $2.05 in Commonwealth notes.[2] A Ken-
tucky correspondent writes, February, 1823 : The
Bank of the Commonwealth " has nearly destroyed
all commerce or trade, extinguished personal credit,
and broken down confidence between man and man,
as well as damped and depressed the industry
of the State; but the people are beginning to
get tired of its blessings, and its paper-mill will
soon cease working, leaving a debt, however,
due to it from the poorest of the people to the
amount of two and a half or three millions of dollars." [3]

In 1823 the notes of the Bank of the Commonwealth began to be withdrawn and burned. Governor Adair, in his message of that year, approved
of the relief system, and denounced the courts for
deciding the replevin laws unconstitutional. This
proceeding of the courts seems to have been then

---

[1] Collins, 89.   [2] 23 Niles, 96.
[3] 23 Niles, 337. Kendall justly described the relief system in
1821. *Autobiography*, 246.

regarded very generally by the people of Kentucky as a usurpation by the judges, and an assault on the liberties of the people. After Adair's term expired, he petitioned for redress, on account of the payment of his salary in depreciated paper.

In 1823 the Court of Appeals of Kentucky declared the relief laws unconstitutional. The Legislature, in January, 1824, affirmed the constitutionality of said laws, and an issue was made up on the right and power of courts to annul, on the ground of unconstitutionality, laws passed by the representatives of the people. The relief system thus brought directly to the test the power of a system of constitutional guarantees, administered by an independent judiciary, to protect rights against an interested and corrupt majority of debtors, which was using its power, under democratic-republican self-government, to rob the minority of creditors. The State election of 1824 was fought on the effort to elect a Legislature, two thirds of which would memorialize the Governor for the removal of the judges who had decided the relief laws unconstitutional. A majority was obtained, but not two thirds. Another course was then taken. The legislative act by which the State judiciary was organized and the Court of Appeals created was repealed. Reference was made, in defence of this action, to the repeal of the federal judiciary act, at the beginning of Jefferson's administration.[1] A new Court of Appeals was constituted by a new

[1] Collins, 90.

act. William T. Barry was appointed chief justice. The old court denied the constitutionality of
the repeal and of the new court, and continued its
existence, so that there were two courts. In 1825
the parties in the State were "Old Court" and
"New Court." [1] The new court party affirmed,
sometimes with vehemence, sometimes with solemnity, that liberty and republicanism were at
stake, and that the contest was to see whether the
judges should be above the law. The old court
party won a majority in the lower House. The
Senate, which held over, was still of the new
court party. The House voted to abolish the
new court, but the Senate did not agree. By this
time the contest had developed a whole school of
ambitious, rising politicians, who appealed with
demagogical address to the passions and distress
of the embarrassed debtors. In November, 1825,
Niles quotes a Kentucky paper that more persons
had left that State than had come to it for many
years. It is plain that two classes of persons were
driven away by the relief system : (1) those who
wanted, by steady industry and accumulation without borrowing, to acquire capital and to be secure
in the possession of it ; and (2) those who could
not, under the prevailing depression, work off the
mortgages which they had eagerly given to the
Bank of the Commonwealth for its notes, in the
hope of thus escaping from old embarrassments.
After five years their condition was hopeless, and

[1] 28 Niles, 277.

if they had any energy they started westward to begin again.

In the mean time there had been a number of decisions by the Supreme Court of the United States which irritated the people of Kentucky, and enhanced their alarm about the assaults of the judiciary on liberty. We have seen how the local banks used the Bank of the United States as a scapegoat for all their sins, and for all the bad legislation of the States. The next swing of the pendulum of popular feeling was over into hatred of the Bank of the United States. Several States, of which Kentucky was one, tried to tax the branches out of existence. In McCulloch *vs.* Maryland (1819),[1] and in Osborn *vs.* Bank of the United States (1824),[2] the Supreme Court of the United States declared that the States could not tax the Bank. In Sturges *vs.* Crowninshield (1819),[3] the same court set limits to the State insolvent laws, and thereby prevented the favor to debtors, which the embarrassed States desired to provide. R. M. Johnson, of Kentucky, proposed an amendment to the Constitution, January 14, 1822, giving appellate jurisdiction to the Senate in any case to which a State was a party, arising under the laws, treaties, etc., of the United States.[4] In Bank of the United States *vs.* Halstead (1825),[5] the Supreme Court decided that it had jurisdiction

---

[1] 4 Wheaton, 316.   [2] 9 Wheaton, 739.
[3] 4 Wheaton, 122.   [4] 7 Benton's *Abridgment*, 145.
[5] 10 Wheaton, 51.

in suits to which the Bank of the United States was a party, and that a law which forbade sales of land under execution for less than three fourths of the appraised value did not apply to writs of execution issued by federal courts. The question of the constitutionality of such a law was avoided. In Wayman *vs.* Southard (1825),[1] the Supreme Court of the United States decided that the replevin and endorsement law of Kentucky did not apply to a writ of execution issued from a federal court. In Bank of the United States *vs.* Planters' Bank of Georgia (1824),[2] it decided that if a State became a party to a banking or commercial enterprise the State could be sued in the course of the business. This decision seemed to threaten the Bank of the Commonwealth of Kentucky. In Green *vs.* Biddle (1823),[3] the Supreme Court of the United States decided that the laws of Kentucky of 1797 and 1812, which reduced the liability of the occupying claimant of land to the successful contestant, on account of rent and profits, as compared with the same liability under the law of Virginia at the time of the separation, and which in a corresponding manner increased the claims of the occupying claimant for improvements, were null and void, being in violation of the contract between Kentucky and Virginia at the time of separation.[4] In Bodley *vs.* Gaither (1825),

[1] 10 Wheaton, 1.   [2] 9 Wheaton, 904.   [3] 8 Wheaton, 1.
[4] Kentucky sent to Congress, May 3, 1824, a remonstrance against this decision. Letcher, of Kentucky, introduced a reso-

the Supreme Court of Kentucky refused to be controlled by the decision in Greene *vs.* Biddle.[1] Inasmuch as the Supreme Court of the United States, in Hawkins *vs.* Barney's Lessee (1831),[2] very materially modified the ruling in Greene *vs.* Biddle, the Kentucky States rights men could claim, as they did, that the federal court had " backed down," and that they were right all the time.[3] In Dartmouth College *vs.* Woodward (1819),[4] the Supreme Court had decided that the charter of a private corporation was a contract which a State Legislature must not violate, and had thus put certain vested rights beyond legislative caprice.[5]

Other decisions had also been made, bearing on State rights and the powers of the federal judiciary in a more general way. In Martin *vs.* Hunter's Lessee (1816),[6] the constitutionality of the 25th section of the judiciary act (power of the Supreme Court to pass upon the constitutionality of State laws) was affirmed, and the authority of the court in a case under a federal treaty was maintained against the Court of Appeals of Virginia. In Gibbons *vs.* Ogden (1824),[7] the court overruled the Supreme Court of New York, and declared an act

lution to amend the law, so that more than a majority of judges should be necessary to declare a State law void. 8 Benton's *Abridgment*, 51.

[1] 3 T. B. Monroe, 58.   [2] 5 Peters, 457.
[3] Butler, 279.   [4] 4 Wheaton, 518.
[5] 1 Webster's *Correspondence*, 283.   [6] 1 Wheaton, 304.
[7] 9 Wheaton, 1.

of the Legislature giving exclusive privileges in
the waters of New York unconstitutional and void.
In Cohens *vs.* Virginia (1821),[1] it was decided that,
if a citizen of a State pleads against a statute
of his own State an act of Congress as defence,
the 25th section of the judiciary act gives the federal Supreme Court jurisdiction to test whether
that defence be good.   In the case of the "Mar-
mion" (1823), the Attorney-General of the United
States (Wirt) had rendered an opinion [2] (1824)
that a law of South Carolina (1822), according to
which any free negro sailors who should come into
that State on board a ship should be imprisoned
until the ship sailed again, was incompatible with
the Constitution and with the international obligations of the United States.   The District Court of
the United States had decided (1823) to the same
effect.[3]

From our present standpoint of established doctrine on the points of constitutional law above
enumerated, it is difficult to understand the shocks
which many or all of these decisions gave to the
Jeffersonian school of politicians.   The assertion
that the reserved rights of the States had been in-
vaded[4] is to be referred to these judicial decisions,
not to executive acts.   The strict construction, State
rights school felt every one of these decisions as a
blow from an adversary against whom there was no

[1] 6 Wheaton, 264.
[2] 1 Opinions of the Attorneys-General, 659.
[3] 25 Niles, 12.   [4] See page 139.

striking back, and the fact undoubtedly is that the Supreme Court, under the lead of Marshall and Story, was consolidating the federal system, and securing it against fanciful dogmas and exaggerated theories which would have made the federal government as ridiculous as the German *Bund*. Readers of to-day are surprised to find that a great many people were alarmed about their liberties under the mild and timid rule of Monroe.[1] It was, however, by no means the scholastic hairsplitters and hobby-riders in constitutional law alone who were astonished and bewildered by the course of the decisions. It needs to be remembered that the system of the Constitution, even after the second war, was yet, to a great degree, unestablished and unformed. Actual experience of any legislative act or constitutional provision is needed to find out how it will work, and what interpretation its terms will take on from the growth of institutions and from their inter-action. It is impossible, upon reading a constitutional provision, to figure to one's self, save in the vaguest way, what will be the character and working of the institution which it creates. It was one of the most fortunate circumstances in the history of the United States that the judicial interpretation and administration of the Constitution was, during its formative period, for a long time in the hands of men who shaped the Constitution in fidelity to its

[1] See Garland's *Randolph*, especially II. 211, on Gibbons *vs.* Ogden.

original meaning and spirit, to secure at once
dignity and strength to the federal system, and
constitutional liberty to the nation. It is fortunate that they were men of profound legal attainments and historic sense, and neither abstractionists
of the French school, nor dialecticians under the
State rights and strict-construction dogmas. The
history of the country has proved the soundness
and wisdom of the constitutional principles they
established, but while they were doing this they had
to meet with a great deal of criticism and abuse.
Kentucky had furnished a number of the cases,
and at least two important interests of hers (relief
system and contested land titles) had been decided
adversely to the interests of the classes which had
least education and property, and most votes.

The message of Governor Desha of Kentucky,
November 7, 1825,[1] deserves attentive reading from
any one who seeks to trace the movement of decisive forces in American political history. The
Governor denounces all banks, and especially the
Bank of the United States, because they are all
hostile to the power and rights of the States. He
says that the Bank of the United States has been
taken under the protection of the federal Supreme
Court, and that these two foreign powers, so allied,
have overthrown the sovereignty of Kentucky. He
complains of the State Court of Appeals, which had
declared the law taxing the Bank of the United
States to be constitutional, for not maintaining its

[1] 29 Niles, 219.

ground, but receding, and deferring to the contrary decision of the Supreme Court of the United
States. He congratulates the State, however, that
the abolition of the old court has removed the
compliant head from the State judiciary, and that
the new court will maintain the sovereignty of
the State against federal encroachments. He declares that the emigration from the State is due to
the decision about the occupying claimant law. He
denounces the federal courts for not recognizing
the State relief laws in regard to writs issued by
themselves, and he regards the State as robbed of
self-government by this intrusion of foreign courts,
which bring with them an independent code of
procedure. He defends the relief system, and
although he does not distinctly say so, what he
means is that the federal courts, by their intrusion,
enable foreign creditors to escape the treatment
which Kentucky creditors have to submit to under
the laws of their country. This was the invasion
of the " sovereignty " of Kentucky which was resented most.

In the same message, Desha suggested that the
Legislature should abolish both the Courts of Appeals, and he promised that, if this should be done,
and a new court should be established, he would
select the judges for it equally from the two existing ones. In 1826 the State election was again
a contest between old court and new court. The
old court carried both Houses.[1] The replevin laws

[1] Collins, 93.

were repealed. The acts of the new court were treated as null. The new court seized the records, and held them by military force. Civil war was avoided only by the moderation of the old court party. The Legislature repealed the law constituting the new court, but the Governor vetoed the repeal.[1] It was passed over his veto, December 30, 1826. By resignations and new appointments among the judges, the court was reconstituted as a single anti-relief body in the years 1828-29.

In 1827 the currency of the States in the Mississippi Valley was fairly good. There remained only $800,000 of Commonwealth paper out, and this was merchandise, not currency.[2] The bank held notes of individuals to the amount of one and a half millions, and real estate worth $30,592. Hence there was due to it a balance from the public, after all its notes should bo paid in, of $600,000. Its debtors had this to pay in specie or its equivalent, or else the bank would get their property. This sum, therefore, fairly represents the net final swindle which the relief system perpetrated on its dupes, to say nothing of its effects on creditors and on the general prosperity of the State. The bank never had over $7,000 capital even spent upon it. Its total issue of bits of paper was printed with the denomination dollars up to three millions. By this issue it had won $600,000 worth of real property, or twenty per cent in five years. Who got this gain? It seems that there

[1] 31 Niles, 310.   [2] 32 Niles, 37.

must have been private and personal interests at
stake to account for the rage which was excited by
the decisions which touched this bank, and by the
intensity of friendship for it which was manifested
by a leading political clique. Undoubtedly the
interest was that of the clique of politicians who
got lucrative offices, power, and influence through
the bank. Wherever a Bank of the State was set
up, the development of such a clique, with all the
attendant corruptions and abuses, took place.

In 1828 the parties were still relief and anti-
relief, the former for Jackson, the latter for Adams. The ideas, however, had changed somewhat.
A " relief " man, in 1828, meant a State rights
man and strict constructionist, who wanted to put
bounds to the supposed encroachments of the federal power, especially the judiciary, and indeed to
the constitutional functions of the judiciary in
general. Metcalf, the anti-relief candidate for
Governor, in 1828, defeated Barry, the relief candidate, after a very hard fight,[1] but the State gave
7,912 majority for Jackson.

Two later decisions of the Supreme Court may
here be mentioned, because they carried forward
the same constitutional tendency which has been
described. They were connected with the political
movements which have been mentioned, and with
those which came later.

In Bank of the Commonwealth of Kentucky
vs. Wister *et al.* (1829),[2] it was held that the

---

[1] Collins, 93.   [2] 2 Peters, 318.

bank must pay specie on demand in return for a deposit which had been made with it of its own notes, although these notes were, when deposited, worth only fifty cents on the dollar. It had been provided in the act establishing the bank that it should pay specie. The bank tried to plead the non-suability of a State, but it was held that, if the State was sole owner and issued as a sovereign, it would be non-suable. Then, however, the notes would be bills of credit. If the State issued as a banker, not a sovereign, then it was suable under the decision in the case of the Planter's Bank of Georgia. In Craig *vs.* Missouri (1830),[1] a law of Missouri (1821) establishing loan offices to loan State currency issues on mortgages was declared unconstitutional as to the notes issued, which were bills of credit. In this decision bills of credit were defined.

[1] 4 Peters, 410.

CHAPTER VII

INTERNAL HISTORY OF JACKSON'S FIRST ADMINISTRATION

JACKSON came to power as the standard-bearer of a new upheaval of democracy, and under a profession of new and fuller realization of the Jeffersonian democratic-republican principles. The causes of the new strength of democracy were economic. It gained strength every year. Everything in the situation of the country favored it. The cotton culture advanced with great rapidity, and led to a rapid settlement of the Southwestern States. The Ohio States filled up with a very strong population. Steamboats came into common use, and they had a value for this country, with its poor roads, but grand rivers, bays, sounds, and lakes, such as they had for no other country. Railroads began to be built just after Jackson's election. The accumulation of capital in the country was not yet great. It was inadequate for the chances which were offered by the opening up of the continent. Hence the industrial organization did not take the form of a wages organization. Individuals, however, found the chances of very free and independent activity, which easily produced a simple abundance. The conditions were such as to give to each a sense of room and power. Individual energy and enterprise were greatly favored. Of course, the effect on the character of the people was certain. They became bold, independent, energetic, and enterprising. They were versatile, and adapted themselves easily to circumstances. They were not disturbed in an emergency; and they were shrewd in dealing with difficulties of every kind. The State constitutions became more and more purely democratic, under the influence of this character of the people. Social usages threw off all the forms which had been inherited from colonial days. The tone of mind was developed which now marks the true, unspoiled American, as distinguished from all Europeans, although it has scarcely been noticed by the critics who have compared the two ; namely, the tone of mind which has no understanding at all of the notion that A could demean himself by talking to B, or that B could be raised in his own estimation or that of other people by being spoken to by A, no matter who A and B might be. Ceremonies, titles, forms of courtesy and etiquette, were distasteful. Niles did not like it that members of Congress were called "honorable." [1] He criticised diplomatic usages. He devoted a paragraph to denunciation of a fashionable marriage in Boston, which took place in King's (!) Chapel, and at which the people cheered the groom. He objected to the

[1] 37 Niles, 378.

term " cabinet," [1] and said, very truly, that there is
no cabinet in our system. He was displeased by
public honors to the President (Monroe). As to
republic, democracy, aristocracy, the " people," and
other political " symbols," as we call them nowa-
days, he held all the vague, half-educated notions
which were then in fashion, compounded of ignorance, tradition, and prejudice, and held in place
by stereotyped phrases and dogmas with a cement
of social envy and political suspicion.

The people of the period found themselves happy
and prosperous. Their lives were easy, and free
from gross cares and from great political anxieties.
They knew little and cared less about other countries. They were generally satisfied with some
crude notions and easy prejudices about institutions
and social states of which they really had no knowledge. Niles knew no more of the English Constitution and English politics than a Cherokee Indian
knew of the politics of the United States. The
American people did not think of their economic
and social condition as peculiar or exceptional.
They supposed that any other nation could be just
like the United States if it chose. They thought
the political institutions, or, more strictly, the political " principles," of this country made all the
difference. They gave their confidence to the
great principles, accordingly, all the more because
those principles flatter human nature. One can
easily discern in Jackson's popularity an element

[1] 40 Niles, 145.

of instinct and personal recognition by the mass of the people. They felt, " He is one of us." " He stands by us." " He is not proud, and does not care for style, but only for plenty of what is sound, strong, and good." " He thinks just as we do about this." The anecdotes about him which had the greatest currency were those which showed him trampling on some conventionality of polite society, or shocking the tastes and prejudices of people from " abroad." In truth Jackson never did these things except for effect, or when carried away by his feelings, but his adherents had a most enjoyable sense of their own power in supporting him in defiance of sober, cultivated people, who disliked him for his violence, ignorance, and lack of cultivation.

The Jackson party flocked to Washington to attend the inauguration. " They really seem," said Webster,[1] " to think that the country has been rescued from some great danger." There was evidently a personal and class feeling involved in their triumph. At the inauguration ball a great crowd of people assembled who had not been accustomed to such festivities. Jackson refused to call on Adams, partly because, as he said, Adams got his office by a bargain, and partly because he thought that Adams could have stopped the campaign references to Mrs. Jackson. That lady had died in the previous December, and Jackson was in a very tender frame of mind in regard to her

[1] 1 Curtis's *Webster*, 340. On the crowd, see 1 Webster's *Correspondence*, 470, 473.

memory.[1] Adams was hurt at the slight put upon
him, and thought that he had deserved other treatment from Jackson.[2] In March, 1832, R. M.
Johnson came to Adams to try to bring about a
reconciliation with Jackson. Nothing came of it.[3]

The inaugural address contained nothing of any
importance. There was a disposition to give Jackson a fair chance. Every one was tired of party
strife,[4] and there was no disposition in any quarter
to make factious opposition. The opposition had
taken the name of national republicans. They
never acknowledged any succession to the federalists. They claimed to belong to the true republican party, but to hold national theories instead
of State rights theories. The Jackson party was
heterogeneous. In opposition it had been held
together by the hope of success, but it had not
been welded together into any true party. No
one yet knew what Jackson thought about any
political question. It had been an unfortunate
necessity to send him to the Senate in 1823. He
had made a record on tariff and internal improvements. His Coleman letter, it is true, left him
safely vague on tariff, but he could only lose, he
could not possibly gain, by making a record on
anything. His advantage over the "statesmen"
was that every one of them was on record a dozen
times on every public question.

---

[1] The New York *American* followed her even beyond the grave
with a scurrilous epitaph.

[2] 8 Adams, 128.   [3] 8 Adams, 484.   [4] 5 *Ann. Reg.* 1.

Calhoun had been reëlected Vice-President. He now understood that Jackson would take only one term, and that he (Calhoun) would have all Jackson's support in 1832. Van Buren, however, who had come into Jackson's political family at a late date, had views and ambitions which crossed this programme of Calhoun. These two men came into collision in the formation of the cabinet. Jackson introduced two innovations. He put the Secretaries back more nearly into the place in which they belong by the original theory of the law. He made them executive clerks or staff officers. The fashion has grown up of calling the Secretaries the President's "constitutional advisers." It is plain that they are not anything of the kind. He is not bound to consult them, and, if he does, it does not detract from his responsibility. Jackson, by the necessity of his character and preparation, and by the nature of the position to which he had been elected, must lean on somebody. He had a number of intimate friends and companions on whom he relied. They did not hold important public positions. They came to be called the "kitchen cabinet." The men were William B. Lewis, Amos Kendall, Duff Green, and Isaac Hill. If the Secretaries had been the "constitutional advisers" of the President, their first right and duty would have been to break off his intimacy with these irresponsible persons, and to prevent their influence. Jackson's second innovation was that he did not hold cabinet councils. Hence his

administration lacked unity and discipline. It did
not have the strength of hearty and conscious
coöperation. Each Secretary went his way, and
gossip and newsmongering had a special field of
activity open to them. The cabinet was not a
strong one. Van Buren was Secretary of State.
S. D. Ingham was Secretary of the Treasury. He
had been an active Pennsylvania politician, and a
member of the House for the last seven years.
John H. Eaton, of Kentucky, was Secretary of
War. He had married, for his first wife, one
of Mrs. Jackson's nieces, and had been an intimate friend of Jackson. He was brother-in-law
of Lewis. He finished, in 1817, a life of Jackson,
which had been begun by Major John Reid. He
had been in the Senate since 1818. John Branch,
of North Carolina, was Secretary of the Navy.
He had been in the Senate since 1823.[1] John M.
Berrien, of Georgia, was Attorney-General. He
had been in the Senate since 1824. William
T. Barry, of Kentucky, who had been chief justice of the new Supreme Court of that State, was
Postmaster-General, with a seat in the cabinet, a
privilege to which that officer had not previously
been admitted. McLean passed into high favor
with the new administration, and was asked to
keep the postmaster-generalship with its new rank.
When the general proscription began he would
not admit it as to his department. He was transferred to the bench of the Supreme Court.[2] Ing-

[1] See page 122 and note 2.   [2] 8 Adams, 112.

ham, Branch, and Berrien were understood to be the Calhoun men in the cabinet.

The men who controlled the administration were the members of the kitchen cabinet. Lewis does not appear to have had any personal ambition. He wanted to return to Tennessee, but Jackson remonstrated that Lewis must not abandon him in the position to which he had been elevated.[1] Lewis was made Second Auditor of the Treasury. He only asked for an office with little work to be done.[2] His character and antecedents have already been noticed. It will appear below that he was far more unwilling to relinquish office than he had been to take it.

Amos Kendall was born in Massachusetts in 1789. He was a graduate of Dartmouth College. In 1814 he went to Washington. In 1815 he was a tutor in Henry Clay's family. He edited a newspaper, the Frankfort "Argus of Western America," and practised law, and was postmaster at Georgetown, Kentucky. He became a leading "relief" man, director in the Bank of the Commonwealth, and as such an enemy of the Bank of the United States. Many of Clay's old supporters, who became relief men, were carried over to Jackson between 1824 and 1828. Kendall was one of these. He had expected an office from Clay, and was offered one, but it did not satisfy him. He had an acrimonious correspondence with Clay in 1828.[3] He was in debt. Clay was one of his

[1] 3 Parton, 180.   [2] Kendall's *Autobiography*, 308.
[3] *Telegraph Extra*, 305.

creditors.   His war with Clay won him Jackson's
favor.   Kendall was an enigmatical combination
of good and bad, great and small traits.   His ability to handle important State questions, and his
skill as a politician, are both beyond question.   He
prostituted his talents to partisan purposes, and
was responsible as much as any other one man
for the bad measures adopted by Jackson.   In his
private character he showed admirable traits of
family devotion and generosity.   As a public man
he belonged to the worst school of American politicians.   He brought the vote of Kentucky to
Washington, and was appointed Fourth Auditor
of the Treasury.   As time went on he proved more
and more the master spirit of the administration.
Harriet Martineau wrote of him, in 1836, as follows: "I was fortunate enough once to catch a
glimpse of the invisible Amos Kendall, one of the
most remarkable men in America.   He is supposed
to be the moving spring of the whole administration, the thinker, planner, and doer; but it is all
in the dark.   Documents are issued of an excellence
which prevents their being attributed to persons
who take the responsibility of them; a correspondence is kept up all over the country for which no
one seems to be answerable; work is done, of goblin
extent and with goblin speed, which makes men
look about them with a superstitious wonder; and
the invisible Amos Kendall has the credit of it
all. . . . He is undoubtedly a great genius.   He
unites with his 'great talent for silence' a splendid

audacity." [1] She goes on to say that he rarely
appeared in public, and seemed to keep up the
mystery. She attributes some of Lewis's work to
Kendall, but the passage is a very fair representation of the opinions of Washington society about
Kendall. He had very great executive and literary
ability. Claiborne said of him, in 1856 : " When I
first saw him, he had a whooping voice, an asth-
matic cough, with a stooping frame and a phthisicky
physiognomy. . . . Yet this little whiffet of a man,
whom the hoosiers would not call even an individual, . . . was the Atlas that bore on his shoulders
the weight of Jackson's administration. He originated, or was consulted in advance, upon every
great measure, and what the prompt decision and
indomitable will of the illustrious chief resolved
upon, the subtle and discriminating intellect of
Kendall elaborated and upheld." [2]

Duff Green was a fighting partisan editor. He
had the virtue of his trade. He was loyal to the
standard to which he had once sworn. He was a
Calhoun man, and he continued to be a retainer of
the most unflinching loyalty. For the first years
of Jackson's administration, Green, as editor of
the " organ," stood on guard all the time to advance the cause of the administration.

[1] 1 Martineau's *Western Travel*, 155. *Cf.* also 1 *Society in
America*, 45.

[2] Quoted in Hudson's *Journalism*, 243. *Cf.* also p. 248, where
Rives's assertion is quoted, in contradiction, that Jackson was
the Atlas of his own administration.

Isaac Hill was born in Massachusetts in 1788. His education was picked up in a printing-office. In 1810 he bought and began to edit the "Patriot,"[1] published at Concord, New Hampshire. He edited his paper with skill and ability, propagating "true republicanism" *in partibus infidelium*, for the people about him were almost all federalists. His main "principle" was that things were in the hands of an "aristocracy," and that he ought to organize the "honest yeomanry" in order to oust that aristocracy from power.[2] He gained adherents. His paper became influential, and he built up a democratic party in New Hampshire.[3] He had long favored strict party proscription. In 1818 he remonstrated with Governor Plumer for appointing a federalist sheriff.[4] He had the rancorous malignity of those men who have been in a contest with persons who have treated them from above downwards. He was not able to carry New Hampshire for Jackson in 1828, but the vote was 24,000 for Adams to 20,600 for Jackson. Hill

[1] Hudson's *Journalism*, 272, on the *Patriot*.

[2] Bradley's *Hill*.

[3] He had kept a boarding-house, at which members of the Legislature, etc., boarded. In 1823 he is referred to as a power. 1 Webster's *Correspondence*, 324. During the New Hampshire election of 1830, forged documents were sent on from Washington to prove Upham, the anti-Jackson candidate for Governor, guilty of smuggling under the embargo. 39 Niles, 156. Mason charged Hill with having sent the papers. 1 Webster's *Correspondence*, 495.

[4] Plumer's *Plumer*, 471.

was immediately taken into the innermost circle at Washington.

The election of Jackson meant that an uneducated Indian fighter had been charged with the power of the presidency, and that these four men wielded it through and for him. Van Buren followed, in order to win the aid of Jackson for the succession. He did not put forth any guiding force. Eaton had some share in the kitchen cabinet. No other member of the cabinet had any influence. Barry, another relief man, but personally quite insignificant, was at the disposal of the kitchen cabinet. Henry Lee had made himself "impossible" by an infamous domestic crime. He was offended at the poor share in the spoils offered to him, and withdrew, relieving the administration of a load. Edward Livingston was in the Senate, but no direct influence by him on the administration, during the first two years, is discernible. The same may be said of Benton.

Some vague expressions in the inaugural about "reform" and the civil service frightened the office-holders, who had already been alarmed by rumors of coming proscription. There was an army of office-seekers and editors in Washington, who had a very clear and positive theory that the victory which they had won, under Jackson's name, meant the acquisition and distribution amongst them of all the honors and emoluments of the federal government. They descended on the federal administration as if upon a conquered domain.

The office-holders of that day had generally staked their existence on the mode of getting a living which the civil service offered. It did not pay well, but it was supposed to be easy, tranquil, and secure. All these persons who were over forty years of age saw ruin staring them in the face. It was too late for them to change their habits or acquire new trades.[1] All the stories by eye-witnesses testify to the distress and terror of the "ins," and the rapacity of the "outs," at that time. It is certain that the public service lost greatly by the changes. Sometimes they were made on account of trivial disrespect to Jackson.[2] It is not clear who was the author or instigator of the policy. Lewis is said to have opposed it. Kendall does not appear to have started with the intention of proscription. March 24, 1829, he wrote to the editor of the Baltimore "Patriot:"[3] "The interests of the country demand that the [Fourth Auditor's] office shall be filled with men of business, and not with babbling politicians. Partisan feelings shall not enter here, if I can keep them out. To others belongs the whole business of electioneering." Probably Jackson believed that the departments were full of corrupt persons, and that Adams and Clay had demoralized the whole civil service,

[1] Washington removed nine persons, one a defaulter; Adams, ten, one a defaulter; Jefferson, thirty-nine; Madison, five, three defaulters; Monroe, nine; Adams, two, both for cause. 5 *Ann. Reg.* 19.

[2] 1 Curtis's *Webster*, 348.

[3] 49 Niles, 43. *Cf.* Kendall's *Autobiography*, 292.

so that a complete change was necessary. It would be quite in character for Jackson to take all the campaign declamation literally. One man, Tobias Watkins, Fourth Auditor, was found short in his accounts.[1] This seemed to offer proof of all that had been affirmed. The proscription was really enforced by the logic of the methods and teachings of the party while in opposition. The leaders had been taken literally by the party behind them, and by the workers, writers, and speakers who had enlisted under them. If they had failed to reward their adherents by the spoils, or if they had avowed the hollowness and artificiality of their charges against the last administration, they would have thrown their party into confusion, and would have destroyed their power. It has been shown above how the spoils system had been developed, since the beginning of the century, in Pennsylvania and New York.[2] It is a crude and incorrect notion that Andrew Jackson corrupted the civil service. His administration is only the date at which a corrupt use of the spoils of the public service, as a

[1] Adams calls this "the bitterest drop in the cup of my afflictions." 8 Adams, 144. Again he says, "The wrong done to me and my administration by the misconduct of Watkins deserves a severer animadversion from me than from Jackson." 8 Adams, 290. He there depicts Jackson's rancor against Watkins. *Cf.* p. 453. Niles describes the virulent political animus of the prosecution. 36 Niles, 421. After Watkins's term of imprisonment was over, he was detained on account of an unpaid fine. By Jackson's personal order a label, "Criminal's Apartment," was put over the door of the room in which he was kept.

[2] Page 131.

cement for party organization, under democratic-republican self-government, having been perfected into a highly finished system in New York and Pennsylvania, was first employed on the federal arena. The student who seeks to penetrate the causes of the corruption of the civil service must go back to study the play of human nature under the political dogmas and institutions of the States named. He cannot rest satisfied with the explanation that "Andrew Jackson did it." In a conversation between two senators, about the reasons for Jackson's popularity, which is reported by a German visitor, it is said that he acted on two maxims: "Give up no friend to win an enemy," and "Be strong with your friends and then you can defy your enemies." [1] These are grand maxims of wise warfare, but they sound like Kendall, not like Jackson. The latter certainly never formulated any philosophical maxims, but he acted on these two.

Thirty-eight of Adams's nominations had been postponed by the Senate, so as to give that patronage to Jackson. Between March 4, 1829, and March 22, 1830, 491 postmasters and 239 other officers were removed, and as the new appointees changed all their clerks, deputies, etc., it was estimated that 2,000 changes in the civil service took place. [2] Jackson, as we have seen, had made a strong point against the appointment of members

[1] 2 *Aristokratie in America*, 177.
[2] Holmes's speech in the Senate, April 28, 1830.

of Congress to offices in the gift of the President.
In one year he appointed more members of Congress to office than any one of his predecessors in
his whole term.[1] The Senate, although democratic,
refused to confirm many of the nominations made.
Henry Lee, appointed consul to Algiers, and James
B. Gardner, register of the land office, were unanimously rejected. Others were rejected by large
votes.[2] Isaac Hill was one of these. Adams was
told that Hill's rejection was caused, in part, by
the publication by him of a pamphlet, containing
"a false and infamous imputation" on Mrs. Adams; so that Adams also had a grievance like
Jackson's.[3] Webster said that, but for the fear of
Jackson's popularity out-of-doors, the Senate would
have rejected half his appointments.[4] The Senate
objected to the obvious distribution of rewards
among the partisan editors who had run country
newspapers in Jackson's influence.[5] Eaton had
visited Binns, and had made to him a distinctly
corrupt proposition to reward him with public
printing,[6] if he would turn to Jackson. The rejection of the editors was construed by the Jackson
men as a proscription of "printers" by the "aristocratic" Senate.[7] Kendall was confirmed by the
casting vote of Calhoun, for fear that he would, if
not confirmed, set up a newspaper in competition

[1] 5 *Ann. Reg.*, 20.   [2] 5 *Ann. Reg.*, 21.
[3] 8 Adams, 217.   [4] 1 Webster's *Correspondence*, 501.
[5] 1 Webster's *Correspondence*, 488.   [6] Binns, 253.
[7] Kendall's *Autobiography*, 370. New York *Courier and Enquirer*, in Bradley's *Hill*, 105.

with Green's "Telegraph" for the position of administration organ.[1] The view of the matter which was promulgated, and which met with general acceptance, was: "The printer and editor Hill, and the schoolmaster and editor Kendall, both enterprising sons of dear Yankee-land, were especially eyesores in the sight of this exclusive aristocracy."[2] On subsequent votes some of the appointments were confirmed, for it was found that Jackson was thrown into a great rage against the Senate which dared reject his appointments. He was delighted when Hill, in 1831, was elected by the Legislature of New Hampshire a member of the Senate, which had refused to confirm him as Second Comptroller of the Treasury. Jackson threw all the administration influence in favor of Hill's election. Here we have an illustration of a method of his of which we shall have many illustrations hereafter. When he was crossed by any one in a course in which he was engaged, he drew back to gather force with which to carry his point in some mode so much more distasteful to his opponents than his first enterprise that it would be a kind of punishment to them and a redress to himself. Hill was elected senator from a motive of this kind. The "Courier and Enquirer" drew a picture of him entering the Senate and saying to the men who violated their oaths by attempting to disfranchise citizens: "Give me room — stand back — do you know me? I am

[1] Kendall's *Autobiography*, 371.
[2] Bradley's *Hill*, 83.

that Isaac Hill, of New Hampshire, who, in this very spot you slandered, vilified, and stript of his rights — the people, your *masters*, have sent me here to take my seat in this very chamber as your equal and your peer." [1] Hill resigned in 1836.

Van Buren and Calhoun at once began to struggle for the control of the patronage which was made disposable by the system of proscription. Their contest for the succession rent the administration; and this ending came about in a very odd way. It was a very noteworthy fact that this administration, which represented a certain contempt for social forms and etiquette, should immediately go to pieces on a question of that kind. So true is it that etiquette is never burdensome until we try to dispense with it. The strange story is as follows: In January, 1829, John H. Eaton married Mrs. Timberlake, widow of a purser in the navy, who had, a short time before, committed suicide, while on service in the Mediterranean, because he could not conquer habits of excessive drinking. Mrs. Timberlake was the daughter of a Washington tavern keeper. As Peggy O'Neil she had been well known about Washington. Eaton had paid her such attention, before her husband's death, as to provoke gossip. He consulted Jackson before the marriage. Jackson, having in mind the case of his own wife, was chivalrously ready to take sides with any woman whose reputation was assailed. He made no objection to the marriage.

[1] Bradley's *Hill*, 105, 107.

When it occurred, several persons remonstrated with Jackson about it, on the ground that Eaton was to be in the cabinet, and that it would hurt the administration. Jackson replied with spirit to the effect that Mrs. Eaton was not to be in the cabinet. If he had kept that attitude towards the matter there might have been no trouble. By Eaton's appointment his wife was introduced to the first circle in Washington. The wives of the other Secretaries and the wife of the Vice-President did not recognize her. She tried to force her way, and General Jackson tried to help her. He made a political question of it. R. M. Johnson was the agent for conferring with the Secretaries to prevail on them to persuade their wives to recognize Mrs. Eaton. The gentlemen were approached individually. Each said that he left such matters to his wife, and could not undertake to overrule her judgment. This answer had no effect on Jackson. Mrs. Donelson, wife of Jackson's nephew and private secretary, and presiding lady at the White House, was as recalcitrant as any one. She was banished to Tennessee for some months. Mrs. Huyghens, wife of the Dutch minister, refused to sit by Mrs. Eaton at a public ball. Jackson threatened to send her husband home. September 8, Lewis, pursuing his favorite method, wrote to inquire of Jackson in regard to a story which he remembered to have heard from Jackson, but which he now wanted to get into writing. Jackson replied on the 10th, giving details of an incident, in 1824, when Mrs. Timber-

lake asked his protection against General Call;
she, Call, Jackson, and Eaton being at the time all
inmates of her father's house. Call's plea in justification may be omitted. " I," writes Jackson,
"gave him a *severe lecture* for taking up such
ideas of *female virtue,* unless on some positive evidence of his own, of which he acknowledged he had
none, only information — and I enforced my admonition by refering him to *the rebuff* he had met
with, which I trusted for the future would guard
him from the like improper conduct. . . . I then
told you & have ever since repeated, that I had
never seen or heard aught against the chastity of
M$^{rs.}$ Timberlake that was calculated to raise even
suspicion of her virtue in the mind of any one
who was not under the influence of *deep prejudices, or prone to jealousy* — that I believed her a
virtuous & much injured female." [1]

The purpose of this letter seems to have been to
get Jackson's personal testimony in favor of Mrs.
Eaton. It certainly revealed the ground of his
own conviction. On the same day on which it was
written Jackson held a meeting of his cabinet,
before which Ely and Campbell, two clergymen
who were held by Jackson partly responsible for
the stories about Mrs. Eaton, were called to appear.
Jackson interrogated them, argued with them, and
strove to refute their statements, as a means of
convincing the members of the cabinet that there
was no ground for the position their wives had

[1] Ford MSS.

taken. Of course this foolish and unbecoming proceeding had no result.

Van Buren, being a widower, was in a certain position of advantage, which he used by showing Mrs. Eaton public and private courtesies. In this way he won Jackson's heart, for as the matter went on Jackson became more and more engaged in it. On the other hand, Calhoun suffered in Jackson's good graces by the fault of Mrs. Calhoun, who had been conspicuous for disapproval of Mrs. Eaton. Jackson had been growing cold towards Calhoun for some time. He doubted if Calhoun was thoroughly loyal to him in 1825,[1] or in 1828. He thought that Calhoun, in 1825, would have made other arrangements than those with Jackson, if any more convenient ones had been offered him. Calhoun did, in fact, declare, in 1825, that he was quite neutral as between Adams and Jackson. He did not interfere at all with the election.[2] The Eaton affair was either a pretext or a cause of widening the breach between them. The factions opposed to Calhoun tried to increase the bad feeling. Jackson was led to believe, and he often affirmed, that the attack on Mrs. Eaton was a plot to drive Eaton out of the cabinet. When forced to justify his own interference, he put it on this ground. He said that Clay was at the bottom of the attack on Mrs. Eaton. All this trouble in

[1] Wise (p. 82) says that Jackson was very angry with Calhoun after the election in 1825.

[2] Cobb, 219.

the cabinet remained for the time unknown to the public.

Lewis's statement, given by Parton,[1] covers the history of all Jackson's relations with Calhoun. Lewis had an inkling, in 1819, that Calhoun had not, as Jackson supposed, been Jackson's friend in Monroe's cabinet, in the Seminole war affair. Lewis wrote to the "Aurora," suggesting that opinion, but Jackson wrote to him from Washington to dismiss any suspicion as to Calhoun's unfriendliness in that matter. It seems to be necessary to read between the lines of Lewis's statement, on pages 315–30. Did he not always retain his suspicion of Calhoun? Was he not on the watch for any evidence to confirm it? He speaks as if he had rested content with Jackson's assurance, and had been corrected later by accident or entirely on the initiative of others. He does not mention the first attempt made by the old Crawford men to get over into the Jackson camp. It was not an easy march, for in 1824 the Crawford men, as the "regulars," hated intensely the Jackson men, as upstarts and disorganizers. Crawford had carried into his retirement a venomous and rancorous spirit, the chief object of which was Calhoun. He could join any one to hurt Calhoun.

Lewis wrote to Hayward, March 28, 1827: "In justice to Mr. Calhoun, however, I must say that I am inclined to think more favorably of him now than formerly. This is a delicate subject and

[1] 3 Parton, 310.

ought to be touched with great caution. It is a
rock upon which we may split." [1]   In April, 1827,
Van Buren and Cambreleng visited Crawford, and
first established ties between him and Jackson.
The first effect was a letter from Crawford to
Balch, a neighbor of Jackson, December 14, 1827,
stating that Calhoun and his friends bandied about
the epithet "military chieftain;" also that Calhoun favored Adams until Clay came out for
Adams; [2] and adding that it would do Jackson a
service to obtain assurances for Crawford that Jackson's advancement would not benefit Calhoun. [3]
This letter was meant to separate Jackson and
Calhoun, and it may have had a general effect.
Specific consequences cannot be traced to it.   In
1828 there was a project to run Crawford for Vice-
President with Adams. [4]   Adams refused. [5]   Crawford also, in 1828, by private letters to the Georgia
electors, tried to persuade them not to vote for
Calhoun. [6]   In the same year he made friends with
Clay, writing to him that the charge of bargain
was absurd.

According to Lewis's story, James A. Hamilton,
on a Jackson electioneering tour, went to see Crawford, in January, 1828, in order to reconcile him
with Jackson.   Lewis instructed Hamilton what to
say to Crawford on Jackson's part.   Hamilton did

[1] Ford MSS.
[2] *Cf.* Lewis, in 3 Parton, 315, on the allusion to Banquo's ghost
in Webster's reply to Hayne.
[3] 40 Niles, 12.   [4] 33 Niles, 315.
[5] 7 Adams, *Diary*, 390.   [6] Cobb, 240.

not see Crawford. He left the business in the hands of Forsyth. Forsyth soon wrote to Hamilton that Crawford affirmed that Jackson's enmity against him was groundless, since it was not he, but Calhoun, in Monroe's cabinet, who had tried to have Jackson censured for his proceedings in Florida in 1818. In April or May Lewis was in New York. Hamilton showed him Forsyth's letter. For the time Lewis kept this information quite to himself. He was too clever to spoil the force of it by using it too soon, and he well understood how, in the changes and chances of politics, a conjuncture might arise in which such a fact would gain tenfold force.

In April, 1828, Henry Lee tried to draw Calhoun into a correspondence about the construction of the orders to Jackson in 1818. Calhoun offered to give Jackson any statements or explanations, but declined to correspond with any one else.[1]

In November, 1829, at the height of the Peggy O'Neil affair, Jackson gave a dinner to Monroe. At this dinner Ringold affirmed that Monroe alone stood by Jackson in 1818. If Ringold did not have his cue, he was by chance contributing astonishingly to Lewis's plans. After dinner Lewis and Eaton kept up a conversation, within ear-shot of Jackson, about what Ringold had said. Of course Jackson's attention was soon arrested, and he began to ask questions. Lewis then told him that he had seen, eighteen months before, the above men-

[1] 40 Niles, 14.

tioned letter of Forsyth to Hamilton. Jackson dis-
patched Lewis to New York the next morning to
get that letter. In all this story, it is plain how
adroitly these men managed the General, and how
skilful they were in producing "accidents." It is
evident that they did not think it was time yet to
bring about the explosion. Lewis came back from
New York without Forsyth's letter, and said that
it was thought best to get a letter directly from
Crawford, containing an explicit statement. In
this position the matter rested all winter. It is
perfectly clear that the Jackson managers lost faith
in Calhoun's loyalty to Jackson and the Jackson
party, and that they were hostile to him in 1827–28,
but could not yet afford to break with him. Jackson clung to his friendships and alliances with a
certain tenacity. As Calhoun was drawn more and
more into nullification, the Jackson clique took a
more positive attitude in opposition to it.

In the autumn of 1829 the clique around Jackson had decided that he must run again, if he
should live, in 1832, in order to consolidate the
party, which no one else could lead to victory at
that time, and that Van Buren must succeed him
in 1836.[1] Lewis was already committed to Van
Buren, and Parton brings us some more of Lewis's invaluable testimony as to this arrangement.[2]
Here, for once, a wire-puller put on paper a clear

[1] Parton says that Benton was booked for the period 1844–52.
3 Parton, 297.
[2] 3 Parton, 293, 297.

description of his proceedings in a typical case. There was fear in the Jackson camp, in 1829, on account of Jackson's very bad health, that he might not live through his term. Lewis says that he and Jackson were both anxious that Van Buren should succeed Jackson, and they believed that, if Jackson should die, a political testament left by him would have great influence. Accordingly Jackson wrote a letter to his old friend, Judge Overton, of Tennessee, dated December 31, 1829, praising Van Buren, and expressing grave doubts about Calhoun. A copy was duly kept, for Judge Overton was not informed of the contingent use for which the letter was intended, and no risk was taken as to his care in preserving the letter. This provision having been made for the case that Jackson should die, the next thing was to provide for his reëlection, in case he should live.

December 19, 1829, the "Courier and Enquirer" came out in favor of Van Buren for the succession, if Jackson should not stand for reëlection. The "Telegraph" was annoyed at this, called it "premature," and likely to produce division.[1] These two papers, representing the Van Buren and Calhoun factions in the administration party, were engaged, during the winter, in acrimonious strife.[2] Niles no doubt expressed the sentiment of sensible people when he said, April, 1830, that he did not see the necessity of action on the subject at that time. His statement, however, only showed how little he un-

[1] 37 Niles, 300.   [2] 38 Niles, 109.

derstood the processes by which the people manifest their power of self-government.

March 11, 1830, Lewis wrote to Colonel Stanbaugh, of Pennsylvania, suggesting that the Pennsylvania Legislature should address to Jackson an appeal to stand for reëlection. To the end that they might send just the proper appeal, Lewis inclosed it to them, already prepared for their signatures. Lewis wrote to Stanbaugh that he did not think it would be wise for Jackson's friends in Washington to [be known to] lead in the movement for his reëlection, and Pennsylvania, the stronghold of his popularity, seemed to be the most advantageous place from which the movement might [appear to] start. The address came back duly signed with sixty-eight names. It was published in the "Pennsylvania Reporter," and copied all over the country as a spontaneous and irrepressible call of the people to the "old hero" not to desert his country. The enterprise did not run off quite so smoothly as Lewis's narrative would imply. There was strong opposition by the Calhoun faction in the Pennsylvania Legislature to Jackson's renomination, and a distinct renomination could not be carried.[1] In April a caucus of the New York Legislature declared that it responded "to the sentiment of the Legislature of Pennsylvania." This caucus was prompted from Washington, and was managed by the editor of the "Courier."[2] So soon as the example was set,

[1] 38 Niles, 170.   [2] *Ibid.*

other Legislatures followed it. In January, 1831, the "Globe" said that General Jackson might be regarded as before the country for reëlection.[1]

April 13, 1830 (Jefferson's birthday), while still the letter from Crawford was not received, but while Jackson's mind was full of suspicion against Calhoun, a banquet was prepared at Washington, which was intended to be a nullification demonstration.[2] Jackson gave as a toast, "Our federal Union: It must be preserved." This was a bomb-shell to the nullifiers, and a declaration of war against Calhoun, who at the same banquet offered a toast and made a speech, the point of which was that liberty was worth more than union. How much the personal element of growing suspicion and ill-will towards Calhoun had to do with the attitude which Jackson took up towards nullification is a matter of conjecture and inference. His opinions, however, deduced from hatred of the Hartford convention, had always been strongly favorable to the Union, and the men in the kitchen cabinet, except Green, were strong unionists, although Jackson and they all were likewise strong State rights men. Ten years earlier Kendall had maintained the major premise of nullification with great zeal.[3]

At the same banquet Isaac Hill offered the following toast and "sentiment:"[4] "Democracy: 'Wherefore do I take my flesh in my teeth, and

[1] 39 Niles, 385. [2] 1 Benton, 148.
[3] *Autobiography*, 222. [4] 38 Niles, 153.

put my life in mine hand? Though he slay me,
yet will I trust in him.' " The quotation is from
Job xiii. 14, and "he" is usually interpreted as
referring to God. This "sentiment" therefore
exalts democracy higher than any other known
expression, but it is best worth remembering as an
illustration of the slave-like spirit which is bred by
adherence to absolutist doctrines, whether the absolute sovereign be an autocrat or a popular majority.
Altogether, the Jefferson's birthday banquet was
a memorable occasion.

A letter from Crawford's own hand, disclosing
the attitude of Calhoun in Monroe's cabinet towards Jackson and his proceedings in Florida in
1818, was at last received about May 1, 1830. In
this letter the John Rhea letter from Jackson to
Monroe first comes into history, and is the pivot
on which the whole Seminole war question, in its
revived form, is made to turn. Crawford said that
that letter was produced in the cabinet, and that it
brought him over to Jackson's side, but that Calhoun persisted in hostility. Monroe and every
member of his cabinet, when appealed to, denied
that the Rhea letter was produced, or brought into
consideration in 1818 at all. Jackson immediately,
May 13th, inclosed a copy of Crawford's letter to
Calhoun, and demanded an explanation of Calhoun's apparent perfidy, as he construed it. Jackson's main point in this letter, which was evidently
"copied" for him, is that Calhoun well knew, by
virtue of his position in the cabinet, and as he had

shown by his orders,[1] that Jackson, in all that he did, had the approval and connivance of the administration. This brought out all the tangled misunderstandings about Jackson's letter to Monroe and John Rhea's supposed reply. Calhoun at once recognized his position. He could not understand the allusions to previous understandings which had never existed, but it was plain that Crawford had opened an irreparable breach between Jackson and him, and that all the hopes which Calhoun had built upon his alliance with Jackson were in ruins. He also saw that the whole movement was a Van Buren victory over him. He replied on May 20th, complaining and explaining. He really had no charge to repel. He had done nothing wrong, and was guiltless of any injustice or perfidy towards Jackson. The whole matter was a cabinet secret. Crawford had violated confidence in making known the nature of the preliminary discussions which preceded the adoption, by Monroe's cabinet, of a definite policy as to Jackson's proceedings. Calhoun was not to blame for any of the misunderstandings about the previous authorization which Jackson thought that he had received. It seems that Calhoun might have set forth this position with dignity. He did not do so. Jackson replied to him, May 30th, in a very haughty tone, declaring a complete breach between them on the ground of Calhoun's duplicity. This letter was plainly prepared by the persons

[1] See *ante*, page 70.

who were working on Jackson's strong personal
feeling about his Florida campaign to bring him
to a breach with Calhoun, and to throw him into a
close alliance with Van Buren. The plan was a
complete success. Lewis says that Jackson sent
Calhoun's letter of May 20th to Van Buren, that
he might read it and give advice about it, but that
Van Buren would not read it because he did not
want to be involved in the affair at all. Lewis
further says that Van Buren had nothing to do
with getting up the quarrel. We may well believe
all this. Lewis was not such a bungling workman
in a job of that kind as to commit his principal
to any inconvenient knowledge or compromising
activity.

The quarrel with Calhoun brought on a quarrel
with Duff Green and the " Telegraph." Jackson
wrote to Lewis from Wheeling: " Board Steam
Boat, June 26, 1830, The truth is, he [Duff Green]
has professed to me to be heart & soul, against
the Bank, but his idol controls him as much as
the shewman does his puppits, and we must get
another organ to announce the policy, & defend
the administration, — in his hands, it is more injured than by all the opposition." [1] Amos Kendall sent for Francis P. Blair, an old Kentucky
friend and co-worker of his, and his successor as
editor of the " Argus." Blair was then thirty-nine
years old. He was another old Clay man, con-

[1] Ford MSS. The mention of the " Bank " here is very note•
worthy.

verted by Kentucky relief politics into a Jackson
man. He was a fanatical opponent of the Bank
of the United States, and strongly opposed to nullification. Parton says that he was forty thousand
dollars in debt. He had been president of the
Bank of the Commonwealth of Kentucky, and was
indebted to the Bank of the United States.[1] Blair
started the "Globe," and took Green's place in
the kitchen cabinet, which now contained a very
large element of Kentucky relief politics. Blair
was the prince of partisan editors, a man made to
run an organ. For he was not a mere mouth-piece.
He was independent and able to go alone, but had
infinite tact, discretion, and shrewdness, so that he
was an easy man to work with. The organ, therefore, worked perfectly. Every expression in it
came directly from the White House. If Blair
spoke without consulting Jackson, the harmony
and sympathy of their ideas was such that Jackson's mind was correctly interpreted. If Jackson
wanted anything to be said, Blair was in such accord that it cost him nothing in the way of concession to say it. He and Kendall went with Jackson
when no one else did, and they were the leading
spirits in the government of the country until
1840. The first number of the "Globe" was
issued December 7, 1830. Since Blair had no
capital, the paper was at first semi-weekly, but
Lewis and Kendall brought their connections to
bear on the office-holders to make them transfer

[1] Kendall's *Autobiography*, 372.

their subscriptions from the "Telegraph" to the "Globe." [1] Parton says that Jackson compelled the departments to give Blair their printing.

Mrs. Eaton accompanied the Jackson party to Tennessee in the summer of 1830. Jackson wrote to Lewis, July 28: "The ladies of the place [Franklin] had received M^{rs}. Eaton in the most friendly manner, and has extended to her that polite attention due to her. This is as it should be, and is a severe comment on the combination at Nashville, & will lead to its prostration — Until I got to Tyre Springs I had no conception of the combination & conspiracy to injure & prostrate Major Eaton — and injure me — I see the great Magicians hand in all this — and what mortifies me more is to find that this combination is holding up & making my family the tools to injure me, disturb my administration, & if possible to betray my friend Major Eaton. This will recoil upon their own heads — but such a combination I am sure never was formed before, and that my Nephew & Nece should permit themselves to be held up as the instruments, & *tools*, of such wickedness, is truly mortifying to me — I was pleadsed to see the marked attention bestowed upon the Major & his family on their journey hither and the secrete plans engendered at the city & concluded here, & practised upon by some of my connections have been prostrated by the independant, & virtuous portion of this community — " [2] Such was the

[1] 40 Niles, 318.   [2] Ford MSS.

persistence with which he pursued this matter, and such the way in which he intertwined it with the interests and prerogatives of his high office. His sycophants and flatterers practiced on his passionate zeal in it.

The quarrel between the President and the Vice-President did not become known until the end of the year 1830. Adams first refers to it in his diary under date of December 22, 1830. Niles mentions it as a rumor, January 29, 1831. In February, 1831, Calhoun published a large pamphlet about the whole matter.[1] The next thing for his enemies to do was to get his three friends, Ingham, Branch, and Berrien, out of the cabinet. To this end those who were in the secret resigned, as a means of breaking up the cabinet and forcing a reconstruction. Barry was asked to remain in his office. Eaton resigned first, April 7, 1831. Van Buren resigned April 11, 1831, in a letter which was so oracular that no one could understand it.[2] The main ideas in his letter of resignation and in Jackson's reply were : — (1) That Jackson did not intend to have any one in his cabinet who was a candidate for the succession. This indicated Van Buren as such a candidate. (2) That the cabinet was originally a "unit," and that Jackson wanted to keep his cabinet a unit. This hint had no effect on the other secretaries. "I found in my first cabinet," wrote Jackson, in 1841, "dessemblers, & hypocrites." He suggests that Ber-

[1] 40 Niles, 11.　　　　　[2] 40 Niles, 145.

rien was the worst.[1] The ministers wanted to be
dismissed, and a separate quarrel was necessary in
the case of each. It was in this connection that
the Peggy O'Neil affair[2] and all the old misunderstanding about the Seminole war came to a public
discussion. Van Buren was appointed minister to
England, and he went out. At the next session
of Congress a great political conflict arose over his
confirmation. When McLane was sent out to
England, in 1829, he had instructions from Van
Buren to reopen the negotiations about the West
India trade, and, as a basis for so doing, to point
out to the English government that the party
which had brought that question into the position
in which it then stood had been condemned by the
people at the election. This introduced the internal party contests of the country into diplomacy,
and instead of representing this nation to foreign
nations as a unit, having, for all its international
relations, a continuous and consistent life, it invited
foreigners to note party changes here, as if they
had to negotiate at one time with one American
nation, and at another time with another. The
fact that Van Buren had given these instructions
was alleged as a reason for not confirming his appointment, but the debate took a wide range. His
confirmation was defeated by the casting vote of
Calhoun. This check to Jackson's plans gave just

[1] Ford MSS.

[2] Webster knew of that affair and its political bearings in
January, 1830. 1 *Correspondence*, 483.

the requisite spur of personal pique to his desire
to make Van Buren President, and he pursued
that purpose from this time on with all his powers.
He was enraged at the Senate. The "Globe"
proposed to reduce the term of senators to two
years, and to take from the Senate the power to
confirm appointments.[1] It was in the debate on
Van Buren's confirmation that William L. Marcy
cynically avowed the doctrine: "To the victors
belong the spoils."

Jackson found that women are the arbiters in
certain social matters, and that men, no matter
how great or domineering they may be, have no
resources by which to overrule their prerogative.
He was defeated. His interference had done only
far greater harm to the person he had tried to be-
friend. He gave her an unenviable, unavoidable,
yet probably undeserved place in history. Eaton
was in a state of ungovernable rage at the discussion
of his wife's reputation by the newspapers from one
end of the country to the other. He challenged
Campbell, one of the clergymen mentioned above
as prominent in connection with the scandal. June
18, 1831, he challenged Ingham, Secretary of the
Treasury. Ingham declined to fight. A few days
later Ingham complained to Jackson that he had
been waylaid and hindered in his duties by Eaton,
Lewis, Randolph, and others. They denied that
they had molested him, or had intended to do

[1] 41 Niles, 444; an editorial exposing the folly of the complaints
and anger.

so.[1] Jackson's plan had been that Hugh L. White, senator from Tennessee, should resign, and that Eaton should take his place. White was to be Secretary of War.[2] White, however, who perhaps was piqued that he was not made Secretary of War in 1829, declined to fulfil his share of this programme. He became alienated from Jackson. Eaton was made Governor of Florida. From 1836 to 1840 he was minister to Spain. Parton says that he quarrelled with Jackson, and was a whig in 1840.[3] He died in 1856. Mrs. Eaton died about 1878.

The new cabinet was: Edward Livingston, of Louisiana, Secretary of State; Louis McLane, of Delaware, Secretary of the Treasury; Lewis Cass, of Michigan, Secretary of War; Levi Woodbury, of New Hampshire (who had given up to Hill his place in the Senate), Secretary of the Navy; Roger B. Taney, of Maryland, Attorney-General. Adams mentions a story that the War Department was offered to William Drayton, leader of the Union party of South Carolina.[4] This cabinet was a "unit," and a unit for Jackson and the successor on whom he had determined.

We have now brought the intimate and personal history of Jackson's first administration down to the time when the campaign for his reelection opened. We have seen how Jackson con-

---

[1] 40 Niles, 302.　　　　　　[2] Hunt's *Livingston*, 358.

[3] 3 Parton, 368, 639. See also below, page 273.

[4] 9 Adams, 132.

strued the presidential office in its immediate bearings, and how he addressed himself to its immediate and personal duties. We turn now to the
public questions and measures of his first administration.

CHAPTER VIII

PUBLIC QUESTIONS OF JACKSON'S FIRST ADMINISTRATION

I. *The trade between the United States and the British West Indies* had been a source of irritation and dissatisfaction ever since the United States had been independent. After independence the United States desired to obtain a commercial treaty which would enable them to trade with the British West Indies as they always had done. This the English resented as an effort to retain the benefits of being in the empire after leaving it. The Americans therefore employed in that trade the illicit methods which they had developed into a high art in trade with the non-British West Indies before the Revolution. After the second war the question was reopened. The English had hardly yet lost faith in the Navigation System, and the Americans had adopted it as far as it would apply to a State with no colonies beyond the sea. As the diplomatic efforts for a treaty failed, resort was had by the United States to retaliatory measures. These had their inevitable effect. The two countries, respectively, advanced step by step into a dead-lock, from which the only issue was that one side or the other must recede. This point was reached in 1827. The opposition in the United States made capital out of the entanglement. In the mean time the illicit trade went merrily on, and the smuggler rectified, in his way, the folly of statesmen. Thus the matter stood when Jackson was elected. Gallatin said that " if he had hinted to the Canning ministry that their course concerning the colonial trade would promote the election of Jackson, they would have given up the point." [1]

One of his first acts was to send McLane to England to reopen negotiations. This he was to do by pointing to the result of the election as a rebuke to the former administration, which had brought about the dead-lock. Pending the negotiations an act of Congress was passed, May 29, 1830, authorizing the President to declare the retaliatory acts of 1818, 1820, and 1823 repealed, whenever American ships should be allowed in the West Indies on the same terms as British ships arriving there from the United States, and when they should be allowed to carry goods from the colonies to any non-British ports to which British ships might go. This act was sent to England. Lord Aberdeen said that it was all that England had ever demanded.[2] The colonial duties were increased, a differential duty in favor of the North American colonies was laid, and the trade was opened. The President issued his proclamation October 5, 1830. The administration boasted of this diplomatic achievement. The truth

[1] 8 Adams, 326.   [2] 39 Niles, 390 *et seq.*

was that the United States set out to force England to let American goods come into the West Indies on the same footing as British North American goods. England was coerced by the acts of 1818 and 1820. Canning said, in 1826, that England had yielded to coercion, but that she escaped from it as soon as she could. By way of escape she opened her trade to all the world. The countervailing system of the United States, then, no longer exercised any coercion, and the United States, to get the trade reopened, abandoned the demands with which it had started on the experiment of countervailing. This last step was what the Jackson administration had accomplished. Niles and the other protectionists scoffed at the new arrangement. They said that the illicit trade was better than the new arrangement.[1] A proof that this was true is found in the fact that the illicit trade went on. The laws forced products of the United States to reach the islands through Canada and Nova Scotia, and this offered just so much premium to illicit trade.

II. *The claims of the United States for spoliations* against France and against all those states of Europe which had been drawn by Napoleon into his continental system, had been a subject of fruitless negotiation ever since 1815.[2] Jackson

[1] 39 Niles, 208; 42 Niles, 148. N. Y. *Advertiser* in 2 *Pol. Reg.* 444.

[2] For succinct statements of the origin and history of these claims, see the report of a minority of the committee of the House, 48 Niles, 6, and the article 47 Niles, 455.

took up these claims with new energy and spirit. He sent W. C. Rives to France in 1829, under instructions which covered the whole history of the claims, to try to get a settlement. In his message of 1829, while these negotiations were pending, Jackson referred to the claims as likely to " furnish a subject of unpleasant discussion and possible collision." This reference was not of a kind to help the negotiations. In 1830 a revolution put Louis Philippe on the throne under a Constitution. New hopes of a settlement of the claims were raised by this turn in affairs. A treaty was finally signed at Paris, July 4, 1831, by which France agreed to pay twenty-five million francs, and the United States agreed to pay one and a half million francs, in final settlement of all outstanding claims of citizens of one country against the government of the other country. The treaty was ratified February 2, 1832. The first instalment became due February 2, 1833. Claims against the other states of the old continental league of Napoleon's time were likewise liquidated, and payment was secured during Jackson's administration. The administration derived great credit from these settlements. There was a great deal more in the matter than the money. European nations, which had similar claims against France, had secured payment soon after the peace, but the claims of the United States had been neglected. Payment now meant a concession of consideration and respect to the United States, and the people felt that Jackson had won this for the nation.

III. *The Authority and Organization of the Federal Judiciary.* During Adams's administration the Kentucky men made several attempts to lead the opposition party to measures favorable to them in their conflicts with the federal judiciary, arising from the " relief " acts. In the session of 1827–28 a bill was introduced to regulate the procedure of the federal courts in the new States, which had been admitted since the passage of the laws of September 29, 1789, and May 8, 1792, which regulated the procedure of the federal courts. To this bill Rowan of Kentucky proposed an amendment which would take away from the federal courts the power to modify or change any of the rules of procedure, or any of the forms of writs of execution, which were to be those of the State in which the court was sitting.[1] If this amendment had been passed, the federal courts would not have been allowed to change rules and forms, but the State Legislatures would have had power to do so, and the federal judiciary would have been handed over to State control. This amendment was adopted by the Senate. Webster, who had been away, returned to find that the whole federal judiciary system had been thrown into confusion[2] by this hasty proposition, which had been made only with reference to some of the whims of Kentucky relief politics. He exposed

[1] *Cf.* page 167.   [2] 7 Adams, 455.

the effects of the bill. It was recommitted and recast, establishing for the new States the procedure then existing, with power in the courts to modify, under the supervision of the Supreme Court, and in this shape was passed.

In 1830 an attempt was made to repeal the twenty-fifth section of the judiciary act, by which the Supreme Court is empowered to pass upon the constitutionality of State laws. The bill was lost in the House by the vote of 137 to 51, but the minority consisted of some of the leading administration men. In 1831 the House refused, 115 to 61, to consider a resolution instructing the judiciary committee to report a bill setting terms of years for federal judges.[1] In 1830 Berrien, the Attorney-General, gave an opinion on the South Carolina Police Act,[2] in which he overturned Wirt's opinion. He held that that act was valid because it was an act of internal police. In this opinion he laid down the doctrine of the extreme Southern State rights men about the limits of federal power. He held that the federal authorities ought not, in exercising their powers, to make laws or treaties to come into collision with anything which the States had done under their reserved powers, unless it was *necessary* to do so. The admission of black men into the State was only convenient, not necessary; hence collision on that point would be improper.[3]

The Jackson party and the Executive Depart-

[1] 39 Niles, 405.   [2] See page 169.
[3] 2 Opinions of the Attorneys-General, 433.

ment were on terms of jealousy and distrust towards the judiciary for several years. Another expression of these feelings was the impeachment of Judge Peck, of Missouri. The democrats were especially jealous of the prerogative powers of the courts; among the rest, of the power to imprison for contempt. Peck wrote out and published in a newspaper, in 1826, a decision which he had rendered. Lawless, counsel for the defeated party, published a review of the opinion. Peck imprisoned him for twenty-four hours, and suspended him from practice in the court for eighteen months, for contempt. Lawless petitioned the federal House of Representatives during three sessions for redress, in vain. In 1829 the democratic House impeached Peck. Buchanan was the leader.[1] The impeachment was in the current of popular feeling, and there was capital to be made out of it. January 31, 1831, the vote was, 21 to convict, 22 to acquit. Adams says that Jackson favored acquittal, lest Buchanan should gain by a conviction, just as Jefferson, in Chase's case, favored acquittal, lest John Randolph should gain power by a conviction.[2] By an act of March 2, 1831, the power of the courts to punish at discretion for contempt was limited to cases of misbehavior in court, or so near to the court as to obstruct the administration of justice.

IV. *The Indians.* — Georgia continually pressed the federal government to buy off the Indian title

[1] Charges and specifications, 38 Niles, 245. *Cf.*, also, 2 Kennedy's *Wirt*, 308.   [2] 8 Adams, 306.

to lands in that State, and it was done from time to time for certain portions. The treaty of 1802 was supposed to cover Georgia's claims for the expenses of the Indian wars of 1793–94, but those claims were urged until 1827, when Congress voted $129,375 to discharge them. At the urgent solicitation of Georgia, Monroe appointed two commissioners to treat with the Creeks, of whose lands nine and a half million acres were still under the Indian title. The lower Creeks were then on the land west of the Flint River, and north of 31° 30′, and the upper Creeks were almost entirely in Alabama, between the Coosa River and the Georgia boundary, and north of an east and west line through the Hickory Ground (Wetumpka). These boundaries were set by Jackson's treaty with the Creeks of 1814, and he guaranteed to them the lands which were then left to them.[1] The Cherokees were in the northwestern corner of Georgia, the northeastern corner of Alabama, and the southeastern corner of Tennessee, between the Chattahoochee, the Etowah, and the Hiwasee rivers.[2] The Creeks voted to put to death any one who should vote to sell any more land, and refused to treat with Monroe's commissioners. After the council broke up, a few chiefs, headed by McIntosh, made the treaty of Indian Spring, February 12, 1825, ceding all their lands in Georgia and Alabama

[1] Folio State Papers, 1 *Indian Affairs*, 827.
[2] An excellent map of the Cherokee territory in 5 *Bur. Ethnology*.

for $400,000. The Senate confirmed this treaty, March 3, 1825. April 30th the Creeks set McIntosh's house on fire, and shot him as he came out. Governor Troup of Georgia claimed the lands for Georgia at once, and began to survey them. He also set up a lottery to dispose of them. President Adams appointed an agent to investigate the negotiation of the treaty. The agent reported that forty-nine fiftieths of the Creeks repudiated the treaty as a fraud on them. The President ordered General Gaines to prevent any trespass on the lands of the Indians, and pointed out to Governor Troup the objections to his proceedings. Troup blustered, and asked if the President would hold himself responsible to the State of Georgia. The Georgia Legislature did not sustain the Governor. The treaty of Indian Spring was annulled, and a new one was made in January, 1826, by which a part of the lands in Georgia were ceded. This treaty was not confirmed, and another, ceding all[1] the lands in Georgia, was finally made, as Benton says, by appealing to the cupidity of the chiefs. The McIntosh party got an indemnity, and a large sum was given to the chiefs. Land was to be provided west of the Mississippi for all who would go there. This treaty did not satisfy the Georgians. Nevertheless, inasmuch as by the last treaty all the lands in Georgia were ceded, and by the second treaty only part of those lands were ceded, the Georgians claimed a substantial victory,[2] although not all the

[1] 1 Benton, 59.   [2] Hodgson, 141.

lands in Georgia and Alabama were ceded, as by the treaty of Indian Spring. The Cherokees still remained undisturbed. In January, 1828, the Georgia Legislature passed a set of resolutions, the truculency of which is unparalleled, demanding that the United States should extinguish the title of the Cherokees.[1]

The Cherokees were the most civilized of the Gulf Indians, and perhaps they had reached a higher pitch of civilization than any other Indians have ever yet reached.[2] They had horses and cattle, goats, sheep, and swine. They raised maize, cotton, tobacco, wheat, oats, and potatoes, and traded with their products to New Orleans. They had gardens, and apple and peach orchards. They had built roads, and they kept inns for travellers. They manufactured cotton and wool; though probably these were very poor in their way. Their numbers were increasing. In 1825 there were 13,563, besides 220 resident whites and 1,277 slaves, in the Cherokee country. One of their number had invented an alphabet for their language. They had a civil government, imitated from that of the United States. The Chickasaws had ten mills and fifty workshops. They lived in the northeast corner of Mississippi. They numbered 4,000, and were increasing. The Choctaws, in Central Mississippi, numbered 21,000, and ranked next to the Cherokees in civilization. The Creeks numbered 40,000, and were the lowest in civilization. The

[1] 3 *Ann. Reg.*, Local History, 143.   [2] 3 *Ann. Reg.* 77.

money paid them for their lands had debauched them. The facts were that the Indians had reached a certain grade of civilization, that they were increasing in numbers, and that they were forming civilized and Christian bodies; and it was these very facts which made all the trouble, for they all led to the probability that the Indians would remain a permanent part of the society, and would occupy definite areas of land in the midst of the States. It certainly was a home question, when, in 1829, Jackson asked whether Maine or New York would tolerate an Indian state within her own civil limits. Peter B. Porter, Secretary of War under Adams, prepared a plan for an Indian territory west of the Mississippi, and for colonizing the Gulf Indians in it. The plan was referred to the next administration. Adams made himself very unpopular in the Southwest by his action to protect the Indians. He did not get a vote in Georgia in 1828. Jackson had abundantly shown [1] that he held the Southwestern white man's views of Indians and Indian rights.

As soon as Jackson was elected, December 20, 1828, Georgia passed a law extending her jurisdiction over the Cherokee lands and dividing them into counties, and enacted that no Indian should testify against a white man. In 1829 she modified this so that an Indian might testify against a white man who lived in the Indian territory. In 1829 Alabama, and in 1830 Mississippi, passed similar

[1] See page 29.

laws, but somewhat milder. The new administration admitted the soundness of the theory of these laws, which were plainly in contravention of the treaties made with the Indians by the federal government. In his message of 1829 Jackson said that he had told the Indians that their pretensions would not be supported. In the spring of 1830 Congress passed an act for encouraging and facilitating the removal of the Gulf Indians to a territory set apart for them west of the Mississippi.

The quarrel between Georgia and the Indians had now narrowed down to a struggle with the Cherokees, who were the most civilized, and who had the strongest treaty guarantees from the federal authority for their territory and their self-government. It was proposed to test the proceedings of Georgia before the Supreme Court of the United States. In the summer of 1830, Judge Clayton, a Georgia State judge, charged the grand jury that he intended to allow no case to be withdrawn from his jurisdiction by any foreign authority, but that he should enforce the State laws about the Indians, and he wanted to know whether he was to be supported by the people.[1] The first test arose on a murder case against George Tassel, a Cherokee, for killing another Cherokee. The Superior Court of Hall County tried, convicted, and sentenced him. The Chief Justice of the Supreme Court of the United States issued a citation to the State of Georgia, December 12, 1830, to appear

[1] 39 Niles, 99.

and show cause, in answer to a writ of error, why the sentence against Tassel should not be corrected.[1] Governor Gilmer laid this document before the Legislature, which ordered him to disregard it, and to resist by force any attempt to interfere with the criminal law of the State. On the 28th of December Tassel was hung.

The Governor of Georgia called on the President to withdraw the federal troops, and to leave Georgia to deal with the Indians and gold-diggers. The President complied. The Georgia militia marched in, and complaints from the Indians at once began to be heard. The President refused to enforce the treaty rights of the Indians. The Cherokees applied to the Supreme Court for an injunction to prevent Georgia from interfering with their treaty rights. In January, 1831, the court, while in effect sustaining the claims and rights of the Cherokees, declared that the remedy prayed for could not be employed. What was needed was not a judicial but a political remedy.[2] The political remedy belonged to the Executive and the President had refused to use it.

Georgia ordered all white residents of the Cherokee country to obtain State licenses, and to take an oath of allegiance to the State. Two missionaries, sent out by a Boston society, Worcester and Butler, amongst others, did not comply with this law. They were arrested, but were at first released, under the belief that they were disbursing

<hr />

[1] 39 Niles, 338.   [2] 5 Peters, 1.

agents of the federal government. The authorities at Washington denied that they were such. Thereupon they were rearrested, tried, convicted, and condemned to four years' hard labor in the penitentiary. In sentencing them Judge Clayton made another stump speech.[1] On a writ of error in 1832, the Supreme Court held that the law under which these men were convicted was unconstitutional, that the laws of Georgia about the Cherokees contravened federal treaties and were void, and ordered that the men be released.[2] Georgia refused to obey. The Georgia doctrine seemed to be that all three departments of the federal government must concur in holding a State law to be unconstitutional in order to set it aside.[3] Jackson refused to take any executive action to give force to the decision of the court. The presidential election was at hand, and he said that he would submit his conduct to the people, who could at the election show whether they approved or disapproved of his refusal to sustain the decision.[4] No case could more distinctly show the vice of the political philosophy which Jackson professed. Twelve persons in all were convicted, in Georgia, of illegal residence in the Indian country.

[1] 41 Niles, 174.   [2] 6 Peters, 515.   [3] 9 Adams, 548.

[4] Greeley has a story that Jackson said, "John Marshall has made his decision. Now let him enforce it." 1 Greeley, 106. Jackson disliked Marshall, although he had no active enmity against him. Scarcely two men could be found less likely to appreciate each other personally or politically.

All were pardoned.[1] The missionaries refused at
first to accept a pardon. In January, 1833, they
withdrew their suit in the Supreme Court, and
were released.[2]

In 1833 Alabama came into collision with the
federal government on account of Indians. Federal troops were employed to expel intruders from
the Indian territory. In executing this duty they
killed one Owens. The State authorities attempted
to try for murder the soldiers through whose action
the man met his death. The military authorities
would not consent. The federal government, taught
by nullification, took a firmer position than in the
case of Georgia. By a compromise, the reservation
was made smaller, and the white intruders were
allowed to buy titles from the Indians.[3]

In September, 1830, a treaty was negotiated at
Dancing Rabbit Creek with the Choctaws, over
whom Mississippi had extended her laws, by which
they ceded their lands and went west of the Mississippi. They were to be provided with land,
transportation, houses, tools, a year's subsistence,
$50,000 for schools, $20,000 a year for twenty
years, $250 during twenty years for each one of
four chiefs, and $500 for another, as president,
should such an officer be chosen. When this treaty
was before the Senate for ratification the preamble
was stricken out, because it recited that "the President of the United States has said that he cannot

[1] 7 *Ann. Reg.* 265.   [2] 43 Niles, 419.
[3] 45 Niles, 155 ; Hodgson, 179.

protect the Choctaw people from the operation of these laws " of Mississippi.[1] During the next eight years the tribes were all half persuaded, half forced, to go. The Indian Territory was roughly defined by an act of June 30, 1834. Part of the Cherokees had gone in 1818, because they wanted to follow their old mode of life. In 1836 all the rights of the Cherokees east of the Mississippi were bought for five million dollars and the expenses of removal.[2] In the same year the Creeks broke into hostilities, and were forced to migrate. The civilized Cherokees migrated in 1838.

V. *Public Lands.* Various plans for dealing with the lands had been proposed previous to Jackson's accession. One was that the States should seize the lands by virtue of their "sovereignty." This short and easy method recommended itself to the politicians of the emphatic and metaphysical school. It meant simply that the first settlers should buy some land, organize a State, and get "sovereignty," and then take possession of the rest of the land within the civil jurisdiction. Another plan was to sell to the States at a nominal price. Another : to sell all the land at graduated prices, for what it would bring. Another : to give the land to actual settlers (since realized in the homestead

---

[1] 40 Niles, 106.

[2] 50 Niles, 265. In 1886 there were 3,000 Indians (of whom 2,000 were full-blood Cherokees) on a reservation of 100,000 acres, in their old home. (Eastern Band of Cherokee Indians *vs.* U. S. and Cherokee Nation in Sup. Ct. U. S. Ind. Comm. Rep. 1886, 208, 404.)

law). Another: to use the lands as a fund for
internal improvements and education (since realized in the railroad subsidies and agricultural
college land grants). It is plain that if the federal government buys territory by treaties like those
of Louisiana and Florida, and surveys the lands,
and maintains civil institutions over all the territory, and then gives the lands away, what it gives
is the outlay necessary to bring the land to the
point where a civilized man can begin to use it.
Of course the new States wanted population, and
were eager that the federal government should encourage immigration by making this outlay and
giving away the product of it. To September 30,
1832, the lands had cost $49,700,000,[1] and the
total revenue received from them had amounted to
$38,300,000. The notion that the Union possessed,
in its unoccupied lands, a great estate, or an asset
of great value, was a delusion. It was only a
form of the still wider social delusion that raw land
is a " boon of nature," with which the human race,
through its individual members, is endowed.

The old States, especially the tariff States, then
saw distinctly the relation of the lands to the tariff.
Everything which enhanced the attractiveness of
the land, and made it easier to get at it, was just
so much force drawing the man who had no land
and no capital away from the old States and out
of the wages class. Every improvement in transportation ; every abolition of taxes and restrictions

[1] Round numbers ; the five right hand figures disregarded.

like the corn laws, which kept American agricultural products out of England, every reduction in
the price of land, increased the chances of the
man who had nothing to become by industry and
economy an independent land-owner. The capi-
talist employer in the old States was forced to
offset this attractiveness of the land by raising
wages. This of course is the reason why wages in
the United States are high, and why no wages class
has ever yet been distinctly differentiated here. It
might justly be argued that it was improper for the
federal government to raise funds by taxation on
the old States, and to expend them in buying, sur-
veying, and policing wild land, and then to give
the land away to either "the poor" or the rich;
but the protectionists distinctly faced the issue
which was raised for their pet dogma, and demanded that the lands should not be surveyed and
sold abundantly and cheaply, but should be kept
out of the market. The effect of this would be to
prevent the population from spreading thinly over
the whole continent, to make it dense in the old
States, to raise the value and rent of land there, to
produce a class dependent on wages, *i. e.*, a supply
of labor, and to keep wages down. At the same
time all the taxes on clothing, furniture, and tools
would reduce the net return of the agriculturist
and lower the attractiveness of the land. Lower
wages would then suffice to hold the laborer in the
East. These two lines of legislation would therefore be consistent and support each other; but they

were sorely unjust to the man who had nothing
with which to fight the battle of life save his stout
hands and his good-will to work.

The free-trade States of the South and the
free-land States of the West, therefore, fell most
naturally into the " coalition " which the tariff men
and national republicans denounced.   The latter
said that the Southerners had agreed to surrender
the lands to the West as a price for the assistance
of the West against the Eastern States and the
tariff.[1]   The sudden and unaccountable popularity
of Jackson in rural Pennsylvania threw that State,
in spite of the tariff interests of her capitalists,
into the combination to which Jackson belonged
sectionally, and the ambitious politicians of New
York, seeing the need of joining Jackson, brought
as much as they could of that State to his support.
These combinations constituted the Jackson party,
in regard to the incoherency of whose elements
something has been said and more will appear.
Clay was operating his political career through
tariff and internal improvements, with the lands
as a fund for colonization, canals, roads, and education.   This gave him no strength in the West, and
he could not break Jackson's phalanx in Pennsylvania, where his own policy should have made
him strong.   Hence he never could consolidate a
party.   Benton antagonized Clay in the West by
taking up the policy of free lands.

In January and February, 1829, Illinois and

[1] 9 Adams, 235.

Indiana adopted resolutions questioning the right of the federal government to the lands in those States. They did not adopt the Georgia tone, but they seemed disposed to adopt the Georgia policy in case of a disagreement with the federal government.

Jackson had no settled policy in regard to land. In his first message he favored distribution of the surplus revenue among the States, so soon as the debt should be paid.

December 29, 1829. Foot, of Connecticut, offered in the Senate a resolution that the Committee on Public Lands should inquire into the expediency of restricting sales of land to what still remained unsold at the minimum price, *i. e.*, the areas which up to that time had been put upon the market. It was in the debate on this resolution that Webster and Hayne became involved in their famous argument on the theory of the confederation. Benton introduced a bill for selling the lands at graduated prices, so that those remaining unsold at $1.25 should not be reserved, but sold at lower prices, after they had been three years on the market. The Senate passed this bill May 7, 1830. It was not acted on in the House.

In January, 1831, the subject came up again in the House, on an appropriation for surveys,[1] and produced a long debate, in which all the views of the question were represented. In his annual report for 1831, McLane, Secretary of the Treasury,

[1] 6 *Ann. Reg.* 81.

proposed that the lands should be sold to the States in which they lay at a fair price, and that the sum thus obtained should be divided amongst the States. March 22, 1832, Bibb moved,[1] in the Senate, that the Committee on Manufactures should report, as a preliminary to the consideration of the tariff, on the expediency of reducing the price of the lands, and also on the expediency of surrendering the lands to the States. Clay reported from that committee against both propositions, and in favor of giving ten per cent of the proceeds of the lands to the new States, in addition to what they were already entitled to, and dividing the residue among all the States. Clay's report was referred to the Committee on Public Lands, which reported, May 18th, adversely to his propositions, and recommended a minimum price of $1.00; lands remaining unsold at that price for five years to be then sold for fifty cents; fifteen per cent of the proceeds to be divided amongst the new States. No action was taken on account of the disagreement of the two Houses, but the administration, by its attitude on the land question, gained strength in the Western States for the presidential election of 1832.

VI. *Internal Improvements.* Jackson, in his first message, indicated hostility to the general policy of internal improvements, and favored distribution. May 27, 1830, he vetoed a bill for subscription, by the United States, to the stock of the

[1] 7 *Ann. Reg.* 57.

Maysville and Lexington road.[1] In his veto message he placed himself on the constitutional doctrine of Madison and Monroe. The local and political interests which had become involved in the system at this time were very numerous and very strong. The evil of special legislation was growing. Politicians and interested speculators combined to further each other's interests at the public expense. Jackson affronted the whole interest; one would say that he affronted it boldly, if it were not that he acted with such spontaneous will and disregard of consequences that there was no conscious exercise of courage. He was not able to put an end to the abuse, but he curtailed it. He used the exceptional strength of his political position to do what no one else would have dared to do, in meeting a strong and growing cause of corruption. He held a bill for the Louisville canal, and another for light-houses, over the session, and then returned them unsigned. At the session of 1830–31 a bill for improvements was passed by such majorities that a veto was useless. In 1831–32 Jackson signed one such bill and " pocketed " another. In the session of 1832–33 an internal improvement bill was defeated by parliamentary tactics. In the message of 1832 Jackson recommended the sale of all the stocks held by the United States in canals, turnpikes, etc. He edu-

[1] This road was to run through the strongest Jackson district in Kentucky. (Clay to Webster. 1 Webster's *Correspondence*, 501.)

cated his party, for that generation at least, up to a position of party hostility to special legislation of every kind.

VII. *Tariff*. In 1825 Huskisson brought forward the first reforms in the system of taxation in England. His propositions, viewed from to-day's stand-point, seem beggarly enough, but at that time they seemed revolutionary. He reduced taxes on raw materials, chemicals, dye-stuffs, and materials of industry. Raw wool was reduced from sixpence to a penny and a half penny per pound, according to quality. After the tariff of 1824 was passed by Congress, the English woollen producers exported some of their cloths to this country in an unfinished state, in order to get them in below the minimum ($33\frac{1}{3}$ cents), and then had them finished here. They also sent agents to this country, to whom they invoiced their cloths below the open market price.

Every one of the above statements, as will be seen, introduces a fact which affected the relations of the American woollen industry, in its competition with the English woollen industry, in a way to counteract any protection by the tariff. A number of persons had begun the manufacture of woollens because the federal legislation encouraged them so to do, not because they understood that business, or had examined the industrial conditions of success in it. They were pleased to consider Huskisson's legislation as hostile to the United States, and they called for measures to countervail it. They also construed as fraud the importation of unfinished cloths, and the practice of invoicing to agents at manufacturer's cost. The "American system," therefore, which had already changed its meaning two or three times, underwent another transformation. It now meant to countervail and offset any foreign legislation, even in the direction of freedom and reform, or advance in civilization, if that legislation favored the American consumer.

The first complaint came from the old free-trade section. After 1824 the New England States, which up to that time had been commercial States, turned to manufactures. They had resisted all the earlier tariffs. They would have been obliged to begin manufacturing, tariff or no tariff, on account of the growing density of the population; but there was force in Webster's assertion, in reply to Hayne, that New England, after protesting against the tariff as long as she could, had conformed to a policy forced upon the country by others, and had embarked her capital in manufacturing.[1] October 23, 1826, the Boston woollen manufacturers petitioned Congress for more protection.[2] They said that they had been led, by the profits of the English woollen industry in 1824 and the tariff of 1824, to begin manufacturing woollens, confident that they should not yield to fair competition, and that such competition would be secured to them by law. They went on to

[1] 3 Webster's Works, 305.   [2] 31 Niles, 145.

say that the English woollen manufacturers had glutted the market in England, and produced distress there, which had reacted on this country. They said that they could not be relieved "without the aid of their national government."

This appeal of the woollen manufacturers brought out new demands from other quarters. Especially the wool-growers came forward. They had not gained anything by the tariff. A few shrewd men, who took to breeding sheep and who sold out their flocks to the farmers (who were eager buyers, because they were sure, since they had a protective tax in their favor, that they were to make fortunes out of wool), won by the tariff. No one else did. It is stated that the woollen manufacturers did not dare to ask for higher duties in 1824, because they feared that the wool-growers would only demand so much more.[1] They thought that their want of success was due to want of experience and skill, and they looked to make improvements. In fact, the tax on wool was raised, in 1824, more than that on woollens.

January 10, 1827, Mallary, of Vermont, introduced the "woollens bill," for "adjusting" the tariff on wool and woollens.[2] Niles had taken up the high tariff doctrine ten years before, and had preached it in his "Register" assiduously. His economic notions were meagre and erroneous throughout, and he had absolutely no training. He had no doubt, however, that he was inculcating

[1] 2 *Ann. Reg.* 102.   [2] 31 Niles, 319.

the rules of prosperity and wise government. He
unquestionably exerted a great influence; for he
never tired of his labored prescriptions for "giving
a circulation to money," and "encouraging industry." He took up the cause of the woollen men
with his whole heart. Of his sincerity and dis-
interestedness there can be no question. To him
and the economists and statesmen of his school the
minimum seemed to be a marvellous invention.
Mallary proposed to use it to the utmost. He
proposed to leave the rates of tax unchanged, but
to apply them on and between minima of 40 cents,
$2.50, and $4.00. Cloth, therefore, which cost 41
cents was to be held to have cost $2.50, and the
tax on it was to be $62\frac{1}{2}$ cents. Wool which cost
over 10 cents was to be held to have cost 40 cents.
The duty on it was to be 35 per cent for a year;
then 40 per cent. The principle now proposed
was, therefore, that the duties should *advance* with
time. In the tariff of 1816, they had been made
to *decline* year by year. The woollens bill passed
the House, 106 to 95. It was tabled in the Senate
by the casting vote of Calhoun. Calhoun was
forced into this vote by a manœuvre of Van Buren,
who "dodged." Calhoun suffered, in consequence,
in Pennsylvania and New York. Politics ran very
high on this bill. In fact, they quite superseded
all the economic interests.[1] The opposition were
afraid of offending either the Pennsylvania supporters of Jackson, or the southern supporters of

[1] 31 Niles, 321; 33 Niles, 385.

Jackson. Passion began now to enter into tariff discussion, not only on the part of the Southerners, but also between the wool men and the woollen men, each of whom thought the other grasping, and that each was to be defeated in their purpose by the other. Niles said that it was more a wool bill than a woollens bill, and the woollen men were much dissatisfied with it.

May 14, 1827, the Pennsylvania Society for the Promotion of Manufactures and the Mechanic Arts called a convention of wool growers and manufacturers. The convention met at Harrisburg, July 30, 1827. It was found necessary to enlarge the scope of the convention, in order to make allies of interests which would otherwise become hostile. The convention adopted the plan of favoring protection on everything which asked for it. The result was that iron, steel, glass, wool, woollens, hemp, and flax were recommended for protection. Louisiana was not represented, and so sugar was left out. It was voted to discourage the importation of foreign spirits and the distillation of spirits from foreign products, by way of protection to western whiskey. The convention proposed, as its idea of a reasonable and proper tax on wool and woollens, the following:[1] On wool which cost 8 cents or less per pound, 20 cents per pound and an advance of $2\frac{1}{2}$ cents per pound per annum until it should be 50 cents; on woollens, four minima were proposed, 50 cents, $2.50, $4.00, and $6.00, on

[1] 32 Niles, 388.

which the tax was to be 40 per cent for a year, 45 per cent the next year, and 50 per cent thereafter. The minimum on cottons was to be raised to 40 cents.

When the 20th Congress met, the tariff was the absorbing question. Popular interest had become engaged in it, and parties were to form on it, but it perplexed the politicians greatly. Stevenson, of Virginia, an anti-tariff man, was chosen Speaker. Adams says that Stevenson won votes by promising to make a committee favorable to the tariff.[1] Stevenson put Mallary at the head of the committee, but he put an anti-tariff majority behind him. The "Annual Register"[2] stated the foreign trade of the country then as follows: Twenty-four million dollars' worth of cotton, rice, and tobacco were exported to England annually. Four million dollars' worth more were exported to other countries. The imports from England were seven or eight millions' worth of woollens, about the same value of cottons, three or four millions' worth of iron, steel, and hardware, and miscellaneous articles, bringing the total up to twenty-eight millions. From this it was plain that the producers of breadstuffs in the United States, who were kept out of England by the corn laws, were forced to take their products to the West Indies and South America, and exchange them there for four millions' worth of colonial produce, which England would receive, in order to balance the account.

[1] 7 Adams, *Diary*, 369.   [2] 3 *Ann. Reg.* 37.

The editor of the "Annual Register" built upon this fact his argument for protection as a retaliation to break down the English corn laws. He saw that the southern staple products must be the fulcrum for the lever by which the English restrictions were to be broken. He offered the Southerners a certain consolation in the hope that there would be a larger consumption of their staples at home, but really concluded that, as between interests, the grain interest of the North and West was worth more than the interests of the South. It is not strange if this mode of reasoning was not relished in the South.[1]

Mallary stated in debate that the consumption of woollens in the United States was then seventy-two million dollars per annum, of which ten millions' worth were imported, twenty-two millions' worth were manufactured in the United States, and forty millions' worth were produced by household spinning and weaving (" domestic industry," as the term was then used). If these statistics are worth anything, the twelve millions of population consumed, on an average, six dollars' worth of woollens per head per annum. What Mallary proposed to do was to prevent the ten millions' worth from being imported. To do this he would increase the cost of the part imported and the part manufactured at home, the result of which would be that still a larger part of the population would have to be clothed in homespun. Thus his project might

[1] See page 248.

easily defeat itself, so far as it aimed to benefit the
American manufacturer, and it would deprive the
American people of the rest, leisure, and greater
satisfaction, as well as abundance, which new machinery and the factory system were winning out
of the textile industries, as compared with the old
household spinning and weaving.

The Committee on Manufactures of the House
had been taking testimony on the tariff during the
recess.   The southern free-traders had brought
this about against the opposition of the northern
protectionists.   There were only twenty-eight wit-
nesses examined, of whom nine were voluntary
and seven were members of Congress.   The evidence amounted to nothing but complaints of hard
times and losses.[1]   The deduction that these facts
were due to a lack of sufficient tariff was taken
for granted.[2]

Silas Wright and other anti-tariff men on the
Committee on Manufactures would not let Mallary
report the propositions of the Harrisburg convention on wool and woollens.[3]   Mallary tried to introduce those propositions as amendments on the floor
of the House.   All the interests, industrial and

[1] 34 Niles, 1.

[2] As a specimen of the value of such complaints: In April,
1828, Niles said that there was dullness in trade and great distress
at Baltimore.   34 Niles, 139.   In October he said that he had
not been through parts of the city for a long time, and that on a
recent walk he had been astonished at the signs of prosperity.
35 Niles, 81.

[3] Hammond's *Wright*, 104.

political, pounced upon the bill to try to amend it to their notions. New England and the Adams men wanted high duties on woollens and cottons, and low duties on wool, iron, hemp, salt, and molasses (the raw material of rum). Pennsylvania, Ohio, and Kentucky wanted high taxes on iron, wool, hemp, molasses (protection to whiskey), and low taxes on woollens and cottons. The Southerners wanted low taxes on everything, but especially on finished goods, and if there were to be heavy taxes on these latter they did not care how heavy the taxes on the raw materials were made. This last point, and the unswerving loyalty of rural Pennsylvania to Jackson, enabled the Jackson party to hold together its discordant elements. The political and economic alliances of the South were plainly inconsistent.[1]

The act, which resulted from the scramble of selfish special interests, was an economic monstrosity. The industrial interests of twelve millions of people had been thrown into an arena where there was little knowledge of economic principles, and no information about the industrial state of the country, or about the special industries. It being assumed that the Legislature could, would, and was about to, confer favors and advantages, there was a scramble to see who should get the most. At the same time party ambitions and strifes seized upon the industrial interests as capital for President-making. May 19, 1828, the bill became a law.

[1] See page 250.

The duty on wool costing less than 10 cents per pound was 15 per cent, on other wool 20 per cent and 30 per cent. That on woollens was 40 per cent for a year, then 45 per cent, there being four minima, 50 cents, $1.00, $2.50, $4.00. All which cost over $4.00 were to be taxed 45 per cent for a year, then 50 per cent. Niles and all the woollen men were enraged at this arrangement. No South Carolinian was more discontented than they. The " dollar minimum " was the especial cause of their rage. Cloth which cost 51 cents they wanted to regard as costing $2.50, and to tax it 40 per cent on that, *i. e.*, $1.00. The dollar minimum let in a large class of cloths which cost from $1.00 to $1.25, and which could be run down to cost from 90 to 99 cents.

The process of rolling iron had not yet been introduced into this country. It was argued that rolled iron was not as good as forged, and this was made the ground for raising the tax on rolled iron from $30.00 to $37.00 per ton, while the tax on forged iron was raised from $18.00 to $22.40. Rolled iron was cheaper, and was available for a great number of uses. The tax, in this case, " countervailed " an improvement in the arts, and robbed the American people of their share in the advantage of a new industrial achievement. The tax on steel was raised from $20.00 to $30.00 per ton ; that on hemp from $35.00 to $45.00 per ton ; that on molasses from 5 cents to 10 cents per gallon ; that on flax from nothing to $35.00 per ton. The taxes

on sugar, salt, and glass remained unchanged, as
did that on tea also, save by a differential tonnage
duty. Coffee was classified and the tax reduced.
The tax on wine, by a separate act, was reduced
one half or more.[1]

This was the " tariff of abominations," so called
on account of the number of especially monstrous
provisions which it contained. In the course of
the debate on it, the dogma was freely used that
protective taxes lower prices, and the exclusion of
American grain by the English corn laws was a
constantly effective argument. Credit varying
from nine to eighteen months was allowed under
this as under the previous tariffs.

VIII. *Nullification.* The Southerners bitterly
denounced the tariff of 1828. They had already
begun to complain of the operation of the system
four or five years before. To understand their
complaint, it is enough to notice with what reckless
extravagance the tariff theory, even if its truth
were admitted, was being handled in 1828. Of
course the public argument in favor of the tariff
necessarily took the form of assertions that, by
some occult process or other, the taxation proposed
would be beneficent to all, and that the protective
theory was a theory of national wealth. The
Southerners were sure that they paid the expenses
of the experiment, and they ventured the inference
that those who were so eager for the tariff saw
their profit in it; but when the attempt was made

[1] See page 402.

to find any compensation to the nation or to the South, no such thing could be found. Up to that point there was the plain fact of capital expended and capital gained ; at that point all turned into dogma and declamation.

March 12, 1828, McDuffie, of South Carolina, presented a report from the Committee on Ways and Means[1] against the tariff. He enumerated the varieties of woollens used by the people, and showed the operation of the minima upon each. He then went on to discuss the economic doctrines and the theory of protection as a mode of increasing the wealth of the country, and more especially the effect of the proposed taxes on the agricultural and exporting sections. The facts and doctrines stated by him were unanswerable, but they did not touch either the political motives or the interested pecuniary motives which were really pushing the tariff. He had all the right and all the reason, but not the power. The agricultural States were forced, under the tariff, either to export their products, exchange them for foreign products, and pay taxes on these latter to the federal treasury before they could bring them home, or else to exchange their products with the northern manufacturers for manufactured products, and to pay taxes to the latter in the price of the goods. All the mysteries of exchange, banking, and brokerage might obscure, they never could alter, these actual economic relations of fact.

[1] 34 Niles, 81.

The protectionists always affected to deride the
southern declaration that the tax fell on the South.
The popular notion was that the tariff tax bore on
the foreigner in some way or other, and helped the
domestic producer to a victory over the foreigner.
Since the object of the tariff was to prevent importations of foreign goods, it would, if it succeeded, make the foreigner stay at home, and keep
his goods there. This of course deprived him of
a certain demand for his goods, and prevented him
from reaching a gain which, under other conditions, he might have won, but it could not possibly
render him or his capital in any way available
for " encouraging American manufactures." The
American consumer of American products is the
only person whom American laws could reach in
order to make him contribute capital to build up
American industry. So far, then, as the American
protected industries were concerned, they preyed
upon each other with such results of net gain and
loss as chance and stupidity might bring about.
So far as American non-protected industries were
concerned, they, being the naturally strong and
independent industries of the country, sustained
the whole body of protected industries, which
were simply parasites upon them. The protective
theory, as a theory of wealth, therefore proposed
to organize national industry as an independent
body with a parasite upon it, while the free-trade
theory proposed to let industry organize itself as
so many independent and vigorous bodies as the

labor, capital, and land of the country could support.

The grievance of the South in 1828 is undeniable. So long as the exports of the country were almost exclusively southern products — cotton and tobacco — and so long as the federal revenue was almost entirely derived from duties on imports, it is certain that the southern industries either supported the federal government or paid tribute to the northern manufacturers. The Southerners could not even get a hearing or patient and proper study of the economic questions at issue. Their interests were being sacrificed to pretended national interests, just as, under the embargo, the interests of New England were sacrificed to national interests. In each case the party which considered its interests sacrificed came to regard the Union only as a cage, in which all were held in order that the stronger combination might plunder the weaker. In each case the party which was in power, and was having its way, refused to heed any remonstrance ; in fact regarded remonstrance as rebellion.

The more thoroughly the economist and the political philosopher recognizes the grievance of the Southerners in 1828, the more he must regret the unwisdom of the southern proceedings. The opponents of the tariff of 1828 adopted the policy of voting in favor of all the " abominations " on points of detail, in the hope that they could so weight down the bill that it would at last fail as a whole.[1]

[1] 35 Niles, 52.

Hence those Southerners who supported Jackson voted with the Pennsylvania and New York high-tariff men for all the worst features of the bill, while New England and the Adams men, who started as high-tariff men, voted on the other side. The southern Jackson men wanted to give way sufficiently on the tariff to secure one or two doubtful States. For instance, they were willing to protect whiskey and hemp to win Kentucky from Clay to Jackson. They were, in fact, playing a game which was far too delicate, between their economic interests and their political party affiliations. They were caught at last. In the vote on the previous question in the House, the yeas were 110, of whom 11 were Adams men and 99 Jackson men; the nays were 91, of whom 80 were Adams men and 11 Jackson men. The nays were those who wanted a tariff, but who wanted to amend the bill before them a great deal more before they passed it; that is, they wanted to take out the abominations which the anti-tariff men had voted into it. On the final passage of the bill, the yeas were 105, of whom 61 were Adams men and 44 Jackson men; the nays were 94, of whom 35 were Adams men and 59 were Jackson men. Of the yeas only 3 were from south of the Potomac. The policy of the southern free-traders, like most attempts at legislative finesse, proved an entire failure. The high-tariff men, although every man had intense objection to something in the bill, voted for it rather than defeat the bill entirely.

The New England men did not know how to vote.
In the end 23 of them voted against the bill and
16 for it.[1] The bill passed the Senate, 26 to 21.
Webster did not know on May 7th how he should
vote.[2] He voted for it, and then went home and
defended the vote on the ground that he had to
take the good and evil of the measure together.[3]
After all, the tariff made no capital for anybody.
The protectionists, by threatening both parties,
forced both to concede the tariff, after which the
protectionists voted with either party, according to
their preferences, just as they would have done if
both had resisted instead of both yielding.

Van Buren obtained "instructions" from Albany
to vote for the tariff, in order to be able to do so
without offending the Southerners.[4] Calhoun declared, in a speech in the Senate, February 23,
1837, that Van Buren was to blame for the tariff
of 1828.[5]

The South had already begun to discuss remedies before the tariff of 1828 was passed. Colonel
Hamilton, of South Carolina, at a public dinner in
the autumn of 1827, proposed "nullification" as a
remedy, the term being borrowed from the Virginia and Kentucky resolutions of 1798. Those

---

[1] 35 Niles, 52.   [2] 7 Adams, 534.   [3] 1 Webster's Works, 165.

[4] Mackeinzie, 103; Hammond's *Wright*, 105.

[5] Green's *Telegraph Extra*, 271, says that Adams wanted to
veto the tariff of 1828, and throw himself on the South, uniting
with Calhoun, but that Clay would not let him do so, because that
would ruin him and the American system. This is a very doubtful story.

resolutions now came to have, for a certain party in the South, the character and authority of an addendum to the Constitution. They were, in truth, only the manifesto of a rancorous opposition, like the resolutions of the Hartford convention. Yet, at that time, to call a man a "federalist" would have been a graver insult throughout the South than it would be now, in the North, to call a man a secessionist.

An examination of the resolutions of 1798, as they were adopted, will fail to find nullification in them. The resolutions, with a number of other most interesting documents connected therewith, are given by Niles in a supplement to his 43d volume. By examination of these it appears that Jefferson's original draft of the Kentucky resolutions contained, in the eighth resolution, these words: "Where powers are assumed which have not been delegated, a nullification of the act is the right remedy." The Legislature of Kentucky cut out this and nearly all the rest of the eighth resolution. The executory resolution, as drawn by Jefferson, ended thus: "The co-States [he means those States which by adopting these resolutions agree to coöperate] . . . will concur in declaring these acts [the alien and sedition laws] void and of no force, and will each take measures of its own for providing that neither of these acts . . . shall be exercised within their respective territories." Here, instead of an undefined term, we have a specific programme, which shows, without ambiguity, what the term meant. Different States, while remaining in the Union, were to prohibit validity within their territories, each to such federal acts as it disapproved, speaking through its constituted authorities. The Legislature struck this out, and adopted, as the executory resolution: "The co-States . . . will concur in declaring these [acts] void and of no force, and will each unite with this commonwealth in requesting their repeal at the next session of Congress." Some of the other States responded to these resolutions, and in 1799 Kentucky passed a resolution in which occurs this statement: "A nullification by those sovereignties of all unauthorized acts done under color of that instrument [the Constitution] is the rightful remedy." Madison's Virginia resolutions do not contain nullification either in form or substance, least of all as a practical remedy. They declared the alien and sedition acts unconstitutional, and that "the necessary and proper measures will be taken by each [of the concurring States] for co-operating with this State" to preserve the reserved rights of the States and people. In 1799 Madison made a long report to the Virginia House of Delegates, in which he analyzed and defended the resolutions of 1798, and especially defended the remedy proposed, namely, a solemn resolution and protest, communicated to the other States. He construed this remedy strictly. In May, 1830, Madison wrote to Livingston, approving of an anti-nullification speech made by him on March

15th of that year. He thus states the error of the nullifiers: "The error in the late comments on the Virginia proceedings has arisen from a failure to distinguish between what is declaratory of opinion and what is *ipso facto* executory; between the rights of the parties and of a single party; and between resorts within the purview of the Constitution and the *ultima ratio* which appeals from a Constitution, cancelled by its abuses, to original rights, paramount to all Constitutions." In 1830 Madison also wrote two long letters, one to Edward Everett, the other to Andrew Stevenson, in which he interpreted the Virginia resolutions. He certainly softens them down somewhat, which is a proof that party heat influenced him when he wrote them. He lays especial stress on the limited and harmless nature of the proposed action of Virginia. His two letters are the best statement of " Madisonian federalism."

It is certain that the nullification of a federal law in a State, by a State authority, as a practical and available remedy against an offensive measure, found no sanction in 1798–99, except in the supplementary resolution of Kentucky, when the heat of the controversy favored an extreme position. It was a notion of Jefferson, in which Madison did not join, and which neither Legislature adopted, except as stated. Never until 1827 was any body of men found to take up the notion, and try to handle it as reasonable and practical. Nullification is jacobinism. It is revolution made a

constant political means, and brought into the
every-day business of civil life. Nothing is more
astonishing in American political history than
the immunity enjoyed by some men, and the unfair responsibility enforced against others. Every
school-boy is taught to execrate the alien and sedition laws, and John Adams bears the odium of
them, but no responsibility worth speaking of for
nullification attaches to Jefferson. He was the
father of it, and the sponsor of it, and the authority
of his name was what recommended it in 1827.

In December, 1827, the South Carolina Legislature raised a committee on the powers of the federal
government in regard to tariff. In the winter
of 1827–28 the Legislatures of several southern
States passed resolutions about protective tariff
legislation. South Carolina had been a federal
State in the previous generation. She had not
been opposed to the federal government save in
the matter of her " police bill." Georgia had been
the turbulent State, — the one which had had the
most frequent collisions with the federal government, and had behaved on those occasions with
violence and folly. South Carolina in Monroe's
time was latitudinarian and anti-radical, and as
such was opposed to Georgia. South Carolina
now declared the tariff, internal improvements,
and appropriations for the colonization society unconstitutional.[1] Georgia declared the tariff and
internal improvements unconstitutional; declared

[1] 38 Niles, 154.

that Georgia would not submit to the action of
Congress, and affirmed the right of secession.[1]
The old Crawford party, however, took sides
against nullification, and prevented Georgia from
ranging herself with South Carolina. At a meeting at Athens, August 6, 1828, presided over by
Crawford, a committee, consisting of Wayne, Berrien, Cobb, Gilmer, Clayton, Troup, and others,
reported an address and resolutions denouncing
the tariff, but disclaiming all disunion sentiments
or purposes, and favoring [2] constitutional remedies.
In 1832 Crawford advocated a theory that secession
was wrong until *after* a convention to amend the
Constitution had been tried and proved a failure.[3]
North Carolina protested, in 1828, against the
new tariff, declaring that it violated the spirit of
the Constitution and opposed the interests of that
State. Alabama denied the constitutionality of
the tariff, and denounced it as pillage of that
State.

The proceedings of South Carolina did not
remedy the matter at all; but they altered the
issue very much to the satisfaction of the protectionists. The Union and the supremacy of the law
were something on which a much better fight could
be made than on the tariff, and the protectionists,
having secured the law, wanted nothing better
than to draw away attention from the criticism of
it by making the fight on nullification. Calhoun
and the South Carolinians had changed the fighting

[1] 3 *Ann. Reg.* 64.   [2] 35 Niles, 14.   [3] 42 Niles, 380.

from free-trade to nullification, and on that they stood alone. They threw away a splendid chance to secure a sound policy on one of the first economic interests of the country. In the debate between Webster and Hayne the latter won a complete victory on tariff and land. Webster made the fighting on the constitutional question, and turned away from the other questions almost entirely. He had no standing ground on tariff and land. He was on record in his earliest speeches as an intelligent free-trader, and his biographer[1] has infinite and fruitless trouble to try to explain away the fact. When Hayne opened the constitutional question, he gave Webster every chance of victory.

The action of Congress in passing the tariff of 1828, in spite of the attitude of the South, seemed to the Southerners to indicate an insolent disregard of their expostulations. In the winter of 1828–29 the South Carolina Legislature sent to the Senate an " Exposition and Protest " against the new law. Georgia wanted to nullify both Indian legislation and tariff. Virginia adopted the principle of nullification. North Carolina denounced the tariff, but nullification also. Alabama denounced the tariff, but recognized the right of Congress to levy revenue duties, with incidental protective effect. In 1829 Alabama went nearer to nullification. This was the high water mark of nullification outside of South Carolina. All these States were taunted, in answer to their remonstrances, with the votes of

[1] 1 Curtis's *Webster*, 207 *et seq.*

the Southern members on the details of the tariff
of abominations.

Neither party could let the tariff rest. A high
tariff is in a state of unstable equilibrium. If
legislators could ever gain full and accurate knowledge of all the circumstances and relations of
trade in their own country, and in all countries
with which it trades; if they had sufficient wit to
establish an artificial tax system which should just
fit the complicated facts, and produce the results
they want without doing any harm to anybody's
interests; and if, furthermore, the circumstances
and relations of trade would remain unchanged, it
would be possible to make a permanent and stable
tariff. Each of these conditions is as monstrously
impossible as anything in economics can be. Hence
constant new efforts are necessary, as well to suit
those to whom the tariff does not yet bring what
they expected from it, as to silence those who are
oppressed by it. The persons whose interests
were violated by the tariff of 1828 tried every
means in their power to evade it. January 27,
1830, Mallary brought in a bill to render the custom house appraisal more stringent and effective.
McDuffie responded with a proposition to reduce
all taxes on woollens, cottons, iron, hemp, flax,
molasses, and indigo to what they were before the
tariff of 1824 was passed. The whole subject was
reopened. McDuffie's bill was defeated, and Mallary's was passed. By separate bills the taxes on
salt, molasses, coffee, cocoa, and tea were reduced.

In April, 1830, came Jackson's Union toast.[1] It was a great disappointment to the mass of the Southerners, who had been his ardent supporters, and who had hoped, from his action in regard to Georgia and the Indians, that he would let the powers of the federal government go by default in the case of the tariff also.[2]   The personal element, which always had such strong influence with Jackson, had become more or less involved in the nullification struggle with which Calhoun was identified.

"I was aware of the hostility of the influential character aluded to [Calhoun] —   I sincerely regret the course taken by Hamilton & Hayne —   The people of South Carolina will not, *nay* cannot sustain such nulifying Doctrines.   They Carolinians are a patriotic & highminded people, and they prize their liberty too high to jeopardize it, at the shrine of an ambitious Demagogue, whether a native of Carolina or of any other country —   This influential character in this heat, has led Hamilton & Hayne astray, and it will, I fear, lead to the injury of Hamilton & loose him his election —   But the ambitious Demagogue aluded to, would sacrifice friends & country, & move heaven & earth, if he had the power, to gratify his unholy ambition —   His course will prostrate him here as well as every where else —   Our friend Mr Grundy says he will abandon him unless he can satisfy him that he has used his influence to put down this nulifying doctrine, which threatens to desolve our happy union." [3]

[1] See page 203.   [2] Hodgson, 166–7.
[3] Jackson to Lewis, Aug. 25, 1830, from Franklin, Tenn.   Ford MSS.

The Georgia case involved only indirectly the authority and prestige of the federal government. The immediate parties in interest were the Indians. Nullification involved directly the power and prestige of the federal government, and he would certainly be a most exceptional person who, being President of the United States, would allow the government of which he was the head to be defied and insulted.

On the 22d of November, 1830, a bill for a State convention failed to get a two thirds vote in the South Carolina Legislature. An attempt was then made to test the constitutionality of the tariff in the courts by refusing to pay duty bonds, and pleading "no consideration" for the taxes levied; but the United States District Court, in 1831, refused to hear evidence of "no consideration," drawn from the character of the tariff of 1828.[1]

June 14, 1831, Jackson wrote a letter to a committee of citizens of Charleston, in answer to an invitation to attend the celebration of the Fourth of July at that city, in which he indicated that a policy of force would be necessary and proper against nullification. The Governor of the State brought this letter to the notice of the Legislature, which adopted resolutions denouncing the act of the President in writing such a letter, and denying the lawfulness of the steps which he described. There were some in South Carolina who, at this

[1] 7 *Ann. Reg.* 260.

time, favored secession, so soon as South Carolina could organize a sufficient combination to go out with her. Cheves was a leader of such.[1]

North Carolina now denounced nullification, but the other States as yet held back.

On the 5th of October, 1831, a free-trade convention met at Philadelphia. On the 26th of October a protectionist convention met at New York. Gallatin wrote the address published by the former. Of course it was all free trade, — no nullification. A. H. Everett wrote the address issued by the New York convention. The public debt was being paid off with great rapidity, and the need for revenue was all the time declining. The free-traders said: In that case, let us abolish the taxes, and not raise a revenue which we do not need. It will be an additional advantage that we can do away, without any complicated devices, with all the protective taxes which one citizen pays to another, and which take shelter under the revenue taxes. Let the people keep and use their own earnings. The protectionists wanted to remove the taxes from all commodities the like of which were not produced here. They argued that, if the country was out of debt, it could afford to enter on great schemes of national development by government expenditure. They therefore proposed to keep up the taxes for protective purposes, and to spend the surplus revenue (in which they regarded the revenue from land as a thing by itself) on in-

[1] 8 Adams, *Diary*, 410.

ternal improvements, pensions, French spoliation
claims, etc. These were not yet strictly party positions, but in general the former was the administration policy and the latter the opposition policy.

The session of 1831–32 was full of tariff. A
presidential election was again at hand. J. Q.
Adams was put at the head of the Committee on
Manufactures with an anti-tariff majority. Mc-
Duffie was chairman of the Committee on Ways
and Means. January 19, 1832, the House instructed the Secretary of the Treasury to collect
information about manufactures. A report was
rendered in two large volumes, in 1833, after the
whole subject had been disposed of. Clay was
nominated for President in December, 1831, and
was preparing his policy and programme. A conference was held at Washington by his supporters,
at which he presented his views, as it appears, in a
somewhat dictatorial manner.[1] He wanted all the
revenue taxes (on tea, coffee, wine, etc.) abolished.
The protective taxes he wanted to make prohibi-
tory, so as to stop revenue. He said that the duties on hemp were useless, as our dew-rotted hemp
never could compete with the water-rotted hemp
which was imported. This was rather hard, considering that the tax on hemp had been laid for
the sake of Kentucky, and now the member from
Kentucky and father of the " American system"
said that protection to hemp was useless. Clay
was willing to allow a drawback on rigging ex-

[1] 8 Adams, *Diary*, 445.

ported. Dearborn said that the tax on hemp had
closed every rope-walk in Boston. Adams said
that the House Committee on Manufactures would
reduce the duties prospectively; that is, to take
effect when the debt should be paid. Clay wanted
to stop paying the debt in order to take away the
administration " cry." Adams took sides with
Jackson on the point of paying the debt. He
thought public opinion favored that policy. He
also thought Clay's programme would appear like
defying the South. Clay said that he did not care
whom he defied. " To preserve, maintain, and
strengthen the American system he would defy
the South, the President, and the Devil." We
may say what we like of the nullifiers, but, so far
as they met with and knew of this disposition on
the part of Clay and his supporters, they would
not have been free men if they had not resisted it;
for it must not be forgotten that the real question
at issue was whether their property should be
taken away from them or not.

In the annual message for 1831 Jackson recommended that the tariff be amended so as to reduce
revenue. February 8, 1832, McDuffie reported
a bill making the taxes on iron, steel, sugar, salt,
hemp, flour, woollens, cottons, and manufactures
of iron twenty-five per cent for a year after June
30, 1832, then eighteen and three fourths per cent
for a year, and then twelve and one half per cent
for an indefinite period. All other goods which
were taxed over twelve and one half per cent at

the time of passing the bill were to be taxed twelve and one half per cent after June 30, 1832. April 27, 1832, the Secretary of the Treasury (McLane) presented a tariff bill in answer to a call by the House. It was planned to raise twelve millions of revenue. It was proposed to collect fifteen per cent on imports in general, with especial and higher rates on the great protected commodities. This was the administration plan. The House Committee on Manufactures reported a bill May 23, which was taken up instead of the others. The battle reopened, and ranged over the whole field of politics and political economy. The act, as finally passed (July 14, 1832), reduced or abolished many of the revenue taxes. It did not materially alter the protective taxes. The tax on iron was reduced, that on cottons was unchanged, that on woollens was raised to fifty per cent; wool costing less than eight cents per pound was made free, other wool was taxed as before. Woollen yarn was now first taxed. This was the position of tariff and nullification when the presidential election was held.

IX. *National Bank.* — In the United States the democratic element in public opinion has always been jealous of and hostile to the money power. The hostility has broken out at different times in different ways, as an assault on banks, corporations, vested rights, and public credit. Sometimes it seems as if the "money power" were regarded superstitiously, as if it were a superhuman entity,

with will and power. The assaults on it are mingled with dread, as of an enemy with whom one
is not yet ready to cope, but whose power is increasing rapidly, so that the chance of ultimate
victory over him is small. This antagonism is but
a premonition of the conflict between democracy
and plutocracy, which is the next great crisis which
the human race has to meet. We are now to study
one of the greatest struggles between democracy
and the money power.

After a renewal of the charter of the first Bank
of the United States had been refused, in 1812,
a great number of local banks were organized,
especially in the Middle States. This movement
unfortunately coincided with the second war with
England. The combination of bank mania and war
financiering produced a very extravagant bank-
note inflation. The party in power was forced
to imitate measure after measure of Hamilton's
financial system, which they had so vigorously denounced twenty years before. At last they came
to a national bank also. The Senate wanted to
make a Bank to suit the administration, that is,
one which could make loans to the Treasury; one,
therefore, which was not bound to pay specie. The
House strenuously resisted the creation of such a
mere paper-money machine. Madison vetoed, in
January, 1815, a bill which had been passed in
conformity with the ideas of the House. Another
bill was introduced at once, which provided for a
bank to conform to the wishes of the administra-

tion. This bill was before the House on the day
on which news of the treaty of Ghent was received
at Washington (February 13). Pitkin says that
the news was received at the moment of voting.[1]
The bill was laid aside and was never revived.

At the next session (1815–16) the proposition
came up for a national bank, not as a financial
resource for the Treasury, but to check the local
banks and force a return to specie payments. The
charter became a law April 10, 1816. It was a
close imitation of Hamilton's Bank. In this Bank
also the government had a big stock note for seven
millions of dollars of stock, which it had subscribed for as a resource to pay its debts, not as
investment for free capital. The Bank was chartered for twenty years. Its capital was thirty-five
millions, seven subscribed by the United States in
a five per cent stock note, seven by the public in
specie, and twenty-one by the public in United
States stocks. It was to pay a bonus of one and
one half millions in two, three, and four years. It
was not to issue notes under $5.00, and not to sus-
pend specie payments under a penalty of twelve
per cent on all notes not redeemed on presentation. Twenty directors were to be elected annually
by the stockholders, and five, being stockholders,
were to be appointed by the President of the
United States and confirmed by the Senate. The
federal government was to charter no other bank
during the period of the charter of this. The

[1] Pitkin, 427.

Secretary of the Treasury might at any time redeem the stocks in the capital of the Bank, including the five per cent subscription stock. He might remove the public deposits if he should see fit, but must state his reasons for so doing to Congress at its next meeting. The Bank engaged to transfer public funds without charge. At first it undertook to equalize the currency by receiving any notes of any branch at any branch, but it was soon forced to abandon the attempt. The old Bank had never done this.[1] Two things were mixed up in this attempt : (1) The equalization of the different degrees of depreciation existing in the bank-notes of different districts. This the Bank could not have corrected save by relentlessly presenting all local notes for redemption, until they were made equal to specie or were withdrawn. So far as the Bank did this, it won the reputation of a "monster" which was crushing out the local banks.[1] (2) The equalization of the domestic exchanges. This was impossible and undesirable, since capital never could be distributed in exact proportion to local needs for it. The failure of the Bank to "equalize the exchanges," and its refusal to take any notes at any branch, earned it more popular condemnation than anything else.

The Bank charter contained a great many faults. To mention only those which affected its career : The capital was too large. There was no reason for lending its capital to the government, *i. e.*,

[1] Carey's *Letters*, 55.   [1] See page 156.

putting it into public stocks, or making the Bank a syndicate of bond-holders. There was every reason why the United States should not hold stock in it, especially when it could not pay for the same. The dividends of the bank from 1816 to 1831, when the government paid its stock note, averaged five per cent per annum, paid semi-annually. The United States paid five per cent on its stock note quarterly. This gave room for another complaint by the enemies of the Bank.

The Bank was established at Philadelphia. It began with nineteen branches, and grew to twenty-five. Specie payments were resumed nominally February 20, 1817, after which date, according to a joint resolution of Congress of April 16, 1816, the Treasury *ought* to receive only specie, or notes of the Bank of the United States, or of specie-paying banks, or Treasury notes. In the first two years of its existence the great Bank was carried to the verge of bankruptcy by as bad banking as ever was heard of. Instead of checking the other banks in their improper proceedings, it led and surpassed them all. A clique inside the Bank was jobbing in its shares, and robbing it to provide the margins. Instead of rectifying the currency, it made the currency worse. Instead of helping the country out of the distress produced by the war, it plunged the country into the commercial crisis of 1819, which caused a general liquidation, lasting four or five years. All the old-school republicans denounced themselves for having abandoned their principles in voting for a national bank. All the ill-doing of the Bank they regarded as essential elements in the character of any national bank. Niles denounced the whole system of banking, and all the banks. He had good reason. It is almost incredible that the legislation of any civilized coun, try could have opened the chance for such abuses of credit, banking, and currency as then existed. The franchise of issuing paper notes to be used by the people as currency, that is to say, the license to appropriate a certain amount of the specie circulation of the country, and to put one's promissory notes in the place of it, was given away, not only without any equivalent, but without any guarantee at all. When Niles and Gouge denounced banking and banks, it was because they had in mind these swindling institutions. The great Bank justly suffered with the rest, because it had made itself in many respects like them. The popular anti-bank party, opposed to the money power, was very strong during the period of liquidation.

Langdon Cheves, of South Carolina, was elected president of the Bank March 6, 1819. He set about restoring it. In three years he had succeeded, although the losses were over three millions. Nicholas Biddle was elected president of the Bank in January, 1823. He was only thirty-seven years old, and had been more a literary man than anything else. He was appointed government director in 1819. His election in Cheves's place was the result of a conflict between a young and progressive

policy, which he represented, and an old and con.
servative policy. At the nearest date to January
1, 1823, the bank had $4,600,000 notes out;
$4,400,000 specie; $2,700,000 public deposits;
$1,500,000 deposits by public officers; $3,300,000
deposits by individuals; $28,700,000 bills dis-
counted. Congress refused to allow the officers of
the branches to sign notes issued by the branches.
It is not clear why this petition was refused, except
that Congress was in no mood to grant any request
of the Bank. The labor, for the president and
cashier of the parent bank, of signing all the notes
of the Bank and branches was very great. Accordingly, in 1827, branch drafts were devised to
avoid this inconvenience. They were the counter-
part of bank-notes. They were drawn for even
sums, by the cashier of any branch, on the parent
bank, to the order of some officer of the branch,
and endorsed by the latter to bearer. They then
circulated like bank-notes. They were at first
made in denominations of $5.00 and $10.00. In
1831 the denomination $20.00 was added. Binney,
Wirt, and Webster gave an opinion that these
drafts were legal. Rush, Secretary of the Treasury, approved of them, and allowed public dues
to be paid in them.[1] These branch drafts were a
most unlucky invention, and to them is to be
traced most of the subsequent real trouble of the
Bank. The branches, especially the distant ones,
when they issued these drafts, did not lend their

[1] Document B.

own capital, but that of the Bank at Philadelphia. At the same time, therefore, they fell in debt to the parent bank. This stimulated their issues. The borrowers used these drafts to sustain what were called "race-horse bills." These were drafts drawn between the different places where there were branches, so that a bill falling due at one place was met by the discount of a bill drawn on another place. This system was equivalent to unlimited renewals. It kept up a constant inflation of credit. Up to the time of Jackson's accession these drafts had not yet done much harm, and had attracted no adverse criticism.

At the session of 1827–28, P. P. Barbour brought forward a proposition to sell the stock owned by the United States in the Bank. A debate arose concerning the Bank, and it seems that there was a desire on the part of a portion of the opposition to put opposition to it into their platform.[1] The project failed. Barbour's resolution was tabled, 174 to 9.

The facts which are now to be narrated were not known to the public until 1832. They are told here as they occurred in the order of time.

June 27, 1829, Levi Woodbury, senator from New Hampshire, wrote to Samuel Ingham, Secretary of the Treasury, making confidential complaints of Jeremiah Mason, the new president of the Portsmouth, New Hampshire, branch of the Bank of the United States, because (1) of the

[1] 33 Niles, 275.

general brusqueness of his manner; (2) of his severity and partiality in the matter of loans and collections. He added that Mason was a friend of Webster. "His political character is doubtless known to you." He also said that the complaints were general and from all political parties. Ingham enclosed the letter to Biddle, pointing out that it seemed to have been called out by the political effects of the action of the branch. He said that the administration wanted no favors from the Bank. Biddle replied that he would investigate.

One great trouble with Biddle, which appeared at once in this correspondence, was that he wrote too easily. When he got a pen in his hand, it ran away with him. In this first reply, he went on to write a long letter, by which he drew out all the venomous rancor of Levi Woodbury and Isaac Hill against the old federalists and Jeremiah Mason and the Bank, all which lurked in Ingham's letter, but came out only in the form of innuendo and suggestion. The innuendoes stung Biddle, and he challenged the suggestions instead of ignoring them. Thus he gave them a chance to come forth without sneaking. He was jauntily innocent and unconscious of what spirit he was dealing with and what impended over him. He stated (1) that Mason had been appointed to a vacancy caused by the resignation, not by the removal, of his predecessor; (2) that the salary of the position had not been increased for Mason; (3) that, after Mason's appointment, Webster was asked to persuade him to accept. He quoted a letter from Woodbury to himself, in July, in which Woodbury said that Mason was as unpopular with one party as the other. Biddle inferred, no doubt correctly, that Mason, as banker, had done his duty by the Bank, without regard to politics. He explained that the branch had previously not been well managed, and that Mason was put in as a competent banker and lawyer to put it right again.[1] It is easy to see that Mason, in order to put the bank right, had to act severely, and that he especially disappointed those who, on account of political sympathy, expected favors, but did not get them. Politics had run high in New Hampshire for ten or twelve years. Mason and Webster on one side, and Hill, Woodbury, and Plumer on the other, had been in strong antagonism. The relations had been amicable between some of them, but Hill and Mason were two men who could not meet without striking fire. Hill was now president of a small bank at Concord, and business jealousy was added to political animosity. Woodbury had been elected

[1] Hill, in a speech, March 3, 1834, said: "After the tariff law of 1828 had passed, the manufacturing stock fell, in many cases sinking the whole investment, so that where the bank had had no other security, bad debts were made. . . . The bank lost, in bad debts, some $80,000. . . . [Mason] in violation of the terms of payment on which loans had been made, called on all the customers of the bank to pay four for one of what they were required to pay by the implied terms of their first contract. . . . It was this arbitrary breach of faith with the customers of the bank that induced the merchants and men of business of all parties to petition for the removal of the man who had caused the distress."

to the Senate as an Adams man, and the personal and political feelings were only more intense, because Adams was called a republican. The federalists were first invited to support him, then they were ignored,[1] and Woodbury and Hill were working for Jackson.

Biddle, as if dissatisfied with whatever prudence he had shown in his first letter, wrote another, in which he declared that the Bank had nothing to do with politics; that people were all the time trying to draw it into politics, but that it always resisted.

July 23d Ingham wrote again to Biddle, insisting that there must be grounds of complaint, and that exemption from party preference was impossible. He added that he represented the views of the administration.

In August, the Secretary of War ordered the pension agency transferred from the Portsmouth branch to the bank at Concord, of which Isaac Hill had been president. The parent bank forbade the branch to comply with this order, on the ground that it was illegal. The order was revoked.

September 15th Biddle wrote again to Ingham. He had visited Buffalo and Portsmouth during the summer. His letter is sharp and independent in tone. He says that two memorials have been sent to him by Isaac Hill, Second Controller of the Treasury, one from the business men of Ports-

[1] 1 Webster's *Correspondence*, 415, 419.

mouth, and the other from sixty members of the
Legislature of New Hampshire, requesting Mason's
removal, and nominating a new board of directors,
" friends of General Jackson in New Hampshire."
Those proceedings were evidently planned by the
anti-Bank clique at Washington to provoke Biddle.
He hastened to crown that purpose with complete
success. He says that public opinion in the community around a bank is no test of bank management, and that the reported opinion at Portsmouth,
upon examination, "degenerated into the personal
hostility of a very limited, and for the most part
very prejudiced, circle." He then takes up three
points which he finds in Ingham's letters, suggested
or assumed, but not formulated. These are: (1)
That the Secretary has some supervision over the
choice of officers of the Bank, which comes to him
from the relations of the government to the Bank.
(2) That there is some action of the government
on the Bank, which is not precisely defined, but of
which the Secretary is the proper agent. (3) That
it is the right and duty of the Secretary to make
known to the president of the Bank the views of
the administration on the political opinions of the
officers of the Bank. He then says that the board
acknowledges no responsibility whatever to the
Secretary in regard to the political opinions of the
officers of the Bank ; that the Bank is responsible
to Congress only, and is carefully shielded by its
charter from executive control. He indignantly
denies that freedom from political bias is impos-

sible, shows the folly of the notion of political
" checks and counter-balances " between the officers
of the Bank, and declares that the Bank ought to
disregard all parties. He won a complete victory
on the argument of his points, but delivered himself, on the main issue, without reserve into the
hands of his enemies.

Ingham's letter of October 5th is a masterly
specimen of cool and insidious malice. In form it
is smooth, courteous, and plausible, but it is full of
menace and deep hostility. He discusses the points
implied by him, but, in form, raised by Biddle.
He says that if the Bank should abuse its powers
the Secretary is authorized to remove the deposits.
Hence the three points which Biddle found in his
former letter are good. It does not appear that
Biddle ever thought of this power as within the
range of the discussion, or of the exercise of this
power as among the possibilities. Ingham says
there are two theories of the Bank: (1) That it is
exclusively for national purposes and for the common benefit of all, and that the " employment of
private interests is only an incident, — perhaps
an evil, — founded in mere convenience for care
and management." (2) That it is intended " to
strengthen the arm of wealth, and counterpoise the
influence of extended suffrage in the disposition of
public affairs," and that the public deposits are
one of its means for performing this function. He
says that there are two means of resisting the latter
theory : the power to remove the deposits, and the

power to appoint five of the directors. He adds that, if the Bank should exercise political influence, that would afford him the strongest motive for removing the deposits. Biddle's reply of October 9th shows that he recognizes at last what temper he has to deal with. He is still gay and good-natured, and he recedes gracefully, only maintaining that it is the policy of the Bank to keep out of politics.

In Ingham's letters of July 23d and October 5th is to be found the key to the "Bank War." Ingham argues that the Bank cannot keep out of politics, that its officers ought to be taken from both parties, and that, if it meddles with politics, he will remove the deposits. The only road left by which to escape from the situation he creates is to go into politics on his side. No evidence is known to exist that the Bank had interfered in politics. The administration men are distinctly seen in this correspondence, trying to drive it to use political influence on their side, and the Bank resists, not on behalf of the other party, but on behalf of its independence. It is the second of the alleged theories in the letter of October 5th, however, which demands particular attention. The Jackson administration always pretended that the managers of the Bank construed the character and function of the Bank according to that theory. It is the Kentucky relief notion of the Bank in its extreme and most malignant form. The statement is, on its face, invidious and malicious. It is not, even in form, a formula of functions attributed to

the Bank. It is a construction of the political
philosophy of a national bank. It is not parallel
with the first statement. It was ridiculous to allege that the stockholders of the Bank had subscribed twenty-eight million dollars, not even for
party purposes, but to go crusading against democracy and universal suffrage. However, the justice
or injustice of the allegations in these letters, which
could be submitted to no tribunal, and which touched
motives, not acts, was immaterial. The administration had determined to make war on the Bank.
The ultimate agents were Amos Kendall, who
brought the Kentucky relief element, and Isaac
Hill, who brought the element of local bank jealousy and party rancor. Ingham published, in
1832,[1] after the above correspondence had been
published, an " Address " in his own defence.
He says that he found, to his surprise, soon after
he entered Jackson's cabinet, that the President
and those nearest in his confidence felt animosity
against the Bank. He saw that the persons who
had the most feeling influenced the President's
mind the most. Allegations of fact were reported
in regard to political interference by the Bank.
Ingham says that when he was urged to action
about the Bank he tried to trace down these stories
to something tangible. He quotes the only statement he ever got. It is a letter by Amos Kendall,
giving second or third hand reports of the use of
money by officers of the Bank in the Kentucky

[1] 42 Niles, 315.

election of 1825, when the old and new court question was at issue.[1] The man whom Kendall gave as his authority failed, when called upon, to substantiate the assertion. In Kendall's Autobiography there is a gap from 1823 to 1829, and the origin of his eager hostility to the Bank is not known. Jackson is not known to have had any opinion about the Bank when he came to Washington. He is not known to have had any collision with the Bank, except that, when he was on his way to Florida, as Governor, the branch at New Orleans refused his request that it would advance money to him on his draft on the Secretary of State at its face value.[2] Hill and Kendall, either by telling Jackson that the Bank had worked against him in the election, or by other means, infused into his mind the hostility to it which had long rankled in theirs. They were soon reën-forced by Blair, who was stronger than either, and more zealously hostile to the Bank than either.

In November, 1829, about a week before Congress met, Amos Kendall sent privately [3] a letter to the " Courier and Enquirer," Jackson organ at New York, in which he insinuated that Jackson would come out against the Bank in the annual message. A head and tail piece were put to this letter, and it was put in as an editorial. It attracted some attention, but, its origin being of course unknown, it was received with a great deal of scepticism.

[1] See page 164. [2] 2 Parton, 596.
[3] *Memoirs of Bennett*, 111.

In its form it consisted of a series of queries,[1] of
which the following may be quoted as the most
significant, and as best illustrating the methods of
procedure introduced in Jackson's administration.
We must remember that these queries were drawn
up by a man in the closest intimacy with the
President, who helped to make the message what
it was, and we must further remember what we
have already learned of William B. Lewis's methods. " Will sundry banks throughout the Union
take measures to satisfy the general government
of their safety in receiving deposits of the revenue, and transacting the banking concerns of the
United States? Will the Legislatures of the
several States adopt resolutions on the subject,
and instruct their senators how to vote? Will a
proposition be made to authorize the government
to issue exchequer bills, to the amount of the annual revenue, redeemable at pleasure, to constitute
a circulating medium equivalent to the notes issued
by the United States Bank?" So far as appears,
no one saw in these queries the oracle which was
foretelling the history of the United States for the
next ten or fifteen years.

Jackson's first annual message contained a paragraph on the Bank which struck the whole country
with astonishment. " We had seen," says Niles,
" one or two dark paragraphs in certain of the
newspapers, which led to a belief that the administration was not friendly to this great moneyed

[1] It is quoted 37 Niles, 378. (January 30, 1830.)

institution, but few had any suspicion that it would form one of the topics of the first message." [1] After mentioning the fact that the charter would expire in 1836, and that a recharter would be asked for, the message said that such an important question could not too soon be brought before Congress. " Both the constitutionality and the expediency of the law creating this bank are well questioned by a large portion of our fellow citizens, and it must be admitted by all that it has failed in the great end of establishing a uniform and sound currency." The question is then raised whether a bank could not be devised, " founded on the credit of the government and its revenues," which should answer all the useful purposes of the Bank of the United States.

No period in the history of the United States could be mentioned when the country was in a state of more profound tranquillity, both in its domestic and foreign relations, and in a condition of more humdrum prosperity in its industry, than 1829. The currency never had been as good as it was then, for the troubles of the early '20's, both in the East and in the West, had been to a great extent overcome.[2] The currency has never, since 1829, been better and more uniform, if we take the whole country over, than it was then. The proceedings, of which the paragraph in the message

[1] 37 Niles, 257.

[2] See the tables in 2 Macgregor, 1140; also Gallatin on the *Currency and Banking System of the United States.*

of 1829 was the first warning, threw the currency
and banking of the country into confusion and un-
certainty, one thing following upon another, and
they have never yet recovered the character of established order and routine operation which they
had then. The Bank charter was not to expire
until March 3, 1836 ; that is, three years beyond
the time when Jackson's term would expire. He
seems to apologize for haste in bringing up the
question of its renewal. It certainly was a premature step, and can be explained only by the degree
of *feeling* which the active agents had mingled
with their opinions about the Bank. It was,
moreover, a new mode of statement for the President to address Congress, not on his own motion,
and in order to set forth his own opinions and recommendations, but as the mouth-piece of " a large
portion of our fellow citizens." Who were they?
How many were they? How had they made their
opinions known to the President? Why did they
not use the press or the Legislature, as usual, for
making known their opinions? Who must be dealt
with in discussing the opinions, the President or
the "large portion," etc. ? What becomes of the
constitutional responsibility of the President, if he
does not speak for himself, but gets his notions
before Congress as a quotation from somebody
else, and that somebody " a large portion of our
fellow citizens"? Then again the question must
arise : Does the President correctly quote anybody?
No proofs can be found that any hundred persons

in the United States had active doubts of the constitutionality and expediency of the Bank, or were looking forward to its recharter as a political crisis to be prepared for. If the theoretical question had been raised, a great many people would have said that they thought a national bank unconstitutional. They would have said, as any one must say now, that there was no power given in the Constitution to buy territory, but they did not propose to give up Louisiana and Florida. Just so in regard to a national bank. The Supreme Court had decided in McCulloch *vs.* Maryland that the Bank charter was constitutional, and that was the end of controversy. The question of the constitutionality of the Bank had no actuality, and occupied no place in public opinion, so far as one can learn from newspapers, books, speeches, diaries, correspondence, or other evidence we have of what occupied the minds of the people. Jackson's statement was only a figure of speech. The observation which is most important for a fair judgment of his policy of active hostility to the Bank is, that any great financial institution or system which is in operation, and is performing its functions endurably, has a great presumption in its favor. The only reasonable question for statesman or financier is that of slow and careful correction and improvement. The man who sets out to overturn and destroy, in obedience to " a principle," especially if he shows that he does not know the possible scope of his own action, or what he intends to construct

afterwards, assumes a responsibility which no public man has any right to take.

The vague and confused proposition of the President for some new kind of bank added alarm to
astonishment.   What did he mean by his bank
based on the credit and revenues of the government?   It sounded like a big paper-money machine.
If there was any intelligible idea in it, it referred
to something like the Bank of the Commonwealth
of Kentucky on a still larger scale.   It will be noticed that this notion of a national bank coincided
with the suggestion, in Kendall's queries,[1] of a currency of exchequer bills.   The stock of the Bank
declined from 125 to 116 on account of the message.[2]   It was supposed that the President must
have knowledge of some facts about the Bank.

The part of the message about the Bank was referred in both Houses.   April 13, 1830,[3] McDuffie
made a long report from the Committee on Ways
and Means.   He argued that the constitutionality
of the Bank was settled by the decision of the
Supreme Court and by prescription.   He defended
the history and expediency of the Bank, and ended
by declaring the bank proposed by the President
to be very dangerous and inexpedient, both financially and politically, — the latter because it would
increase the power of the Executive.   In the Senate, Smith, of Maryland, reported from the Committee on Finance in favor of the Bank.[4]   The

[1] See page 280.   [2] 38 Niles, 177.
[3] 38 Niles, 183.   [4] 38 Niles, 126.

House, May 10, 1830, tabled, by 89 to 66, resolutions that the House would not consent to renew the charter of the Bank ; and on May 29th it tabled, 95 to 67, a series of resolutions calling for a comprehensive report of the proceedings of the Bank. As yet there were no allegations against the management of the Bank. The stock rose to 130 on the reports of the committees of Congress.

A great many politicians had to " turn a sharp corner," as Niles expressed it, when Jackson came out against the Bank. His supporters in Pennsylvania cities were nearly all Bank men. Van Buren, Marcy, and Butler had signed a petition, in 1826, for a branch of the bank at Albany.[1] The petition was refused. In January, 1829, Van Buren, as Governor of New York, referred to banks under federal control as objectionable. The administration party was not yet consolidated. It was still only that group of factions which had united in opposition to Adams. The Bank question was one of the great questions through which Jackson's popularity and his will drilled them into a solid party phalanx. All had to conform to the lines which he drew for the party, under the influence of Kendall, Lewis, and Hill. If they did not do so, they met with speedy discipline.

In his message for 1830, Jackson again inserted a paragraph about the Bank, and proposed a Bank as a " branch of the Treasury Department." The outline is very vague, but it approaches the sub-

[1] Mackeinzie, 98.

treasury idea. No notice was taken of this part
of the message in the session of 1830-31. On a
test question, whether to refer the part of the message relating to the Bank to the Committee on
Ways and Means or to a select committee, the
Bank triumphed, 108 to 67.

At the time of Tyler's struggle with Congress,
about his "Exchequer" plan, 1841, he tried to
win strength for it by connecting it with the recommendation of Jackson. This led Jackson to
write to Lewis, January 1, 1842, as follows: —

"I informed you in my last, that I regretted that part
of the Presidents message, that recommended a paper
currency of treasury notes, and as the President has
observed that it was shadowed forth by my message of
1830, I sincerely regret that he did not fully embrace
the propositions therein set forth — Turn to it, and you
will find that there is no expression there that will
justify the idea of Congress making a paper currency of
any kind, much less by issue of Treasury notes — and it
is impossible to make out of any paper system, a sound
circulating and uniform currency. You are certainly
right that the mode presented is much better than a
national Bank, such as Biddles, because it admits expressly that congress has the right to alter or repeal it."

A fortnight later, he added: —

"I discover that Mr Rives has adverted to my message of 1830 in support of the measures recommended.
I regretted to see this — it shows him uncandid, because
there is no likeness between them. In my message there
is no recommendation to issue treasury notes, or to dis-

count bills of exchange or to purchase property, with power only to remit the funds of the government. My explanatory remarks shews this — I remark, "This not being a corporate body, having no stockholders, debtors, or property, could not become dangerous to our country &c &c, as incorporated Banks with all their mamoth powers &c &c — In mine there were to be no paper, no debtors, a cash business, where there could be no loss to the government — The word Bank was used by me in its proper sense to distinguish it from an incorporated Bank — *a place where the money of the government was to be kept*, to clearly show that it was to have no stockholders, no power to issue paper, discount or exchange and if Mr Rives will read all my messages and my farewell address which was intended to give my full views on Banking he will find he has done me great injustice in referring to my messages, as authority for the fiscal plan proposed by President Tyler. Every one who knows me, must be aware of my universal hostility against all government paper currency — The old continental currency, was sufficient to convince me that a greater curse could not visit a nation than a paper currency —"[1]

There is a bank-plan in print which is attributed to Jackson.[2]

Benton offered a joint resolution, in the Senate, February 2, 1831, "That the charter of the Bank of the United States ought not to be renewed." The Senate refused leave, 23 to 20, to introduce it. In July, 1831, the Secretary of War ordered the pension funds for the State of New York to be

[1] Ford MSS.   [2] Ingersoll, 283.

removed from the New York branch. Biddle remonstrated, because there was no authority of law for the order, and the Auditor had refused to accept such an order as a voucher in a previous case. Secretary Cass revoked the order, March 1, 1832. In the message of 1831 Jackson referred to the Bank question as one on which he had discharged his duty and freed his responsibility. The Secretary of the Treasury, McLane, in his annual report, December, 1831, made a long and strong argument in favor of the Bank. If we may judge from the tone of the message of 1831, Jackson was willing to allow the Bank question to drop, at least until the presidential election should be over. There is even room for a suspicion that McLane's argument in favor of the Bank was a sort of "hedging;" for although the Secretary's report was not necessarily submitted to the President,[1] Jackson was hardly the man to allow a report to be sent in of which he disapproved.

[1] See page 353.

Margaret Eaton

H Biddle

CHAPTER IX

THE CAMPAIGN OF 1832

CLAY was the leading man in the opposition, but the opposition was by no means united. A new factor had been gaining importance in politics for the last few years. The politicians had ignored it and sneered at it, but it had continued to grow, and was now strong enough to mar, if it could not make, a national election.

In 1826 a bricklayer, named William Morgan, who lived at Batavia, N. Y., and was very poor, thought that he could earn something by writing an exposure of the secrets of free-masonry,[1] he being a mason. The masons learned that he had written such a book. They caused his arrest and imprisonment over Sunday on a frivolous civil complaint, and searched his house for the manuscript during his absence. A month later he was arrested again for a debt of $2.10, and imprisoned under an execution for $2.69, debt and costs. The next day the creditor declared the debt satisfied. Morgan was released, passed at the prison door into the hands of masked men, was placed in

[1] Report of the Special Agent of the State of New York. 5 *Ann. Reg.* 537.

a carriage, taken to Fort Niagara, and detained there. A few days later a body was found floating in the river, which was identified as Morgan's body. The masons always denied that this identification was correct. Morgan has never been seen or heard of since. In January, 1827, certain persons were tried for conspiracy and abduction. They pleaded guilty, and so prevented a disclosure of details.[1] The masons confessed and admitted abduction, but declared that Morgan was not dead. The opinion that Morgan had been murdered, and that the body found was his, took possession of the minds of those people of western New York who were not masons. Popular legend and political passion have become so interwoven with the original mystery that the truth cannot now be known.

The outrage on Morgan aroused great indignation in western New York, then still a simple frontier country. Public opinion acted on all subjects. A committee appointed at a mass-meeting undertook an extra-legal investigation, and soon brought the matter into such shape that no legal tribunal ever after had much chance of unravelling it. After the fashion of the time, and of the place also, a political color was immediately given to the affair. As Spencer, the special agent appointed by the State to investigate the matter, declared in his report, the fact of this political coloring was disastrous to the cause of justice. The politicians

[1] 2 Hammond, 376. See, however, the trial reported 4 *Ann. Reg.* 68.

tried to put down the whole excitement, because it
traversed their plans and combinations. They
asked, with astonishment and with justice, what
the affair had to do with politics. The popular
feeling, however, was very strong, and it was fed
by public meetings, committee reports, etc. The
monstrous outrage deserved that a strong public
opinion should sustain the institutions of justice in
finding out and punishing the perpetrators. Some
of the officers were too lax and indifferent in the
discharge of their duties to suit the public temper.
They were masons. Hence the inference that a
man who was a mason was not fit or competent to
be entrusted with public duties. The political
connection was thus rendered logical and at least
plausible. Many persons resolved not to vote for
any one who was a mason for any public office.
Moreover, the excitement offered an unexampled
opportunity to the ambitious young orators and
politicians of the day. It was a case where pure
heat and emphasis were the only requirements of
the orator. He need not learn anything, or have
any ideas. A number of men rose to prominence
on the movement who had no claims whatever to
public influence. They of course stimulated as
much as they could the popular excitement against
masonry, which furnished them their opportunity
and their capital. Many masons withdrew from
the order. Others foolishly made light of the
outrage itself. For the most part, however, the
masons argued that masonry was no more respon-

sible, as an institution, for the outrage on Morgan than the Christian church is responsible for the wrongs done in its name by particular persons and groups.   These discussions only sharpened the issue, and masons and anti-masons came to be a division which cut across all the old party lines in the State of New York.   In 1828 the anti-masons were the old Clintonians,[1] the rump of the federalists, and many buck-tails, with whom horror at the Morgan outrage was a controlling motive.   Jackson, Clinton, and Van Buren were then allied. Jackson and Clinton were masons.   The Clintonians who would not follow Clinton to the support of Jackson, either because they disliked the man, or because he was a mason, and the buck-tails who would not vote for a mason, were Adams men. The great body of the buck-tails (amongst whom party discipline was stronger than in any other faction), the Clintonians who followed Clinton into the Jackson camp, and the masons who let defence of the order control their politics, were Jackson men.   Hence the New York vote (which was taken by districts in 1828) was divided.

The regency buck-tail democrats, being in control of the State government, tried to put down the excitement by indirect means, because of its disorganizing effects.   This made them appear to suppress inquiry, and to be indifferent to the outrage.   It only fanned the flame of popular indignation, and strengthened anti-masonry.   The

[1] Clinton died February 11, 1828.

anti-masons came out as an anti-administration
party in 1830. They held a convention at Utica
in August, and framed a platform of national
principles. This is the first "platform," as distinguished from the old-fashioned address. The
anti-masons had come together under no other
bond than opposition to masonry. If they were to
be a permanent party, and a national party, they
needed to find or make some political principles.
This was their great political weakness and the
sure cause of their decay. Their party had no
root in political convictions. It had its root elsewhere, and in very thin soil too, for a great political
organization. Since the masons were not constantly and by the life principle of their order perpetrators of outrages and murders, they could not
furnish regular fuel to keep up the indignation of
the anti-masons. The anti-masons, then, adopted
their principles as an after-thought; and for this
reason they needed an explicit statement of them
in a categorical form, i. e., a platform, far more
than this would be needed by a party which had
an historical origin, and traditions derived from
old political controversies. Anti-masonry spread
rapidly through New York and large parts of Pennsylvania and Massachusetts. Vermont became a
stronghold of it. It is by no means extinct there
now. It had considerable strength in Connecticut and Ohio. It widened into hostility to all
secret societies and extra-judicial oaths. Perhaps
it reached its acme when it could lead men like

J. Q. Adams and Joseph Story to spend days
in discussing plans for abolishing the secrecy of
the Phi Beta Kappa society of Harvard College.[1]
That action of theirs only showed to what extent
every man is carried away by the currents of
thought and interest which prevail for the time
being in the community.

The anti-masons next invented the national political convention.[2] They held one at Philadelphia,
September 11, 1830,[3] which called another, to
meet September 26, 1831, at Baltimore, to nominate candidates for President and Vice-President.
At the latter date 112 delegates met.[4] William
Wirt, of Maryland, was nominated for President,
and Amos Ellmaker, of Pennsylvania, for Vice-
President, almost unanimously. Wirt had been a
mason, and had neglected, not abandoned, the
order. In his letter of acceptance[5] he said that
he had often spoken of " masonry and anti-masonry
as a fitter subject for farce than tragedy." He
circumscribed and tamed down the whole anti-
masonic movement, and put himself on no platform

[1] 8 Adams, 383.

[2] A convention of delegates from eleven States nominated De
Witt Clinton, in 1812.   Binns (page 244) claims to have invented
the national convention, but his was a project for introducing
into the congressional caucus of the republican party special delegates from the non-republican States, so as to make that body
represent the whole party.

[3] 39 Niles, 58.

[4] 41 Niles, 83, 107.   Twelve States were represented.   W. H.
Seward and Thaddeus Stevens were in the convention.

[5] 2 Kennedy's *Wirt*, 350.

save hostility to oaths which might interfere with a man's civic duties. He put the whole Morgan case aside, except so far as, on the trial, it appeared that masonry hindered justice. The anti-masons were, in fact, aiming at political power. They had before them the names of McLean, Calhoun, and J. Q. Adams.[1] New York wanted McLean. He declined.[2] The anti-masonic convention published a long address, setting forth the history and principles of the party.[3] There was a hope, in which Wirt seems to have shared, that when the anti-masons presented a separate nomination Clay would withdraw, and the national republicans would take up Wirt.[4] When this hope had passed away, Wirt wanted to withdraw, but could not do so.[5] He had from the first desired Clay's election, and had agreed to stand, only when assured that Clay could not unite the anti-Jackson men. Clay refused to answer the interrogatories of the anti-masons. He said, "I do not know a solitary provision in the Constitution of the United States which conveys the slightest authority to the general government to interfere, one way or the other, with either masonry or anti-masonry." He said that if the President should meddle with that matter he would be a usurper and a tyrant.[6]

[1] 8 Adams, 412, 416.   [2] 41 Niles, 259.   [3] 41 Niles, 166.
[4] Judge Spencer thought that Wirt could unite the opposition, if Clay would stand back, and that Wirt could be elected over Jackson. 1 Curtis's *Webster*, 402.
[5] 2 Kennedy's *Wirt*, 356, 362, 366.
[6] 41 Niles, 260; 8 Adams, 430.

The opposition therefore went into the contest divided and discordant. The anti-masons were strong enough to produce that state of things, and of course their conduct showed that the opposition was not united on any political policy whatever. Jackson, on the contrary, had been consolidating a *party*, which had a strong consciousness of its power and its purpose, and a vigorous party will. Jackson had the credit of recovering the West India trade, settling the spoliation claims, and placing all foreign relations on a good footing. He also claimed that he had carried the administration of the government back to the Jeffersonian ideas. In general this meant that he held to the non-interference theory of government, and to the policy of leaving people to be happy in their own way. He had not yet been forced to commit himself on land and tariff, although he had favored a liberal policy about land ; but on internal improvements he had spoken clearly, and inferences were freely drawn as to what he would do on land and tariff. He had favored State rights and strict construction in all the cases which had arisen. He had discountenanced all heavy expenditures on so-called national objects, and had prosecuted as rapidly as possible the payment of the debt. Here was a strong record and a consistent one on a number of great points of policy, and that, of course, is what is needed to form a party. The record also furnished two or three good party cries. Further, the general non-interference policy strengthens any government which recurs to it; though all governments in time depart from it, because they always credit themselves with power to do better for the people than the people can do for themselves. In 1831–32 Jackson had not yet reached this stage in his career. The delicate points in his record were tariff and Bank. If he assailed the tariff, would he not lose Pennsylvania, Ohio, and Kentucky? If he favored it, would he not lose the South? This was the old division in the body of his supporters, and it seemed that he might now be ruined if that cleft were opened. Also, if he went on with the " Bank War," would he not lose Pennsylvania? His mild message on the Bank in 1831 seemed to indicate fear.

Clay declared unhesitatingly that the campaign required that the opposition should force the fighting on tariff and Bank, especially on the latter. We have seen [1] what his demeanor and demands were in the conference at Washington. For the fight out-of-doors he thought that the recharter of the Bank was the strongest issue he could make. Of course Benton's assertion [2] that the Bank attacked Jackson is a ridiculous misrepresentation. Clay did, however, seize upon the question which Jackson had raised about the Bank, and he risked that important financial institution on the fortunes of a political campaign. The Bank was very unwilling to be so used. Its disinterested friends in both parties strongly dissuaded Biddle from allow-

[1] Page 262.   [2] 1 Benton, 227.

ing the question of recharter to be brought into the campaign.[1] Clay's advisers also tried to dissuade him. The Bank, however, could not oppose the public man on whom it depended most, and the party leaders deferred at last to their chief. Jackson never was more dictatorial and obstinate than Clay was at this juncture. Clay was the champion of the system of state-craft which makes public men undertake a tutelage of the nation, and teaches them not to be content to let the nation grow by its own forces, and according to the shaping of the forces and the conditions. His system of statesmanship is one which always offers shelter to numbers of interested schemes and corrupt enterprises. The public regarded the Bank, under his political advocacy, as a part of that system of state-craft.

The national Republican convention met at Baltimore, December 12, 1831. It consisted [2] of 155 delegates from seventeen States. Abner Lacock, of Pennsylvania, who as senator had made a very strong report against Jackson on the Seminole war, was president of the convention. John Sergeant, of Pennsylvania, was nominated for Vice-President. The convention issued an address, in which the Bank question was put forward. It was declared that the President " is fully and three times over pledged to the people to negative any bill that may be passed for rechartering the Bank, and there is little doubt that the additional influence which he would acquire by a reëlection would

---

[1] Ingersoll, 208.   [2] 41 Niles, 301.

be employed to carry through Congress the extraordinary substitute which he has repeatedly proposed." The appeal, therefore, was to defeat Jackson in order to save the Bank and to prevent the device proposed by Jackson from being tried.

Such a challenge as that could have but one effect on Jackson. It called every faculty he possessed into activity to compass the destruction of the Bank. Instead of retiring from the position he had taken, the moment there was a fight to be fought, he did what he had done at New Orleans. He moved his lines up to the last point he could command on the side towards the enemy. The anti-Bank men, Kendall, Blair, and Hill, must have been delighted to see the adversary put spurs into Jackson's animosity. The proceedings seemed to prove just what the anti-Bank men had asserted: that the Bank was a great monster, which aimed to control elections, and to set up and put down Presidents. The campaign of 1832 was a struggle between the popularity of the Bank and the popularity of Jackson. His popularity in rural Pennsylvania had never had any rational basis, and hence could not be overthrown by rational deductions. His spirit and boldness in meeting the issue offered by Clay won him support. His party was not broken; it was consolidated. The opposition to him was divided, discordant, uncertain of itself, vague in its principle, and hesitating as to its programme. The Bank could never be a strong popular interest, nor the maintenance of it a positive purpose which could avail to consolidate a party. Opposition to secret societies was a whim which never could inspire a party; it could only avail to put the kind of people who take up whims in the attitude of stubborn opposition, which makes it impracticable to coöperate with them in organization.

On the 9th of January, 1832, in prosecution of the programme, the memorial of the Bank for a renewal of its charter was presented in the Senate by Dallas, and in the House by McDuffie. These men were both " Bank democrats." This name is ambiguous, unless we distinguish between *Bank* democrats and *bank* democrats, for the latter name began to be given to those who were interested in local banks and who went over to Jackson when he attacked their great rival. Sargent[1] says Biddle told him that the Bank wanted Webster, or some such unequivocal friend of the Bank, to present the memorial, but that Dallas claimed the duty as belonging to a Pennsylvanian. There was great and just dissatisfaction with Dallas for the way in which he managed the business. He intimated a doubt whether the application was not premature, and a doubt about the policy of the memorial, lest " it might be drawn into a real or imaginary conflict with some higher, some more favorite, some more immediate wish or purpose of the American people." In the Senate the petition was referred to a select committee, and in the House to the Committee on Ways and Means. The Senate

[1] 1 Sargent, 215.

committee reported favorably, March 13th, and
recommended only a few changes in the old charter. They proposed to demand a bonus of one and
a half millions in three annual instalments. In
the House, McDuffie reported February 9th.[1] He
said that the proposition to recharter had called out
a number of wild propositions. The old Bank was
too large, yet now one was proposed with a capital
of fifty millions. He criticised the notion that all
citizens should have an equal right to subscribe to
the stock of the Bank. If A has $100 on balance,
and B owes $100 on balance, their "equal right"
to subscribe to bank stock is a strange thing to
discuss.

Benton[2] says that the opponents of the Bank in
Congress agreed upon a policy. They determined
to fight the charter at every point, and to bring
the Bank into odium as much as possible. He
says that he organized a movement to this effect in
the House, incited Clayton, of Georgia, to demand
an investigation of the Bank, and furnished him
with the charges and specifications on which to
base that demand. Clayton moved for an investigation, February 23d. He presented Benton's
charges, seven important and fifteen minor ones.
McDuffie answered the charges at once, but the
investigation was ordered to be made by a special
committee. They reported, April 30th. The majority reported that the Bank ought not to be
rechartered until the debt was all paid and the

[1] Document C.   [2] 1 Benton, 236.

revenue readjusted. R. M. Johnson signed this
report, so as to make a majority, out of good-
nature. He rose in his place in Congress and said
that he had not looked at a document at Philadelphia. The minority reported that the Bank
ought to be rechartered; that it was sound and
useful. John Quincy Adams made a third report,
in which he brought his characteristic industry to
bear on the question, and discussed all the points
raised in the attack on the Bank. It is to his
report that we are indebted for a knowledge of
the correspondence of 1829 between Biddle and
Ingham, and the controversy over the Portsmouth
branch, which was the first skirmish in the "Bank
War."[1]

The charges against the Bank, and the truth
about them, so far as we can discover it, were as
follows: —

(1.) Usury. The bank sold Bank of Kentucky
notes to certain persons on long credit. When
these persons afterwards claimed an allowance for
depreciation, it was granted. A case which came to
trial went off on technicalities, which were claimed
to amount to a confession by the Bank that it had
made an unlawful contract.[2] The Bank had also
charged discount and exchange for domestic bills,
on such a basis that the two amounted to more than
six per cent, the rate to which it was restrained by

[1] Document B.
[2] *Cf.* Bank of the United States *vs.* William Owens *et al.* 2
Peters, 527.

its charter. This charge was no doubt true. The device was used by all banks to evade the usury law.

(2.) Branch drafts issued as currency. The amount of these outstanding was $7,400,000. The majority of the committee doubted the lawfulness of the branch drafts, but said nothing about the danger from them as instruments of credit. Adams said that they were useful, but likely to do mischief. These drafts were in form redeemable where issued, but in intention and practice they were redeemed hundreds of miles away, and they had no true convertibility. There was no check whatever on the inflation of the currency by them so long as credit was active. Cambreleng very pointedly asked Biddle how the branch draft arrangement differed from an obligation of a Philadelphia bank to redeem all the notes of all the banks in Pennsylvania. Biddle replied that the Bank of the United States *controlled* all the branches which issued branch drafts on it. That was, to be sure, the assumption, but he had had hard experience all winter that it was not true in fact.[1]

(3.) Sales of coin, especially American coin. The Bank had bought and sold foreign coin by weight, and had sold $84,734.44 of American gold coin. The majority held that such coins were not bullion, because Congress had fixed their value by law. Adams easily showed the fallacy of this. All

[1] See below, pages 311–12.

gold coins, then, American included, were a commodity, not money.[1]

(4.) Sales of public stocks. The Bank was forbidden by the charter to sell public stocks, the object being to prevent it from manipulating the price of the same. In 1824, in aid of a refunding scheme, the Bank took some public stocks from the government, and had special permission by act of Congress to sell them. Nevertheless, the majority disapproved of the sale.

(5.) Gifts to roads, canals, etc. The Bank had made two subscriptions of $1,500 each to the stock of turnpike companies. The other cases were all petty gifts to fire companies, etc. The majority argued that, since the administration had pronounced against internal improvements, the Bank ought not to have assisted any such works. Adams said that the administration had opposed internal improvements, on the ground that they were unconstitutional when undertaken by the federal government; but he asked what argument that furnished against such works when undertaken by anybody else.

(6.) Building houses to let or sell. The Bank had been obliged, in some cases, to take real estate for debts. When it could not sell, it had, in a few cases, improved.

These points were the alleged violations of the charter. Biddle denied the seventh charge, of *non-user*, in failing to issue notes in the South and

[1] See page 390.

West for seven years. Adams pointed out that these charges would only afford ground for a *scire facias* to go before a jury on the facts.

The charges of mismanagement, and the truth about them, so far as we can ascertain, were as follows : —

(1.) Subsidizing the press. Webb and Noah, of the "Courier and Enquirer" (administration organ until April, 1831; then in favor of the Bank), Gales and Seaton, of the "National Intelligencer" (independent opposition), Duff Green, of the "Telegraph" (administration organ until the spring of 1831), and Thomas Ritchie, of the Richmond "Enquirer" (administration), were on the books of the Bank as borrowers. The change of front by the "Courier and Enquirer" was regarded as very significant. Adams said that there was no law against subsidizing the press, and that the phrase meant nothing. He protested against the examination of the editors. The case stood so that, if the Bank discounted a note for an administration editor, it was said to bribe him ; if for an opposition editor, it was said to subsidize him.

(2.) Favoritism to Thomas Biddle, second cousin of the president of the Bank. T. Biddle was the broker of the Bank. N. Biddle admitted that the Bank had followed a usage, adopted by other banks, of allowing cash in the drawer to be loaned out to particular persons, and replaced by securities, which were passed as cash, for a few days. He said the practice had been discontinued.

Reuben M. Whitney made a very circumstantial
charge that T. Biddle had been allowed to do this,
and that he had paid no interest for the funds of
the bank of which he thus got the use.   The loans
to him were very large.   October 15, 1830, he had
$1,131,672 at five per cent.   N. Biddle proved that
he was in Washington when Whitney's statement
implied his presence in Philadelphia.   Adams said
that Whitney lied.   It was certainly true, and was
admitted, that T. Biddle had had enormous confidential transactions with the Bank, but Whitney
was placed, in respect to all the important part of
his evidence, in the position of a convicted calum-
niator.   He went to Washington, where he was
taken into the kitchen cabinet and made special
agent of the deposit banks.   In 1837 he published
an "Address to the American People," in which
he reiterated the charges against Biddle.[1]

(3.) Exporting specie, and drawing specie from
the South and West.   The minority state that the
usual current was, that silver was imported from
Mexico to New Orleans, and passed up the Mississippi and Ohio, and was exported to China from
the East.   From 1820 to 1832, $22,500,000 were
drawn from the South and West to New York.
The Bank was charged with draining the West of
specie.   So far as the current of silver was normal,
the Bank had nothing to do with it.   If there had
been no banks of issue, the West would have kept
enough specie for its use, and the current would

[1] 52 Niles, 106.

have flowed through and past, leaving always enough. The paper issues in the valley drove out the specie, and little stayed. The branch drafts, after 1827, helped to produce this result, and the charge was, in so far, just.[1] The Bank was also charged with exporting specie as a result of its exchange operations. It sold drafts on London for use in China, payable six months after sight. They were sold for the note of the buyer at one year. The goods could be imported and sold to meet the draft. This produced an inflation of credit, since one who had no capital, if he could get the bank accommodation, could extend credit indefinitely. The majority made a point on this, but they added the following contribution to financial science : " The legitimate object of banks the committee believe to be granting facilities, not loaning capital." On that theory there would have been no fault to be found with the China drafts, which must have been a great " facility " to those who could get them, and who had no other capital.

(4.) The improper increase of branches. It was true that there were too many. Cheves, in his time, thought some of them disadvantageous to the Bank; but it had been importuned to establish them, and there was complaint if a branch was lacking where the government or influential indi-

[1] Gouge says that, in 1828, there was no local bank in operation in Kentucky, Indiana, Illinois, or Missouri, and only one each in Tennessee, Mississippi, and Alabama. Gouge, 39.

viduals wanted one. To abolish one was not to be thought of at all. The whole history of the Bank proves the evil of branches, unless the canons of banking which are recognized are the soundest, and the discipline the most stringent.

(5.) Expansion of the circulation by $1,300,000 between September 1, 1831, and April 1, 1832, although the discounts had been reduced during the winter. The Bank was struggling already with the branch drafts, and the facts alleged were produced by its efforts to cope with the effects of the drafts.

(6.) Failure of the Bank to serve the nation. The majority made another extraordinary blunder here. They said that the duties were paid at New York and Philadelphia, and that drafts on these cities were always at a premium. Hence they argued that the Bank gained more the further it transferred funds for the government. The minority ridiculed this as an annihilation of space, a means of making a thing worth more the further it was from where it was wanted.

(7.) Mismanagement of the public deposits. The majority state what they think the Bank ought to do. It ought to use its capital as a permanent fund, and loan the public deposits on time, so as to be payable near the time when they would be required by the government for the debt payments. If the Bank had done this it would have carried to a maximum the disturbances in the money market which were actually produced by the semi-annual payments on the debt.   It would have inflated and contracted its discounts by an enormous sum every six months.

(8.) Postponement of the payment of the three per cents.   These stocks were issued in 1792 for the accrued interest on the Revolutionary debt. They were to be paid at par.   The Secretary informed the Bank, March 24th, just before the Bank committee was raised, that he should pay half the three per cents ($6,000,000) in July. Biddle hastened to Washington to secure a postponement; not, as he affirmed, for the sake of the Bank, but for two other reasons: (1) that $9,000,000 duty bonds would be payable July 1st, and the merchants would be put to inconvenience if the debt payment fell at that time; (2) a visitation of cholera was to be feared, which would derange industry; and the payment of the debt, with the recall of so much capital loaned to merchants, would add to the distress.   The friends of the Bank said that these reasons were good and sufficient.   Its enemies said that they were specious, but were only pretexts.   The Secretary agreed to defer the payment of $5,000,000 of the three per cents until October 1st, the Bank agreeing to pay the interest for three months.[1]   This matter will be discussed below.

(9.) Incomplete number of directors.   Biddle was both government director and elected director, so that there were only twenty-four in all.   The

[1] Document D.

government directors might be reappointed indefinitely. The elected ones rotated. Biddle was
both, so that he might always be eligible to the
Presidency.

(10.) Large expenditures for printing: $6,700
in 1830: $9,100 in 1831. From 1829, the date
of Jackson's first attack, the Bank spent money on
pamphlets and newspapers to influence public
opinion in its favor.

(11.) Large contingent expenditures. There
was a contingent fund account, the footings of
which, in 1832, were $6,000,000, to sink the losses
of the first few years, the bonus, premiums on
public stocks bought, banking house, etc., etc.
The suggestion was that this was a convenient
place in which to hide corrupt expenditures, and
that the sum was so large as to raise a suspicion
that such were included in it.

(12.) Loans to members of Congress in advance of appropriations. Adams objected to this
as an evil practice. He said afterwards that the
investigation into this point was dropped, because
it was found that a large number of congressmen
of both parties had had loans.

(13.) Refusal to give a list of stockholders resident in Connecticut, so that that State might collect taxes from them on their stock.

(14.) Usurpation of the control of the Bank by
the exchange committee of the board of directors,
to the exclusion of the other directors. This
charge was denied.

In all this tedious catalogue of charges we can find nothing but frivolous complaints and ignorant criticism successfully refuted, except when we touch the branch drafts. The majority of the committee, if all their points are taken together, thought that the Bank ought to lend the public deposits liberally, and draw them in promptly when wanted to pay the debt, yet ought to refuse no accommodation (especially to any one who was embarrassed), ought not to sell its public stocks, nor increase its circulation, nor draw in its loans, nor part with its specie, nor draw on the debtor branches in the West, nor press the debtor State banks, nor contract any temporary loans. The student of the evidence and reports of 1832, *if he believes the Bank's statements in the evidence,* will say that the Bank was triumphantly vindicated. Two facts, however, are very striking: (1) The most important of the charges against which the Bank successfully defended itself in 1832 were the very acts of which it was guilty in 1837–38, and they were what ruined it; these were the second charge, which involved Whitney's veracity, and the fourteenth charge, which the bank denied. (2) Whether the Bank was thoroughly sincere and above-board in these matters is a question on which an unpleasant doubt is thrown by the certainty that it was not thoroughly honest in some other matters.   In regard to the three per cents (under 8), it is certain that Biddle wanted to defer the payment for the sake of the Bank.   He was embarrassed already by the debt of the western branches, which had been produced by the operation of the branch drafts. Their effect was just beginning to tell seriously. There was a great movement of free capital in the form of specie to this country in 1830, on account of revolutions in Europe. In 1830 and 1831 the United States paid its stock note in the capital of the Bank. Capital was easy to borrow. In October, 1831, a certain stringency set in. The branch drafts were transferring the capital of the Bank to the western branches, and locking it up there in accommodation paper, indefinitely extended by drawing and redrawing. Biddle could not make the western branches pay. He was forced to curtail the eastern branches. At such a juncture it was impossible for him to see with equanimity the public bonds which bore only three per cent interest paid off at par, when the market rate for money was seven or eight per cent. He wanted to get possession of that capital. Even before he received notice that the three per cents were to be paid, he tried to negotiate with Ludlow, the representative of a large number of holders of the three per cents, for the purchase of the same. Ludlow had not power to sell.[1] Great consequences hung on the strait into which the branch drafts had pushed the Bank, and upon this measure of relief to which Biddle had recourse. Biddle was too plausible. In any emergency he was ready to write a letter or report, to smooth

[1] Polk's Minority Report, 1833, Document E.

things over, and present a good face in spite of facts. Any one who has carefully studied the history of the Bank, and Biddle's "statements," will come to every statement of his with a disagreeable sense of suspicion. It is by no means certain, whatever the true explanation of the contradiction may be, that Whitney told a lie in the matter in which his word and Biddle's were opposed.

Biddle's theory of bank-note issues was vicious and false. He thought that the business of a bank was to furnish a paper medium for trade and commerce. He thought that this medium served as a token and record of transactions, so that the transactions to be accomplished called out the paper, and when accomplished brought the paper back. The art of the banker consisted in a kind of legerdemain, by which he kept bolstering up one transaction by another, and swelling the total amount of them on which he won profits. There could then be no inflation of the paper, if it was only put out as demanded for real transactions. Therefore he never distinguished between bills of exchange and money, or the true paper substitute for money, which is constantly and directly interchangeable with money, so that it cannot degenerate into a negotiable instrument like notes and bills. His management of the Bank was a test of his theory on a grand scale. The branch drafts were a special test of it. It was proved that they had none of the character of convertible bank-notes or money, but were instruments of credit, and, like all instruments of credit which have cut loose from actual redemption in capital, there was no more limit to their possible inflation than to the infinity of human hopes and human desires. Only a few months after the congressional investigation, November, 1832, the president of the Nashville branch wrote to Biddle: "Be assured, sir, that we are as well convinced as you are that too many bills are offered and purchased, — amounting to more than the present crop of cotton and tobacco will pay; I mean, before all these papers are taken up." It does not appear that, in the spring of 1832, Biddle yet perceived the operation of the branch drafts, and it could not be said that sincerity required that he should avow a mistake to a hostile committee; but his letter to Clayton, appended to the report of 1832, is meretricious and dazzling, calculated to repel investigation and cover up weakness by a sensational assertion. "The whole policy of the Bank for the last six months has been exclusively protective and conservative, calculated to mitigate suffering and yet avert danger." He sketches out in broad and bold outlines the national and international relations of American industry and commerce and the financial relations of the Treasury, with the Bank enthroned over all as the financial providence of the country. This kind of writing had a great effect on the uninitiated. Who could dispute with a man who thus handled all the public and private finance of the whole country as a

school-master would tell boys how to do a sum in
long division? However, it was all humbug, and
especially that part which represented the Bank
as watching over and caring for the public. As
Gouge most justly remarked, after quoting some
of Biddle's rhetoric: "The true basis of the in-
terior trade of the United States is the fertility of
the soil and the industry of the people. The sun
would shine, the streams would flow, and the earth
would yield her increase, if the Bank of the United
States was not in existence."[1] If the Bank had
been strong, Biddle's explanations would all have
been meretricious; as it was, the Bank had been
quite fully occupied in 1831–32 in taking care of
itself, mitigating its own sufferings and averting
its own dangers.

No doubt the Bank was the chief sufferer from
the shocks inflicted on the money market by the
sudden and heavy payments on the public debt.
Long credits were given for duties. When paid
they passed into the Bank as public deposits.
They were loaned again to merchants to pay new
duties, so that one credit was piled upon another
already in this part of the arrangement. Then
the deposits were called in to meet drafts of the
Treasury to pay the debt, and so passed to the
former fund-holders. These latter next entered
the money market as investors, and the capital
passed into new employments. Therefore Benton's argument, which all the anti-Bank men caught

[1] Gouge, 56.

up, that the financial heats and chills of this period were certainly due to the malice of the Bank, is of no force at all. The disturbances were such, they necessarily lasted so long, and they finally settled down to such uncalculable final effects that all such deductions as Benton made were unwarranted. A public debt is not a blessing, but it is not as great a curse as a public surplus, and it is very possible to pay off a debt too rapidly. We shall, on two or three further occasions in this history, find the " public deposits " banging about the money market like a cannon ball loose in the hold of a ship in a high wind.

While the committee was investigating the Bank the political strife was growing more intense, and every chance of dealing dispassionately with the question of recharter had passed away. In January, Van Buren's nomination as minister to England was rejected by the Senate.[1] The Legislature of New York had passed resolutions against the recharter of the Bank.[2] This hurt Van Buren in Pennsylvania. Such was the strange combination of feelings and convictions at this time that Jackson could demolish the Bank without shaking his hold on Pennsylvania, but Van Buren was never forgiven for the action of his State against the Bank. It illustrated again the observation made above, that the popular idol enjoys an unreasonable immunity, while others may be held to an unreasonable responsibility. All Jackson's intensest

---

[1] See page 210.   [2] 2 Hammond, 351.

personal feelings, as well as the choice of the kitchen cabinet, now converged on Van Buren's nomination. The Seminole war grudge, hatred of Calhoun, the Eaton scandal, and animosity to the Senate contributed towards this end.

Parton gives us one of Lewis's letters, which shows the wire-pulling which preceded the first democratic convention. Kendall was in New Hampshire in the spring of 1831. Lewis wrote to him to propose that a convention should be held in May, 1832, to nominate Van Buren for Vice-President. He suggested that the New Hampshire Legislature should be prompted to propose it. Kendall arranged this and wrote a letter, giving an account of the meeting, resolutions, etc., which was published anonymously in the "Globe," July 6, 1831. The "Globe" took up the proposition and approved of it. The convention met at Baltimore, May 21, 1832. John H. Eaton was a delegate to the convention. He intended to vote against Van Buren, for, although Van Buren had taken Mrs. Eaton's part, he had not won Eaton's affection. Lewis wrote to Eaton that he must not vote against Van Buren "unless he was prepared to quarrel with the general." Van Buren was nominated by 260 votes out of 326. The "spontaneous unanimity" of this convention was produced by the will of Andrew Jackson and the energetic discipline of the kitchen cabinet. It may well be doubted whether, without Jackson's support, Van Buren could have got 260 votes for President or Vice-

President in the whole United States, in 1832.
The "Globe" dragooned the whole Jackson party
into the support of Van Buren, not without considerable trouble. The convention adopted an address prepared by Kendall, containing a review of
Jackson's first administration.[1]

May 7, 1832, a national republican convention
of young men met in Washington. William Cost
Johnson was president. The convention ratified
the nominations of Clay and Sergeant, and passed
a series of resolutions in favor of tariff and internal
improvements, and approving the rejection of Van
Buren's nomination as minister to England.[2]

During the spring and summer Biddle took
quarters in Washington, from which he directed
the congressional campaign on behalf of the recharter. He was then at the zenith of his power
and fame, and enjoyed real renown in Europe and
America. He and Jackson were pitted against
each other personally. Biddle, however, put a
letter in Livingston's [3] hands, stating that he would
accept any charter to which Jackson would consent.[4] Jackson never fought for compromises, and
nothing was heard of this letter. Jackson drew
up a queer plan of a "bank," which he thought
constitutional and suitable, but it remained in his

[1] Kendall's *Autobiography*, 296.   [2] 42 Niles, 206, 236.
[3] Livingston was on the side of the Bank. Hunt's *Livingston*,
253.
[4] Ingersoll, 268. On the same page it is said that Biddle was
talked of for President of the United States.

drawer.[1] The anti-Bank men affirmed that Biddle was corrupting Congress.

The charter passed the Senate June 11th, 28 to 20, and the House, July 3d, 107 to 85. It was sent to the President July 4th. The Senate voted to adjourn July 16th. It was a clever device of theirs to force Jackson to sign or veto by giving him more than ten days. They wanted to force him to a direct issue. It is not probable that there was room for his will to be any further stimulated by this kind of manœuvring, but he never flinched from a direct issue, and the only effect was to put him where he would have risked his reëlection and everything else on a defiant reply to the challenge offered. Niles says [2] that, a week before the bill passed, the best informed were " as six to half a dozen," whether the bill, if passed, would be vetoed, but that, for the two or three days before the bill was sent up, a veto was confidently expected. The veto was sent in, July 10th.[3] The reasons given for it were : (1) The Bank would have a monopoly for which the bonus was no equivalent. (2) One fifth of the stockholders were foreigners. (3) Banks were to be allowed to pay the Bank of the United States in branch drafts, which individuals could not do. (4) The States were allowed to tax the stock of the Bank owned by their citizens, which would cause the stock to go out of the country.

[1] Ingersoll, 283.   [2] 42 Niles, 337.
[3] Congress has chartered national banks as follows : 1791, 1815 (vetoed), 1816, 1832 (vetoed), 1841, two bills, both vetoed, 1863.

(5) The few stockholders here would then control
it.   (6) The charter was unconstitutional.   (7)
The business of the Bank would be exempt from
taxation.   (8) There were strong suspicions of
mismanagement in the Bank.   (9) The President
could have given a better plan.   (10) The Bank
would increase the distinction between rich and
poor.

The bill was voted upon again in the Senate July
13th, yeas 22, nays 19.   The veto therefore remained in force; and if the Bank was to continue to
exist Jackson must be defeated.   The local bank
interest, however, had now been aroused to the great
gain it would make if the Bank of the United States
should be overthrown.   The Jackson party thereby
won the adhesion of an important faction.   The
safety-fund banks of New York were bound into a
solid phalanx by their system, and they constituted
a great political power.   The chief crime alleged
against the Bank of the United States was med-
dling with politics.   The safety-fund banks of New
York were an active political power organized
under Van Buren's control, and they went into this
election animated by the hope of a share in the
deposits.   The great Bank also distributed pamphlets and subsidized newspapers, fighting for its
existence.   The Jackson men always denounced this
action of the Bank of the United States as corrupt,
and as proof of the truth of Jackson's charges.

Jackson got 219 electoral votes; Clay, 49;
Floyd, 11, from South Carolina, the nullification

ticket; Wirt, 7, from Vermont. There were two
vacancies — in Maryland. Clay carried Massachusetts, Rhode Island, Connecticut, Delaware,
and Kentucky, and five votes in Maryland. For
Vice-President Van Buren got 189. Pennsylvania
would not vote for him. She gave her 30 votes to
William Wilkins. Sergeant got 49 votes; Henry
Lee, of Massachusetts, 11, from South Carolina;
Ellmaker, 7. At this election South Carolina alone
threw her vote by her Legislature. The popular
vote was 707,217 for Jackson; 328,561 for Clay;
254,720 for Wirt. Jackson's majority, in a total
vote (excluding South Carolina) of 1,290,498, was
123,936. In Alabama there was no anti-Jackson
ticket.

CHAPTER X

GENERAL JACKSON now advanced to another
development of his political philosophy and his
political art. No government which has felt itself
strong has ever had the self-control to practise
faithfully the non-interference theory. A popular
idol at the head of a democratic republic is one
of the last political organs to do so. The belief in
himself is of course for him a natural product of
the situation, and he is quite ready to believe, as
he is constantly told, that he can make the people
happy, and can "save the country" from evil
and designing persons, namely, those who do not
join the chorus of adulation. A President of the
United States, under existing social and economic
circumstances, has no chance whatever to play the
rôle of Cæsar or Napoleon, but he may practise
the methods of personal government within the
limits of the situation. Jackson held that his
reëlection was a triumphant vindication of him in
all the points in which he had been engaged in
controversy with anybody, and a kind of charter
to him, as representative, or rather tribune, of the

people, to go on and govern on his own judgment over and against everybody, including Congress. His action about the Cherokee Indians, his attitude towards the Supreme Court, his construction of his duties under the Constitution, his vetoes of internal improvements and the Bank, his defence of Mrs. Eaton, his relations with Calhoun and Clay, his discontent with the Senate, all things, great and small, in which he had been active and interested, were held to be covered and passed upon by the voice of the people in his reëlection.[1] Adulation and success had already done much to make Jackson a dangerous man. After his reëlection, his self-confidence and self-will became tenfold greater.[2] Moreover, his intimates and confidential advisers, Kendall, Lewis, Blair, and Hill, won more confidence in themselves, and handled their

---

[1] We may test this theory in regard to one point, the Bank. The Legislature of Pennsylvania, on the 2d of February, 1832, within eight months of the election at which Jackson got three fifths of the vote of Pennsylvania, instructed the senators and representatives in Congress from that State, by a unanimous vote in the Senate, and by 77 to 7 in the House, to secure the recharter of the Bank.

[2] "The truth is, I consider the President intoxicated with power and flattery." "All the circumstances around him [when he came to office] were calculated to make him entertain an exalted opinion of himself, and a contemptuous one of others. His own natural passions contributed to this result." Duane, 133, under date October, 1833. "There is a tone of insolence and insult in his intercourse with both Houses of Congress, especially since his reëlection, which never was witnessed between the Executive and the Legislature before." 9 Adams, *Diary*, 51; December 12, 1833.

power with greater freedom and certainty. " I do not believe that the world ever saw a more perfectly unprincipled set of men than that which surrounded Jackson at Washington." [1]   It has already been shown in this history that they were perfect masters of the art of party organization, and that they had a strong hatred of the Bank; but they had no statesmanlike ideas in finance or public policy, and they governed by playing on the prejudices and vanity of Jackson.

Jackson's modes of action in his second term were those of personal government.   He proceeded avowedly, on his own initiative and responsibility, to experiment, as Napoleon did, with great public institutions and interests.   It came in his way to do some good, to check some bad tendencies and to strengthen some good ones; but the moment the historian tries to analyze these acts, and to bring them, for purposes of generalization, into relations with the stand-point or doctrine by which Jackson acted, that moment he perceives that Jackson acted from spite, pique, instinct, prejudice, or emotion, and the influence he exerted sinks to the nature of an incident or an accident.   Then, although we believe in personal liberty with responsibility, and in free institutions; although we believe that no modern free state can exist without wide popular rights; although we believe in the non-interference theory, and oppose the extension of state action to internal improvements and tariffs; although we

[1] John Tyler, in 1856.   2 Tyler's *Tylers*, 414.

recognize the dreadful evils of bad banking and fluctuating currency; and although we believe that the Union is absolutely the first political interest of the American people, yet, if we think that intelligent deliberation and disciplined reason ought to control the civil affairs of a civilized state, we must say of Jackson that he stumbled along through a magnificent career, now and then taking up a chance without really appreciating it, and leaving behind him distorted and discordant elements of good and ill, just fit to produce turmoil and disaster in the future. We have already seen, in some cases, what was the tyranny of his popularity. It crushed out reason and common sense. To the gravest arguments and remonstrances, the answer was, literally, " Hurrah for Jackson! " Is, then, that a sound state of things for any civilized state? Is that the sense of democracy? Is a democratic republic working fairly and truly by its theory in such a case? Representative institutions are degraded on the Jacksonian theory, just as they are on the divine-right theory, or on the theory of the democratic empire.

One of the most remarkable modes of personal rule employed by Jackson was the perfection and refinement given to the " organ " as an institution of democratic government. In the hands of Blair the " Globe " came to be a terrible power. Every office-holder signed his allegiance by taking the " Globe." In it both friend and foe found daily utterances from the White House à *propos* of every topic of political interest. The suggestions, innuendoes, queries, quips, and sarcasms of the " Globe " were scanned by the men who desired to recommend themselves by the zeal which antici- pates a command, and the subserviency which can even dispense with it. The editorials scarcely veiled their inspiration and authorization. The President issued a message to his party every day. He told the political news confidentially, and in advance of the mere newspapers, while deriding and denouncing his enemies, praising the adherents who pleased him, and checking, warning, or stimu- lating all, as he thought best to promote discipline and efficiency. When we say " he " did it, we speak, of course, figuratively. If it was Blair's voice, Jackson ratified it. If it was Jackson's will, Blair promulgated it. We have an instance, in a letter of Jackson to Lewis, August 9, 1832, from Tennessee : —

" With my sincere respects to Kendall & Blair, tell them the veto works well, & that the Globe revolves with all its usual splendor — That instead, as was predicted & expected by my enemies, & some of my friends, that the veto would destroy me, it has destroyed the Bank.

" I have just read the address of the nulifying mem- bers of S°. Carolina to their constituents — I hope Kendall, or Blair will criticize it well ; it is one of the most jesuistical and uncandid productions I ever read, and is easily exposed." [1]

The South Carolinians thought that the limit

[1] Ford MSS.

of proper delay and constitutional agitation had
been reached when the tariff of July, 1832, was
passed. In the year 1832 the nullifiers, for the
first time, got control of South Carolina. The
Legislature was convened, by special proclamation,
for the 22d of October, 1832, — a month earlier
than usual. An act was passed, October 25th,
ordering a convention to be held on the 19th of
November. The Legislature then adjourned until
its regular day of meeting, the fourth Monday in
November. The convention met as ordered; Governor Hamilton was president of it. It adopted
an ordinance that the acts of Congress of May 19,
1828, and July 14, 1832, were null and void in
South Carolina. These proceedings conformed to
a theory of the practice of nullification which
the South Carolina doctrinaires had wrought out;
namely, that the Legislature could not nullify, but
that a convention, being the State in some more
original capacity, and embodying the "sovereignty"
in a purer emanation, could do so. The theory
and practice of nullification was a triumph of
metaphysical politics. The South Carolinians went
through the evolutions, by which, as they had
persuaded themselves, nullification could be made
a constitutional remedy, with a solemnity which
was either edifying or ridiculous, according as one
forgot or remembered that the adverse party attached no significance to the evolutions.

The ordinance provided that no appeal from a
South Carolina court to a federal court should be

allowed in any case arising under any of the laws passed in pursuance of the ordinance; such an appeal to be a contempt of court. All officers and jurors were to take an oath to the ordinance. South Carolina would secede if the United States should attempt to enforce anything contrary to the ordinance. November 27th the Legislature met again, and passed the laws requisite to put the ordinance in operation. Goods seized by the custom-house officers might be replevied. Militia and volunteers might be called out. A thousand stand of arms were to be purchased.

A Union convention met at Columbia early in December. It declared itself ready to support the federal government. It appeared, therefore, that there would be civil war in South Carolina. The Union men were strong in Charleston and in the Western counties.

Jackson immediately took up the defiance which South Carolina had offered to the federal government. He ordered General Scott to Charleston, and caused troops to collect within convenient distance, although not so as to provoke a collision. He ordered two war vessels to Charleston. He issued, December 10th, a proclamation to the people of South Carolina. It was written by Livingston, who, as we have seen,[1] had taken up a position against nullification more than two years before. He represented the only tariff State in the South, — Louisiana. It has been asserted that

[1] See page 253.

Jackson did not like the constitutional doctrines of the proclamation, which are Madisonian federalist, and not such as he had held, but that he let the paper pass on account of the lack of time to modify it.[1] There is nothing of the Jacksonian temper in the document. It is strong, moderate, eloquent, and, at last, even pathetic.[2] It is very long. The following passage is perhaps the most important in it: "I consider the power to annul a law of the United States, assumed by one State, incompatible with the existence of the Union, contradicted expressly by the letter of the Constitution, unauthorized by its spirit, inconsistent with every principle on which it was founded, and destructive of the great object for which it was formed." This proclamation voiced the opinion and feeling of the whole country, except the nullifiers in South Carolina and a few of their comrades in other Southern States. The dignified tone of the paper was especially satisfactory. It was the right tone to take to men who had allowed their passionate temper to commit them to unworthy and boyish proceedings, and who had sought a remedy for civil grievances in acts which made liberty and security impossible. Jackson found himself a national civil hero for once, and he enjoyed the

[1] Lewis in 3 Parton, 466; Tyler's *Taney*, 188. Taney recorded, in 1861, that he should have objected to some of the doctrines of the proclamation, if he had been in Washington at the time. *Ibid*.

[2] Jackson contributed a suggestion of the pathos. Hunt's *Livingston*, 373.

plaudits of those persons who had detested him
the most earnestly. He lives in popular memory
and tradition chiefly as the man who put down
this treason. But the historian must remember
that, if Jackson had done his duty in regard to
Georgia and the Indians, nullification would never
have attained any strength. The Southerners were
astonished at the proclamation. It seemed to them
inconsistent, even treacherous.[1] The constitutional
theories were not at all such as Jackson had been
understood to hold. They ascribed Jackson's attitude on this question to hatred of Calhoun. Old
John Randolph, who was in a dying condition,
roused himself as the champion of State rights,
although he had been a strong adherent of Jackson,
and went through the counties of Virginia, in which
he had once been a power, in his carriage, to try
to arouse the people to resist the dangerous doctrines of the proclamation,[2] and yet to uphold
the Union. This southern dissatisfaction alarmed
Jackson's managers. Lewis wrote to Ritchie of
Richmond, Sept. 17, 1833 : —

"I am very much in hopes he [Blair] will be able to
convince you [Ritchie], and other southern friends, that
the character of the proclamation has been greatly misunderstood, as well as the views of the President with
regard to it." [3]

[1] Hodgson, 173. *Cf.* Resolution of the South Carolina Legislature, 43 Niles, 300.   Duff Green's *Pol. Reg.* vol. 2, *passim.*
[2] 2 Garland's *Randolph,* 360.
[3] Copy in Ford MSS.

December 20th, Governor Hayne of South Carolina issued a proclamation in answer to Jackson's. Calhoun resigned the vice-presidency, December 28th. He was elected senator in Hayne's place. He had been Vice-President for eight years. He now returned to the floor and to active work. He never afterwards took position in any party. He was an isolated man, who formed alliances to further his ends. South Carolina also remained an isolated State until 1840, when she voted for Van Buren and came back into the ranks. Calhoun seemed to have lost the talent for practical statesmanship which he had shown in his earlier years. He involved himself tighter and tighter in spinnings of political mysticism and fantastic speculation. Harriet Martineau calls him a cast-iron man, and describes his eager, absorbed, over-speculative type of conversation and bearing, even in society.[1] "I know of no man who lives in such utter intellectual solitude. He meets men and harangues them by the fireside as in the Senate. He is wrought like a piece of machinery, set going vehemently by a weight, and stops while you answer. He either passes by what you say, or twists it into suitability with what is in his head, and begins to lecture again." He "is as full as ever of his nullification doctrines [1836], and those who know the force that is in him, and his utter incapacity of modification by other minds, . . . will no more expect repose and self-retention from him than

[1] 1 Martineau, *Western Travel*, 148.

from a volcano in full force. Relaxation is no longer in the power of his will. I never saw any one who so completely gave me the idea of possession."

In his message of 1832, Jackson said that the protective system must ultimately be limited to the commodities needed in war. Beyond this limit that system had already produced discontent. He suggested that the subject should be reviewed in a disposition to dispose of it justly. December 13th the Senate called on the Secretary of the Treasury to propose a tariff bill. December 27th, in the House, the Committee on Ways and Means reported a bill based on the Secretary's views. It proposed an immediate and sweeping reduction, with a further reduction, after 1834, to a "horizontal" rate of fifteen per cent or twenty per cent. January 16, 1833, Jackson sent in a message, in which he informed Congress of the proceedings of South Carolina, and asked for power to remove the custom house and to hold goods for customs by military force; also for provisions that federal courts should have exclusive jurisdiction of revenue cases, and that the Circuit Court of the United States might remove revenue cases from State courts. Calhoun, in reply to this message, declared that South Carolina was not hostile to the Union, and he made one unanswerable point against Jackson's position. Jackson had referred to the Supreme Court as the proper authority to decide the constitutionality of the tariff. The nullifiers had always wished to get the tariff before the Supreme Court, but there was no way to do so. The first tariff of 1789 was preceded by a preamble, in which the protection of domestic manufactures was specified as one of the purposes of the act; but this form had not been continued. The anti-tariff men tried to have such a preamble prefixed to the tariff act of 1828, but the tariff majority voted it down. Congress had unquestioned power to lay taxes. How could it be ascertained what the purpose of the majority in Congress was, when they voted for a certain tax law? How could the constitutionality of a law be tried, when it turned on the question of this purpose, which, in the nature of the case, was mixed and unavowed?[1] It was not, therefore, fair to represent the nullifiers as neglecting an obvious and adequate legal remedy. A grand debate on constitutional theories arose out of Calhoun's criticism of Jackson's message and proclamation. Calhoun, Grundy, and Clayton each offered a set of resolutions,[2] and a flood of metaphysical dogmatizing about constitutional law was let loose. As it began nowhere, it ended nowhere. In these disputes, the disputants always carefully lay down, in their resolutions about "the great underlying principles of the Constitution," those premises which will sustain the deductions which

[1] The principle is covered fully by the decision in Loan Association vs. Topeka, 20 Wallace, 655; but the practical difficulty probably remains.

[2] 43 Niles, Supp. 222. The debate is there given.

they want to arrive at for the support of their interests. In the mean time the merits of the particular question are untouched. To inform one's self on the merits of the question would require patient labor. To dogmatize on "great principles" and settle the question by an inference is easy. Consequently, the latter method will not soon be abandoned.

On the 21st of January, 1833, a bill for enforcing the collection of the revenue was reported to the Senate. It gave the powers and made the provisions which Jackson had asked for. On the next day Calhoun introduced his resolutions : that the States are united "as parties to a constitutional compact;" that the acts of the general government, outside of the defined powers given to it, are void ; that each State may judge when the compact is broken ; that the theory that the people of the United States "are now or ever have been united on the principle of the social compact, and as such are now formed into one nation or people," is erroneous, false in history and reason. It would only be tedious to cite the other resolutions offered. Webster was good enough lawyer to get tired of the metaphysics very soon. Hodgson says that he withdrew, defeated by Calhoun.[1] The appearance of the "social compact" as an understood and accepted element of political philosophy is worth noting.

The State Legislatures also passed resolutions.

[1] Hodgson, 174.

Massachusetts, Connecticut, Delaware, New York, Missouri, Tennessee, and Indiana pronounced against nullification; North Carolina and Alabama against nullification and tariff; Georgia against the tariff, also that nullification is unconstitutional, and that a convention of the Gulf States should be held; New Hampshire, that the tariff should be reduced; Massachusetts, Rhode Island, Vermont, New Jersey, and Pennsylvania, that the tariff ought not to be reduced. Virginia offered to mediate between the United States and South Carolina.[1]

The House was at work on the tariff during January. February 12th, Clay introduced the compromise tariff in the Senate, to supersede all other propositions and be a final solution of all pending troubles. Of all the duties which were over twenty per cent, by the act of July 14, 1832, one tenth of the excess over twenty per cent was to be struck off after September 30, 1835, and one tenth each alternate year thereafter until 1841. Then one half the remaining excess was to be taken off, and in 1842 the tax would be reduced to twenty per cent as a horizontal rate, with a large free list, home valuation, and no credit. Credit for duties worked very mischievously. An importer sold his goods before he paid his duties. The price he obtained contained the duties which he had not yet paid. Hence he was able to get capital from the public with which to carry on his

1 8 *Ann. Reg.* 48.

business. In the end perhaps he became bankrupt, and did not pay the duties at all. In 1831 a report from the Treasury stated the duty bonds in suit at $6,800,000, of which only $1,000,000 was estimated to be collectible. Clay's compromise, as first drawn, had a preamble, in which it was stated that, after March 3, 1840, all duties should be equal, " and solely for the purpose and with the intent of providing such revenue as may be necessary to an economical expenditure by the government, without regard to the protection or encouragement of any branch of domestic industry whatever." [1]

Webster objected to the horizontal rate, and to an attempt to pledge future Congresses. He was now reduced, after having previously made some of the most masterly arguments ever made for free trade, to defend protection by such devices as he could. Now he derided Adam Smith and the other economists.[2] He first paltered with his convictions on the tariff, and broke his moral stamina by so doing. Many of the people who have been so much astonished at his "sudden" apostasy on slavery would understand it more easily, if their own judgment was more open to appreciate his earlier apostasy on free trade. February 13th, he introduced resolutions against the compromise.[3]

The enforcing act passed the Senate, February 20, 1833, by 32 to 8. On the 21st the compromise

[1] 1 Curtis's *Webster*, 434, 455.
[2] 1 Webster's *Correspondence*, 501.   [3] 43 Niles, 406.

tariff was taken up in the Senate. On the 25th the House recommitted the tariff bill which was there pending, with instructions to the committee to report the compromise bill. On the 26th the latter was passed, 119 to 85. On the same day the Senate laid Clay's bill on the table, took up the same bill in the copy sent up from the House, and passed it, 29 to 16. On the 27th the House passed the enforcing bill, 111 to 40. Thus the olive branch and the rod were bound up together.

There was one moment, in January, when ex-Governor Hamilton seemed ready to precipitate a conflict, and when Governor Hayne seemed ready to support him ;[1] but the leading nullifiers determined to wait until Congress adjourned. February 1st was the day appointed for nullification to go into effect, but all action was postponed. The Legislature replied to Jackson's proclamation by a series of resolutions which charged him with usurpation and tyranny.[2] Jackson was annoyed by these resolutions, and made threats against the leading nullifiers in January. The Governor had summoned the convention to meet again on March 11th. The compromise tariff was regarded as a substantial victory for the South. It became a law on March 3d, the day on which the tariff of July 14, 1832, went into effect. The re-assembled convention repealed the ordinance of nullification, passed another ordinance nullifying the enforcement act, and adjourned. It is not quite clear

[1] 8 *Ann. Reg.* 290.   [2] 43 Niles, 300.

whether the last act was a bit of fireworks to cele-
brate the conclusion of the trouble, or was seriously
meant. If it was serious, it strongly illustrated
the defective sense of humor which characterized
all the proceedings of the nullifiers. The gentlemen who had nullified a tax, and then nullified a
contingent declaration of war, would probably, in
the next stage, have tried, by ordinance, to nullify
a battle and a defeat. Adams quoted a remark of
Mangum, in 1833, that "the course of the southern
politicians for the last six or eight years had been
one of very great and mischievous errors. This is
now admitted by almost all of them." [1] They
threw away the grandest chance any men have ever
had to serve their country.

The compromise tariff settled nothing. The fact
was that Clay had been driven, by the rapacity of
the protected interests, to a point from which he
could neither advance nor recede, and Calhoun had
been driven by the nullification enterprise into a
similar untenable position. Benton says that Calhoun was afraid of Jackson, who had threatened to
hang the nullifiers. Curtis, on the authority of
Crittenden, says that Calhoun, in alarm, sought an
interview with Clay, and that Clay intervened.[2]
It is claimed that John Tyler brought them together.[3] They met and patched up the compromise, by which they opened an escape for each
other. For ten years afterwards they wrangled,

[1] 9 Adams, 58.   [2] 1 Curtis's *Webster*, 444.
[3] 1 Tyler's *Tylers*, 458.

in the Senate, over the question who had been in the worse predicament, and who won most, in 1833. Clay claimed that he rescued protection from the slaughter which awaited it in Verplanck's bill. Calhoun claimed that the compromise tariff was a free-trade victory, won by nullification. Clay said that he made the compromise out of pity for Calhoun and South Carolina, who were in peril. Calhoun said that nullification killed the tariff, and that Clay was flat on his back until Calhoun helped him to rise and escape by the compromise. The protected interests were as angry with Clay as if he had never served them. They accused him of treachery. He never gained anything by his devotion to protection. He was right at least in saying that protection would have been overthrown in 1833 if it had not been for the compromise tariff.[1]

Jackson's animosity towards the Bank, in the autumn of 1832, had gathered the intensity and bull-dog ferocity which he always felt for an enemy engaged in active resistance. In the matter of the three per cents, the Bank gave him a chance of attack. In July, General Cadwallader was sent to Europe to try to negotiate with the holders of the three per cents for an extension of the loan for a year beyond October, the Bank becoming the debtor, and paying, if necessary, four per cent on the extension. The Bank, then, instead of

[1] See a speech by Clayton on Hugh L. White's action, October 5, 1842; 63 Niles, 106. Parton, III. 478, has the same story.

paying the debt for the government, desired to intrude itself into the position of the Treasury, and extend a loan which the Treasury wanted to pay. Its object of course was to get a loan at three (or four) per cent. This proceeding was obviously open to grave censure. The obligation of the Treasury would not cease, although the Bank would have taken the public money appropriated to the payment of the debt. Five million dollars were in fact transferred, in October, on the books of the Bank, to the Redemption of the Public Debt Account. It seems to be indisputable that the Bank, in this matter, abused its relation to the Treasury as depository of the public funds. August 22d General Cadwallader made an arrangement with the Barings, by which they were to pay off all the holders of the stocks who were not willing to extend them and take the Bank as debtor. The Barings bought $1,798,597, and extended $2,376,481. The arrangement with the Barings was to be secret, but it was published in a New York paper, October 11th. October 15th, Biddle repudiated the contract, because under it the Bank would become a purchaser of public stocks, contrary to the charter. Would he have repudiated the contract if it had not been published?

The message of 1832 was temperate in tone, but very severe against the Bank. The President interpreted the eagerness of the Bank to get possession of the three per cents as a sign of weakness, and he urged Congress to make a " serious investigation " to see whether the public deposits were safe. An agent, Henry Toland, was appointed to investigate on behalf of the Treasury. He reported favorably to the Bank. The Committee on Ways and Means also investigated the Bank. The President's message created considerable alarm for a time, and, at some places, there were signs of a run on the branches.[1] February 13, 1833, Polk reported a bill to sell the stock owned by the nation in the Bank. It was rejected, 102 to 91. The majority of the Committee on Ways and Means reported (Verplanck's report) that the Bank was sound and that the deposits were safe. On January 1, 1833, the assets were $80,800,000, the liabilities $37,800,000 ; leaving $43,000,000 to pay $35,000,000 of capital. The circulation was $17,500,000 ; specie $9,000,000. The local banks were estimated to have $68,000,000 circulation and $10,000,000 or $11,000,000 specie. The minority report (Polk's) doubted if the assets were all good, and hence doubted the solvency of the Bank. It referred to the western debts, and gave, in a supplemental report, evidence of the character of these debts. The committee investigated the proceedings of the Bank in relation to the three per cents. The minority reported that they could not find out clearly what was the final arrangement made by the Bank, but it appeared that the certificates had been surrendered, and that the Bank had, by and through the former transaction, obtained

[1] 43 Niles, 315.

a loan in Europe. The majority said that the Bank had receded from the project, and that there was nothing more to say about it.[1]

October 4, 1832, Biddle informed the directors that the Bank was strong enough to relax the orders, which had been given to the western branches in the previous winter, to contract their loans and remit eastward. He then supposed that the arrangement with the Barings about the three per cents had been concluded. The western affairs, however, were at this time approaching a crisis. The supplementary report (Polk's) by the minority of the Committee on Ways and Means, March 2, 1833,[2] contains conclusive evidence that the western branches were in a very critical condition; that there had been drawing and redrawing between the branches, and that Biddle knew it. The directors had testified to the committee that they knew nothing of any such proceedings. Some of the most important points in evidence are as follows: September 11, 1832, the cashier of the branch at Lexington, Kentucky, wrote that he was enduring a run. Two hundred and seventy-five thousand dollars were sent to him from Philadelphia, Louisville, St. Louis, New Orleans, and Natchez. A letter from Biddle to the president of the Nashville branch, dated November 20, 1832, shows plainly that he knew that redrawing was going on. In a letter from the president of the Nashville branch, November 22d, the following passage

[1] Document E.   [2] Ibid.

occurs : " We will not be able to get the debts due
this office paid; indeed, if any, it will be a small
part ; the means are not in the country." The
same branch officer, in a letter of November 24th,
plainly states that he had been forced to collect
drafts drawn on him by the parent bank, and the
New York, Baltimore, Washington, Richmond,
Pittsburgh, Cincinnati, Louisville, and Lexington
branches, and that he could not prevent a protest
save by redrawing on New Orleans. Again, November 26th, he states that he had, within a year,
collected drafts for a million dollars for the bank
and branches, " which, with small exceptions, have
been paid through our bill operations." The majority of the committee of 1832–33 had interpreted
the fluctuations in the amount of bills at Nashville
as proof that, when the crops came in, the debts
were cancelled. The minority show that these fluctuations were due to the presence of the " racers "
at one or the other end of the course. It is quite
beyond question that a mass of accommodation
bills were chasing each other from branch to branch
in the years 1832–33, and that they formed a mass
of debt, which the Bank could not, for the time,
control.

March 2, 1833, the House adopted, 109 to 46, a
resolution that the deposits might safely be continued in the Bank. The reports of the committee
had not been carefully considered by anybody.
The Bank question was now a party question, and
men voted on it according to party, not according

to evidence. Whatever force might be attributed
to any of the facts brought out by Polk in the
minority report, it does not appear that anybody in
Congress really thought that the Bank was insolvent
and the deposits in danger. His supplemental report bears date March 2d, that is to say, the day
on which the House acted. Polk did not propose
to withdraw the deposits. He wanted to avoid any
positive action. McDuffie objected to this policy
that, if Congress took no action, Jackson would
remove the deposits on the principle that silence
gives consent.[1]

The first instalment of the payment by France
was due February 2, 1833.[2] The Secretary of the
Treasury did not draw until February 7th. Then
he drew a sight draft, which he sold to the Bank for
$961,240.30. Congress, March 2d, passed an act
ordering the Secretary to loan this sum at interest.
The treaty of July 4, 1831, was unpopular in
France, and the French Chambers had not passed
any appropriation to meet the payments provided
for in it. The draft was therefore protested, and
was taken up by Hottinguer for the Bank, because
it bore the indorsement of the Bank. The Bank
had put the money to the credit of the Treasury,
and it claimed to prove, by quoting the account,
that the funds had been drawn. Hence it declared
that it was out of funds for twice the amount of
the bill. It demanded fifteen per cent damages
under an old law of Maryland, which was the law

[1] 44 Niles, 108.   [2] See p. 217.

of the District of Columbia. The Treasury paid the amount of the bill, and offered to pay the actual loss incurred. July 8, 1834, Biddle informed the Secretary of the Treasury that the sum of $170,041 would be retained out of a three and a half per cent dividend, payable July 17th, on the stock owned by the United States. March 2, 1838, the United States brought suit against the Bank, in the federal Circuit Court of Pennsylvania, for the amount so withheld. It got judgment for $251,243.54. The Bank appealed to the Supreme Court, which, in 1844, reversed the judgment, finding that the Bank was the true holder of the bill and entitled to damages.[1] On a new trial the Circuit Court gave judgment for the Bank. The United States then appealed on the ground that a bill drawn by a government on a government was not subject to the law merchant.[2] The Supreme Court sustained this view, in 1847, and again reversed the decision of the Circuit Court.[3] No further action was taken.

In the spring of 1833, McLane was transferred from the Treasury to the State Department. He was opposed to the removal of the deposits by executive act, which was now beginning to be urged in the inmost administration circles. William J. Duane, of Pennsylvania, was appointed Secretary of the Treasury. This appointment was Jackson's

[1] 2 Howard, 711.
[2] Suppose that France had drawn on the United States for the sum due in 1787.   [3] 5 Howard, 382.

own personal act. He had admired Duane's father, the editor of the "Aurora," and he declared that the son was a chip of the old block. In this he was mistaken. Duane was a very different man from his father.[1] He was a lawyer of very good standing. He had never been a politician or office-holder, but had shunned that career. Lewis says that he does not know who first proposed the removal of the deposits, but that it began to be talked of in the inner administration circles soon after Jackson's second election. In the cabinet McLane and Cass were so earnestly opposed to the project that it was feared they would resign. McLane sent for Kendall to know why it was desired to execute such a project. This was before McLane left the Treasury. Kendall endeavored to persuade him. Cass finally said that he did not understand the question. Woodbury was neutral. Barry assented to the act, but brought no force to support it. Taney strongly supported the project. He was an old federalist, who had come into Jackson's party in 1824, on account of Jackson's letters to Monroe about non-partisan appointments.[2] He was Jackson's most trusted adviser in 1833: so his biographer says, and it seems to be true. Van Buren warmly opposed the removal at first. Kendall persuaded him. He seems to have faltered

[1] Parton obtained from William B. Lewis an inside account of the removal of the deposits. Duane wrote a full account of it, and there is another account in Kendall's *Autobiography*, but it is by the editor, and only at second hand from Kendall.

[2] Tyler's *Taney*, 158.

afterwards, but Kendall held him up to the point.[1] Benton warmly approved of the removal, but was not active in bringing it about. Lewis opposed it.

The proceeding is traced, by all the evidence, to Kendall and Blair as the moving spirits,[2] with Reuben M. Whitney as a coadjutor. These men had no public official responsibility. They certainly were not recognized by the nation as the men who ought to have a controlling influence on public affairs. They were animated by prejudice and rancor sixteen years old. Andrew Jackson's power and popularity, moving now under the impulse of the passions which animate an Indian on the war-path, were the engine with which these men battered down a great financial institution. The Bank had been guilty of great financial errors, but they were not by any means beyond remedy. The Bank of England, at the same period, was guilty of great financial errors. Blair and Kendall were not working for sound finance. Blair's doctrine was that the Bank would use the public deposits as a means of corrupting the political institutions of the country. If that were true, it proved the error of having a great surplus of public money in the Treasury, i. e., in the Bank. He said that the Bank would corrupt Congress.[3] In August Duane wrote: "It is true that there is an irresponsible cabal that has more power than the

---

[1] Kendall's *Autobiography*, 383.
[2] Kendall's *Autobiography*, 375.   [3] Lewis in 3 Parton, 503.

people are aware of." "What I object to is that
there is an under-current, a sly, whispering, slan-
dering system pursued."[1] In his history of the
matter, written five years later, he says: "I had
heard rumors of the existence of an influence at
Washington, unknown to the Constitution and to
the country; and the conviction that they were
well founded now became irresistible. I knew
that four of the six members of the last cabinet,
and that four of the six members of the present
cabinet, opposed a removal of the deposits, and
yet their exertions were nullified by individuals,
whose intercourse with the President was clandes-
tine. During his absence [in New England]
several of those individuals called on me, and
made many of the identical observations, in the
identical language used by himself. They represented Congress as corruptible, and the new
members as in need of special guidance. . . . In
short, I felt satisfied from all that I saw and
heard, that factious and selfish views alone guided
those who had influence with the Executive, and
that the true welfare and honor of the country
constituted no part of their objects."[2] Lewis gives
a report of a conversation with Jackson, in which
he (Lewis) tried to persuade Jackson to desist
from the project. Jackson's points were, "I have
no confidence in Congress." "If the Bank is permitted to have the public money, there is no power
that can prevent it from obtaining a charter; it

will have it, if it has to buy up all Congress, and
the public funds would enable it to do so!"   "If
we leave the means of corruption in its hands,
the presidential veto will avail nothing." [1]   The
statements in Kendall's "Autobiography" are in
perfect accord with these.   It is perfectly plain
who was at the bottom of this project, what their
motives were, how they set to work, how they gave
a bias to Jackson's mind, and furnished him with
arguments and phrases.   It is also worthy of the
most careful attention that they and Jackson were
now busy "saving the country," holding in check
the constitutional organs of the country, above all
Congress; and that they were proceeding upon assumptions about the motives and purposes of the
Bank which were not true and had not even been
tested, and upon assumptions in regard to the
character of Congress which were insulting to the
nation.   The Jeffersonian non-interference theories
were now all left far behind.   Jacksonian democracy was approaching already the Napoleonic type
of the democratic empire, in which "the elect of
the nation" is charged to protect the state against
everybody, chiefly, however, against any constitutional organs.

On the first day of Duane's official life, June 1,
1833, Whitney called on him, obviously in a certain ambassadorial capacity, and made known to
him the project to remove the deposits from the
Bank, and to use local banks as depositories and

[1] Lewis in 3 Parton, 505 *et seq.*

fiscal agents. A few days later Jackson started
on a progress through New England. The recent
overthrow of nullification had rendered him very
popular.[1] No one knew of any new trouble brew-
ing, and there was a general outburst of enthusiasm and satisfaction that a great cause of political
discord had been removed, and that peace and
quiet might be enjoyed. Jackson was fêted en-
thusiastically and generally. Harvard College
made him a Doctor of Laws. Adams said that it
was " a sycophantic compliment." "As myself
an affectionate child of our Alma Mater, I would
not be present to witness her disgrace in conferring
her highest literary honors upon a barbarian, who
could not write a sentence of grammar and hardly
could spell his own name." [2] Jackson was very ill
at this time.[3] Adams wrote a spiteful page in the
" Diary," alleging that " four fifths of his sickness
is trickery, and the other fifth mere fatigue." " He
is so ravenous of notoriety that he craves the sympathy for sickness as a portion of his glory." [4]
The low personal injustice which is born of party
hatred is here strikingly illustrated.

Duane did not accept the *rôle* for which he had
been selected. He objected to the removal of the
deposits. Jackson sent to him from Boston a long
argument, written by Kendall, to try to persuade
him. Jackson returned early in July. The question of the removal was then debated between him

[1] Quincy's *Figures*, 354.   [2] 8 Adams, 546.
[3] Quincy's *Figures*, 368 *et seq.*   [4] 4 Adams, 5.

and Duane very seriously, Duane standing his ground. It is evident that Taney was then asked to take the Treasury in case Duane should continue recalcitrant. Jackson left Washington on an excursion to the Rip Raps without having come to an arrangement with Duane.[1]

In July rumors became current that the President intended to remove the deposits.[2] August 5, 1833, while Jackson was absent, Taney wrote to him, encouraging him to prosecute the project of removal, and thoroughly approving of it. It is a sycophantic letter.[3] In August, Kendall went on a tour through the Middle and Eastern States to negotiate with the local banks, so as to find out whether they would undertake the fiscal duties. His first project seems to have been based on the New York Safety Fund system. He got no encouragement for this.[4] To more general inquiries as to a willingness to enter into some arrangement he got a number of favorable replies.[5] Commenting on these replies, Duane says : " It was into this chaos that I was asked to plunge the fiscal concerns of the country at a moment when they were

[1] In May, 1833, Jackson laid the corner-stone of a monument to Washington's mother. On his way to the site of the monument, while the steamboat was at Alexandria, Lieutenant Randolph, who had been dismissed from the navy because he could not make his accounts good, committed an assault on the President, and attempted to pull his nose. Considerable political heat was excited by the extra legal measures taken to punish Randolph for his outrage. 44 Niles, 170.

[2] 44 Niles, 353.   [3] Tyler's *Taney*, 195.
[4] Document F, page 10.   [5] Document F.

conducted by the legitimate agent with the utmost
simplicity, safety, and despatch." [1]

Rives published a story, in 1856, in the " Globe,"
to the effect that, while Jackson was at the Rip
Raps, where Blair was with him, a letter was received from Kendall saying that he had had such
ill success that the project of removing the deposits
must be given up. Jackson declared that the
Bank was broken. Blair tried to soothe him, saying that it was politically dangerous, but not
broken. Jackson insisted. He now had formed
an opinion of his own. Better than anybody else
he had seen through Biddle's plausible and sophis-
tical reasons for desiring to postpone the payment of the three per cents, and he had adopted a
conviction that the Bank was financially weak.
He reasoned that Biddle was proud and brave, and
that he never would have come to Washington to
beg Jackson to defer the payment, if the Bank had
not been so weak that he was forced to it. Rives
added that Kendall, when asked, denied that he
ever wrote any letter despairing of the removal.[2]

On Jackson's return he took up the business at
once. Of course Kendall's negotiations could not
be kept secret. Niles's " Register " for September
7, 1833, contains a long list of extracts from different newspapers presenting different speculations as
to the probability of the removal of the deposits.
The money market was, of course, immediately
affected. The Bank had ordered its branches to

[1] Duane, 96.   [2] Hudson's *Journalism*, 250.

buy no drafts having over ninety days to run.
This was too short a time for " racers," considering
the difficulty of communication. The western
debts had now been considerably curtailed by the
strenuous efforts which had been made during the
year. In the cabinet, Duane was still resisting.
The sixteenth section of the Bank charter gave to
the Secretary of the Treasury, by specific desig-
nation, the power to remove the deposits.

By the acts of July 2, 1789, and May 10, 1800,
the Secretary of the Treasury reports to the House
of Representatives. John Adams objected to the
position thus created for the Secretary of the Treasury.[1] At other times also it has caused complaint.[2] His position certainly was anomalous.
His powers and responsibilities were in no consistent relation to each other. He was independent
of the President in his functions, yet might be
removed by him. He reported to Congress what
he had done, yet could not be removed by Congress
except by impeachment. Jackson now advanced
another step in his imperial theory. He said to
Duane : I take the responsibility ; and he extended
his responsibility over Duane on the theory that
the Secretary was a subordinate, bound only to
obey orders. What then was the sense of providing in the charter that the Secretary might use

[1] 1 Gibbs, 569. 8 J. Adams's *Life and Works*, 555.
[2] 4 Adams, 501. See a history of the Treasury Department in
a report of the Committee on Ways and Means, March 4, 1834.
46 Niles, 39.

a certain discretion, and that he should state to
Congress his reasons for any use he made of it?
Jackson's responsibility was only a figure of speech;
he was elected for a set term, and could not and
would not stand again. As Congress stood there
was no danger of impeachment. His position,
therefore, was simply that he was determined to
do what he thought best to do, because there was
no power at hand to stop him.

On the 18th of September the President read,
in the meeting of his cabinet, a paper prepared by
Taney,[1] in which he argued that the deposits ought
to be removed. The grounds were, the three per
cents, the French bill, the political activity of the
Bank, and its unconstitutionality. He said that
he would not dictate to the Secretary, but he took
all the responsibility of deciding that, after October 1st, no more public money should be deposited
in the Bank, and that the current drafts should be
allowed to withdraw all money then in it. Duane
refused to give the order and refused to resign.
He was dismissed, September 23d. Taney was
transferred to the Treasury. He gave the order.
Taney told Kendall that he was not a politician,
and that, in taking a political office, he sacrificed
his ambition, which was to be a judge of the
Supreme Court.[2]

Duane at once published the final correspondence between the President and himself, in which
he gave fifteen reasons why the deposits ought not

[1] Tyler's *Taney*, 204.   [2] Kendall's *Autobiography*, 186.

to be removed.[1] One of them was, "I believe
that the efforts made in various quarters to hasten
the removal of the deposits did not originate with
patriots or statesmen, but in schemes to promote
factious and selfish purposes." The administration press immediately turned upon Duane with
fierce abuse.[2]

The removal of the deposits was a violent and
unnecessary step, even from Jackson's stand-point,
as Lewis tried to persuade him.[3] The Bank had
no chance of a recharter, unless one is prepared to
believe that it could and would buy enough congressmen to get a two-thirds majority. If it had
been willing to do that, it had enough money of its
own for the purpose, even after the deposits were
withdrawn. The removal caused a great commotion, — even a panic.[4] Bank stock fell one and
one half per cent at New York, but it recovered
when the paper read in the cabinet was received,
because the grounds were only the old charges.
The public confidence in the Bank had not been
shaken by the charges, investigations, and reports.
The Bank replied to the President's paper by a
long manifesto, in which it pursued him point by
point.[5] No doubt Biddle wrote this paper. In

[1] 45 Niles, 236.

[2] In a letter dated June 7, 1837, Duane complained that he
found himself completely "ostracized, disowned, outlawed on all
sides." "My position is a warning to all persons to adhere to
party, right or wrong." New York Times, May 13, 1894.

[3] Lewis in 3 Parton, 506.   [4] 45 Niles, 65.

[5] 45 Niles, 248.

order to defend the Bank in the matter of the three per cents, he resorted to the tactics noticed before. He said that there was heavy indebtedness to Europe in 1832, on account of the importations of 1831. He wanted to prevent an exportation of specie and give the country leisure to pay that debt. He said that the Bank was at ease, and would have kept quiet if it had considered only its own interests. Nothing less than the movements which involve continents and cover years would do for him to explain his policy. No motive less than universal benevolence would suffice to account for the action of the Bank. These pretences were, as similar ones almost always are, not true.

The average monthly balance in the Bank, to the credit of the Treasury, from 1818 to 1833, was $6,700,000. In 1832 it was $11,300,000. In 1833 it was $8,500,000. In September, 1833, it was $9,100,000.[1] Kendall reported to a cabinet meeting the results of his negotiations with the banks. One bank was objected to " on political grounds." [2] Twenty-three were selected before the end of the year. The chance for favoritism was speedily perceived. The first intention was to use the Bank of the Metropolis, Washington, as the head of the system of deposit banks, although no system was devised. In fact, the administration had taken the work of destruction in hand with great vigor, but it never planned a system to take the place of the old one. The Bank of the United

---

[1] Document H.   [2] Kendall's *Autobiography*, 387.

States had, of course, been compelled to devise its own measures for carrying on the business of the Treasury, so far as it was charged with that business. The Treasury was now forced to oversee, if it did not originate, the system of relations between the deposit banks. January 30, 1834, Silas Wright made a statement which was understood to be authoritative. He said that the Executive had entered again upon the control of the public money which belonged to him before the national Bank was chartered; that the administration would bring forward no law to regulate the deposits, but that the Executive would proceed with the experiment of using local banks. Webster expressed strong disappointment and disapproval, claiming that there should be a law.[1] March 18, 1834, Webster proposed a bill to extend the charter of the Bank of the United States for six years, without monopoly, the public money to be deposited in it, it to pay to the Treasury $200,000 annually on March 4th, none of its notes to be for less than $20.00. The Bank men would not agree to support it. It was tabled and never called up.[2] April 15, 1834, six months after the deposits were removed, Taney sent to the Committee on Ways and Means a plan for the organization of the deposit bank system, but it was a mere vague outline.[3]

[1] 45 Niles, 400.
[2] 46 Niles, 52; 1 Curtis's *Webster*, 485; 4 Webster's *Works*, 82.
[3] 46 Niles, 157.

December 15, 1834, Woodbury sent in a long essay
on currency and banking, but no positive scheme
or arrangement. It was not until June, 1836, that
the system was regulated by measures aiming at
efficiency and responsibility.

Taney desired that Kendall should be president
of the Bank of the Metropolis and organize the
system, but Kendall's readiness, which had not before failed, had now reached its limit. The Bank
of the Metropolis was then asked to admit Whitney as agent and correspondent of the deposit
banks. The bank refused to do this, and the plan
of making that bank the head was given up.[1] The
banks were recommended to employ Whitney as
agent and correspondent at Washington for their
dealings with the Treasury. He was thus placed
in a position of great power and influence. He
did not escape the charge of having abused it, and
an investigation, in 1837, produced evidence very
adverse to his good character. Part of the correspondence between him and the banks was then
published. From that correspondence it is plain
that the chief argument brought to support an application for a share of the deposits, or other favor,
was devotion to Jackson and hatred of the Bank
of the United States.[2] It is not proved that the
deposits were ever used by the Bank of the United
States for any political purpose whatever. It is
conclusively proved that the deposits were used
by Jackson's administration, through Whitney's

[1] Kendall's *Autobiography*, 388.   [2] 52 Niles, 91.

agency, to reward adherents and to win supporters. The first banks which took up the system also, in some cases, used the deposits which were given to them to put themselves in the position which they were required, by the theory of the deposit system, to occupy. Taney assumed that the Bank of the United States would make a spiteful attempt to injure the deposit banks by calling on them to pay balances. It was then considered wrong and cruel for one bank to call on another to pay balances promptly. Taney, therefore, placed some large drafts on the Bank of the United States in the hands of officers of the deposit banks at New York, Philadelphia, and Baltimore, so that they might offset any such malicious demand. Otherwise, the drafts were not to be used. The Bank took no steps which afforded even a pretext for using these drafts, but the president of the Union Bank of Maryland cashed one of them for $100,000 a few days after he got it, and used the money in stock speculations.[1] For fear of scandal this act was passed over by the Executive, but it led to an investigation by Congress. Taney was a stockholder in the Union Bank.[2] The Manhattan Company used one of these drafts for $500,000.[3]

[1] Kendall's *Autobiography*, 389. *Cf.* Document H, page 339. It is well worth while to read these two passages together in order to see how much deceit there was in the proceedings about the removal of the deposits.

[2] Quincy's *Adams*, 227. He sold his stock February 18, 1834. Document M.

[3] Document H.

Taney claimed the power to make these transfers. He referred it back to a precedent set by Crawford,[1] who, in his turn, when he had been called to account for it, had referred it back to Gallatin. The source of the stream, however, was not Gallatin, but William Jones, Acting Secretary.[2] The baneful effects of the large surplus of public money are plain enough.

At the session of 1833-34 the message alleged, as the occasion of removing the deposits, the report of the government directors of the Bank, which showed, as Jackson said, that the Bank had been turned into an electioneering engine. It was never alleged that the Bank had spent money otherwise than in distributing Gallatin's pamphlet on currency, McDuffie's report of 1830, and similar documents. Some might think that it was not wise and right for the Bank so to defend itself, since politics were involved; but its judge was now the most interested party in the contest, the one to whom that offence would seem most heinous, and he insisted on imposing a penalty at his own discretion, on an *ex parte* statement of his own appointees, and a penalty which could not be considered appropriate or duly measured to the offence. He also charged the Bank with manufacturing a panic. Taney reported "his" reasons for the

[1] Document F.
[2] American State Papers, 4 Finance, 266, 279. *Cf.* 1 Gallatin's *Writings*, 80. It has been asserted that Hamilton used the same power. Ingersoll, 279; *cf.* 6 Hamilton's *Works*, 175.

removal. He argued that the Secretary must discharge his duties under the supervision of the President; that the Secretary alone had power to remove the deposits; that Congress could not order it to be done; that the Secretary could do it, if he thought best, for any reason, not necessarily only when the Bank had misconducted itself. He put the removal which had been executed on the ground of public interest. The people had shown, in the election, that they did not want the Bank rechartered. It was not best to remove the deposits suddenly when the charter should expire. He blamed the Bank for increasing its loans from December 1, 1832, to August 2, 1833, from $61,500,000 to $64,100,000, and then reducing them, from that date until October 2, 1833, to $60,000,000. He said that the Bank had forfeited public confidence, had excluded the government directors from knowledge to which they were entitled, had shown selfishness in the affair of the French bill, had done wrongly about the three per cents, had granted favors to editors, and had distributed documents to control elections. He favored the use of the local banks as fiscal agents of the government.

December 9th the Bank memorialized Congress against the removal of the deposits as a breach of contract. A great struggle over the Bank question occupied the whole session. The Senate refused, 25 to 20, to confirm the reappointment of the government directors, who were said to have acted as the President's spies. Jackson sent the names in again with a long message,[1] and they were rejected, 30 to 11. Taney's appointment as Secretary of the Treasury was rejected, to Jackson's great indignation. Taney was then nominated for judge of the Supreme Court, and again rejected. Marshall died in July, 1835. Taney was appointed Chief Justice, December 28, 1835, and confirmed, March 15, 1836.

December 11th Clay moved a call for a copy of the paper read in the cabinet. Jackson refused it on the ground that Congress had no business with it. The document, in fact, had no standing in our system of government. It was another extension of personal government, by the adoption of a Napoleonic procedure. The Emperor made known his will by a letter of instructions to his minister, and this, when published, informed the public. Jackson used his "paper read in the cabinet" in just that way. By publishing it he violated the secrecy and privilege of the cabinet, and made it a public document, but when it was called for he fell back on cabinet privilege.[2] If Jackson's doctrine was sound, there would be modes of governing this country without any responsibility to Congress, and the "cabinet," as such, would come to have recognized functions as a body for registering and publishing the rescripts of the President. It was a thoroughly consistent extension of the same doctrine that Jackson, in his reply, in which he refused

[1] 46 Niles, 180.   [2] 45 Niles, 247.

to comply with the call of the Senate, professed his responsibility to the American people, and his willingness to explain to them the grounds of his conduct. Such a profession was an insult to the constitutional organ of the mind and will of the American people worthy of a military autocrat, and although it might have a jingle which would tickle the ears of men miseducated by the catchwords of democracy, nevertheless a people which would accept it as a proper and lawful expression from their executive chief would not yet have learned the alphabet of constitutional government.

In January, 1834, Jackson sent in a message complaining that the Bank still kept the books, papers, and funds belonging to the pension agency with which it had hitherto been charged. The Senate voted, May 26th, 26 to 17, that the Secretary of War had no authority to remove the pension funds from the Bank.

Clay introduced resolutions which finally took this shape: " Resolved, (1) That the President, in the late executive proceedings in relation to the public revenue, has assumed upon himself authority and power not conferred by the Constitution and the laws, but in derogation of both. (2) That the reasons assigned by the Secretary for the removal are unsatisfactory and insufficient." Benton offered a resolution that Biddle should be called to the bar of the Senate to give the reasons for the recent curtailments of the Bank, and to answer

for the use of its funds for electioneering.[1] February 5, 1834, Webster reported from the Committee on Finance in regard to the removal of the
deposits.   Clay's second resolution was at once
adopted, 28 to 18.   March 28th the first resolution
was adopted, 26 to 20.   April 15th, Jackson sent
in a protest against the latter resolution.   The
Senate refused to receive it, 27 to 16, declaring it
a breach of privilege.   The main points in the
protest were that the President meant to maintain
intact the rights of the Executive, and that the
Senate would be the judges in case of impeachment, but for that reason ought not to express an
opinion until the House saw fit to impeach.   The
Bank charter provided that the Secretary should
report his reasons to Congress.   On the doctrine of
the protest, however, one House of Congress could
adopt no expression of opinion on the report submitted, because it must wait for the other.   The administration press kept up truculent denunciations
of the Senate all winter.   The "Pennsylvanian"
said: "The democrats never heartily sanctioned it,
and now, having the power, should amend or get
rid of it once and forever."[2]   The New York
"Standard" called the senators "usurpers."[3]

The debates of the winter were acrimonious in
the extreme.   Probably no session of Congress before 1860–61 was marked by such fierce contention
in Congress and such excitement out-of-doors.
Chevalier, who was an acute and unprejudiced

[1] 45 Niles, 332.　　[2] 46 Niles, 131.　　[3] Ibid. 147.

observer, said that the speeches of the administration men resembled the French republican tirades of 1791–92. They had the same distinguishing trait, — emphasis. " Most generally the pictures presented in these declamations are fantastical delineations of the moneyed aristocracy overrunning the country, with seduction, corruption, and slavery in its train, or of Mr. Biddle aiming at the crown." [1] The chief weapon of debate was emphasis instead of fact and reason. With an "old hero" to support and the "money power" to assail, the politicians and orators of the emphatic school had a grand opportunity. There is also an unformulated dogma, which seems to command a great deal of faith, to this effect, that, if a man is only sufficiently ignorant, his whims and notions constitute "plain common sense." There are no questions on which this dogma acts more perniciously than on questions of banking and currency. Wild and whimsical notions about these topics, propounded with vehemence and obstinacy in Congress, helped to increase the alarm out-of-doors.

Senators Bibb, of Kentucky, and White, of Tennessee, went into opposition. Calhoun, also, for the time, allied himself heartily with the opposition.

The Virginia Legislature passed resolutions condemning the dismissal of Duane and the removal of the deposits. In pursuance of the dogmas of Virginia democracy, Rives, senator from that

[1] Chevalier, 61.

State, and supporter of the administration measures, resigned. B. W. Leigh was elected in his
place.

As soon as the resolution of censure was passed,
Benton gave notice of a motion to expunge the
same from the records. He introduced such a resolution at the next session, and the Jackson party
was more firmly consolidated than ever before in
the determination to carry it. The personal element was present in that enterprise, with the desire
for revenge, and the wish to demonstrate loyalty.
March 3, 1835, the words " ordered to be expunged "
were stricken from Benton's resolution, 39 to 7,
and the resolution was tabled, 27 to 20. The
agitation was then carried back into the State elections, and " expunging " came to be a test of party
fealty. Benton renewed the motion December 26,
1836. The Legislature of Virginia adopted instructions in favor of it. John Tyler would not
vote for it, and resigned. Leigh would not do so,
and would not resign. He never recovered party
standing.[1] Rives was sent back in Tyler's place.
This martyrdom, and Tyler's report on the Bank,
mentioned below, made Tyler Vice - President.[2]
The vice of the doctrine of instructions was well
illustrated in these proceedings. If the Virginia
doctrine were admitted, senators would be elected,
not for six years, but until the politics of the State
represented might change. The senator would
not be a true representative, under the theory of

[1] See his letter of reply : 50 Niles, 28.   [2] Wise, 158.

representative institutions, but a delegate, or ambassador. It would be another victory of pure democracy over constitutional institutions.

The administration had a majority in the Senate in 1836, but Benton says that a caucus was held on expunging. The resolution was passed, 24 to 19, that black lines should be drawn around the record on the journal of the Senate, and that the words " expunged, by order of the Senate, this 16th day of January, 1837," should be written across it. It was a great personal victory for Jackson. The Senate had risen up to condemn him for something which he had seen fit to do, and he had successfully resented and silenced its reproof. It gratified him more than any other incident of the latter part of his life. It was still another step forward in the development of his political methods, according to which his personality came more and more into play as a political force, and the constitutional institutions of the country were set aside. The day after the resolution was expunged, leave was refused, in the House, to bring in a resolution that it is unconstitutional to expunge any part of any record of either House.[1]

[1] There was a case of expunging in Jefferson's time. A resolution which had been passed contained a statement that certain filibusters thought that they had executive sanction. This was expunged. 1 Adams, 439. A case is mentioned in Massachusetts. Quincy's resolution against rejoicing in naval victories was expunged. Ingersoll, 23. For a discussion of other precedents see the speeches of Rives and Leigh. 50 Niles, 168, 173.

March 4, 1834, Polk reported from the Committee on Ways and Means on the removal of the deposits, supporting Jackson and Taney in all their positions. He offered four resolutions, which were passed, April 4th, as follows: (1) that the Bank ought not to be rechartered, 132 to 82; (2) that the deposits ought not to be restored, 118 to 103; (3) that the local banks ought to be depositories of the public funds, 117 to 105; (4) that a select committee should be raised on the Bank and the commercial crisis, 171 to 42. The committee last mentioned reported May 22d.[1] The majority said that the Bank had resisted all their attempts to investigate. They proposed that the directors should be arrested and brought to the bar of the House. The position of the Bank seemed to be, at this time, that since the Bank charter was to expire, and the deposits had been withdrawn, any further investigations were only vexatious. The minority of the committee (Edward Everett and W. W. Ellsworth) reported that the committee had made improper demands, and that the instruction given to the committee to examine the Bank in regard to the commercial crisis was based on improper assumptions. The Senate, June 30th, instructed the Committee on Finance to make another investigation of all the allegations against the Bank made by Jackson and Taney in justification of the removal. That committee reported December 18, 1834, by John Tyler.[2] The report

[1] 46 Niles, 221, 225.   [2] Document 1.

goes over all the points, with conclusions favorable
to the Bank on each. The time was long gone by,
however, when anybody cared for reports.

The excitement about the removal of the deposits was greatly exaggerated. The public was
thrown into a panic, because it did not quite see
what the effect would be. It is untrue that the
Bank made a panic, and it is untrue to say that
there was no real crisis. The statistics of loans,
etc., which the hostile committees were fond of
gathering, proved nothing, because they proved
anything. If the Bank loans increased, the Bank
was extending its loans to curry favor. If they
decreased, the Bank was punishing the public, and
making a panic. As bank loans always fluctuate,
the argument never slackened. The figures appended to Tyler's report cover the whole history of
the Bank. There are no fluctuations there which
can be attributed to malicious action by the Bank.
The root of all the wrong-doing of the Bank, out
of which sprang nearly all the charges which were
in any measure just, was in the branch drafts and
the bad banking in the West. The loans increased
up to May, 1832, when they were $70,400,000.
The increase, so far as it was remarkable, was in the
western branches. The operation of the " racers "
is also distinctly traceable in the accounts of the
parent bank and some of the branches. The effect
of the general restraint imposed can also be seen,
and the movement can be traced by which the
Bank, drawing back from the perilous position

into which it was drifting in 1832, got its branches
into better condition, and improved its whole status
from October, 1832, to October, 1833. It was
this course which afforded all the grounds there
were for the charge of panic-making.

The Bank was very strong when the deposits
were removed. The loans were $42,200,000;
domestic exchange, $17,800,000 ; foreign ex-
change, 2,300,000; specie, $10,600,000; due from
local banks, $2,200,000; notes of local banks,
$62,400,000; public deposits, $9,000,000; private
deposits, $8,000,000; circulation, $19,100,000. It
also held real estate worth $3,000,000. During
the winter of 1833–34 there was a stringent money
market and commercial distress. The local banks
were in no condition to take the public deposits.
They were trying to strengthen themselves, and
to put themselves on the level of the Treasury
requirements in the hope of getting a share of the
deposits. It was they who operated a bank con-
traction during that winter. It was six months,
and then only by the favor and concession of the
Treasury, before the local banks, "pet banks" as
they soon came to be called, could get into a
position to take the place of the Bank of the
United States. This was the "chaos" into which
Duane, like an honest man, and man of sense, had
refused to plunge the fiscal interests of the country.
The administration, however, charged everything
to Biddle and the Bank. Petitions were sent to
Congress. Benton and the others said that there

was no crisis, and that the petitions were gotten up for effect, to frighten Jackson into restoring the deposits. The proofs of the genuineness and severity of the crisis, in the forty-fifth volume of Niles's " Register," are ample. In January, 1834, exchange on England was at one hundred and one and a half (par one hundred and seven) ; capital was loaning at from one and a half per cent to three per cent per month ; bank-notes were quoted at varying rates of discount.[1] Delegations went to Washington to represent to Jackson the state of the country. He became violent ; told the delegations to go to Biddle ; that he had all the money ; that the Bank was a " monster," to which all the trouble was due. In answer to a delegation from Philadelphia, February 11, 1834, Jackson sketched out the bullionist program, which the administration pursued from this time forth as an offset to the complaints about the removal of the deposits.[2] Up to this time it had been supposed that Jackson rather leaned to paper-money notions. He now proposed, as an " experiment " (so he called it), to induce the banks, by promising them a share in the deposits, to give up the use of notes under $5.00, later to do away with all under $10.00, and finally to restrict bank-notes to $20.00 and upwards, so as to bring about a circulation of which

[1] 46 Niles, 133.

[2] Taney made the first official statement of the plan of the administration in a letter to the Committee on Ways and Means, April 15, 1834.

a reasonable part should be specie.   Jackson's personal interest had been enlisted in this scheme. He wrote to Lewis, while on a journey to Tennessee, July 15, 1834: "supper is announced and I am hungry — but I cannot forego saying to you that all things appear well in Virginia — the Gold bill & a Specie currency are doing wonders — " [1] The notion was good as far as it went, but had precisely the fault of a good financial notion in the hands of incompetent men ; the scheme did not take into account *all* the consequences of distributing the deposits as proposed.   It persuaded the banks to conform to external rules about circulation, but, under the circumstances, these rules did not have the force they were supposed to have, and the bank loans were stimulated to an enormous inflation, which threw the whole business of the country into a fever, and then produced a great commercial crisis.   For a short period, in the summer of 1834, the currency was in a very sound condition.   The Bank of the United States was, by the necessity of its position, under strong precautions.   The local banks, by their efforts to meet the Treasury requirements, were stronger than ever before.   The popular sentiment, however, had now swung over again to the mania for banks. Each district wanted a deposit bank, so as to get a share in the stream of wealth from the public treasury.   If a deposit could not be obtained, then the bank was formed in order to participate

[1] Ford MSS.

in the carnival of credit and speculation, for a
non-deposit bank could manage its affairs as recklessly as it chose. The deposit banks speedily
drew together to try to prevent any more from
being admitted to share in the public deposits.
The mania for banking was such that formal riots
occurred at the subscription to the stock of new
banks.[1] The favored few, who could subscribe
the whole, sold to the rest at an advance. To be
a commissioner was worth from $500 to $1,000.[2]
There was a notion, borrowed perhaps from the
proceedings of the government of the United
States in the organization of both national banks,
that to make a bank was a resource by which a
group of insolvent debtors could extricate themselves from their embarrassments. The Tammany
society being in debt, a plan was formed for paying
the debt by making a bank.[3] When the great fire
occurred in New York, December, 1835, a proposition was made to create a bank, as a mode of
relieving the sufferers. " To make a bank," said
Niles, " is the great panacea for every ill that can
befall the people of the United States, and yet it
adds not one cent to the capital of the community."[4] The effect of this multiplication of banks,
and of the scramble between them for the public
deposits, was that an enormous amount of capital was arbitrarily distributed over the country,

[1] 42 Niles, 257; 44 Niles, 371. See some of these facts and
the use made of them in Brothers's *United States*, p. 51.
[2] 46 Niles, 188.   [3] Mackeinzie, 70.   [4] 49 Niles, 298.

according to political favoritism and local influence, and in entire disregard of the industrial and commercial conditions. The public debt was all paid January 1, 1835. After that date the public deposits increased with great rapidity, and there was no occasion to spend them. The state of things was therefore this: an immense amount of capital was being collected by taxes, and then distributed to favored corporations, as a free loan for an indefinite period, on which they could earn profits by lending it at interest. No monster bank, under the most malicious management, could have produced as much harm, either political or financial, as this system produced while it lasted.

November 5, 1834, Secretary Woodbury informed the Bank of the United States that the Treasury would not receive branch drafts after January 1, 1835. This led to a spirited correspondence with Biddle, in which the latter defended the drafts as good, both in law and finance.[1] In the message of 1834 Jackson recapitulated the old complaints against the Bank, and recommended that, on account of its "high-handed proceedings," its notes should no longer be received by the Treasury, and that the stock owned by the nation should be sold. The session of 1834–35 was, however, fruitless as to banking and currency. January 12, 1835, on Benton's motion, the Committee on Finance was ordered to investigate the specie transactions of the Bank. Tyler took fire at this,

[1] Document J.

because it reflected on the report which he had just made. In view of subsequent history, it is worth while to notice the profession of faith which was drawn from Tyler at this time. He said that he was opposed to any national bank on constitutional grounds, but that he was free from Jacksonism, and that he wanted to be just to the existing Bank. January 10th Polk introduced a bill to forbid the receipt of notes of the Bank of the United States at the Treasury, unless the Bank would pay at once the dividend which had been withheld in 1834. Bills were also proposed for regulating the deposits in the deposit banks. No action resulted.

In the message of 1835 Jackson referred to the war which (as he said) the Bank had waged on the government for four years, as a proof of the evil effects of such an institution. He declared that the Bank belonged to a system of distrust of the popular will as a regulator of political power, and to a policy which would supplant our system by a consolidated government. Here, then, at the end of the Bank war, we meet again with the second of the theories of the Bank which Ingham formulated in his letter to Biddle of October 5, 1829,[1] at the beginning of the Bank war. Ingham said that some people held that theory. The assumption that the Bank held that theory concerning itself had been made the rule of action of the government, and the laws and administration of the coun-

[1] See page 276.

try had been made to conform to that assumption as an established fact. At the session of 1835–36 an attempt was made to investigate the transactions of members of Congress with the Bank. It was abandoned when Adams declared that a similar attempt in 1832 had been abandoned, because it cut both ways.

CHAPTER XI

SPECULATION, DISTRIBUTION, CURRENCY LEGISLATION, AND END OF THE BANK OF THE UNITED STATES

Speculation and Inflation. — In the spring of 1835 the phenomena of a period of speculation began to be distinctly marked. There was great monetary ease and prosperity in England and France, as well as here. Some important improvements in machinery, the first railroads, greater political satisfaction and security, and joint stock banks were especially favorable elements which were then affecting France and England. The price of cotton advanced sharply during 1834–35. Speculation seized upon cotton lands in Mississippi and Louisiana, and on negroes. Next it affected real estate in the cities at which cotton was handled commercially. The success of the Erie Canal led to numerous enterprises of a like nature in Pennsylvania, Maryland, Ohio, Indiana, and Illinois. Capital for these enterprises was not at hand. The States endeavored to draw the capital from Europe by the use of their credit. The natural consequence was great recklessness in contracting debt, and much "financiering" by agents and middle-men. The abundant and cheap capital, here and abroad, of 1835–36 favored all the improvement enterprises. These enterprises were, however, in their nature, investments, returns from which could not be expected for a long period. In the mean time, they locked up capital. It appears that labor and capital were withdrawn for a time from agriculture, and devoted to means of transportation. Wheat and flour were imported in 1836.[1] The land of the Western States had greatly risen in value since the Erie Canal had been open. Speculation in this land became very active. Timber lands in Maine were another mania.[2] The loans of capital from Europe increased month by month. The entire payment of the public debt of the United States had a great effect upon the imagination of people in Europe. It raised the credit of the United States. It was thought that a country which could pay off its debt with such rapidity must be a good country in which to invest capital. The credit extended to the United States depressed the exchanges, and gave an unusual protection to the excessive bank-note issues in the United States. Those issues sustained and stimulated the excessive credit which the public deposits were bringing into existence. The banks had an arbitrary rule that a reserve of specie to the amount of one third of the circulation would secure them beyond any danger. So long as the exchanges were depressed by the exportation

[1] 50 Niles, 50, 74; 51 Niles, 17.   [2] 48 Niles, 167.

of capital from Europe to America, no shipment of
specie occurred, and the system was not tested.
All prices were rising; all was active and hopeful;
debt was the road to wealth. If one could obtain capital for margins, and speculate on differences in stocks, commodities, and real estate, he
had a chance to win enormous profits while the
credit system went on. Large classes. of persons
were drawn to city occupations, exchange, banking,
and brokerage, because these industries were most
profitable. Cities grew, rents advanced, real estate
rose in value. Down to October 1, 1836, the following States had forbidden notes under $5.00:
New York, Pennsylvania, Virginia, Georgia, Louisiana, Indiana, Alabama, New Jersey, Maryland,
North Carolina, Tennessee, Kentucky, and Maine.
It appears, however, that small notes of earlier
issue were still in circulation, and the state of
things which the legislation meant to bring about
never was reached, so far as one can now learn.

In the autumn of 1835, the money market became more stringent. This fact was. charged to
the pet banks and to fears of trouble with France.[1]
The pet banks had every interest to arrest inflation.
If they were held to conservative rules, while the
non-deposit banks about them were not so held,
the former only left free room for the latter, and
then the former had to receive the notes of the
latter. In January, 1836, the rate of discount at
Philadelphia was two per cent per month.[2] Banks

1 49 Niles, 225, 281.   2 49 Niles, 313.

were still being multiplied.[1] During 1836 prices
continued to rise, speculation was active, rates for
capital increased; there was complaint of a scar-
city of money, and a demand for more banks.
Governor Marcy, of New York, in his message
for 1836, pointed out the "unregulated spirit of
speculation" which prevailed, and he warned the
Legislature, against the fallacies involved in the
demand for more banks.[2] In April the best commercial paper was quoted, at New York, at thirty
per cent to forty per cent per annum; second rate,
at one half of one per cent per day.[3] At Boston
the rate was one per cent per month. Exchange
on England, at New York, was one hundred and
five (par one hundred and nine and three fifths),
showing the current of capital in spite of the inflation. In May Niles said, "There is an awful
pressure for money in most of the cities,"[4] yet he
also describes the unprecedented activity of business in Baltimore.

Land and Distribution. — In the first message
after his reëlection, in 1832, Jackson proposed, in
regard to the public lands, that they should be
sold to the new States and to actual settlers at a
very low price. December 12th of that year Clay
reintroduced his land bill.[5] He succeeded in getting it passed, but it was sent to the President
within ten days of the end of the session. Jackson

---

[1] 49 Niles, 435.   [2] 2 Hammond, 449.
[3] *Evening Post*, in 50 Niles, 134.   [4] 50 Niles, 185.
[5] See page 234.

did not sign it. In December, 1833, he sent in a message stating his reasons for not doing so. He objected especially to the policy of giving away the proceeds of the lands while levying heavy duties on imports. The session of 1833–34 was fully occupied with the Bank question and the removal of the deposits. At the session of 1834–35 Clay again brought in a land bill, but no action was taken. Relations with France occupied the attention of Congress during that session, which was a short one. At the session of 1835–36 Clay introduced a bill to distribute the net proceeds of the lands, after taking out ten per cent for the ten new States. Calhoun introduced a joint resolution to amend the Constitution so that the surplus revenue could be distributed among the States. He also introduced a bill to regulate the public deposits. A bill to distribute the surplus revenue was also introduced. The land bill passed the Senate May 4, 1836, by 25 to 20. It was tabled in the House, 104 to 85, June 22d. The distribution bill and the deposit bill were consolidated into one, and passed by the Senate June 17th, 38 to 6. On the 20th of June, in the House, an effort was made to divide the bill, so as to separate the regulation of the deposits from the distribution, but the effort failed. The House then changed the plan of distributing the surplus to the States as a gift, into a plan for "depositing" it with them subject to recall. In this shape the bill passed, 155 to 38, and became a law by the concurrence of the Senate and the President.

The " Globe "[1] said that Jackson would have vetoed the bill as it came from the Senate. He thought that the plan of "depositing" the surplus was free from constitutional objections, but the " Globe " gave notice to all whom it might concern that the President would not sign any bill the effect of which would be to raise revenue by federal taxation, and distribute the proceeds among the States. The distribution measure was one of those errors which are apt to be committed on the eve of a presidential election, when politicians do not dare to oppose measures which gratify class or local feelings or interests. Webster opposed distribution, unless the land income could be separated. He said that taxes must be reduced even at the risk of injuring some industries.[2] It was provided in the bill that there should be in each State a deposit bank, if a bank could be found which would fulfil the prescribed conditions. Each of these banks was to redeem all its notes in specie, and to issue no notes for less than $5.00 after July 4, 1836. The Treasury was not to receive, after that date, the notes of any bank which did issue notes under $5.00. It was to pay out no note under $10.00 after the passage of the act, and no note under $20.00 after March 3, 1837. If the public deposits in any bank should exceed one fourth of the capital of the bank, it was to pay two per cent interest on the excess. No transfer of deposits from bank to bank was to be made by the Secre-

[1] 50 Niles, 281.   [2] 1 Curtis's *Webster*, 537.

tary, except when and because the convenience of the Treasury required it. In that case, he was to transfer from one deposit bank to the next deposit bank in the neighborhood, and so on; *i. e.*, not from one end of the country to the other. As to distribution, the bill provided that all the money in the Treasury, January 1, 1837, in excess of $5,000,000, was to be deposited with the States in the proportion of their membership in the electoral college, and in four instalments, January, April, July, and October, 1837. The States were to give *negotiable* certificates of deposit, payable to the Secretary or his assigns on demand. If the Secretary should negotiate any certificate, it should bear five per cent interest from the date of assignment. While not assigned, the certificates bore no interest.[1]

In his message of 1836 Jackson offered a long and very just criticism on this act. His objections were so pertinent and so strong that we are forced to believe that he did not veto only on account of the pending election. A number of doubtful States were "improvement States;" that is, they had plunged recklessly into debt for canals, etc., which were not finished, and credit was declining while the money market was growing stringent. Those States were very eager (or, at least, many people in them were) to get the money in the federal treasury with which to go on with the works. Jackson argued in favor of the reduction and

[1] 50 Niles, 290.

abolition of all the taxes with which the compromise tariff allowed Congress to deal, and he exposed completely the silly device by which the whigs tried to justify distribution, separating the revenue in imagination, and pretending to distribute the part which came from land. Jackson made a lame attempt to explain the recommendations which he had made in his early messages in favor of distribution. He gave a table showing the effect of distribution according to the ratio of membership in the electoral college as compared with that on the ratio of federal population. The small and new States gained enormously by the plan adopted.

The best that can be said in excuse for distribution is that the surplus was doing so much mischief that the best thing to do with it was to throw it away. Unfortunately, it could not be thrown away without doing other harm. We have already noticed the shocks given to the money market by the debt-paying operation.[1] The removal of the deposits took place before that was completed, and produced a new complication. The credit relations formerly existing towards and around the great Bank were rudely cut off, and left to reconstruct themselves as best they could. As soon as the new state of things had become a little established, there was an accumulation of a great surplus, nominally in the deposit banks, really loaned out to individuals, and fully engaged in speculative importations with credit for duties, or in speculative

[1] See page 315.

contracts, payment on which was to be received in State bonds and scrip, or in still other indescribable repetitions of debt and contract. The capital, when thus fully absorbed, was next all called in again, in order to be transferred to the States. The States did not intend to loan the capital; they intended to spend it in public works; that is, for the most part, considering the actual facts as they existed, to sink it entirely. In one way or another these funds were squandered by all the States, or worse than squandered, since they served corruption and abuse. In 1877 it was declared that the Comptroller of New York did not know what had become of the deposit fund of the State. For many years the commissioners of only nine counties had made any report. The Comptroller asked for $15,000 with which to find out what had become of the $4,000,000 which was the share of New York. The fact that the funds were squandered was the least of the purely financial evils attendant on distribution. The effect on all the relations of capital, credit, and currency, that is, the effect on every man's rights and interests, was the most far-reaching and serious consequence.[1]

On the 1st of June, 1836,[2] the deposit banks stood thus: capital, $46,400,000; due to the Treasurer of the United States, $37,200,000; due to public officers, $3,700,000; circulation, $27,900,000; other deposits, $16,000,000; due

---

[1] Bourne, *Surplus Revenue of* 1837.   [2] 50 Niles, 313.

to other banks, $17,100,000. *Contra:* loans, $71,200,000 ; domestic exchange, $37,100,000 ; due from banks, $17,800,000 ; notes of other banks, $10,900,000 ; specie, $10,400,000. It appears then that these banks owed the United States $41,000,000, while their whole capital was only $46,000,000 ; that is to say, the public deposits furnished them with a capital nearly equal to their own. If their "other deposits" had been all cash capital deposited, four elevenths of all their loanable funds would have been public deposits, which would have been "called" by the act of June 23, 1836. It is also noticeable what a large sum is due to and from other banks. The feeling that banks ought to forbear demands on each other seems to have been an outgrowth of the war against the Bank of the United States. The consequence was that the banks were all locked together, and when the trouble came they all went down together.

In December, 1836, Calhoun introduced another distribution bill to distribute any surplus which might be in the Treasury on January 1, 1838. It was finally added as a "rider" to an appropriation bill, providing money for fortifications. The House passed the bill and rider, but the Senate rejected the whole. Clay also introduced another land distribution bill. Schemes of distribution were great whig measures down to Tyler's time.

The first and second instalments of the distribution of 1837 were paid in specie, in January

and April. The commercial crisis began in March.
The banks suspended in May. The third instalment was paid in notes in July. Before August
the Treasury, which was giving away $35,000,000,
was in the greatest straits. Van Buren was forced
to call an extra session of Congress. That body
had no more urgent business than to forbid the
Secretary to negotiate any of his "deposit" certificates, or to call on any of the States for the
money deposited with them. The payment of the
fourth instalment was postponed until January 1,
1839. At that date there was debt, not surplus,
and the fourth instalment never was paid. Congress has never recalled any part of the other three
instalments. Even when the civil war broke out,
it did not venture to do this. The amount of the
three instalments, $28,000,000, stands on the books
as unavailable funds. The Secretary of the Treasury was obliged to draw his first three instalments
where he could get them, so he drew them from the
North and East, the banks of the Southwest being
really ruined. The fourth instalment remained
due from the banks of the Southwestern States.
It was years before any part of it could be recovered. The Southwestern States participated in
the distribution of the three instalments.[1]

Specie Currency. — Reference has been made
above[2] to the plans of the administration for a
specie currency, as a complement or offset to the
removal of the deposits and destruction of the

[1] See table, 53 Niles, 35.   [2] See page 371.

Bank.[1] Benton, who was the strongest bullionist
in the administration circle, was under an exaggerated opinion of the efficacy of a metallic currency to prevent abuses of credit. A metallic
currency is not liable to certain abuses, and it re-
quires no skill for its management. In contrast
with paper, therefore, it is surer and safer. It,
however, offers no guarantees against bad banking.
At most it could relieve the non-capitalist wage-
receiver from any direct share or risk in bad banking. In contending against plutocracy, democracy
ought to put a metallic currency high up on its
banner. The most subtle and inexcusable abuse of
the public which has ever been devised is that
of granting to corporations, without exacting an
equivalent, the privilege of taking out of the circulation the value currency, for which the public
must always pay, whether they get it or not, and
putting into it their own promises to pay. The
subtlety of this device, and the fallacies which clus-
ter about it and impose upon uneducated people,
are a full justification for men of democratic convictions, if they say: We do not understand it well
enough to control it. We cannot spend time and
attention to watch it. We will not allow it at all.
Such confession of ignorance and abnegation of
power, however, is hardly in the spirit of democracy. As a matter of history, the bullionist tendencies of a section of the Jacksonian party were
at war with other parts of the policy of the same

[1] The *Globe* in 46 Niles, 331.

party, notably the distribution of the public deposits in eighty banks, with encouragement to loan freely.

The opposition party, on the other hand, took up cudgels in behalf of banks and bank paper, as if there would be no currency if bank paper were withdrawn, and as if there would be no credit if there were no banks of issue. In their arguments against the bullionist party, they talked as if they believed that, if the public Treasury did its own business, and did it in gold, it would get possession of all the gold in the country, and that this would give it control of all the credit in the country, because the paper issue was based on gold.

In 1834 the administration was determined to have a gold currency. The Committee on Ways and Means reported, April 22, 1834,[1] that it was useless to coin gold while the rating remained as it was fixed by the laws of 1792 and 1793. The coinage law had often been discussed before. Lowndes studied it and reported on it in 1819; J. Q. Adams in 1820. In 1830 Sanford, of New York, proposed a gold currency with subsidiary silver. In the same year Ingham made a report, recommending the ratio 1: 15.625. In 1831 a coinage bill passed the Senate, but was not acted on in the House. At the session of 1831–32 White and Verplanck, of New York, wanted silver made sole money. On account of the difficulty and delicacy of the subject no action had been reached. In 1834 a new

[1] 46 Niles, 159.

interest came in. The gold product of the Southern Alleghanies was increasing. In 1832 there came to the mint from that region $678,000 value of gold, and in 1833 $868,000. There was a protectionist movement in behalf of gold, the interest of which was that gold should supplant silver, to which end an incorrect rating was desired.[1] By the laws of 1792 and 1793 the gold eagle weighed 270 grains and was $\frac{11}{12}$ fine. The silver dollar weighed 416 grains and was $\frac{1485}{1664}$ fine, giving a ratio of $1:15$. The market ratio was, from 1792 to 1830, about $1:15.6$. Therefore gold was not money, but merchandise. From 1828 to 1833 the average premium on gold at Philadelphia was $4\frac{3}{8}$ per cent.[2] The reports before Congress, in 1834, showed that the real ratio was between $1:15.6$ and $1:15.8$. The mint put $1:15.8$ as the highest ratio admissible. Duncan, of Illinois, in a speech, showed that the ratio since 1821 had been, on an average, $1:15.625$.[3] These authorities were all disregarded.

The administration politicians had determined to have gold as a matter of taste, and the southern gold interest wanted it. The law of June 28, 1834, made the gold eagle weigh 258 grains, of which 232 grains were to be pure; fineness, .8992. The silver dollar was unaltered. The ratio of gold to silver, by this law, was therefore $1:16.002$. The old eagles were worth in the new ones $10.681, or old gold coins were worth 94.827 cents per pennyweight in the new. Taking gold to silver at

[1] Raguet, 236.   [2] Raguet, 250.   [3] 47 Niles, 29.

1 : 15.625, an old silver dollar was worth $1.024 in
the new gold one, and as the silver dollar had
been the standard of prices and contracts, and the
new gold one now was such, the money of account
had been depreciated $2\frac{1}{4}$ per cent. In the new
standard, a pound sterling was worth, metal for
metal, $4.87073; and if the old arbitrary par, £1=
4.44\frac{4}{9}$, were 100, the true par of exchange would
be 109.59. Of course the supposed gain to the
gold producers from the incorrect rating was a
pure delusion. They got no more goods for their
gold than they would have got before, save in so
far as the United States added some small incre-
ment to the previous demand in the whole world
for gold. The bullion brokers won by exchan-
ging gold coins for silver coins and exporting the
latter.

In December, 1834, Woodbury, who had become
Secretary of the Treasury, gave the following statistics of the circulation on December 1st: local
bank paper, from $57,000,000 to $68,000,000;
Bank of the United States paper, $16,000,000;
gold, $4,000,000; silver, $16,000,000; total active circulation per head, $7.00. In bank: specie,
$18,250,000; paper, $35,000,000; grand total per
head, $10.00.[1] The currency was then in a very
sound condition.[2]

The bank paper increased before the gold could
be brought into circulation, and the gold currency
never was made a fact. Silver rose to a premium,

[1] Document K, p. 64.   [2] See page 372.

and was melted or exported.[1] The new mint law
therefore produced the inconvenience of driving
out silver just when the administration was trying
to abolish small notes. A gold dollar had been
proposed in the new law, but the provision for it
was stricken out. The silver dollars then on hand
appear to have been all clipped or worn.[2] The
first which had been coined since 1805 were coined
in 1836.[3] They could not, however, be kept in circulation. By the act of January 18, 1837, two
tenths of a grain were added to the pure contents
of the eagle. This made the fineness just .900.
The pure contents of the silver dollar were left
unaltered, but the gross weight was reduced to
$412\frac{1}{2}$ grains, so that the fineness of this coin also
was .900. The ratio of the metals in the coinage
was then 1 : 15.988. One pound sterling was then
worth \$4.8665, or, if \$4.44$\frac{4}{9}$ be assumed 100, par of
exchange was 109$\frac{4}{9}$. As soon as the crisis broke
out, in 1837, all specie disappeared, and notes and
tickets for the smallest denominations came into
use.

At the session of 1835–36 Benton tried to get a
resolution passed that nothing but gold or silver
should be taken for public lands. He did not succeed. After Congress adjourned, July 11, 1836,
the Secretary of the Treasury issued, by the President's order, a circular to all the land offices, known
afterwards as the "Specie Circular," ordering that
only gold, or silver, or land scrip should be received

[1] 47 Niles, 147.   [2] 37 Niles, 393.   [3] 51 Niles, 241.

for public lands. The occasion for this order was serious. The sales of public lands were increasing at an extraordinary rate. Lands were sold for $4,800,000 in 1834; for $14,700,000 in 1835; for $24,800,000 in 1836. The receipts for the lands consisted largely of notes of irresponsible banks. Land speculators organized a "bank," got it appointed a deposit bank if they could, issued notes, borrowed them and bought land; the notes were deposited; they borrowed them again, and so on indefinitely. The guarantees required of the deposit banks were idle against such a scheme. There was, of course, little specie in the West on account of the flood of paper there. The circular caused inconvenience, and bad temper on the part of those who were checked in their transactions. It also caused trouble and expense in transporting specie from the East, and it no doubt made a demand for specie in the East against the banks there. In the existing state of the eastern banks this demand was probably just the touch needed to push down the rickety pretense of solvency which they were keeping up. Specie could not be drawn in from Europe, except by a great fall in prices and a large contraction of the currency. Either through demand for specie or fall in prices, the inflated currency must collapse, and the crisis was at hand. Moreover, the banks were under notice to surrender, on January 1st, one fourth of the public deposits. Thousands of people who were carrying commodities or property for a rise, or who were en-

gaged in enterprises, to finish which they depended
on bank loans, found themselves arrested by the
exorbitant rate for loans. The speculative period
in England had also run its course, and the inflation here could no longer be sustained by borrowing there. From all these facts, it is plain that
the specie circular may have played the *rôle* of
the spark which produces an explosion, when all
the conditions and materials have been prepared ;
but those who called the circular the *cause* of the
crisis made a mistake which is only too common in
the criticism of economic events. A similar circular was issued in Adams's administration, which
had hardly been noticed.[1] There was a great deal
of outcry against the President for high-handed
proceedings in this matter, but without reason.
There were only two forms of currency which were
at this time by law receivable for lands, — specie
and notes of specie value.[2] The notes which were
being received in the West were not of specie
value.

A bill to annul the specie circular passed the
Senate, 41 to 5, and the House, 143 to 59. The
President sent it to the State Department at 11.45
P. M., March 3, 1837, and filed his reasons for not
signing it, it having been sent to him less than ten
days before the end of the session. His reason for
not signing the bill was that it was obscure.

[1] 7 Adams, 427.
[2] Report by Silas Wright, May 16, 1838, with history of the
laws about currency receivable at the Treasury, 55 Niles, 106.

The End of the Bank of the United States.—
The charter of the Bank of the United States was
to expire March 3, 1836. The history of the internal affairs of the Bank, after Tyler's report in
1834, was not known to the public until 1841,
when committees of the stockholders published reports, from which we are able to state the internal
history of the Bank in its true historical connection.
March 6, 1835, by a resolution of the directors,
the exchange committee was directed to loan the
capital of the Bank, so fast as it should be released,
on call, on stock collateral. The exchange committee, from this time on, secured entire control of
the Bank. During the year 1835, branches were
sold for bonds having from one to five years to
run. Down to November, fifteen branches had
been sold.[1] In November, projects began to be
talked about for getting a State charter from
Pennsylvania.[2] There was a great deal of jealousy
at this time between New York and Philadelphia.
There was a proposition for a great fifty-million-
dollar bank at New York, and it seemed that if
Philadelphia lost her bank, and New York got
one, the financial hegemony would be permanently
transferred. In December, 1835, after the great
fire in New York, the Bank of the United States
was asked to give aid. It did so by opening credits
for $2,000,000 in favor of the insurance companies.[3]

The act of the Pennsylvania Legislature, by
which the United States Bank of Pennsylvania

[1] 49 Niles, 182. [2] 49 Niles, 162. [3] 49 Niles, 307.

was chartered, is, on its face, a piece of corrupt
legislation. Its corruption was addressed to the
people of the State, not to private individuals. It
comprised three projects in an obvious log-rolling
combination, — remission of taxes, public improvements, and bank charter. The Bank was chartered for thirty years.[1] It was to pay a bonus of
$2,500,000, pay $100,000 per year for twenty
years for schools, loan the State not over a million a year in temporary loans at four per cent,
and subscribe $640,000 to railroads and turnpikes.
Personal taxes were repealed by other sections of
the bill, and $1,368,147 were appropriated, out of
the Bank bonus, for various canals and turnpikes.
Either this bill was corruptly put together to win
strength by enlisting local and personal interests
in favor of it, or else the Pennsylvanians, having
got their big Bank to themselves, set to work to
plunder it. The charter passed the State Senate,
19 to 12, and the House, 57 to 30.[2] Inasmuch as
the democrats had a majority in the Senate, it was
charged that private corruption had passed the
bill. An investigation resulted in nothing. There
was found, in 1841, an entry, of about the date of
the charter, of $400,000 expenditure, vouchers for
which could not be produced.[3] Biddle represented
the case as if the proposition that the State should
charter the Bank had originated with leading members of the Legislature, who asked the Bank if it

[1] 49 Niles, 377, 396.   [2] 49 Niles, 434.
[3] Second report, 1841, 60 Niles, 202.

would accept a State charter.[1]   The act was dated
February 18, 1836.   The Bank accepted the charter, and presented a service of plate to Biddle.[2]

In the story of the Bank war, which has been
given in the preceding pages, the reader has perceived that the writer does not believe that Jackson's administration had a case against the Bank,
or that the charges it made were proved.   To say
this is to say that Jackson's administration unjustly, passionately, ignorantly, and without regard
to truth, assailed a great and valuable financial
institution, and calumniated its management.   Such
was the opinion of people of that generation, at
least until March 3, 1836.   Jackson's charges
against the Bank were held to be not proved.   The
effect of them naturally was to make confidence in
the Bank blind and deaf.   In January, 1836, when
it was expected that the Bank would wind up in
two months, its stock stood at 116.   For four years
afterwards, nothing seemed able to destroy public
confidence in the Bank.   One thing alone suggests
a doubt, and makes one hold back from the adoption of a positive judgment in favor of the Bank,
even down to the end of its national charter:
that is, a doubt of Biddle's sincerity.   If he was
not sincere, we have no measure for the degree of
misrepresentation there may have been in his plausible statements and explanations, or for how much
may have been hidden under the financial expositions he was so fond of making, and which were,

[1] Biddle to Adams, 51 Niles, 230.   [2] 49 Niles, 441.

like the expositions of a juggler, meant to mystify the audience still more.

The final catastrophe of the Bank has always affected the judgment which all students of its history have formed of the merits of its struggle with Jackson. The Jackson men always claimed that the end proved that Jackson and his coterie were right all the time. This has probably been the general verdict. The whigs felt the weight of the inference, and they tried to distinguish between the Bank of the United States and the United States Bank of Pennsylvania. A little reflection will show that both these views are erroneous. A bank may go on well and be sound for twenty years, and then go wrong. It may make mistakes and recover, and then make more mistakes and perish. We must go by the facts all the way along. The State bank and the national bank of the United States had a continuous, an integral life. The attempt to save one and condemn the other, aside from an investigation of the merits, is a partisan proceeding. It is not sound historically or financially. We have now reached as just an opinion as we can form about the Bank up to the time of its State charter.

The State Bank started on its career under very bad auspices. It never threw off the suspicion which attached to its legislative birth. It was too large for its new sphere, yet pride prevented its reduction. It had other aims than to win profits by sound banking. It wanted to prove itself

necessary, or to show itself a public benefactor, or
to sustain the rivalry of Philadelphia with New
York. Biddle, freed from the restraints of the
old organization, launched out into sensational
banking, and tested his theories of banking to the
utmost. There is scarcely anything vicious and
unsound in banking which the great Bank did not
illustrate during the next five years. Its officers
plundered it. Its end was so ignominious that no
one wanted to remember that he had ever believed
in it.

On the 1st of February, 1836, the account of
the Bank [1] showed a surplus of $7,800,000, which
was expected to pay off the bonus, notes, etc.
There were $20,000,000 loaned on stocks, and
there was the State bonus, the government stock,
and the circulation of the old bank to be paid.
New stock was sold to pay off the government
stock. £1,000,000 were borrowed in London,
and 12,500,000 francs in Paris.[2] Jaudon was sent
to England as agent of the Bank. In May, the
money market at New York being very stringent,
the Bank was asked for aid, which it gave.[3] By
an act of June 15, 1836, Congress repealed the
14th section of the Bank charter. This put an
end to the receipt of the notes of the old Bank by
the Treasury, and crippled the circulation of the
Bank. In October there was a report that the
Bank would surrender its State charter if it could

[1] 60 Niles, 106.   [2] First report, 1841, 60 Niles, 105.
[3] 50 Niles, 267.

get back its bonus.[1] In that same month, however, Biddle wrote another letter to Adams to show the wrong of trying to repeal the State charter. June 23d, Congress authorized the Secretary of the Treasury to treat with the Bank for the payment of the government stock. No agreement was reached, but, February 25, 1837, the Bank sent a memorial to the Speaker, in which it offered to pay off the public shares, at $115.58 per share, in four instalments, September, 1837–38–39–40. This proposition was accepted, March 3, 1837, and the instalments were all paid.

In his message, 1836, Jackson discharged a last broadside at the Bank. He seemed to be as angry that the Bank had escaped annihilation as he was in 1818 that Billy Bowlegs got across the Suwanee river. He complained that the Bank had not paid off the public stock, and was reissuing its old notes. This latter proceeding was stopped by an act of July 6, 1838. The Bank failed three times during the years of commercial distress which followed, namely, May 10, 1837, with all the other banks; October 9, 1839, when it carried down with it all which had resumed, except those in New York and a few in New England; February 4, 1841, when it was entirely ruined. Its stockholders lost all their capital.

Biddle had resigned March 29, 1839, but he had been so identified with the Bank that its ruin was attributed to him. He fell into disgrace. He

[1] 51 Niles, 113.

was arraigned for conspiracy to plunder the stockholders, but escaped on a technicality. He died, insolvent and broken-hearted, February 27, 1844, aged fifty-eight.[1]

Webster declared, in 1842, that a bank of the United States founded on a private subscription was an " obsolete idea; "[2] but perhaps the unkindest cut of all was that the Whig Almanac for 1843 could refer to " Nick Biddle " as a rascal, and to " his Bank " as one which was " corruptly managed."

[1] Ingersoll, 285 ; a very touching description of Biddle's last years.

[2] 2 Webster's Works, 135.

CHAPTER XII

THE NEW SPIRIT IN VARIOUS POINTS OF FOREIGN AND DOMESTIC POLICY

Quarrel with France. — The neglect of France to fulfil the stipulations of the treaty of July 4, 1831, offered the occasion for the most important diplomatic negotiation in which Jackson was engaged. In his message of 1834, he gave a full account of the treaty and of the neglect of the French Chambers, at two sessions, to appropriate money to meet engagements which had been made, on behalf of the French nation, by the constitutional authorities of France. The King had shown strong personal interest in the matter,[1] and had exerted himself to secure a satisfactory settlement and to prevent any bad feeling from arising between the two nations. In the mean time the United States had reduced the duties on wine, according to the engagement in the treaty, by an act of July 13, 1832, and France was getting the benefit of the treaty without performing her share of it. It seemed to Jackson that this state of things called for spirited action. Moreover,

[1] Livingston's dispatch, 47 Niles, 417. Rives came home in 1831. Livingston went out in 1833.

Livingston wrote a very important dispatch from Paris, November 22, 1834,[1] in which he said that there was a disposition in France to wait and see what the message would be ; also that the moderate tone of the United States up to this time had had a bad effect. " From all this you may imagine the anxiety I shall feel for the arrival of the President's message. On its tone will depend, very much, not only the payment of our claims, but our national reputation for energy." The message of 1834, which must have been prepared before this dispatch was received, did not sin by moderation and lack of energy.[2] The Duc de Broglie, the French minister, afterwards declared that the appropriation would have been passed in December, 1834, if copies of this message had not just then been received. Jackson was under erroneous information as to the time of meeting of the French Chambers. The Duc de Broglie had also, in the March previous, when the bill drawn by the American Treasury went to protest, found fault with the American government for selling the bill to a bank, instead of receiving the money through a diplomatic agent.[3] He argued that the United

---

[1] 47 Niles, 417.

[2] Curtis (*Buchanan*, i. 235) gives, without mentioning authority, a story that Judge Catron was sent to Jackson, by friends, at this time, to ask him to make his message, so far as it referred to the difficulty with France, mild, and that Jackson took from his drawer a letter from Louis Philippe, urging that the message should contain a threat of war, lest the payment be defeated in France.   [3] 47 Niles, 327.

ANDREW JACKSON

States ought not to have regarded the treaty as definitive until all the organs of the French government had assented to it. In his message, before mentioned, Jackson suggested that, if Congress inferred from the inaction of France that she did not intend to fulfil the treaty, it might proceed to measures of coercion, amongst which he mentioned reprisals, as suitable and "peaceable." He proposed that a law should be passed authorizing reprisals, if France should neglect the fulfilment of the treaty beyond a certain time. He added that this suggestion ought not to be regarded by France as a "menace." Chevalier thought that Jackson, having had his bout with the nullifiers, found his blood heated and his appetite for war reawakened; that he satisfied this appetite first in the Bank war, and then in the difficulty with France.[1]

The message caused great excitement in France. The French journals all regarded it as a menace. The feeling was aroused that France could not then pay without dishonor.[2] Additional embarrassment arose from the fact that the King's active interest was revealed by the documents published in America. The bad temper of the French was still further increased when they read Rives's letters, in which he seemed to boast of having outwitted the French minister, and Livingston's letter, in which he suggested that France never would pay unless the message brought her behavior before

---

[1] Chevalier, 177. See his estimate of Jackson's character.
[2] French newspapers quoted, 47 Niles, 327.

Congress in a spirited way. The Committee on
Foreign Relations of the Senate made a report,[1]
in which they expressed full agreement with the
President on all the essential points; but they regarded the proposition to employ reprisals as premature, and likely to embarrass the negotiations.
In the House, two reports were made,[2] but they
were not important. The Senate voted unanimously, January 14, 1835, that it was not expedient to adopt any legislative measures in regard
to the relations with France. In the House, J. Q.
Adams took the lead in sustaining Jackson's position, and was largely influential in securing the
adoption by the House, unanimously, March 2,
1835, of a resolution that the execution of the
treaty should be insisted on. The French minister to the United States was recalled. His final
note of January 14, 1835, was not received by
Jackson, but was referred back to the French government; they approved of it.

In December, 1834, the French Chambers rejected a bill appropriating money to pay the indem-
nities. A cabinet crisis followed, not on account
of this vote, but also not entirely, as it appears,
without reference to it. The Duc de Broglie, however, returned to office with the understanding that
provision was to be made for fulfilling the treaty.
April 25, 1835, the French Chambers passed the
appropriation, but with a condition that no money
should be paid until " satisfactory explanations "

[1] 47 Niles, 344.   [2] 48 Niles, 5 and 6.

of the President's message of 1834 should be received. The original condition in the law was, " until it shall have been ascertained that the government of the United States has adopted no measures injurious to French interests; " [1] but it was afterwards changed to the other form [2] by amendment. Livingston wrote a note, April 25, 1835, declaring that the message was a domestic document, for which no responsibility to any foreign power would be admitted; that the message of 1834 itself contained a sufficient disclaimer; and that the condition which had been incorporated in the act of the French Chambers would prevent it from being a satisfactory settlement. [3] He then came home. In Congress, whose session ended March 4th, an amendment to the usual appropriation bill for fortifications was proposed, by which $3,000,000 were appropriated for extraordinary expenditures for defence, in case such should become necessary before the next session. The whole bill was lost, borne down, as it appears, by this amendment. As the relations with France were still more critical when Congress next met, and nothing had been done for defence, on account of the failure of that bill, a great deal of crimination and recrimination took place in an effort to fix the blame and responsibility. No result was reached. [4]

In the message of 1835, Jackson reviewed the

[1] 47 Niles, 436.
[2] 48 Niles, 220.
[3] 48 Niles, 318.
[4] 49 Niles, 446.

whole affair, insisted that he had never used menace, and alluded to Livingston's final note to the French minister as having clearly so stated. He said that he would never apologize. A long dispatch of the Duc de Broglie to the French *chargé* here, in June, 1835, set forth the French case. It was read to Forsyth, but he declined to receive a copy.[1] Jackson directed Barton, *chargé d'affaires* at Paris, to make a specific inquiry what France intended to do. The Duc de Broglie replied that France would pay whenever the United States would say that it regretted the misunderstanding, that the misunderstanding arose from mistake, that the good faith of France had not been questioned, and that no menace was ever intended. This question and answer were exchanged in October, 1835.[2] Barton came home in January, 1836, and Pageot, the French *chargé*, was recalled at the same time, so that diplomatic relations were entirely broken off.

January 18, 1836, Jackson sent in a special message on the relations with France,[3] sending copies of Barton's correspondence. Livingston toned down[4] this message somewhat from the first intention; nevertheless Jackson in it again recommended coercive measures. He proposed to exclude French ships and products from the ports of the United States; that is to say, his reserve of force by which to sustain his spirited diplomacy

[1] 49 Niles, 353.   [2] 49 Niles, 347.
[3] 49 Niles, 345.   [4] Hunt's *Livingston*, 428.

was the old, imbecile, and worn-out device of a commercial war. He said that France was strengthening her navy; if against us, an apology from us was out of the question.

Thus this question had been pushed into the worst kind of a diplomatic dead-lock, out of which neither party could advance without fighting, and neither could recede without (supposed) dishonor. That is the evil of spirited diplomacy, for good diplomacy would avoid such a dead-lock as one of the worst blunders possible in the profession. The English government now intervened, and offered its good offices as mediator. The French government declared to the English that the President's message of 1835 had removed the bad impressions of that of 1834. This declaration was made known to Forsyth by the English minister at Washington, and was transmitted to Congress, with a message by the President, February 22, 1836.[1] It was very good-natured of France to regard the message of 1835 as compliance with the demands which had been made to Barton in October. She simply covered her retreat, for she had been in the wrong on the merits of the question from the beginning, and she justly bore half the blame of the diplomatic dead-lock. March 19, 1836, the King of France ordered four instalments of the indemnity to be paid at once, in order to settle the matter down to date, according to the terms of the treaty.

[1] 49 Niles, 442.

The Post-Office.— Barry, the Postmaster-General, was the only member of the cabinet retained in 1831. In his hands the administration of the Post-Office Department, both in its business and its finances, steadily declined. The complaints in 1834–35 of the irregularity and delay of the mails were very numerous and bitter. The department was also running into arrears financially. Both Houses of Congress, at the session of 1834–35, investigated the department. Barry's personal honesty does not seem to have been questioned, but his chief clerk, Rev. Obadiah B. Brown,[1] became for the time a very distinguished man, on account of relations with mail contractors, which, if innocent, were very improper. The contractors had made use of familiar devices, "straw bids," "unbalanced bids," "expedited service," etc., if not of corrupt influences on subordinates in the department, by which chicanery shrewd men take advantage of inefficient public officers.[2] Barry refused to answer some of the questions put to him, and in place thereof, after the fashion of the time, published an "Appeal to the American People."[3] Brown resigned in an official document, imitated apparently from Van Buren's resignation of 1831.[4] He too published an "Appeal," etc. Jackson selected Kendall for Barry's successor, May 1, 1835. Kendall's administrative ability was great, and he speedily reorganized the department, and

---

[1] See page 443.
[2] 47 Niles, 381, 393.
[3] 46 Niles, 338.
[4] 47 Niles, 395.

restored its efficiency. There was great doubt, however, when he was appointed, whether he would be confirmed. Barry was sent as minister to Spain, but died on his way thither.

Slavery. — The emancipation of slaves in the British West Indies in 1833 gave a great impulse in the United States to abolition sentiment and effort, which had not been active since the compromise of 1820 was adopted. The new spirit was manifested in the organization of societies, distribution of pamphlets and newspapers, petitions to Congress to abolish slavery in the District of Columbia, and other forms of agitation. The first efforts of this kind were frowned down all over the North, but the general movement grew. The sentiments of democracy and of religion were both against slavery, and every step which was taken to arrest the agitation — the gag law in Congress, by which petitions about slavery were practically shut out, and the mob violence which was employed against the agitators — only strengthened it. Towards the end of Jackson's second administration the antislavery agitation was a real growing movement, and an element in the social and civil life of the nation. The story of these things has been often told in detail, and may be passed over here. The history of the United States has, in fact, been studied chiefly with regard to the slavery question. Jackson's administration was not called upon to act on the slavery issue save in one or two points.

The abolition societies adopted the policy of

sending documents, papers, and pictures against slavery to the southern States. If the intention was, as was charged, to incite the slaves to revolt, the device, as it seems to us now, must have fallen far short of its object, for the chance that anything could get from the post-office into the hands of a black man, without going through the hands of a white man, was poor indeed. These publications, however, caused a panic and a wild indignation in the South. The postmaster at Charleston, being lectured by the people there on his duty, turned to the Postmaster-General for orders. August 4, 1835, Kendall gave an ambiguous reply, so far as orders were concerned. He, however, threw the postmaster on his own discretion, and then said for himself : " By no act or direction of mine, official or private, could I be induced to aid, knowingly, in giving circulation to papers of this description, directly or indirectly " (*i. e.*, papers alleged by the postmaster to be " the most inflammatory and incendiary, and insurrectionary to the last degree "). " We owe an obligation to the laws, but a higher one to the communities in which we live, and, if the former be perverted to destroy the latter, it is patriotism to disregard them. Entertaining these views, I cannot sanction, and will not condemn, the step you have taken " in refusing to deliver certain mail-matter. August 22d Kendall wrote a long letter to Gouverneur, postmaster at New York, elaborating and defending his position.[1]

[1] 49 Niles, 8.

Politics were already combined with the slavery question in this incident. Kendall's confirmation by the Senate was very doubtful, and Van Buren's southern support was ready to abandon him at a moment's notice, if slavery came into account. Kendall won enough southern votes to carry his confirmation.

Texas and Mexico. — Monroe, as Secretary of State, in 1816, instructed the Minister to Spain that President Madison would consent to the Sabine from its mouth to its source as the boundary between the United States and the Spanish provinces.[1] When J. Q. Adams, in 1819, was negotiating with the Spanish minister the treaty by which the western boundary of the United States was defined, he could get no encouragement from Monroe or any of his ministers to try to push the boundary westward.[2] Monroe appeared to think that the United States would be weakened by including territory west of the Sabine.[3] It was not long, however, before the southern slave-holding interest began to see the error of this view of the matter. After the Missouri Compromise was adopted, it appeared that wild land for the formation of new free States was owned north of that line from the Mississippi to the Pacific, while south of that line similar land, available for new slave States, extended only to the Sabine and the 100-degree meridian. The Richmond " Enquirer," March 7, 1820, said: The southern and western

[1] 12 Adams, 64.   [2] See page 84.   [3] 11 Adams, 348.

representatives " owe it to themselves to keep their
eyes firmly fixed on Texas. If we are cooped
up on the north, we must have elbow room to
the west." [1]   Only a few persons, however, as
yet perceived this view of the matter. On June
23, 1819, one James Long proclaimed the independence of Texas.[2] In 1821 Austin colonized
three hundred families in Texas, by permission
of Mexico. In 1826 some American immigrants
at Nacogdoches declared Texas independent. In
1824 the Emperor of Russia tried to establish exclusive control over the Northern Pacific, and the
attention of the most far-seeing statesmen was
drawn to the interests of the United States in the
Northwest and on the Pacific. It seems necessary
to bear in mind, all through the history of the
annexation of Texas, the connection of that question with the acquisition of California, including
the port of San Francisco, which was then the
chief reason for wanting California. Adams, when
President, in 1827, sent to Poinsett, minister of
the United States in Mexico, orders to try to buy
Texas for a million dollars. Poinsett did not
make the attempt. He gave as his reason the
danger of irritating Mexico by a proposition which
was sure to be rejected.[3]

In 1824 Mexico took the first steps towards the
abolition of slavery. By a decree of September

---

[1] Quoted 1 Tyler's *Tylers*, 325.   [2] 17 Niles, 31; Jay.
[3] The attempt to buy Texas seems to have been Clay's act.
Cf. 7 Adams, 239, 240; 9 Adams, 379; especially 11 Adams, 348.

15, 1829, slavery was definitively abolished. In
the mean time, Americans had emigrated to Texas,
chiefly from the southern States, and had taken
slaves thither. They resisted the abolition decree,
and the Mexican government saw itself forced to
except the State of Texas from the decree. It,
however, united Texas with Coahuila, as a means
of holding the foreign and insubordinate settlers
in check. The abolition of slavery by Mexico
affected the southern States doubly : first, it les-
sened the area open to slavery; second, it put a
free State on the flank and rear of the slave territory. The interest of the southwestern States in
the independence of Texas, or its annexation, was
at once aroused. A fanciful doctrine, in the taste
of the southwestern statesmen, was immediately
invented to give a basis for stump-speaking in
defence of a real act of violence. It was declared
that the United States must RE-annex what had
once been maliciously given away by a northern
statesman. The gravity and care with which
re-annexation was talked about had its parallel
only in the theatrical legislation of nullification.
In 1780 Spain claimed that the eastern boundary
of Louisiana was such as to include nearly all the
present State of Alabama, and the Hiawasee, Tennessee, Clinch, and Cumberland rivers through
what is now Tennessee and Kentucky.[1] Inside of
this claim she would take what she could get.
The boundaries to the westward were still more

[1] Ramsey, 523.

vague. Therefore, any one who chose to dabble
in the authorities could prove anything he liked,
and think himself no contemptible scholar into the
bargain. "Texas," as a State of the Mexican
confederation, embraced only the southeastern corner of the territory now included in the State of
that name.[1]

The anxiety about Texas was increasing just
when Jackson came into power. The South expected him to secure it. "If the discussion of the
acquisition of Texas brings on the agitation of the
slave question, as we are sure that it will, a rupture
with the northern States will become almost inevitable."[2]   Erving, who had been minister to
Spain in 1819, claimed to show to Jackson that he
had, at that time, laid the basis for a negotiation
at Madrid, which would have set the boundary at
the Colorado, or even at the Rio Grande, but that
the negotiation was transferred to Washington,
where American rights were surrendered.[3]   In the
summer of 1829 Van Buren sent instructions to
Poinsett to try to buy Texas, and five million
dollars were offered for it.   In 1830 Mexico,
which had at first welcomed the immigrants, forbade Americans to settle in Texas.   Of course this
law had no effect.

[1] Carey & Lea's *Atlas*, 1822. *Cf.* Carey's map of 1814, on
which Texas seems to be delineated as extending from the Nueces
to the Sabine.

[2] Columbia, S. C., *Telescope*, Nov. 6, 1829, in 37 Niles, 213.

[3] Letters in the Ford MSS. See p. 459.

We are indebted to a Dr. Mayo, who was a hanger-on at Washington during Jackson's time, for a little book in which most of the Texas intrigue is laid bare. Mayo was in the way of picking up certain information, and more came to him by accident. He gives also many documents. He was intimate with ex-Governor Samuel Houston, of Tennessee, an old companion in arms of Jackson, who came to Washington in 1829 to get Jackson's connivance at an enterprise which Houston had in mind for revolutionizing Texas. That Jackson did connive at this enterprise, just as he supposed Monroe connived at his own proceedings in Florida, cannot be established by proof, but it is sustained by very strong inference.[1]

April 5, 1832, two treaties with Mexico were published, — one of commerce and one of boundaries, — confirming the boundary of the Florida treaty.

In 1833 a revolution broke out in Mexico, which threw the whole country into anarchy, Texas with the rest. Santa Anna gradually established his authority. In the autumn of 1835 he tried to extend it over Texas, but he met with armed resistance, and was defeated. In July, 1835, Jackson authorized an offer of an additional half million dollars if Mexico would allow the boundary, after

[1] See 11 Adams, 41, 347, 357, 363; and his Fifteen Day Speech, of June, 1838. Wise (*Decades*, 148), affirms it very positively. He is better authority on this point than on some others about which he is very positive, *e. g.*, the Adams-Clay bargain.

the cession of Texas, to follow the Rio Grande up to the thirty-seventh degree, and then run on that parallel to the Pacific.[1] All propositions to purchase failed. After the Texans proved able to beat the Mexicans in battle, no further propositions of that kind were made.

March 2, 1836, a Declaration of Independence, on behalf of Texas, was adopted. March 6th the fort of the Alamo was taken by the Mexicans, and its defenders massacred. On the 27th Colonels Fannin and Ward, with other Texan (or American) prisoners, were massacred. On the 17th of March the Constitution of Texas was adopted. It contained the strongest provisions in favor of slavery. The massacres aroused great indignation in the Southwest, and hundreds of adventurers hastened to Texas, where Houston was now chief in command, to help him win independence.[2] The decisive battle was fought at San Jacinto, April 21st, when Santa Anna was routed and captured. He promised everything in captivity, but cancelled his promises after he was released.[3]

[1] 11 Adams, 362. [2] Jay, 28.

[3] There is in the Ford MSS. a copy of a letter from Lewis to Houston, in which the former proposes the plan which was followed: " To turn Santa Anna loose upon those gentry who have possessed themselves of his place. . . . If he were to return to Mexico, I have no doubt he would give them enough to do at home, instead of collecting and marching their forces against you." He added that, if Santa Anna did not keep faith, foreign nations would acknowledge Texas. He states that the letter was written at the suggestion of the President, that it had been read to him, and that he desired that it should be sent.

" The mission of Col. Butler having failed, I then
determined to use my influence, after the battle of San
Jacinto, to have the independence of Texas acknowledged, and to receive her into the Union. But that
arch enemy, J. Q. Adams, rallied all his forces to prevent its annexation to the U. States — We must regain
Texas; *peacebly* if *we can; forcibly if we must !* . . .
I repeat that the safety, as well as the perpetuation of
our glorious Union depends upon the retrocession of the
whole of that country, as far as the *ancient limits* of
Louisiana, to the U. States." [1]

In June, 1836, Judge Catron wrote to Webster,
from Tennessee, that the spirit was abroad through
the whole Mississippi Valley to march to Texas.[2]
Perhaps the disposition to march was not so strong
elsewhere, but immense speculations in land had
already been organized, and great speculations in
Texan [3] securities soon after began, which enlisted
the pecuniary interests of great numbers of people
in the independence of Texas.

A correspondence now began between the representatives of the governments of the United States
and Mexico, which no American ought to read without shame. It would be hard to find an equally
gross instance of bullying on the part of a large
State towards a small one. Jackson had ordered

[1] Ford MSS.; Jackson to Lewis, September 18, 1843.

[2] 1 Webster's *Correspondence*, 523.

[3] The first issue of Texan bonds was authorized in November,
1836. The first Treasury notes were issued November 1, 1837.
Gouge's *Texas*, 57, 71.

that General Gaines should enter the territory of
Texas, and march to Nacogdoches, if he thought
that there was any danger of hostilities on the part
of the Indians, and if there was suspicion that the
Mexican general was stirring up the Indians to war
on the United States. Here we have another re-
miniscence of Florida revived. Gaines understood
his orders, and entered the Mexican territory.
Understanding also, no doubt, that the Jacksonian
proceedings of 1818 had now been legitimized as
the correct American line of procedure for a military officer, he called on the governors of the
neighboring States for militia. Although com-
panies were forming and marching to Texas under
full organization, this " call " was overruled by the
War Department. The energetic remonstrances
of the Mexican minister finally led to an order to
Gaines to retire from Texan territory, not, however,
until after the Mexican minister had broken off
diplomatic relations.

In July, 1836, both Houses voted, the Senate
unanimously, that the independence of Texas ought
to be acknowledged as soon as Texas had proved
that she could maintain it. Texas was already
represented by agents applying for annexation.
Jackson recommended longer delay in a message
of December 21, 1836. The fact was that the
geographical definition of " Texas " was not yet
satisfactorily established, and it was not desirable
to have annexation settled too soon. An act was
passed by the Legislature of Texas, December 19,

1836, by which the Rio Grande was declared to be the western boundary of Texas. In his message of December 22d, Jackson submitted the report of his agent that the boundaries of Texas, before the last revolution, were the Nueces, the Red, and the Sabine rivers, but that she now claimed as her boundary the Rio del Norte to its source, and from that point eastward and southward the existing boundary of the United States.[1] That is as if Maine should secede and claim that her boundaries were the Alleghanies and the Potomac. Jackson's message distinctly pointed out that in taking Texas then, or later, the United States would take her with her new boundary claims. That is as if Maine should join the Dominion of Canada, and England should set up a claim to the New England and Middle States based on the "declaration" of Maine above supposed. The policy was to keep the Texas question open until California could be obtained. The Mexican war ultimately became necessary for that purpose, and for no other; for Texas, even to the Rio Grande, could have been obtained without it.[2] Another reason for delay was that opposition to the annexation of Texas had been aroused in the North, and there was not yet strength enough to carry it. May 25, 1836, Adams[3] made a speech against a war with Mexico to conquer Texas, which had great influence in the North.

[1] Document L.
[2] 3 Von Holst, 67, 81, 103, 108, 112; Jay, 130.
[3] 50 Niles, 276.

March 1, 1837, the Senate recognized the independence of Texas, 23 to 19. The House did not concur in full form, but did in effect.

In 1836 the government of the United States opened a new battery against that of Mexico in the shape of a series of claims and charges. The diplomatic agent of the former power, Powhatan Ellis, performed his duties in such a rude and peremptory manner that one is forced to suspect that he acted by orders, especially as his rank was only that of *chargé d'affaires*. The charges were at first 15 in number, then 46, then 57. They were frivolous and forced, and bear the character of attempts to make a quarrel.[1] Ellis abruptly came home. In August, 1837, the agent of Texas, Memucan Hunt, made a formal proposal for annexation. Van Buren declined it. Mexico next proposed a new negotiation, with arbitration in regard to the claims and charges made against her by the United States. The opposition to annexation in the North had grown so strong that delay was necessary, and negotiations were opened which resulted in the convention of August 17, 1840. Mexico could not fulfil the engagements she entered into in that treaty, or in a subsequent one of 1843, and so the question was reopened, and finally was manœuvred into a war. It appears that Van Buren had the feeling which any President will be sure to have, adverse to any war during his administration. The Mexican war was forced on

[1] Jay, 36 *et seq.*

by a cabinet intrigue, and Tyler forced it on
Polk.

The Texas intrigue and the Mexican war were
full of Jacksonian acts and principles.   There are
constant outcroppings of the old Seminole war proceedings and doctrines.   The army and navy were
corrupted by swagger and insubordination, and by
the anxiety of the officers to win popularity by the
methods of which Jackson had set the example.[1]
The filibustering spirit, one law for ourselves and
another for every one else, gained a popularity for
which Jackson was much to blame.   During the
Texas intrigue, Jackson engaged in private and
personal correspondence on public questions with
diplomatic agents, who were not always accredited.[2]

*Briscoe vs. The Bank of the Commonwealth of
Kentucky.* — In 1834 the case of Briscoe *vs.* The
Bank of the Commonwealth of Kentucky was argued before the Supreme Court.[3]   Briscoe and
others gave a note, in 1830, which they did not
pay at maturity.   In the State Circuit Court,
Briscoe pleaded " no consideration," on the ground
that the note was given for a loan of notes of the
Bank of the Commonwealth, which were " bills of
credit " within the prohibition of the Constitution,
and therefore of no value.   The State court found

---

[1] In 1824 Commodore Porter was guilty of an outrage at Fo-
xardo, Porto Rico.   When court-martialled, he made an elaborate
comparison of his proceedings with those of Jackson in Florida,
by way of defence.   28 Niles, 370.   He was cashiered.

[2] 11 Adams, 357.   [3] 8 Peters, 118.

for the bank. The State Court of Appeals affirmed that decision. The case was carried to the Supreme Court of the United States on a writ of error. The court consisted, in 1834, of Chief Justice Marshall, of Virginia, appointed by Adams in 1801; and Associate Justices Johnson, of South Carolina, appointed by Jefferson in 1804; Duvall, of Maryland, appointed by Madison in 1811; Story, of Massachusetts, appointed in the same year by the same; Thompson, of New York, appointed by Monroe in 1823; McLean, of Ohio, appointed by Jackson in 1829; and Baldwin, of Pennsylvania, appointed by Jackson in 1830. Johnson was absent all the term. Duvall was absent part of the term. Of the five who heard the argument in Briscoe's case, a majority thought that the notes of the Bank of the Commonwealth were bills of credit under the decision in Craig vs. Missouri,[1] but there were not four, a majority of the whole, who concurred in this opinion. The rule of the court was, not to pronounce a State law invalid for unconstitutionality unless a majority of the whole court should concur. Hence no decision was rendered.

The Circuit Court of Mercer County, Kentucky, decided in 1834, under the decision in Craig vs. Missouri, that the notes of the Bank of the Commonwealth were bills of credit.[2]

Judge Johnson died in 1834. Duvall resigned in January, 1835. Wayne took his seat January 14, 1835. Hence there was one vacancy in 1835,

[1] See page 175. [2] 46 Niles, 210.

and Briscoe's case went over. Marshall died July
6, 1835. In 1836 there were only five judges on
the bench of the court. Taney was confirmed
March 15, 1836. P. P. Barbour, of Virginia, was
confirmed on the same day. This made the court
complete again. Three changes had taken place
since 1834, and five of the seven judges were now
Jackson's appointees.

Briscoe *vs.* The Bank was decided in January,
1837. The decision was by McLean. It was held
that a bill of credit " is a paper issued by the sovereign power, containing a pledge of its faith and
designed to circulate as money." Notes, to be bills
of credit, must be issued by the State and bind
the faith of the State. Commissioners of issue
must not impart any credit by signature, nor be
responsible. Hence it was held that the notes
of the Bank of the Commonwealth were not bills of
credit. Story rendered a very strong and unusu-
ally eager dissenting opinion. In it he gave a
summary history and analysis of " bills of credit "
as they existed before the Revolution, and as they
were understood by the Constitution-makers. He
explicitly referred to the former hearing of the
case, and said that Marshall had been in the majority against the constitutionality of the issues.

The decision in Briscoe's case marks the beginning of a new era in the history of the constitutional law of the United States. Up to that time
the court had not failed to pursue the organic development of the Constitution, and it had, on every

occasion on which it was put to the test, proved the bulwark of constitutional liberty, by the steadiness and solidity of judgment with which it had established the interpretation of the Constitution, and checked every partial and interested effort to wrest the instrument from its true character. Our children are familiarized, in their school-books, with the names of statesmen and generals, and popular tradition carries forward the fame of men who have been conspicuous in public life; but no one who really knows how the national life of the United States has developed will dispute the assertion, that no man can be named to whom the nation is more indebted for solid and far-reaching services than it is to John Marshall. The proceedings of the Supreme Court are almost always overlooked in ordinary narrations of history, but he who looks for real construction or growth in the institutions of the country should look to those proceedings first of all. Especially in the midst of a surging democracy, exposed to the chicane of political mountebanks and the devices of interested cliques, the firmness and correctness with which the court had held its course on behalf of constitutional liberty and order has been of inestimable value to the nation. The series of great constitutional decisions, to which reference has been made in the preceding pages, have now entered into the commonplaces of our law. They have been tested through three quarters of a century. To see in the retrospect that they were wise, and that the contrary decisions would have produced mischief, is one thing; to see at the time, in the heat of controversy and under the clamor of interests, what was the sound and correct interpretation, and to pronounce it in spite of abuse, was another thing.

In Briscoe's case the court broke the line of its decisions, and made the prohibition of bills of credit nugatory.[1] If the degree of responsibility and independent authority which the directors of the Bank of the Commonwealth of Kentucky possessed, and the amount of credit they gave to the notes, aside from the credit of the State, was sufficient to put those notes outside the prohibition of the Constitution, then no State could find any difficulty in making a device for escaping the constitutional prohibition. Wild-cat banking was granted standing ground under the Constitution, and the boast that the Constitutional Convention had closed and barred the door against the paper money with which the colonies had been cursed was without foundation. The great "banks" set up by the southwestern States between 1835 and 1837 were protected by this decision. They went on their course, and carried those States down to bankruptcy and repudiation. The wild-cat banking which devastated the Ohio States between 1837 and 1860, and miseducated the people of those

[1] "A virtual and incidental enforcement of the depreciated notes of the State banks, by their crowding out a sound medium, though a great evil, was not foreseen." Madison to C. J. Ingersoll, February 22, 1831; 4 Elliott, 641.

States until they thought irredeemable government issues an unhoped-for blessing, never could have existed if Story's opinion had been law. The legal-tender notes of 1862, and the decisions of the Supreme Court on the constitutionality of the legal-tender act, must have borne an entirely different color, if Marshall's opinion had prevailed in Briscoe's case.

Jackson's appointments introduced the mode of action by the Executive, through the selection of the judges, on the interpretation of the Constitution by the Supreme Court. Briscoe's case marked the victory of Kentucky relief finance and State rights politics over the judiciary. The effect of political appointments to the bench is easily traceable, after two or three years, in the reports, which come to read like a collection of old stump speeches. The climax of the tendency which Jackson inaugurated was reached when the court went to pieces on the Dred Scott case, trying to reach a decision which should be politically expedient, rather than one which should be legally sound. A later and similar instance is furnished by the legal-tender cases. As for the immediate effect of Jackson's appointments, it may be most decorously stated by quoting from Story's reasons, in 1845, for proposing to resign: "I have been long convinced that the doctrines and opinions of the old court were daily losing ground, and especially those on great constitutional questions. New men and new opinions have succeeded. The doctrines of the

Constitution, so vital to the country, which, in former times, received the support of the whole court, no longer maintain their ascendency. I am the last member now living of the old court, and I cannot consent to remain where I can no longer hope to see those doctrines recognized and enforced." [1]

Civil and Social Phenomena. — During Jackson's second term the growth of the nation in wealth and prosperity was very great. It is plain, from the history we have been pursuing, that, in spite of all the pettiness and provincialism which marked political controversies, the civil life of the nation was growing wider and richer. It was just because there was an immeasurable source of national life in the physical circumstances, and in the energy of the people, that the political follies and abuses could be endured. If the politicians and statesmen would only let the nation alone it would go on, not only prosperously, but smoothly; that is why the non-interference dogma of the democrats, which the whigs denounced as nongovernment, was in fact the highest political wisdom. On reflection it will not be found strange that the period 1829 to 1837 should have been marked by a great deal of violence and turbulence. It is not possible that a growing nation should spread over new territory, and feel the thrill of its own young energies contending successfully with nature in all her rude force, without social

[1] 2 Story's *Story*, 527.

commotions and a certain recklessness and uproar. The contagion of these forms of disorder produces other and less excusable forms. On account of the allowance to be made for violence and lawlessness under the circumstances, and also on account of the disagreeableness of recalling, if it can be avoided, old follies, no recapitulation of the outrages, mobs, riots, etc., of the period will here be attempted. Suffice it to say that they were worse and more numerous than either before or since. Brawls and duels between congressmen, and assaults on congressmen by persons who considered themselves aggrieved by words spoken in debate, were very frequent at Washington. The cities possessed, as yet, no police. The proposition to introduce police was resented as an assault on liberty. Rowdies, native Americans, protestants, firemen, anti-abolitionists, trades-unionists, anti-bank men, etc., etc., in turn produced riots in the streets of the great eastern cities. From the South came hideous stories of burning negroes, hanging abolitionists, and less heinous violence against the mails. From Charlestown, Massachusetts, came the story of the cruel burning of a convent. Niles, in August, 1835, gathered three pages of reports of recent outrages against law and order.[1] A month later he has another catalogue, and he exclaims in astonishment that the world seems upside down.[2] The fashion of the time seemed to be to pass at once from the feeling to

[1] 48 Niles, 430.　　　　　　　　[2] 49 Niles, 40.

the act. That Jackson's character and example
had done something to set this fashion is hardly
to be denied. Harriet Martineau and Richard
Cobden, both friendly critics, were shocked and
disappointed at the social condition. Adams, in
1834, wrote thus: "The prosperity of the country, independent of all agency of the government,
is so great that the people have nothing to disturb
them but their own waywardness and corruption.
They quarrel upon dissensions of a doit, and split
up in gangs of partisans of A, B, and C, without
knowing why they prefer one to another. Cau-
cuses, county, State, and national conventions,
public dinners and dinner-table speeches, two or
three hours long, constitute the operative power
of electioneering; and the parties are of working
men, temperance reformers, anti-masons, Union
and State rights men, nullifiers, and, above all,
Jackson men, Van Buren men, Clay men, Calhoun
men, Webster men, and McLean men, whigs and
tories, republicans and democrats, without one
ounce of honest principle to choose between
them." [1] In his long catalogue he yet omitted
abolitionists and native Americans, the latter of
whom began to be heard of as soon as foreign immigration became great. Great parties did not
organize on the important political questions.
Men were led off on some petty side issue, or they
attached themselves to a great man, with whom
they hoped to come to power. The zeal of these

[1] 9 Adams, 187.

little cliques was astonishing. One feels that there must have been a desire to say to them: No doubt the thing you have taken up as your hobby is fairly important, but why get so excited about it, and why not pursue your reformatory and philanthropic work outside of politics? Why not go about your proposed improvement soberly and in due measure? The truth was that nearly all the cliques wanted to reach their object by the short cut of legislation, that is, to force other people to do what they were convinced it was a wise thing to do, and a great many of them also wanted to make political capital out of their " causes." There was something provincial about the gossip and news-mongering over small things, and about the dinners and ovations to fourth-rate men. One wonders if the people had not enough interesting things to occupy them. They could not have been very busy or hard-worked, if they had time to spend on all these things. There was something bombastic, too, about the way in which an orator took up a trifle. Everything in the surroundings forced him to be inflated and meretricious, in order to swell up to the dimensions of the occasion the trifle with which he was forced to deal. At the same time serious things, like nullification, were treated by the same inflated method, which made them ridiculous. On every occasion of general interest the people ran together for a public meeting. Their method of doing their thinking on any topic seemed to be to hear some speeches about it. No doubt this was one reason why there was so much heat mixed up with all opinons. The prevailing disposition to boast, and the over-sensitiveness to foreign criticism which was manifested, were additional symptoms of immaturity.

January 30, 1835,[1] Jackson attended the funeral, at the Capitol, of Warren R. Davis, of South Carolina. As he came out through the rotunda, a man named Richard Lawrence snapped two pistols in succession at him. Neither was discharged. Lawrence gave half a dozen inconsistent reasons for the act. He was plainly insane. Jackson immediately gave the attack a political significance. Some days after it occurred, Harriet Martineau called upon him, and referred to the " insane attempt." " He protested, in the presence of many strangers, that there was no insanity in the case. I was silent, of course. He protested that there was a plot, and that the man was a tool." [2] He went so far as to name senator Poindexter, of Mississippi, as the instigator. He was at feud with Poindexter, although the latter had been with him at New Orleans, and had defended him in Congress in the Seminole war affair. Harriet Martineau says that it was expected at Washington that they would have a duel as soon as Jackson's term was out. This was probably based on a reputed speech of Poindexter, to which the

[1] 47 Niles, 340 ; 1 Tyler's *Tylers*, 508.
[2] 1 Martineau, *Western Travel*, 162. She was in the Capitol when the attack occurred.

"Globe" gave currency.[1] That paper, nearly a month after the attempted assassination, treated the charge against Poindexter as not at all incredible. Poindexter obtained an investigation by the Senate, when the charge was, of course, easily proved to rest upon the most frivolous and untrustworthy assertions, no one of which would bear the slightest examination, and some of which were distinctly false. The incident, however, illustrated one trait of Jackson's character, which has been noted several times before. The most extravagant and baseless suspicion of a personal enemy, in connection with an injury to himself, struck his mind with such a degree of self-evident truth that external evidence to the contrary had no influence on him. In the present case, this fault laid him open to a charge of encouraging persons who had committed perjury, and had suborned[2] others to do so. Lawrence, on his trial, continually interrupted the proceedings. He was acquitted, and remanded to custody as an insane person.

The Equal Rights Party or Loco-focos. — A faction arose in New York city in 1834–35, which called itself the "equal rights party," or the "Jeffersonian anti-monopolists." The organization of the Tammany Hall democrats, under Van Buren and the regency, had become rigid and tyrannical. The equal rights faction revolted, and declared that Tammany was aristocratic. They represented a new upheaval of democracy. They

[1] 48 Niles, 33.   [2] 9 Adams, 229.

took literally the dogmas which had been taught them, just as the original Jackson men had done ten years before, only that now, to them, the Jackson party seated in power seemed to have drifted away from the pure principles of democracy, just as Monroe had once appeared to the Jackson men to have done. The equal rights men wanted "to return to the Jeffersonian fountain" again, and make some new deductions. They revived and extended the old doctrines which Duane, of the "Aurora," taught at the beginning of the century in his "Politics for Farmers," and similar pamphlets. In general the doctrines and propositions might be described as an attempt to apply the procedure of a township democracy to a great state. The equal rights men held meetings at first secretly, at four different places, and not more than two successive times at the same place.[1] They were, in a party point of view, conspirators, rebels, — "disorganizers," in short; and they were plotting the highest crime known to the political code in which they had been educated, and which they accepted. Their platform was : No distinction between men save merit ; gold and silver the only legitimate and proper circulating medium ; no perpetuities or monopolies ; strict construction of the Constitution ; no bank charters by States (because banks of issue favor gambling, and are "calculated to build up and strengthen in our country the odious distribution of wealth and power against

[1] Byrdsall, 16.

merits and equal rights ") ; approval of Jackson's
administration ; election of President by direct
popular vote. They favored the doctrine of instructions. They also advocated free trade and
direct taxes.[1] They had some very sincere and
pure-minded men among them, a large number of
over-heated brains, and a still larger number of
demagogues, who were seeking to organize the faction as a means of making themselves so valuable
that the regular managers would buy them. The
equal rights men gained strength so rapidly that,
on the 29th of October, 1835, they were able to
offer battle to the old faction at a primary meeting
in Tammany Hall, for the nomination of a con-
gressman and other officers. The " regular "
party entered the hall by the back entrance, and
organized the meeting before the doors were
opened. The anti-monopolists poured in, nominated a chairman and elected him, ignoring the
previous organization. The question of " equal
rights " between the two chairmen was then settled in the old original method which has prevailed
ever since there has been life on earth. The equal
rights men dispossessed the other faction by force,
and so proved the justice of their principles. The
non-equal rights party then left the hall, but they
" caused " the equal rights men " to be subjected
to a deprivation of the right " to light by turning
out the gas. The equal rights men were thus
forced to test that theory of natural rights which

[1] Byrdsall, 103.

affirms that said rights are only the chance to have good things, *if one can get them.* In spite of their dogma of the equality of all men, which would make a prudent man no better than a careless one, and a man with capital no better than one without capital, the equal rights men had foreseen the emergency, and had provided themselves with capital in the shape of candles and loco-foco matches. They thus established their right to light, against nature and against their enemies. They duly adopted their platform, nominated a ticket, and adjourned. The regular leaders met elsewhere, nominated the ticket which they had previously prepared, and dispensed, for that occasion, with the ornamental and ceremonious formality of a primary meeting to nominate it.

On the next day the " Courier and Enquirer " dubbed the equal rights party the loco-focos, and the name clung to them.[1] Hammond quotes a correspondent[2] who correctly declared that " the workingmen's party and the equal rights party have operated as causes, producing effects that will shape the course of the two great parties of the United States, and consequently the destinies of this great republic." The faction, at least in its better elements, evidently had convictions and a programme. It continued to grow. The " Evening Post " became its organ. That paper quarrelled with the administration on Kendall's order about the mails, and was thereupon formally read out of

[1] 49 Niles, 162.   [2] 2 Hammond, 503.

the party by the " Globe." [1]   The loco-focos ceased
to be a revolting faction. They acquired belligerent rights. The faction, however, in its internal
economy ran the course of all factions. It went
to extremes, and then began to split up. In January, 1836, it declared its independence of the
democratic-republican party. This alienated all
who hated the party tyranny, but who wanted reform in the party. The faction declared itself
opposed to all acts of incorporation, and held that
all such acts were repealable. It declared that
representative institutions were only a practical
convenience, and that Legislatures could not create vested rights.[2] Then it went on to adopt a
platform of " equality of *position*, as well as of
rights."

In October, 1836, Tammany made overtures to
the equal rights men for a reunion, in preparation
for the presidential election. Some of the loco-focos
wanted to unite; others refused. The latter were
the men of conviction; the former were the traders.
The former called the latter " rumps; " the latter
called the former " buffaloes." [3] Only one stage
now remained to complete the old and oft-repeated
drama of faction. A man named Slamm, a blatant
ignoramus, who, to his great joy, had been arrested
by order of the Assembly of New York for contempt and breach of privilege, and who had pro-
fited to the utmost by this incident to make a long
" argument " against the " privilege " of an Ameri-

[1] 49 Niles, 78.   [2] Byrdsall, 41.   [3] Byrdsall, 178.

can Legislature, and to pose as a martyr to equal rights, secured his own election to the position of secretary of the equal rights party. He then secured a vote that no constitutional election could be held unless called by the secretary. He never would call one. There were those who thought that he sold out the party.

Thus the faction perished ignominiously, but it was not without reason that its name passed, a little later, to the whole Jackson - Van Buren party ; i. e., to the radical anti-paper currency, not simply anti-United States Bank, wing of the national democratic party. The equal rights men maintained impracticable doctrines of civil authority, and fantastic dogmas about equality, but when these were stripped away there remained in their platform sound doctrines and imperishable ideas. They first put the democratic party on the platform which for five or six years it had been trying to find. When it did find that platform it was most true to itself, and it contributed most to the welfare of the country. The democratic party was for a generation, by tradition, a party of hard money, free trade, the non-interference theory of government, and no special legislation. If that tradition be traced up to its source, it will lead back, not to the Jackson party of 1829, but to the loco-focos of 1835.

CHAPTER XIII

THE ELECTION OF 1836. — END OF JACKSON'S CAREER

THE attempt was made in 1834 to unite and organize the whole opposition to Jackson. Niles first mentions the party name "whig" in April, 1834.[1] He says that it had come into use in Connecticut and New York. It was adopted with antagonistic reference to the high prerogative and (as alleged) tory doctrines of Jackson. The anti-masons and national republicans ultimately merged in the new whig party, but time was required to bring about that result. In 1834 it was impossible. The anti-masons insisted on acting independently. Their candidate for President then was Francis Granger.[2] Clay would not run in 1836, because he could not unite the opposition. He was disgusted with public life, and desired to retire.[3]

The administration party, on the other hand, was perfectly organized. The corps of federal office-holders had been drilled by the "Globe" into thorough discipline and perfect accord of energy and will. Each officer was held to "revere

[1] 46 Niles, 101.   [2] 50 Niles, 234.   [3] 9 Adams, 170.

the chief," and to act in obedience to the indications of his will which came through the " Globe." They did so. There was no faltering. There was only zealous obedience. It caused some bewilderment to remember that this was the party which had denounced Adams for using the federal officers to electioneer. Lewis had been known to interfere directly in elections, and Blair had done the same in his private capacity.[1] The party had been wonderfully held together. In 1830 there were only four anti-Jackson Legislatures in the Union, namely, in Vermont, Massachusetts, Connecticut, and Delaware. In the six years from 1830 to 1835, both inclusive, twenty-seven States held 162 sessions of their Legislatures. Of these, 118 had Jackson majorities, 40 anti-Jackson, and 4 Calhoun.[2] There was some talk of a third term for Jackson, but it never grew strong. The precedents were cited against it. Jackson's bad health and Van Buren's aspirations were perhaps stronger objections. Adams says that Jackson had " wearied out the sordid subserviency of his supporters." [3] That is not at all improbable.

The democratic convention was held at Baltimore, May 20, 1835. Jackson had written to Tennessee, recommending that a convention should be held of "candidates fresh from the people." There were not wanting those who called this convention a caucus, and said that it was the old congressional monster in a new mask. Tennessee did not send

[1] 40 Niles, 299.   [2] 63 Niles, 308.   [3] 9 Adams, 312.

any delegates.   Even Jackson could not bring that
State to support Van Buren.   Tennessee was a whig
State until 1856.   Her hostility to Van Buren was
adroitly combined with that of Pennsylvania, in
1844, by the selection of Polk as a candidate, to
defeat Van Buren; otherwise stated, it was the
desire to combine these two States, in order to defeat Van Buren, which led to the nomination of
Polk.   In 1835 a caucus of the New Hampshire
Legislature, which nominated Hill for Governor,
passed a resolution begging Tennessee not to divide
the party.[1]   Tennessee, however, had another very
popular candidate, Hugh L. White, a former friend
of Jackson, whom Jackson now hated as a traitor
and renegade.[2]   John Bell, the Speaker, was a
supporter of White, and he and his friends claimed
that they were not in opposition; that they and
White were good republicans, and that they preferred White to the man whom Jackson had selected.[3]   The "Globe" attacked Bell with bitter-
ness.   Jackson was greatly enraged, and exerted
himself personally and directly against White.[4]
One Tennessee man, being in Baltimore when the
convention was held, took upon himself to represent that State.   His name was Rucker, and to
"ruckerize" passed into the political slang of the
day, meaning to assume functions without creden-
tials.

The Baltimore convention was largely composed

[1] 48 Niles, 322.   [2] See page 212.
[3] Bell's speech in 48 Niles, 334.   [4] 49 Niles, 35.

of office-holders. Twenty-one States were represented.[1] Andrew Stevenson, of Virginia, was chairman. The two-thirds rule was adopted, because
Van Buren was sure of two thirds. He actually
got a unanimous vote, 265. For Vice-President,
R. M. Johnson, of Kentucky, got 178 votes ; W. C.
Rives, of Virginia, 87. The Virginia delegation
declared, on the floor of the convention, that Virginia would never vote for Johnson, because he
favored tariff, bank, and internal improvements,
and because they had no confidence in his principles or character.[2] Van Buren, in his letter of
acceptance,[3] said that he had been mentioned as
Jackson's successor "more through the ill-will of
opponents than the partiality of friends." That
statement was so adroit that it would take a page
to tell whether it was true or not. He made a full
and eager declaration that he had asked for no
man's support. He said that he would "endeavor
to tread generally in the footsteps of President
Jackson, — happy if I shall be able to perfect the
work which he has so gloriously begun." Johnson,
in his letter of acceptance,[4] declared that he was
opposed to the old Bank, or to one like it, but
thought that such a bank as Jackson talked of in
his earliest messages might be a good thing. On
tariff and internal improvements he said that he
agreed with Jackson. Van Buren was fifty-four
years of age and Johnson fifty-six. Johnson had

[1] 48 Niles, 207, 227, 244.   [2] *Ibid.* 248.
[3] *Ibid.* 257.   [4] *Ibid.* 329.

been in Congress ever since 1807, except during
the second war with England, when he took the
field. He served with some distinction, but a
ridiculous attempt to credit him with the killing
of Tecumseh has caused his real merits to be forgotten. As a public man he managed to be as
near as possible to the head of every popular movement, and to get his name connected with it, but
he never contributed assistance to any public business. His name is also met with frequently as a
messenger, middle-man, manipulator, and general
efficiency man of the Jackson party. He made a
report, in 1829, on the question of running the
mails on Sunday, which was one of his claims to
fame. It was written for him by the Rev. O. B.
Brown.[1] A chance was found in this report to
utter some noble sentiments on religious liberty,
and to lay down some specifications of American
principles in that regard which were not likely to
provoke contradiction. This valuable production
was printed on cloth, and hung up in stage offices
and bar-rooms all over the country. Johnson had
nourished presidential aspirations for some years.
He did not abandon them till 1844.

The anti-Jackson men, in 1834–35, were opposed,
on principle, to a national convention. They said
that the convention was King Caucus revived.
The anti-masons held a State convention at Harrisburg, December 16, 1835.[2] It was decided not to

[1] See page 409. Kendall's *Autobiography*, 107.
[2] 49 Niles, 265, 287.

call a national convention. They thought the free
action of the people would be best brought out by
State conventions. They nominated William H.
Harrison by 89 votes to 29 for Webster and 3 for
Granger. For Vice-President, Granger got 102
votes; Hugh L. White, 5; William Slade, of Vermont, 5; and William A. Palmer, of Vermont, 7.
The whigs of Pennsylvania adopted the nominations of the anti-masons, and coalesced with them.
Webster was very anxious, at this time, to be
nominated and supported by the whigs. It pleases
some people to think that Webster ought not to
have had this ambition. He was a strange com-
pound of the greatest powers and some mean traits.
To such a man the presidential ambition is very
sure to mean moral shipwreck. Still it was not
wrong for Webster to want the proofs of success
in his career. His dissatisfaction was well founded
when, after his splendid services, he saw William
Henry Harrison preferred before him; and it is a
point which deserves careful attention, that, if
Webster's just ambition had been fairly gratified,
he would have been a better man. He was nominated by the Legislature of Massachusetts.

Hugh L. White, of Tennessee, was nominated
by the Legislatures of Alabama, Tennessee, and
Illinois. Judge McLean was nominated in Ohio.
He had had presidential aspirations ever since
1828.[1] The Northern whigs supported Harrison,
and the Southern whigs supported White. Thus

[1] Kendall's *Autobiography*, 304.

the opposition went into the campaign disorganized and devoted to defeat. When we consider the earnestness with which they all opposed Jackson and Jacksonism, and also the demonstration they had suffered, in 1832, of the consequences of division and tactical imbecility, it is amazing that they should have entered upon another campaign so divided and discordant as to be defeated before they began.

Harrison and White were of the same age, sixty-three. Harrison was a man of no education. He had done some good service as an Indian fighter. The anti-Jackson men, who had derided Jackson's candidature because he was not a statesman, selected, in Harrison, the man nearest like him whom they could find. They hoped to work up a popularity for him on the model of Jackson's popularity.[1] Harrison answered the anti-masons that he was not a mason, and did not like masonry, but that the federal government had nothing to do with that subject. This did not satisfy Thaddeus Stevens, who wanted Webster.[2] White has been mentioned several times. He had a fair education and a good character, and he was very much respected, but he was a person of only ordinary ability.

During the winter of 1835–36 there was a great struggle in the House over a contested election in

[1] For an estimate of Harrison, written in 1828, which is perhaps too highly colored to quote, see 7 Adams, 530.
[2] 9 Adams, 273.

North Carolina. It was thought very probable that the presidential election might be thrown into the House, and the vote of North Carolina might decide the result. The sitting member (Graham) was unseated, and the case was referred back for a new election.

There were two States whose admission was pending when the election approached, — Arkansas and Michigan. In 1835 Michigan became involved in a boundary dispute with Ohio. The act which organized the territory of Michigan, January 11, 1805, described, as its southern boundary, a due east and west line running through the southernmost point of Lake Michigan. The Constitution of Ohio gave that State, as its northern boundary, a line drawn from the southernmost point of Lake Michigan to the northernmost cape of Maumee Bay. Indiana's northern boundary had been described as a due east and west line ten miles north of the southernmost point of Lake Michigan. The northern boundary of Illinois had been placed on the parallel of 42° 30'. Michigan, therefore, found her territory reduced. Jackson, at first, on the advice of Butler, the Attorney-General, took the side of Michigan. The people of Michigan held a convention in September, 1835, and framed a Constitution, which was to go into effect in November. In October, the Assistant Secretary of State, Asbury Dickens, wrote, at the President's orders, that no such reorganization of the government could take place without the consent of Congress.

It was a case of squatterism.[1] In 1835–36 there was some danger of an armed collision between Ohio and Michigan; but it is not easy, on account of the rhetoric which was then in fashion, to judge how great this danger was. June 15, 1836, Arkansas and Michigan were admitted together; but Michigan was put under the condition that she must accept the southern boundary which would result from the northern lines of Indiana and Ohio, and accept compensation on the peninsula north of Lake Michigan.[2] The Legislature of Michigan, in July, called a convention, which met September 26th, and rejected the condition. On the 5th and 6th of December, by the spontaneous action of the people, delegates were elected to a convention, which met December 14, 1836, and assented to the condition. Jackson, in a message, December 26th, informed Congress of the action of Michigan.[3] Michigan was admitted January 26, 1837. She offered a vote in the presidential election. In announcing the vote, the vote of Michigan was included in the alternative form.

In the spring of 1836, Sherrod Williams interrogated the candidates for President. Harrison[4] favored distribution of the surplus revenue and of the revenue from lands; opposed internal improvements, except for works of national scope and importance; would charter a bank, but with great

---

[1] See page 9.
[2] J. Q. Adams was greatly incensed at the wrong to Michigan. 9 Adams, 342.   [3] 51 Niles, 278.   [4] 51 Niles, 23.

reservations; thought that neither House of Congress had a right to expunge anything from its records. Van Buren opposed national bank, internal improvements, and all distribution. The equal rights men interrogated the candidates. The committee reported that they were greatly pleased with Johnson's replies, but that Van Buren's were unsatisfactory. Many " irreconcilable " equal rights men refused to vote for Van Buren. He had not yet become fully identified with that wing of the national democratic party which took up the essential features of the loco-foco doctrine.

In the election [1] Van Buren received 170 votes, counting 3 of Michigan; Harrison, 73 ; White, 26 (Georgia and Tennessee) ; Webster, 14 (Massachusetts) ; W. P. Mangum, of North Carolina, 11 (South Carolina). Van Buren's majority over all was 46. Van Buren's and Harrison's votes were well distributed geographically. Van Buren carried Maine, New Hampshire, Rhode Island, Connecticut, New York, Pennsylvania, Virginia, North Carolina, Alabama, Mississippi, Louisiana, Illinois, Missouri, Arkansas, Michigan. Harrison carried Vermont, New Jersey, Delaware, Maryland, Kentucky, Ohio, and Indiana. The popular vote was: for Van Buren, 761,549 ; for all others, 736,656 ; Van Buren's majority, 24,893.[2] For Vice-President, R. M. Johnson got 147 votes;

[1] 58 Niles, 392.

[2] *American Almanac* for 1880. The figures in Niles are full of obvious errors.

Francis Granger, 77; John Tyler, 47; William Smith, of Alabama, 23 (Virginia). As no one had a majority, the Senate elected Johnson. In January, 1837, Webster wrote to Massachusetts[1] that he should resign his seat. He intended to retire from public life, at least temporarily.

Van Buren was now at the height of his ambition; but the financial and commercial storm which had been gathering for two or three years, the accumulated result of rash ignorance and violent self-will acting on some of the most delicate social interests, was just ready to burst. High prices and high rents had already before the election produced strikes, trades-union conflicts, and labor riots,[2] things which were almost unprecedented in the United States. The price of flour was so high that 493,100 bushels of wheat were imported at New York in 1836, and 857,000 bushels before April, in 1837.[3] Socialistic notions of course found root, and flourished like weeds at such a time. An Englishwoman, named Fanny Wright, became notorious for public teachings of an "emancipated" type. The loco-focos were charged with socialistic notions, not without justice. There were socialists amongst them. The meeting held in the City Hall Park, at New York, February 13, 1837, out of which the "bread riots" sprang, was said to have been called by them. They certainly had habituated the city populace to public

[1] 2 Webster's *Correspondence*, 25 *et seq.*
[2] 48 Niles, 171; 50 Niles, 130.   [3] 52 Niles, 147.

meetings, at which the chance crowd of idlers was addressed as "the people," with all the current catch-words and phrases, and at which blatant orators, eager for popularity and power, harangued the crowd about banks, currency, and vested rights. Of course in these harangues violence of manner and language made up for poverty of ideas, and the minds of the hearers were inflamed all the more because they could understand nothing of what the orators said, except that those addressed were being wronged by somebody. On that day in February the crowd got an idea which it understood.[1] Some one said: Let us go to Hart [a provision merchant], and offer him eight dollars a barrel for his flour. If he will not take it — ! In a few hours the mob destroyed five hundred barrels of flour and one thousand bushels of wheat. The militia were needed to restore order.[2] The park meetings were continued.

The commercial crisis burst on the country just at the beginning of March, when Jackson's term ended. There was a kind of poetic justice in the fact that Van Buren had to bear the weight of all the consequences of Jackson's acts which Van Buren had allowed to be committed, because he would not hazard his standing in Jackson's favor by resisting them. Van Buren disliked the reputation of a wire-puller and intriguer, but he had well

[1] Byrdsall (103) says that the riot was not the fault of the locofocos.
[2] 51 Niles, 403.

earned his title, the "little magician," by the
dexterity with which he had manœuvred himself
across the slippery arena of Washington politics
and up to the first place. He had just the temper
for a politician. Nothing ruffled him. He was
thick-skinned, elastic, and tough. He did not win
confidence from anybody. He was, however, a
man of more than average ability, and he appears
to have been conscious of lowering himself by the
political manœuvring which he had practised. As
President he showed the honorable desire to have a
statesman-like and high-toned administration, and
perhaps to prove that he was more than a creature
of Jackson's whim. He could not get a fair chance.
The inheritances of party virulence and distrust
which he had taken over from Jackson were too
heavy a weight. He lost his grip on the machine
without winning the power of a statesman. He
never was able to regain control in the party.
American public life is constituted out of great
forces, which move on in a powerful stream, under
constantly changing phases and combinations, which
it is hard to foresee. Chance plays a great *rôle*.
If a man, by a chance combination of circumstances, finds himself in one of the greater currents of the stream, he may be carried far and
high, and may go on long; but if another chance
throws him out, his career is, almost always, ended
forever. The course of our political history is
strewn with men who were for a moment carried
high enough to have great ambitions and hopes

excited, but who, by some turn in the tide, were stranded, and left to a forgotten and disappointed old age. Van Buren illustrated these cases.

Parton quotes a letter of Jackson to Trist,[1] written March 2, 1837, in which he says : " On the 4th I hope to be able to go to the Capitol to witness the glorious scene of Mr. Van Buren, once rejected by the Senate, sworn into office by Chief Justice Taney, also being rejected by the factious Senate." The election of Van Buren is thus presented as another personal triumph of Jackson, and another illustration of his remorseless pursuit of success and vengeance in a line in which any one had dared to cross him. This exultation was the temper in which he left office. He was satisfied and triumphant. Not another President in the whole list ever went out of office in a satisfied frame of mind, much less with a feeling of having completed a certain career in triumph.[2]

On the 7th of March Jackson set out for Tennessee. He was surrounded to the last with affection and respect. On his way home he met more than the old marks of attention and popularity. He was welcomed back to Nashville as he had been every time that he had returned for twenty years past. These facts were not astonishing. He retained his popularity. Hence he was still a

[1] 3 Parton, 624.

[2] When Jackson went out of office many satirical copper coins, like cents, in derision of his sayings and doings, were issued. *Amer. Journ. Numism.* Oct. 1869, 42.

power. It was still worth while to court him and to get his name in favor of a man or a measure. Nevertheless, it does not appear that he actually exerted any great influence at Washington. He could not get an appointment for his nephew as a naval cadet, although he applied for it frequently, — at least, if he did succeed, the evidence of it is not in the letters before us. In 1842, he, like nearly all his neighbors, was in pecuniary distress. Two or three persons came forward to offer loans to him, out of respect and affection, but the negotiations fell through for reasons which are not explained. At last Lewis obtained a loan for him from Blair.

Financial revulsions always bring to light many defalcations and embezzlements. The number of these revealed, 1837–42, was very great, including a number by public officers. That of Swartwout furnished a striking parallel to the case of Watkins, under Adams, which Jackson had so ruthlessly exploited against his predecessor.[1] The Swartwout case is several times referred to in the Ford MSS. in letters to Lewis.

" I shall enquire of M.[r] Love Executioner of his fathers estate, to be informed whether any of Major Lees manuscript is left there. I hope for the cause you have named, Major Lee has not destroyed the manuscript — you know, I readily would have renewed his nomination to the Senate, had I at any time been informed that the Senate would have confirmed the nomination — but it

[1] See page 189.

appears to me that those I have had the greatest confidence in, and served most, have acted with bad faith, — and violated that confidence reposed! Is it true that Mr Samuel Swartwant is really a defaulter — and if a defaulter, to what amount, please to give me the time, & the amount. . . . Is it known when he commenced the use of the Public funds — where he is, & if expected back to america —

"I had great confidence in his honesty, honor & integrity, and appointed him to the office on the sheer grounds of his integrity & against a powerful influence — and I still hope he will relieve me from the slanders the Whigg papers are heaping upon me that 'I knew of his using the public money in speculation, & in aid of the Texians' — a greater & more foul slander never was uttered." (Dec. 10, 1838.) "The defalcation of Swartwant & Price has given great pain — how he could so far depart from his sacred pledges often made to me that he would touch not, handle not of the public money for any thing but as prescribed by law. As an honorable man he ought to come out & do justice to the administration & unfold to the public how the money has been applyed & in whose hands it is — the greatest part must be in the hands of the merchants — give me your views on this subject." (March 4, 1839.) "I rejoice to learn that Mr Swartwant is likely to wipe away part of the indebtedness & to close his indebtedness with the Government. I had great confidence in him, and that business gave me more pain than any, & all others during my administration — I still wish him well." (May 23, 1842.)

Jackson and Lewis nearly came to a quarrel in 1839. Jackson wanted Lewis to resign his office, but Lewis clung to it, and argued like a good civil service reformer against his own removal. He was a " conservative," and differed from Van Buren on financial measures.

" I have not heard," wrote Jackson, " one of your true friends, but regretted your remaining at Washington, and you must well conceive that your remaining until removed would be truly mortifying to me, all things considered — . . . You must well recollect how much complaint there were and murmuring by your acquaintances in Nashvill for my placing you in office and keeping you there — I ballanced not, but kept you there regardless of their *growls* to the end of my term at which you had always said you would retire."

One cannot avoid a recognition of retributive justice to find Lewis writing : —

" I have been here too long and am too well acquainted with the manner in which *public sentiment*, so called, is manifactured in *this city*, to place the least confidence in news paper articles upon such subjects. The most of them I know are, and have been heretofore, written in the Departments here, (the Treasury and Post Office Depts are filled with newspaper editors) and sent to Penn^a Ohio, and other states for publication, which are then carefully collected and republished in a little dirty paper in this city (which is no doubt sent to you) as *evidence* of *public sentiment !* These things may impose upon the ignorant, or *unsuspecting*, but they cannot decieve me — nor do they decieve any other person here who is acquainted with the unprincipled and reckless course of those whose business it is to blacken the character of every body whose office they desire for themselves, or their particular friends."

Lewis was removed by Polk, in 1845. He did not like it, and he took to writing complaints and protests in the newspapers, just like an ordinary mortal.

A large part of the letters in the Ford collection belong to the period after Jackson's retirement. They do not show Jackson beset by visitors anxious to get the benefit of his influence, although he is shown as greatly interested in public affairs. He rejoiced greatly when Tyler quarrelled with the whigs.

"The Presidents message, [of 1841], for the most part is good & well said. That part of it which relates to a fiscal agent, the moment I read it, I regretted to see it introduced, — the paper money system — treasury notes to be issued as a circulating paper currency. . . . When the system was adopted by congress, to substitute treasury notes, instead of borrowing, I was opposed to the plan upon constitutional grounds and so wrote my friends in congress, both as to its unconstitutionality and to its expediency. Congress has the express power to borrow, but not to issue bills of credit, or make a paper currency — The government cannot pay a debt legally, but in gold & silver coin, how absurd then to collect the revenue in paper in which it cannot comply with the powers with which it is invested. . . . Ours was intended to be a hard money government. . . . The duty of the government is to leave commerce to its own capital & credit as well as all other branches of business — protecting all in their legal pursuits, granting

exclusive privileges to none — Foster the labour of
our country by an undeviating metalic currency for its
surplus, allway recollecting that if labour is depressed
neither commerce, or manufactories, can flourish, as
they are both based upon the production of labour, produced from the earth, or the mineral world. It is
unjust to them by legislation to depress labour by a
depreciated currency with the idea of prospering commerce &c which is in reallity injured by it — "

The subject which interested him most of all,
however, was the annexation of Texas. He was
very ill and infirm, and every letter contains its
paragraph of description of his ailments and distress, yet he writes letter after letter to Lewis, reiterating the same ideas in almost the same words.
This interest was so obvious, and so consistent
with his favorite life-long ideas, that we wonder
why, when he was President, the acquisition of
Texas was not the chief object of his policy.

"How degrading," he writes, in 1842, "the scenes
in the House of Representatives — it is painful that
old man [J. Q. Adams] who must be deranged or
superlatively wicked, should be permitted to disgrace our
country by such behaviour — his constituents ought to
call him home — and the House at once should censure
him and proceed with business; and if he again mis-
behaves expell him."

"I would regret much that President Tyler should
go against the annexation of Texas, and leave it under
the influence of great Britain, which may be converted

to our great injury & jeopardize the safety of Neworleans
& our slaves — should he do this act of folly, his political
star sets forever." (Oct., 1843.)

These are the ideas of constant repetition, the
slave consideration being foremost in importance.[1]

"If possible this treaty [of March, 1844] ought not
be known of until it is sent to the senate — If it is,
that wicked & reckless old man John Q. Adams, will
write hundreds of memorials & send them over the
whole country to get signers — and all the abolitionists
& many more will sign them — I hope the senate will
act so promptly, that before he can get his memorials &
petitions distributed & signed & returned to congress
the treaty will be ratified."

In 1843 a public letter was obtained from him
favoring the annexation of Texas. This letter was
evidently prepared for him after the fashion of
Lewis. It was held back for a year, and then
published with a false date. So Jackson was used
by the annexation clique to ruin his friend Van
Buren. The party, which he and Van Buren had
consolidated, passed, by the Texas intrigue, away
from Van Buren and under the control of the
slavery wing of it. The last-mentioned letter of
Jackson brought him again into collision with
Adams, for in it Jackson repeated his former assertions that he had always disapproved of the
treaty of 1819, and of the boundary of the Sabine.
Adams produced the entries in his "Diary" as

[1] See a letter from Jackson, reiterating the same ideas, published in the N. Y. *Times*, June 16, 1897.

proof to the contrary. The passage from the Diary [1] shows that Jackson thought that the boundary ought to be the Rio Grande, but that he consented to the Sabine as the best which could be got. He remembered the former position; Adams insisted on the second. Jackson also made use of Erving's statements to him, in 1829,[2] as foundation for a charge which his agents pushed with great energy, in 1844, that Adams had given away his country's interests in 1819.[3] Adams was able to show that Erving's statements had been misunderstood or were incorrect.

As the election of 1844 approached, Jackson became more and more interested in it. He wrote to Lewis, September 12, 1843: —

"If the Madisonian had left M[r]. Tyler to be judged of by his acts, he would have met with a much better support from the Democracy — but the people believe, that these papers are trying to raise a third party under the name of Tyler, not for his benefit, but for M[r] Calhouns, and you now see the meetings begin to shew their choice to be Van Buren, and this will increase until the Baltimore convention settle the question, and that will be on Van Buren — *mark this prophesy* — This diffidence of our friend Cass, was ill timed, & very injudicious, and for the present, has done him, *in Ohio*, a great political injury — and the attack of the Calhoun papers on V. B. has done Calhoun a greater injury and united the Democracy upon V. B. — "

[1] Cited above, page 84. [2] See page 415.
[3] 12 Adams, 93, 101, 123.

When, however, Van Buren flinched on annexation, Jackson abandoned him. Letters signed by him, favoring Polk, were constantly circulated through the newspapers. Probably he was mortified that Clay carried Tennessee, although by only 113 majority in a vote of 120,000. His share in this campaign was his last public activity. He died June 8, 1845. He had had honors beyond anything which his own heart had ever coveted. His successes had outrun his ambition. He had held more power than any other American had ever possessed. He had named his successor. He had been idolized by the great majority of his countrymen, and had been surfeited with adulation. He had been thwarted in hardly anything on which he had set his heart. He had had his desire upon all his enemies. He lived to see Clay defeated again, and to help to bring it about. He saw Calhoun retire in despair and disgust. He saw the Bank in ruins; Biddle arraigned on a criminal charge, and then dead brokenhearted. In his last years he joined the church, and, on that occasion, under the exhortations of his spiritual adviser, he professed to forgive all his enemies in a body, although it is otherwise asserted that he excepted those who had slandered his wife. It does not appear that he ever repented of anything, ever thought that he had been in the wrong in anything, or ever forgave an enemy as a specific individual.

Brothers: The United States of North America as They Are, Not as they are Generally Described : Being a Cure for Radicalism; by Thomas Brothers. Longman & Co.: London, 1840.

Byrdsall : The History of the Loco-Foco or Equal Rights Party ; by F. Byrdsall. Clement & Packard : New York, 1842.

Cable: A History of New Orleans in 10th Census, Social Statistics II.

Carey's Letters : Nine Letters to Dr. Adam Seybert; by Matthew Carey. Author : Philadelphia, 1810.

Carey's Olive Branch: The Olive Branch; or, Faults on Both Sides, Federal and Democratic ; by Matthew Carey. Author: Philadelphia, 1818. (10th Edition.)

Chevalier: Society, Manners, and Politics in the United States: Being a Series of Letters on North America; by Michael Chevalier (translated). Weeks, Jordan & Co : Boston, 1839.

Cobb : Leisure Labors ; or, Miscellanies, Historical, Literary, and Political ; by Joseph B. Cobb. Appleton : New York, 1858.

Cobbett's Jackson: Life of Andrew Jackson; by William Cobbett. Harpers: New York, 1834.

Collins : Historical Sketches of Kentucky; by Lewis Collins. Cincinnati, 1847.

Colton's Clay : The Life and Times of Henry Clay ; by C. Colton. 2 vols. Barnes : New York, 1846.

Curtis's Webster : Life of Daniel Webster; by George Ticknor Curtis. 2 vols. Appleton : New York, 1870.

Curtis's Buchanan : Life of James Buchanan; by G. T. Curtis. 2 vols. New York, 1883.

Documents Relating to New England Federalism, 1800 to 1815; edited by Henry Adams. Little, Brown & Co. : Boston, 1877.

Document A. 15th Congress, 2d Session, Reports, No. 100.

Document B. 22d Congress, 1st Session, 4 Reports, No. 460.

Document C. 22d Congress, 1st Session, 2 Reports, No. 283.

Document D. 22d Congress, 2d Session, 1 Exec. Docs. No. 9.

Document E. 22d Congress, 2d Session, Reports, No. 121.

Document F. 23d Congress, 1st Session, 1 Senate Docs. No. 17.

Document G. 23d Congress, 1st Session, 1 Senate Docs. No. 2.

Document H. 23d Congress, 1st Session, 1 Senate Docs. No. 16.

Document I. 23d Congress, 2d Session, 1 Senate Docs. No. 17.

Document J. 23d Congress, 2d Session, 1 Exec. Docs. No. 9.

FULL TITLES OF BOOKS REFERRED TO IN THIS
VOLUME, IN THE ALPHABETICAL ORDER OF
THE SHORTER DESIGNATIONS BY WHICH THEY
HAVE BEEN CITED.

Adams: Memoirs of John Quincy Adams, Comprising Portions
of his Diary from 1795 to 1848; edited by Charles Francis
Adams. 12 vols. Lippincott: Philadelphia, 1876.

Adams's Life and Works: Works of John Adams, with a Life
and Notes by Charles Francis Adams. Boston, 1856.

Alison: Dropped Stitches in Tennessee History.

American Annual Register for 1796. Philadelphia.

American Register. 7 vols. 1806–1810. Conrad: Philadelphia.

American Whig Review.

Annual Register: The American Annual Register. 8 vols.
[numbered for the purposes of the present work as follows]:
I. 1825–6; II. 1826–7; III. 1827–8–9, Part I.; IV. 1827–8–9,
Part II.; V. 1829–30; VI. 1830–1; VII. 1831–2; VIII.
1832–3.

Aristokratie in America, aus dem Tagebuch eines deutschen
Edelmanns, herausgegeben von F. T. Grund. 2 vols. Stutt-
gart, 1839.

Benton: Thirty Years' View; or, A History of the Working of
the American Government for Thirty Years, from 1820 to
1850; by a Senator of Thirty Years [Thomas H. Benton].
2 vols. Appleton: New York, 1854.

Binns: Recollections of the Life of John Binns; written by himself. Philadelphia, 1854.

Bourne: The History of the Surplus Revenue of 1837; by E. G.
Bourne. New York, 1885.

Bradley: Biography of Isaac Hill [C. P. Bradley]. Concord,
1835.

Butler: A History of the Commonwealth of Kentucky; by Mann
Butler. Louisville, 1834.

Document K. 23d Congress, 2d Session, 2 Senate Docs. No. 13.

Document L. 24th Congress, 2d Session, 2 Exec. Docs.

Document M. 23d Congress, 1st Session, Senate Docs. No. 238.

Drake's Tecumseh: Life of Tecumseh, and of his Brother, the Prophet, with a Historical Sketch of the Shawanoe Indians; by Benjamin Drake. Morgan: Cincinnati, 1841.

The Duplicate Letters, the Fisheries, and the Mississippi; Documents Relating to Transactions at the Negotiation of Ghent; Collected and Published by John Quincy Adams. Davis & Force: Washington, 1822.

Duane: Narrative and Correspondence Concerning the Removal of the Deposits and Occurrences Connected Therewith. [W. J. Duane.] Philadelphia, 1838.

Duane's Pamphlets: Duane's Collection of Select Pamphlets. [W. Duane.] Philadelphia, 1814.

Eaton's Jackson: The Life of Andrew Jackson; Commenced by John Reid, Completed by John H. Eaton. Carey: Philadelphia, 1817.

Edwards: History of Illinois, from 1778 to 1833; and Life and Times of Ninian Edwards; by his Son, Ninian W. Edwards. Illinois State Journal Co.: Springfield, Illinois, 1870.

Elliott: The Debates in the Several State Conventions on the Adoption of the Federal Constitution. 4 vols. Edited by Jonathan Elliott: Washington, 1836.

Felt: An Historical Account of Massachusetts Currency; by J. B. Felt, Boston, 1839.

Folio State Papers: American State Papers; Documents Legislative and Executive of the Congress of the United States from the 1st Session of the 18th Congress to the 1st Session of the 20th Congress. Gales & Seaton: Washington, 1859. Subdivisions: Finance, Indian Affairs, etc., etc.

Ford: A History of Illinois; by T. Ford, Chicago, 1854.

Gallatin: Considerations on the Currency and Banking System of the United States; by Albert Gallatin. Carey & Lea: Philadelphia, 1831 Reprinted from the American Quarterly Review for December, 1830.

Gallatin's Writings: The Writings of Albert Gallatin; edited by Henry Adams. Lippincott: Philadelphia, 1879.

Garland's Randolph: The Life of John Randolph of Roanoke; by Hugh A. Garland. 2 vols. Appleton: New York, 1851.

Gayarré : Louisiana under American Domination ; by C. Gayarré. New York, 1866.

Gibbs: Memoirs of the Administrations of Washington and John Adams; edited from the Papers of Oliver Wolcott, Secretary of the Treasury; by George Gibbs. 2 vols. New York, 1846.

Gilmore : The Advance Guard of Western Civilization. New York, 1888.

Gleig : The Campaigns of the British Army at Washington and New Orleans [G. R. Gleig]. London, 1836.

Goodrich: Recollections of a Life-Time; by S. G. Goodrich. 2 vols. Miller : New York, 1851.

Goodwin's Jackson : Biography of Andrew Jackson ; by Philo A. Goodwin. Clapp & Benton : Hartford, 1832.

Gouge : A Short History of Paper Money and Banking in the United States ; by William M. Gouge. Collins : New York, 1835.

Gouge's Texas : The Fiscal History of Texas ; by William Gouge. Lippincott: Philadelphia, 1852.

Greeley: The American Conflict; by Horace Greeley. Case : Hartford, 1873.

Hamilton's Works : The Works of Alexander Hamilton. Francis : New York, 1851.

Hammond : The History of Political Parties in the State of New York, from the Ratification of the Federal Constitution to December, 1840. 2 vols. By Jabez D. Hammond ; fourth Edition, with notes by General Root. Phinney : Buffalo, 1850.

Hammond's Wright: Life and Times of Silas Wright; by Jabez D. Hammond. Barnes : New York, 1848.

Hanger: Life, Adventures, and Opinions ; by George Hanger [officer with Cornwallis]. London, 1801.

Harper's Calhoun : Life of John C. Calhoun. (Anonymous Pamphlet.) Harpers : New York, 1843.

Haywood : The Civil and Political History of Tennessee to 1796 [written 1823]. Nashville, 1891.

Hewitt : An Historical Account of the Rise and Progress of the Colonies of South Carolina and Georgia. 2 vols. Anonymous [Alexander Hewitt]. Donaldson : London, 1779.

Hodgson : The Cradle of the Confederacy, or the Times of Troup, Quitman, and Yancey ; by Joseph Hodgson, of Mobile. Register Office : Mobile, 1876.

Howard : Reports of Cases Argued and Adjudged in the Supreme Court of the United States.

Hudson : Journalism in the United States : New York, 1873.

Hunt's Livingston : Life of Edward Livingston ; by Charles Havens Hunt.   Appleton : New York, 1864.

Ingersoll : Historical Sketch of the Second War between the United States of America and Great Britain ; by Charles J. Ingersoll.   Events of 1814.   Lea & Blanchard : Philadelphia, 1849.

Jay : A Review of the Causes and Consequences of the Mexican War ; by William Jay.   Mussey : Boston, 1849.

Kendall's Autobiography : Autobiography of Amos Kendall ; edited by his Son-in-law, William Stickney.   Lee & Shepard : Boston, 1872.

Kendall's Jackson : Life of Andrew Jackson, Private, Military, and Civil ; by Amos Kendall.   Harpers : New York, 1843. (Unfinished.)

Kennedy's Wirt : Memoirs of the Life of William Wirt ; by John P. Kennedy.   2 vols.   Lea & Blanchard : Philadelphia, 1849.

Kirke : The Rear Guard of the Revolution ; by Edmund Kirke. [J. R. Gilmore] : New York, 1886.

Lambert's Travels : [1806-8].   2 vols.   London, 1816.

Latour : Historical Memoir of the War in West Florida and Louisiana in 1814–15 ; by Major A. L. Latour.   Conrad : Philadelphia, 1816.

Lodge's Cabot : Life and Letters of George Cabot ; by Henry Cabot Lodge.   Little, Brown & Co. : Boston, 1877.

Macgregor : The Progress of America, from the Discovery by Columbus to the Year 1846 ; by John Macgregor.   2 vols. Whittaker : London, 1847.

Mackeinzie : The Lives and Opinions of Benjamin F. Butler and Jesse Hoyt ; by William L. Mackeinzie.   Cook & Co. : Boston, 1845.

Martin : History of Louisiana ; by F. X. Martin : New Orleans, 1882.

Martineau's Society, etc. : Society in America ; by Harriet Martineau.   2 vols.   Saunders & Otley : New York and London, 1837.

Martineau's Western Travel : Retrospect of Western Travel ; by Harriet Martineau.   2 vols.   Harpers : New York, 1838.

Mayo: Political Sketches of Eight Years in Washington; by Robert Mayo: Baltimore, 1839.

Memoirs of Bennett: Memoirs of James Gordon Bennett and his Times; by a Journalist. Stringer & Townsend: New York, 1855.

Mills's Letters; Selections from the Letters of the Hon. E. H. Mills, reprinted from the Transactions of the Mass. Hist. Soc. Cambridge, 1881.

Monette: History of the Mississippi Valley. New York, 1846.

Morse's Adams: John Quincy Adams; by John T. Morse, Jr. Houghton, Mifflin & Co.: Boston, 1882.

Niles: Niles's Weekly Register, 1811 to 1848.

Opinions of the Attorneys-General: Official Opinions of the Attorneys-General of the United States. Washington, 1852.

Overton's Reports: 1 Tennessee Reports. [Nashville ?], 1813.

Parton: Life of Andrew Jackson; by James Parton. 3 vols. Mason Brothers: New York, 1861.

Perkins: Historical Sketches of the United States from the Peace of 1815 to 1830; by Samuel Perkins. Converse: New York, 1830.

Peters: See Howard.

Pickett: History of Alabama and Incidentally of Georgia and Mississippi, from the Earliest Period; by A. J. Pickett. 2 vols. Walker & James: Charleston, 1851.

Pitkin: A Statistical View of the Commerce of the United States of America; by Timothy Pitkin. Durrie & Peck: New Haven, 1835.

Plumer's Plumer: Life of William Plumer; by his son, William Plumer, Jr. Phillips, Sampson & Co.: Boston, 1856.

Political Register: Edited by Duff Green. 2 vols. Washington, 1832–33.

Putnam: History of Middle Tennessee, or Life and Times of General James Robertson; by A. W. Putnam. Nashville, 1859.

Quincy: Figures of the Past from the Leaves of Old Journals; by Josiah Quincy. Boston, 1883.

Quincy's Adams: Memoirs of the Life of John Quincy Adams; by Josiah Quincy. Phillips, Sampson & Co.: Boston, 1858.

Raguet: A Treatise on Currency and Banking; by Condy Raguet. Grigg & Elliott: Philadelphia, 1839.

Ramsey: The Annals of Tennessee to the End of the Eighteenth Century; by J. G. M. Ramsey. Russell: Charleston, 1853.

Randall's Jefferson: Life of Thomas Jefferson; by H. S. Randall. New York, 1858.

Robertson: Reports of the Trial of Aaron Burr for Treason. 2 vols.; by D. Robertson. Philadelphia, 1808.

Rush: Memoranda of a Residence at the Court of London; by Richard Rush. I. Key and Biddle: Philadelphia, 1833. II. Lea & Blanchard: Philadelphia, 1845.

Safford: Life of H. Blennerhasset; by W. H. Safford. Cincinnati, 1859.

Sargent: Public Men and Events from the Commencement of Mr. Monroe's Administration in 1817 to the Close of Mr. Fillmore's Administration in 1853; by Nathan Sargent. 2 vols. Lippincott: Philadelphia, 1875.

Seybert: Statistical Annals of the United States from 1789 to 1818; by Adam Seybert. Dobson: Philadelphia, 1818.

Southern Bivouac.

Sparks's Morris: Life of Gouverneur Morris, with Selections from his Correspondence and Miscellaneous Papers; by Jared Sparks. 3 vols. Gray & Bowen: Boston, 1832.

[The] Statesman's Manual. 3 vols. Williams: New York, 1854.

Stevens: A History of Georgia from its First Discovery by Europeans to 1798; by William Bacon Stevens. 2 vols. Butler: Philadelphia, 1859.

Story's Story: Life and Letters of Joseph Story; by his Son, W. W. Story. Little, Brown & Co.: Boston, 1851.

Sumner: A History of Banking in the United States; by W. G. Sumner. New York, 1896.

Telegraph, Extra: United States Telegraph, Extra; March to November, 1828. Weekly. Green & Jarvis: Washington.

Truth's Advocate and Monthly Anti-Jackson Expositor. Cincinnati, 1828.

Tyler's Taney: Memoirs of Roger Brook Taney; by Samuel Tyler. Murphy: Baltimore, 1872.

Tyler's Tylers: The Letters and Times of the Tylers; by L. G. Tyler. 2 vols. Richmond, 1884.

Von Holst: The Constitutional and Political History of the United States; by Dr. H. von Holst, (translated). 3 vols. Callaghan: Chicago, 1878–81.

Walker: Life of Andrew Jackson; by A. Walker. Philadelphia, 1860.

Webster's Correspondence: The Private Correspondence of Daniel Webster; edited by Fletcher Webster. 2 vols. Little, Brown & Co.: Boston, 1857.

Webster's Works: The Works of Daniel Webster. 6 vols. Little, Brown & Co.: Boston, 1851.

Wheaton: See Howard.

Whig Almanac: The Whig Almanac (from 1838). Horace Greeley: New York.

Wilkinson: Memoirs of my Own Times; by James Wilkinson. Philadelphia, 1816.

Wilson's Works: The Works of James Wilson, LL. D. 3 vols. Philadelphia, 1804.

Wise: Seven Decades of the Union; by Henry A. Wise. Lippincott: Philadelphia, 1872.

INDEX

INDEX

nation by casting vote, 210; defeats woollen tariff by casting vote, 239; loses support in Pennsylvania and New York, 239; holds Van Buren responsible for tariff of 1828, 251; his political error in opposing tariff on nullification ground, 256, 257; Jackson's opinion of his course, 259; considered as possible candidate for President by anti-masons, 295; resigns vice-presidency and enters Senate, 331; becomes absorbed in political mysticism, 331; his intense earnestness, 331, 332; denies that South Carolina is hostile to Union, 332; offers resolutions on nature of Constitution, 333, 334; said to have been driven by fear of Jackson into an agreement with Clay, 338; later claims to have won victory by compromise tariff, 339; joins whigs in Bank struggle, 365; proposes to amend Constitution so as to allow distribution of surplus, 381, 386; suspected by Jackson of plan to defeat Van Buren's nomination in 1844, 459.

California, the real object of Mexican war, 413, 420.

Call, General Richard K., censured by Jackson for insulting Mrs. Eaton, 195.

Callava, Spanish ex-governor of Florida, refuses to deliver papers to Jackson, sent to calaboose, 87; goes to Washington to protest, 88.

Cambreleng, C., visits Crawford, 198; criticises branch bank drafts, Biddle's ineffective reply, 303.

Campbell, George W., letters of Jackson to, 26, 27.

Campbell, Rev. J. N., called before cabinet by Jackson for defaming Mrs. Eaton, 195; challenged by Eaton, 211.

Canning, George, admits that England was coerced into opening West India trade, 216.

Cass, Lewis, Secretary of War, 212; revokes order transferring pension funds from New York branch bank, 288; opposes removal of deposits, 346.

Catron, John, tells Webster of desire in West to free Texas, 418.

Cherokees, land bought from, by Jackson, 60; their land claimed by Georgia, 223; their number, character, and civilization, 223; laws of Georgia claiming jurisdiction over, 224–226; their removal provided for by Congress, 225; appeal to Supreme Court, 225, 226; abandoned by Jackson, 226, 227; finally sell their lands and remove to Indian Territory, 229.

Chevalier, Michael, compares debates of 1834 to those of French Revolution, 364; on Jackson's reasons for defying France, 404.

Cheves, Langdon, favors secession in 1831, 261; his successful presidency of Bank, 269; thinks many branches disadvantageous, 307.

Chickasaws, their situation in Mississippi, 223.

Choctaws, their lands in Mississippi, 223; cede their lands in 1830, 228; terms of their removal to Indian Territory, 229.

Civil service, appointments to, Jackson's early ideas upon, 62, 63; four-years' term introduced by Crawford, 107; Adams's administration of, 141–143, 146; its degradation under Jackson, 187–192, 409, 453, 454.

Claiborne, General W. C. C., serves in Creek war, 38; wishes martial law abolished, 54; describes Amos Kendall, 185.

Clark, Judge, declares Kentucky replevin law unconstitutional, 162; attempt made to remove him, 163.

Clay, Henry, leads new generation of republicans, 34; opposes Monroe's administration out of pique at failure to receive State Department, 81; attacks Jackson's Florida career, 81; possibly regards Jackson as a presidential rival, 82; alleged plan to nominate for Vice-President in 1820, 92; his reputation and position as presidential candidate in 1824, 108; his political principles, 108; his gambling habits, 108, 109;

Economist, sociologist and teacher, WILLIAM GRAHAM SUMNER was one of Yale's most brilliant professors. He was appointed to the newly established chair of political and social science at that university in 1872, and held the position until 1910. During his tenure he wrote extensively; among his more notable works are *A History of American Currency*, *What Social Classes Owe to Each Other*, and the monumental four-volume *Science of Society*.

ROBERT V. REMINI is Professor of History and Research Professor of Humanities at the University of Illinois. He has written widely on Jackson's career and has recently completed the first volume of a three-volume biography entitled *Andrew Jackson and the Course of the American Empire*.